JÜRGEN HABERMAS

ON SOCIETY

AND POLITICS

JÜRGEN HABERMAS

ON SOCIETY

AND POLITICS

A READER

EDITED BY STEVEN

SEIDMAN

Beacon Press   *Boston*

Beacon Press
25 Beacon Street
Boston, Massachusetts 02108-2800

Beacon Press books
are published under the auspices of
the Unitarian Universalist Association of Congregations.

96 95 94   8 7 6 5 4

Text design by Linda Koegel

Library of Congress Cataloging-in-Publication Data

Habermas, Jürgen.
   [Selections. English. 1989]
   Jürgen Habermas on society and politics : a reader / edited by
Steven Seidman.
      p. cm.
   Selections translated from the German.
   Bibliography: p.
   ISBN 0-8070-2001-X
   1. Sociology—Philosophy. 2. Sociology—Methodology. 3. Social
structure. 4. Political sociology. I. Seidman, Steven.
HM24.H2613   1989
301'.01—dc20   88-43321

Contents

Part Three
THE ANALYSIS AND CRITIQUE OF MODERN SOCIETY

Editor's Note

Three considerations guided my text selection. First, this volume is designed to focus on topics and themes of interest to social scientists and social theorists. It was developed in response to my own pedagogical difficulties in selecting a Habermas text for my undergraduate and graduate theory courses. Its justification lies in whatever aid it provides for students, professors, and nonspecialists in gaining better access to Habermas's work. In this regard, I'll simply note that a second Habermas reader is planned whose focus will be on philosophical concerns. Second, I wanted, wherever feasible, to include the full text of a selection. I have, accordingly, refrained as much as is possible from chopping up selections. This reduced the number of selections but it contributes, I believe, to capturing the full force of Habermas's arguments. Third, I have tried to include selections from all of the major texts. The absence of a selection from *Legitimation Crisis* reflects the preference of Habermas.

I wish to acknowledge Thomas McCarthy's contribution to the overall structure of this volume as well as specific selections. My thanks to Tom and to Linda Nicholson for their comments on my introduction.

Introduction

In the more than three decades that Habermas has been writing, we can observe a sustained project: to provide conceptual and normative foundations for a reconstructed Marxist social theory that provides a critical analysis of modernity. Motivating this project are moral and political concerns that go to the root of his work. Habermas has sought to defend the notion that only in a society in which a general notion of reason can be invoked can we hope to sustain a good society. Without an appeal to general standards of truth and goodness, social life gravitates toward an endless power struggle among antagonistic interest groups. This social condition lends itself to the Hobbesian solution of an authoritarian state called upon to impose order.

Habermas's commitment to a strident rationalism is evident in the fact that, although he supported the student movements of the 1960s, he criticized their assault on theoretical self-reflection. He warned students that their identification of theory with ideology legitimates coercive social strategies to resolve social conflicts. Similarly, *Knowledge and Human Interests* is, at least in part, a response to the relativist implications of interpretive and historicist modes of social inquiry. The belief that reason is a mere local convention or political rhetoric involves a devaluation of reason and consensus-building norms. Again, Habermas's elaboration of a communicative theory of rationality is intended to counter trends toward subjectivist and contextualist thinking which, in his view, contribute to the enfeeblement of critical reason. Indeed, Habermas's notion of communicative rationality is an effort to defend a comprehensive notion of reason—one that includes cognitive truths as well as normative claims. The defense of reason is, for Habermas, inseparable from the project of promoting a democratic social order.

In the aftermath of the decline of logical positivism and the general assault on theoretical rationalism by pragmatism, hermeneutics, historicism, and post-structuralism, Habermas takes up the defense of general standards of truth and goodness. To be sure, he rejects traditional philosophical strategies that have sought an ontological or transcendental grounding to truth or norms. Habermas looks to social scientific theory and research to uncover structures of rationality embedded in everyday life. Because Habermas believes that reason is embodied in the institutional and cultural orders of society, he takes issue with social critics on the right and left for whom the modern world is without redeeming value. In contrast to many contemporary intellectuals who have opted for an anti- or postmodernist position, Habermas sees in the institutional orders of modernity structures of rationality. Whereas many intellectuals have become cynical about the emancipatory potential of modernity and, indeed, have turned to myth, religion, or libidinal desire for social renewal, Habermas continues to insist on the utopian potential of modernity.[1] In a social context in which faith in the Enlightenment project of a good society promoted by reason seems a fading hope and spurned idol, Habermas remains one of its strongest defenders.[2] It is, then, appropriate that we begin our overview of Habermas's work with a discussion of the Enlightenment effort to employ reason to build a free and rational society.

Enlightenment and Emancipation: On the Structure of a Critical Theory of Society

The philosophes were, in the main, firm in their belief in social progress. Modern civilization, they thought, represented a definite advance in the history of humanity. As the rationality embodied in science, law, moral philosophy and art penetrated into daily life, social progress would be an inevitable outcome. Modernization was viewed as exhibiting a movement of increasing rationality and social progress. Yet the philosophes were not reluctant to criticize current forms of modernity. In general, they sought to defend the overall development of modernity against antimodernist critics while criticizing its present defects.[3] Indeed, their criticisms of particular aspects of modernity were intended to be a social force promoting progress. Social criticism was, in other words, to be a social force contributing to a freer, more just society.

Habermas takes Baron d'Holbach as paradigmatic of the philosophes' aim to join reason to emancipation. D'Holbach held that the lack of freedom and happiness was a pervasive condition in contemporary France. This was a product of the dominance of false beliefs. D'Holbach highlights the role of religious and metaphysical dogmas in keeping individuals in a state of ignorance and oppression. Dogmatic traditions function, in effect, as ideologies reifying and legitimating the existing hierarchical social arrangments. In the face of an unfreedom rooted in ignorance, social criticism appeals to experience or to empirical observations in order to discredit dogmatic beliefs and norms. The power of reason to yield truths about the human, natural, and social worlds provides a vantage point from which to critically reflect upon reified social conventions and to achieve some release from their constraining power. The ultimate aim of reason, then, was to advance individual freedom by promoting critical self-reflection.

According to Habermas, the Enlightenment left an ambivalent heritage.[4] On the one hand, it perpetuated a long-standing Western tradition that connects reason to self-reflection and emancipation. On the other hand, there were serious limitations in the way the Enlightenment joined reason and freedom. Although the philosophes linked their critique of false consciousness or ignorance to a critique of social conditions (e.g., the power of the clergy or aristocracy), their social theory was underdeveloped. Little or no attempt was made to provide a systematic or theoretical account of societal dynamics. Moreover, the appeal by the philosophes to experience as a way to justify social criticism opened the way to a positivist reformulation of inquiry that uncoupled reason and emancipation. This intellectual ambivalence in Enlightenment social thought was subsequently manifested in the split between a tradition of Marxian critical theory and the establishment of a positivist orthodoxy in the social sciences.

The principal heir in the nineteenth century to the critical impulse of the Enlightenment was Marx. Like the philosophes, Marx believed the modern epoch to be progressive. Modernization includes processes of secularization, democratization, individuation, and technological advance which make possible human emancipation. His critique is directed at the blockage of this emancipatory potential by the capitalist form of modernization. Accordingly, the center of critique shifts from an epistemological to a materialist one.

Marx elaborates the connection between reason and emancipation in the form of a critical theory of society. Because the philosophes and their heirs in the nineteenth century (e.g., Fichte or Fourier) held that unfreedom is rooted in false beliefs, they believed they had only to reform consciousness to set the individual on the path to autonomy. Changing consciousness, moreover, meant eliminating error or substituting true for false ideas. It is as if the philosophes believed that simply by showing error (e.g., proving religion is a human and not a divine creation) individuals would be freed from dogma and social domination. Marx contests the idealist underpinnings of this position. Critique cannot be restricted to consciousness alone because consciousness is deeply implicated in social existence. Changing consciousness as a condition of freedom must be connected to the critique and reform of social conditions. Indeed, Marx demonstrates that the lack of freedom is not merely a matter of false consciousness but is, in essence, a social condition, that is, it involves social inequality, exploitation, economic insecurity, etc. Epistemological critique is, then, limited in a twofold way. First, it fails to connect the critique of consciousness with the critique of the social structural conditions that shape consciousness. Second, it fails to theorize domination as a condition of the social structure. Because unfreedom is anchored in the social structure, criticism must pass from an idealist critique of consciousness to a materialist critique of society.

In Marx, critique becomes a critical theory of society. It assumes the form of a theoretical analysis of societal dynamics with an eye to identifying the social structural sources of unfreedom and the potential sites of social crisis, conflict, and change. Marx's critical theory focused on the dialectics of social labor, that is, the processes by which humans make and remake themselves through their labor, processes that are highly contradictory yet reveal a trajectory of progress. *Capital* nicely illustrates the materialist formulation of the link between reason, self-reflection, and emancipation. Although Marx held a scientistic understanding of *Capital,* its basic categories (e.g., surplus value, fetishism of commodities, exploitation, class, economic crisis) and explanatory models (e.g., the thesis of the falling rate of profit, the model of general accumulation, the pauperization thesis or the tendency of capital toward the socialization of property) reveal a critical social analysis. Marx provided a critique of capitalism which would allow the working class to understand the social origin of their own malaise. He believed that social criticism would contribute to making the working class into a radical political movement. The critique of political economy aimed, ultimately, at changing capitalism. The power of critique to effect change hinges on its capacity to politicize the working class, a class whose social position and interests dispose them toward an oppositional standpoint with regard to capitalism. Critique may be a catalyst in social change but it cannot, in Marx's view, create the social conditions that give rise to oppositional groups. Nor can critique determine the form of political practice or the future form of a free society. Its chief role is that of promoting self-reflection or making individuals aware of the processes that shape their lives. Materialist critique has the potential to dereify the social world and thereby to anticipate social conditions involving enhanced freedom and happiness.[5]

A question remains: From what vantage point does Marx criticize society and what is the status of his critical theory? The social critic, according to Marx, cannot stand outside the society being criticized. The critic is a part of the society to be changed. Indeed, the Marxian critic assumes that the critic and the critic's theory is a product of the very society being criticized. The internal conflicts or contradictions of society make possible the critique by providing individuals whose social position gives them an interest in criticism and the categories of social critique. Furthermore, the very standards of criticisms are internal to the society of which the critic is a part. The beliefs, norms, and ideals in terms of which society is criticized are indigenous. In other words, the critic takes seriously the ideological claims in terms of which a society legitimates itself. The critic measures society by the very standards that it asks to be judged by. This strategy of "immanent critique" is apparent in *Capital.* Marx aims to show a disjunction between liberal bourgeois ideals and the reality of inequality and injustice. By revealing a social order resting upon coercion and domination and therefore illegitimate by its own standards, critique aims to stimulate critical self-reflection and the politicization of the working class.

Marx's critique of political economy established a tradition of critical theory. It was, however, a heterogeneous tradition and quite ambiguous with regard to the relation of theory to practice. On the one side, Marxism was reconceived in a positivist way and functioned to legitimate communist party rule. On the other side, the positivist Marxism of the Second International and the orthodox Marxism of the Soviet Communist Party was criticized by "Hegelian Marxists" like Korsch, Lukács, and Gramsci. Although this latter tradition of critical Marxism has assumed diverse forms (e.g., the existential Marxism of Sartre, the humanism of the praxis school, the phenomenological Marxism of Paci or Merleau Ponty), the critical theory of the so-called Frankfurt School was perhaps its most important expression between the two world wars. It is, in any event, the Frankfurt School's revision of Marxism that is crucial for understanding Habermas's views on the structure of critical theory.

By the 1940s the Frankfurt School, or at least its chief architects, Adorno and Horkheimer, abandoned the analysis of political economy in favor of a critique of instrumental reason. Drawing on the work of Simmel, Weber, and Lukács, the Frankfurt School gradually concluded that it was not capitalism that was the principal source of unfreedom but a particular identitarian and instrumental concept of reason that assumed cultural hegemony in the West. This instrumental notion of Western reason abolishes individuality. Hence, Adorno and Horkheimer conclude that Enlightenment reason itself turns out to be a more powerful force of domination than the mythical-religious dogmas it struggled to liberate us from.[6] Through the agencies of capitalism, bureaucracy, and science, Western reason creates a global civilizational dynamic that obliterates all forms of autonomy and individuality.

The shift from a critique of political economy to a critique of reason had two significant consequences for the structure of critical theory. First, a social scientific formulation of critical theory was replaced by a historico-philosophical one. With the publication of the *Dialectic of Enlightenment* and subsequently Horkheimer's *Eclipse of Reason,* social critique increasingly appeared as a philosophical critique of structures of consciousness. Second, the critique of instrumental reason ended up embracing a position close to the antimodernism of some German romantics. Modernity was described as an epoch in decline, a spiritually and morally exhausted era. If the path of modernization diverged from that of enhanced rationality, then modern societies were bereft of any emancipatory potential. The struggle for freedom required a complete civilizational transformation. As reason retreats from modernity, the link between critique, self-reflection, and emancipation is broken. There are no structures of rationality to be unleashed and no "subjects" to whom critique can appeal. Critique now functions as a mere shadow of what it was in Marx: it bears witness to the absence of reason in the present and keeps alive a memory of the interest of reason in freedom by finding traces of it in philosophy, art, and critical theory itself.[7]

Reaching maturity during the democratic rebuilding of West Germany and witnessing the rise of radical social movements in the face of a revitalized capitalist economy, Habermas contests key positions of the first generation of critical theorists. In order to demonstrate the continued viability of the Enlightenment project, Habermas presses for a crucial distinction. He distinguishes a critique which acknowledges the positive achievements of modernity but assails its limitations from a critique which describes modernization as a movement away from reason and freedom. The latter gravitates toward an antimodernist standpoint. Adorno and Horkheimer's thesis of the dialectic of enlightenment or Marcuse's theme of one-dimensionality typifies the latter type of critique. Habermas maintains that their critique of modernity fails to concede its very significant accomplishments, e.g., its institutionalization of the rule of law, formal democratic principles, civil, political, and social rights, cultural pluralism. In the end, the healthy suspicion of the Enlightenment by the Frankfurt School turned into cynicism and antimodernism. Habermas wishes to preserve their suspicion toward the Enlightenment but also wishes to endorse modernity as a progressive era.

Habermas's affirmative view of modernity allows him to defend the Enlightenment notion that critique can be a practical force contributing to the release of its emancipatory potential. In order for reason to play this role, it must, he believes, return to a social scientific standpoint. Habermas's reasoning follows Marx. Unfreedom is a condition of the social structure, not merely a product of structures of consciousness. Epistemological critique must be a part of a more comprehensive critical theory of society. Its aim is to stimulate critical self-reflection on the part of disempowered groups by identifying the social sources of unfreedom and highlighting possible social sites of crisis, conflict, and change. It follows that critique must draw from empirical social research in order to analyze societal dynamics and potential social crises. For Habermas, like Marx and the early Frankfurt School, critical theory must assume the form of a critical social science.[8]

From *The Logic of the Social Sciences* to *Knowledge and Human Interests* and *The Theory of Communicative Action,* Habermas has proposed varied formulations of the idea of a critical social science. I do not wish to review these successive proposals, which would take us into a range of epistemological debates that, in any event, have been adequately reviewed by others.[9] Instead, I want to focus on what I take to be Habermas's central position regarding the categorical structure of critical theory.

Habermas has consistently maintained that, methodologically speaking, a critical social science must integrate an interpretive or hermeneutic and a causal or empirical-analytic approach. The rationale for the former arises from the symbolic and meaningful nature of social reality. Individuals assign meaning to their action; these meanings are public or intersubjective; they are lodged in language, daily practices, institutional roles, norms, laws, and world views; they are, finally, constitutive of social life. Social analysis must interpret these configurations of meaning. The grounding of social inquiry in an interpretive approach is especially crucial for critical theory since its aim is to promote critical self-reflection. It can succeed only if individuals are able to recognize their own lives in the descriptions provided by the theory. In other words, the categorical structure of a critical theory must be sufficiently close to or resonant with people's historically specific, meaningfully constituted experience in order to accomplish the critical reflexivity that it intends.

Yet, critical theory cannot be confined to deciphering meanings. Interpretive sociologies are unable to explain the origin, structure, and development of cultural meanings. This requires that we relate cultural meanings to political and economic conditions which can be best studied by means of a social structural analysis that focuses on resource distribution, institutional roles, class dynamics, power relations, etc. Similarly, interpretive approaches that are concerned exclusively with understanding meaning must renounce the project of a critique of ideology. The latter presupposes that meanings do not only give coherence and direction to behavior but simultaneously contribute to producing social patterns involving domination and oppression. If we assume that the full significance of cultural meanings is not comprehended by their symbolic contents but that they have an ideological function, then we need an explanatory social analysis that relates meanings to conditions of power, social conflict, and domination. In other words, society is not simply a configuration produced by cultural traditions but is shaped by labor and power relations. Interpretive analysis must be joined to a structural explanation:

The objective framework within which social action can be comprehended without surrendering its intentionality is not merely a web of transmitted meanings and linguistically articulated traditions. The dimensions of labor and domination cannot be suppressed in favor of subjectively intended symbolic contents. A functionalist framework can also give non-normative conditions their due. Cultural tradition then loses the appearance of an absolute that a self sufficient hermeneutics falsely lends to it. Tradition as a whole can be assigned its place; it can be conceived in its relation to the systems of social labor and political domination. It thus becomes possible to grasp functions that the cultural tradition assumes within the system as a whole, functions that are not made explicit as such in tradition—i.e. ideological relations. . . . [10]

This discussion can be clarified by looking at Habermas's use of psychoanalysis as a model of critical theory.[11] Psychoanalysis resembles hermeneutics in that it seeks to understand a text or behavior whose meaning is obscure or ambiguous. Hermeneutics tries to render the text coherent by piecing together the available linguistic fragments and relating them to their broader social and intellectual context. Textual distortions are considered accidental, for example, a result of gaps in the text or lack of information about the author or context. In the logic of hermeneutics, interpretation does not go beyond making intelligible the manifest or explicit meanings of a verbal or linguistic utterance. Its aim is to arrive at a correct interpretation.

The psychoanalyst is likewise confronted with a text that is, in significant respects, unintelligible. Here, it is the analysand whose behavior is obscure to both him/herself and the analyst. However, the analyst assumes that the distortions (e.g., parapraxes, compulsions, or phobias) are immanent to the behavior or text. They arise from the present psychological state of the analysand. Indeed, the psychoanalyst views these distortions as meaningful; they are taken as external signs or symptoms of an internal psychological state. Specifically, they are manifestations of unconscious processes which shape the individual's thoughts, feelings, and behavior. In other words, observable, meaningful utterances or gestures carry a dual sense. They indicate a manifest meaning that pertains to what is explicitly being communicated and a latent or symbolic meaning in which linguistic utterances serve as signs of nonobservable unconscious dynamics, for example, repressed wishes, conflictual desires, or oedipal struggles. Interpretive work for the analyst presupposes, then, a theoretical framework which posits causal processes as a condition of understanding behavior.

Habermas distinguishes three levels in psychoanalytic theory. First, a metapsychological level which contains its basic categories (e.g., id, ego, superego, instinct, the unconscious) and its basic assumptions (e.g., the theory of instincts, the tripartite model of the psychic apparatus, the theory of neurosis). The metapsychology emerges out of reflection on the communication between analyst and analysand. On the basis of this metapsychology, psychoanalysts have elaborated models of psychosexual development. Habermas calls these models "general interpretations." They are analogous to theories in the empirical-analytic sciences in that they combine metacategories with empirical data in order to posit causal relationships, for example, between types of psychic conflict and symptomatic pathological behavior. The difference between psychoanalysis as a prototype of a critical science and empirical-analytic science becomes apparent when we turn to the third level: the application of general interpretations to the reconstruction of individual life histories. General interpretations are used to piece together the fragments of a life history provided by the analysand into a coherent interpretation. They make possible an interpretation of the analysand's behavior that she or he is unable to provide. In contrast to the natural and cultural sciences, the validity of psychoanalysis is not a matter of correspondence between theory and observations or of reaching a consensus about an interpretation. Rather, psychoanalytic theories are verified only if they are accepted by the analysand or incorporated into the analysand's self-understanding. Ultimately, the validity of general interpretations rests on their power to promote critical self-reflection or to make conscious what was unconscious. This critical reflexivity is a necessary condition of the analysand being released from unconscious processes that blocks her/ his autonomy. Psychoanalysis is, then, a type of science that aims to contribute to emancipation through promoting self-reflection.

Between *Knowledge and Human Interests* and *The Theory of Communicative Action* the general notion of critical theory as a unity of science and critique does not change. Yet at least two noteworthy alterations in the structure of critical theory can be observed. First, Habermas shifts from a quasi-transcendental effort to ground critical theory to a communicative-action theoretic justification. The appeal to an emancipatory cognitive interest is replaced by the claim that reason inheres in speech and linguistic communication. Second, Habermas sets out a much stronger theoretical agenda for critical theory. Indeed, in response to the relativist implications of hermeneutics, pragmatism, and poststructuralism, Habermas abandons the view of theory as a general interpretive framework since this suggests a historical-hermeneutic and therefore relativist standpoint. He wants to defend the proposition that there can be a purely objective theoretical standpoint. In his reconstruction of historical materialism, Habermas attempts to develop a theory of social evolution that draws on the "reconstructive sciences" elaborated by Chomsky, Piaget, and Kohlberg. Pure theory is now identified with these efforts to specify developmental logics or universal competences in speech, action, and communication. This does not, at least in principle, reflect a rejection on Habermas's part of his earlier position that linked critical theory to reflexivity and emancipatory practice. Reconstructive sciences deepen the theoretical and explanatory aspect of critical theory; the latter remains focused on providing historical accounts of contemporary societies that aim to promote critical self-reflection. The shift to a stronger theoretical program may not entail a significant departure from his earlier model of the structure of critical theory but it is indicative of a decisive change in the categorical structure of critical theory. Between *Knowledge and Human Interests* and *The Theory of Communicative Action* Habermas considerably reassesses the tradition of critical theory from an epistemological and normative standpoint. Central to this reconsideration is the effort both to ground critical theory and to elaborate its categorical structure within a communicative-action paradigm.[12] Following the focus of this volume, I'll concentrate on Habermas's critical revision of Marxism as a theory of society and history.

Reconstructing Historical Materialism:
From the Paradigm of Production to Communication

Habermas has consistently maintained that the revitalization of critical theory hinges on its return to a social scientific standpoint. The critique of instrumental reason led critical theory to abandon the categories of political economy and sociology. As a historico-philosophical critique, critical theory renounced its claim to identify potential system crises and sites of social conflict. To that extent critical theory gave up its role in promoting critical self-reflection and, for all practical purposes, severed the link between reason and emancipation. Habermas wants to redirect critical theory back to its Marxian aspiration to incorporate philosophical concerns with rationality in a critical theory of society.

Returning to the Marxian roots of critical theory does not mean, however, uncritically adopting Marx's theoretical perspective. In Habermas's view, nothing less than a complete overhaul of Marx's social theory is necessary. He wishes not merely to upgrade or revise Marxism but to reconstruct it. In the end, Habermas's reconstruction bears so little resemblance to Marx's original formulation that one is forced to conclude that it is purely for political reasons that it can be described as "Marxism" at all.

Reworking historical materialism is justified by its failure to anticipate and account for the principal events of recent history. Not only did worker revolutions fail to occur in Western capitalist societies but these societies have proven to be resilient. Capitalist development has coincided, moreover, with the integration of the working class. Today the chief sites of crisis and conflict are in noneconomic domains and the key oppositional groups are not social classes but heterogeneous social movements. Socialist revolutions have, of course, occurred in non-European, noncapitalist societies— a fact that is, once again, inconsistent with the main interpretive tradition of historical materialism. In short, Marx's social theory has failed to adequately analyze major contemporary developments. It is the obsolesence of classical Marxism that compels its reconstruction.

In Habermas's various efforts at reformulating historical materialism there is an abiding theme. Despite Marx's intent to build into his general theory of society and history a bifocal concern with the material reproduction of society through labor and institutional-normative social reproduction through communicative or symbolic interaction, he does not succeed. Marx's work, at both a metatheoretical and an empirical-theoretical level, minimizes the importance of the institutional-normative aspect of social reproduction.[13] For example, Marx programmatically conceptualizes historical change in terms of both the development of the productive forces propelled by scientific-technological advancement and developments in the institutional-normative and cultural order effected by class conflict. Yet not only does the concept of the mode of production not give us sufficient access to institutional and cultural dynamics but, repeatedly, Marx assumes that changes in the productive forces are the engine driving social development. Similarly, the base-superstructure model of society, a model Marx at times clearly endorses, reduces cultural dynamics to mere superstructural effects. The same reductionism is revealed to the extent that Marx identifies cultural meanings with ideology which in turn is conceptualized as a component of power relations between classes. It is not accidental that Marx nowhere provides an analysis of processes of identity formation, social integration, the normative regulation of action, the development of world views, or social solidarity. To gain access to these dynamics presupposes a categorical framework that fully acknowledges the symbolic grounding of society. Marx's productivist paradigm devalues or suppresses this dimension of social process.

Habermas believes that this reductionism in Marx has contributed to the dominance of a one-dimensional productivist paradigm in twentieth-century Marxism. This has, in turn, led to Marxism's diminishing theoretical and empirical value and credibility. Furthermore, as Marxism assumes a productivist form it provides a technocratic legitimation for an authoritarian politic. As a science of history revealing its laws and direction, Marxists claim—on the basis of their superior knowledge—legitimacy for their rule over the uninformed masses. Finally, within a productivist paradigm, socialism is defined as a planned society providing jobs, material security, and social stability. Considerations of democratization, community building, and individuation become secondary or are explicitly devalued. To the extent that Marxism is framed within a productivist paradigm, it becomes, ironically, a social force obstructing progressive change. Its critique becomes an integral part of the struggle for a free society.

This line of criticism points to the general direction of Habermas's reconstruction of historical materialism. Habermas wishes to recover the idealist dimension of Marxian social theory. He intends to recast the categorical framework of historical materialism in a way that allows him to account fully for sociocultural dynamics. This entails bringing culture back into the basic categories of historical materialism. In the course of this revision, Habermas reconsiders the relation between individual action, culture, and social structure. Ultimately, he is led to abandon virtually the whole conceptual apparatus of classical Marxism in favor of a conceptual structure that integrates action and systems theory.

In his writings prior to 1970, Habermas concentrated on the concept of action that was presupposed in the basic concepts and premises of historical materialism. He suggests that the chief ambiguities and tensions in Marx's social theory derive from his starting point: the concept of labor. Central to Marx's social theory is the assumption that the human species makes itself through its laboring activity. History is interpreted as consisting of successive social formations each defined by a specific mode of production. It is the internal dynamics of modes of production—the dialectic of the forces and relations of production—that explain social change. Yet the concept of labor is ambiguous and is susceptible to a reductionist account of social processes. On the one hand, labor highlights the instrumental aspect of action. A single individual relates to external nature, as subject to object, oriented toward its efficient mastery. On the other hand, conceptualizing labor as a social process points to a communicative model of action. Individuals relate to other individuals, as subject to subject; their behavior is guided by shared expectations, beliefs, and norms. In principle, then, Marx takes into account both material productive activity and the institutional-normative context of work. Unfortunately, Marx was not always clear about these two dimensions. In various programmatic statements, he identifies labor with its instrumental, task-oriented aspect. The origins of the productivism of Marxism is in Marx.

To avoid a productivist rendering of historical materialism, Habermas believes it is necessary to reconceive labor in the more abstract terms of action theory. Although he proposes several formulations in his early writings, the essential distinction is the one I alluded to between instrumental action which is a goal-oriented, monologic type of action guided by norms of efficiency and predictability and a more interactionist, understanding-oriented type of communicative action. It is crucial to note that the shift to a more abstract action-theoretical level is a key move. Habermas assumes that the concept of action is a basic frame of reference for social theory. What one assumes about the nature of action ramifies throughout the entire theoretical edifice. For example, if one begins with an instrumental concept of action that neglects the ends of action or its life-world context, then one's theory will lack categories and models that provide access to dynamics concerned with personal and societal identity, social integration, and solidarity. If an adequate conception of action entails recognizing its instrumental, task-aspect as a necessary condition of material reproduction and its communicative aspect as a necessary condition of institutional-normative reproduction, then social dynamics must be analyzed along these two dimensions. Societal development is framed as a process of expanding control over the natural and social environment through the growth of scientific-technological knowledge and as a process of institutional and cultural transformation rooted in changes in our practical-moral knowledge. From this multidimensional theoretical standpoint, emancipation involves the release from the material constraints of scarcity and a process of increasing reflexivity, consensual strategies of conflict resolution, and the democratization of the public realm.

Habermas's early writings are more in the mode of theoretical revisionism. The action-theoretic framework functioned as a way to avoid reductionism, not as a basis for a new conceptual reworking of historical materialism. The basic concepts and premises of historical materialism are not systematically overhauled but revised and elaborated in new ways. For example, Habermas draws on Freud to reconceive ideology and its relation to power but this is done largely within the framework of a more or less orthodox "Western" interpretation of historical materialism. The real break from the Marxist tradition comes with the publication of *Communication and the Evolution of Society.*[14]

The key piece in this collection is the essay "Toward a Reconstruction of Historical Materialism" (reprinted here as chapter 6). Habermas reconsiders the basic concepts and premises of historical materialism. In the course of his critical analysis he provides an outline of a reconstructed version of a Marxist theory of society.

The concept of labor served Marx not only as the basic epistemological category within which to interpret history but as the basic category of his philosophical anthropology. It was, to put it simply, the fact that humans make their nature through their labor that make humans unique. Drawing on recent anthropological research, Habermas argues that labor is not unique to humans since it is characteristic of hominoids as well. Labor distinguishes hominoids from primates but it does not define a uniquely human type of reproduction. What is unique to the earliest stage of the human species is that labor is organized along kinship lines. Moreover, this development presupposes linguistic communication since kinship structures are a symbolically and linguistically constituted and organized world. By arguing that labor and language or work and communicative action are fundamental to humans, Habermas is building into his basic concepts of historical materialism a concern with both material reproduction and institutional-normative reproduction.

The effort to elaborate a multidimensional social theory leads Habermas to advance similar criticisms of Marx's concept of the mode of production. Marx's attempt to conceive of the history of humanity in terms of the dialectic of social labor received a social theoretical articulation through the concept of a mode of production. History was divided into social formations; each was defined by a hegemonic mode of production. The internal dynamics of the mode of production explains social development. The concept of the mode of production is, then, the most basic social theoretical category of historical materialism. It refers, on the one hand, to productive forces (the labor power of the producers and technical and organizational knowledge) and, on the other hand, to relations of production which comprise the institutional framework that regulates access to the means of production and the distribution of wealth. Habermas indicates that the concept of relations of production entails a notion of communicative action as it refers to a shared framework of meanings and norms. He claims, however, that as the only point of conceptual access to sociocultural dynamics, it is inadequate. It is not a sufficiently differentiated concept to give us access to the kinds of processes (e.g., socialization, identity formation, social integration) that a general theory must be able to conceptualize in complex ways. The concept of relations of production cannot, for example, get at a range of institutional changes that rely on the development of world views since it has no notion of cultural development. Moreover, the concept of the mode of production is difficult to apply empirically. For example, many societies combine elements of different modes of production and therefore the concept is of limited value as a basis for developing a social typology. Habermas claims that, contrary to Marx's view, the development of the productive forces can account only for institutional crises, not their resolution and transformation. Habermas concludes that the concept of the mode of production cannot be defended as an adequate basis on which to differentiate social formations and analyze the causes and dynamics of their succession.

Habermas introduces the concept of "organizational principle" as a more comprehensive and historically sensitive concept than that of the mode of production:

By principles of organization I understand innovations that become possible through developmental-logically reconstructible stages of learning, and which institutionalize new levels of societal learning. The organizational principle of a society circumscribes ranges of possibility. It determines in particular: within which structures changes in the system of institutions are possible; to what extent the available capacities of productive forces are socially utilized and the development of new productive forces can be stimulated; to what extent system complexity and adaptive achievements can be heightened. A principle of organization consists of regulations so abstract that in the social formation which it determines a number of functionally equivalent modes of production are possible. Accordingly, the economic structure of a given society would have to be examined at two analytic levels: firstly in terms of the modes of production that have been concretely combined in it; and then in terms of that social formation to which the dominant mode of production belongs.[15]

Organizational principles can be identified by their institutional core. This regulates access to the means of production and determines the dominant form of social integration. Habermas tentatively specifies four social formations (primitive, traditional, capitalist, and postcapitalist), each differentiated by a unique organizational principle or institutional core. The idea of an organizational principle is intended to give us access not only to property and class relations but to sociocultural processes centered on legitimation, identity formation, or social solidarity.

Consistent with his aim to break away from the productivist bias of Marxism, Habermas further maintains that the institutional core cannot always be identified with the economic base of a society. The economy cannot always be considered the "base" or the basic domain of a social formation. In the main interpretive tradition of Marxism, the institutional-normative framework of society or the relations of production are identified with economic property relations. Accordingly, society could be described in terms of its class division and its historical trajectory analyzed in terms of the dynamics of class conflict. Habermas takes issue with this position. He maintains that only in liberal capitalist societies do the relations of production assume a directly economic form; only in this social formation is the economy the social base. In other societies, a noneconomic domain regulates access to the means of production, determines the distribution of social wealth, and defines the dominant form of social integration. For example, in "primitive" societies it is kinship structures which form the institutional core and therefore function as the base of society.

Building a multidimensional focus into his social theory requires that Habermas rework Marx's view of societal development. Marx held that social change stems from the internal contradictions of a mode of production. Specifically, in every society the productive forces reach a stage of development that renders the relations of production or the institutional-normative framework restrictive. The result of this imbalance between the productive forces and the relations of production is a systems crisis exhibited in structural dysfunctions (e.g., economic crises) and in severe social disturbances (e.g., class struggle). Social change involves an adjustment of the relations of production to the new level reached by the productive forces. Class conflict is the mechanism by which this is accomplished. Habermas argues that while the imbalance between the forces and relations of production may explain system crises, it cannot account for its resolution in the form of institutional-normative change or the creation of a new type of social integration. Innovation at the level of institutional norms or roles involves a novel application of moral-practical knowledge. In other words, when individuals are faced with an institutional crisis, they cannot draw on the scientific-technical knowledge embodied in the productive forces to resolve the crisis. Institutional change is not simply a matter of applying technical knowledge about how social processes work but entails changes in norms of justice, social roles, and personal identities. Institutional change requires that individuals draw on moral-practical knowledge as it is available in cultural traditions, legal systems, constitutions, ideologies, and world views. The transformation of modes of social integration may be conceptualized, at the highest level of abstraction, as an analytically autonomous process involving the development of moral-practical knowledge. Whereas the development of the productive forces hinges on the kind of learning that is embodied in scientific-technical knowledge, the development of new forms of social integration, institutional order, normative regulation, and public life depends on the kind of learning that is embodied in moral-practical knowledge. Indeed, the extent of Habermas's revisionism is dramatized by his claim that it is the development of normative knowledge and related changes in forms of social integration that is the "pacesetter" of social evolution.

Social evolution can be comprehended at a depth-analytical level as a learning process:

Only an analytic answer can explain why a society takes an evolutionary step and how we are to understand that social struggles under certain conditions lead to a new level of social development. I would like to propose the following answer: the species learns not only in the dimension of technically useful knowledge decisive for the development of productive forces but also in the dimension of moral-practical consciousness decisive for structures of interaction. The rules of communicative action do develop in reaction to changes in the domain of instrumental and strategic action; but in doing so they follow their own logic.[16]

Innovation at either the level of productive forces or relations of production presupposes a learning process. The transformation of the former requires the application of scientific, technical, or organizational knowledge; change in the latter entails the application of moral-practical knowledge. From this vantage point, a theory of social evolution must be able to explain the dynamics and stages of development of learning in these two dimensions. It is for this reason that Habermas has recourse to the reconstructive schemes of cognitive and moral development advanced by Kholberg and Piaget. Habermas believes that these developmental logics intended to account for individual cognitive and moral development can be used, with some qualifications, to analyze the development of scientific-technical knowledge and the development of world views, cultural traditions, and legal systems. Just as stages of individual development imply a sequence of stages in which constraints and opportunities for behavior accompany each stage, this holds at a societal level. The reconstructive sciences make possible a depth-structural explanation of societal development. The stage of cognitive and normative development embodied in social and cultural structures defines the opportunities and limits of sociocultural innovation. It is important to emphasize that this developmental approach is simply one dimension of a theory of social evolution. To explain actual historical changes an empirical analysis of historically specific social dynamics would be indispensable. Such an analysis would, of course, draw from these developmental approaches in order to explain a change in organizational principles.

After "Toward a Reconstruction of Historical Materialism," Habermas proceeded to elaborate more fully the presuppositions and conceptual framework of his social theory. This theoretical articulation has received its most comprehensive form in *The Theory of Communicative Action*. This text attempts to integrate Habermas's philosophical interest in developing a theory of rationality with his social theoretical interest in providing a conceptual scheme from which to analyze potential system crises in contemporary Western societies. By way of concluding this section, I highlight some of the central social theoretical themes of this work.[17]

From the vantage point of social theory, Habermas's aim is to integrate the focus on action that one finds in interpretive sociologies with social structural or systems analysis that has been the primary concern of the major social theoretical paradigms (e.g., Marxism, functionalism, or French structuralism). To accomplish this synthesis, Habermas endeavors to rethink the elementary premises of both action and systems theory. Toward this end he draws on recent developments in the philosophy of language, phenomenology, French structuralism, and systems theory. In the end, Habermas's theoretical aim is to provide an overarching conceptual framework that sets out the basic problems, premises, and concepts of a synthetic social inquiry. In this regard, *The Theory of Communicative Action* extends a tradition of general social theory linking Habermas to Marx and Parsons and, more recently, to Luhmann and Giddens. It is social theory conceived in "modernist" terms as a foundationalist enterprise.

Following his most eminent predecessors—Marx, Weber, Mead, and Parsons—Habermas begins his theoretical elaboration with the concept of action.[18] Concepts of action are fundamental to the general theoretical framework one develops. Habermas maintains that, in the main, Western social theory has adopted a purposive-rational or instrumental action model. This posits an individual who must take into account objects (people and things) in the environment in the pursuit of a pregiven goal. Efficiency in coordinating the means and ends is the guiding norm of action. Habermas criticizes this model on the grounds that it does not sufficiently take into account the interpersonal aspect of action or its linguistically mediated character. It does not consider action from the standpoint of behavior oriented to mutual understanding and agreement. Habermas believes that the work of Mead, Wittgenstein, and contemporary ordinary language philosophers points to an alternative model of action, which he calls communicative action. Central to the concept of communicative action is an idea of action as always embedded in an interactive context. To the extent that acts are linguistically constituted, language embeds us in an interpersonal communicative context. Furthermore, focusing on the linguistically mediated nature of interaction we can observe that communication presupposes agreement on a range of claims about ourselves and the world. Social interaction occurs smoothly to the extent that individuals negotiate some consensus about these claims. Communicative action presupposes, in other words, that action is oriented to agreement about certain basic claims and that some level of consensus is a condition of social reproduction.

For Habermas, all human action involves language use and raises validity claims. Every speech act or every act of communication implicitly raises several types of validity claims. For example, a speaker may raise the claim that the statements made are true or that the act is correct in terms of the prevailing normative context or that the speaker is sincere in what she or he is saying. Ongoing interaction presupposes a level of agreement regarding these validity claims. Moreover, each validity claim entails a specific relation between the self and the world. For example, truth claims presuppose a relation between the self and the "objective world" about which true statements are possible. Normative claims involve a relation of the self to a social world of normatively regulated action. Claims regarding the sincerity of what one says point to a relation between the self and a "subjective world." Corresponding to these validity claims are specific modes of argumentation or discourse. When validity claims are disputed or when beliefs about any of the three "worlds" are challenged, individuals may be forced to give reasons for their claims in order to restore agreement. Insofar as claims are problematized in a way that calls for reflexive deliberation, Habermas calls this "argumentation." For example, Habermas calls argumentation involved in disputes about truth claims "theoretical discourse." When claims about the rightness of norms are contested, individuals will, if they do not resort to manipulation or force (strategic action), resort to "practical discourse" in order to restore a consensus.

We need to pause for a moment so as not to lose sight of the point behind this elaboration of the concept of communicative action. At one level, Habermas is simply trying to build into his social theory a conceptual point of departure that attends to sociocultural dynamics. There is, however, another, more philosophical, impulse informing this conceptual elaboration. Habermas wants to press the claim that communicative action cannot be conceptualized without acknowledging that reason is a force in it. He argues that in communicative action individuals are oriented toward reaching an agreement on the beliefs about which validity claims can be raised. Moreover, in order for this behavior to remain a case of communicative action and not, for example, change into strategic action, the agreement must be consensual. This consensus must be based solely on the force of the reasons given for the beliefs, not on coercion or manipulation. Habermas concludes that in communicative action reason or the demand to justify beliefs and behavior by giving reasons is a motivating force. Furthermore, to the extent that the orientation to agreement is not restricted to truth claims but includes beliefs about the correctness of norms or aesthetic judgments, a more comprehensive notion of rationality is advanced than is typically defended in contemporary Western culture. Rationality covers not only science; consensus is possible regarding normative and aesthetic disputes as well. This comprehensive notion of rationality functions as a standard of social criticism. A rational society or rational way of life, in other words, is one in which reasons are continuously given to justify behavior and where public spaces exist to permit free or uncoerced debate over questions of cognitive, normative and aesthetic truth. One of Habermas's more controversial claims is that in modern Western societies these possibilities for a rational society are most fully available.[19]

Developing a theory of action is, in Habermas's view, an integral part of building a general theory of society. In particular, the distinction between instrumental or purposive-rational action and communicative action ensures a dual focus on "material" and symbolic social processes. However, action theory must be joined to a categorical level that can conceptualize the social structural aspects of social life. In this regard, Habermas links action theory to a phenomenological and systems theoretical level.[20]

Communicative action presupposes a framework of common understandings. These shared convictions—e.g., situational definitions, norms, and values—are typically held in a prereflexive way and can be made only partially explicit. These background meanings are embodied in language, customs, and cultural traditions. They make up the realm of the "lifeworld." This consists of a dense network of shared meanings that individuals draw from to construct identities, to negotiate situational definitions, or to create social solidarity. Because the motivational/orientational structures reproduced in the lifeworld are a necessary condition of institutional order, the maintenance of the lifeworld is essential for societal reproduction.

The concept of the lifeworld is limited as a way to conceptualize social structural dynamics. Habermas introduces the concept of system to supplement it. The notion of a systems level of analysis arises from the analysis of the lifeworld. Habermas argues that the institutional core of the lifeworld is the household. Historically, kinship structures have been limited as a basis of societal organization. Population pressures, intersocietal contacts, or the demands for luxury goods create a need to organize complex activities in a more efficient manner. The result is the emergence of functionally differentiated systems out of the lifeworld. At an institutional level, the appearance of economic and political administrative structures which are functionally independent of the kinship unit is the key evolutionary development. These functional systems, with their emphasis on efficiency, predictability, and control, highlight the instrumental aspect of action and social coordination.

From this conceptual vantage point, social evolution is viewed as a two-sided rationalization process of the social system and the lifeworld. The development of social systems can be charted as a process of increasing internal differentiation, complexity, growing organizational predictability, and so on. The rationalization of the lifeworld is analyzed in terms of enhanced reflexivity, the universalization of beliefs and the differentiation of the value or knowledge spheres (science, morality, and art). In general, Habermas sees societal development as progressive. The differentiation of functional systems make possible higher levels of institutional mastery over natural and social processes which can potentially enhance our autonomy. The rationalization of the lifeworld makes possible higher levels of reflexivity, the criticizibility of interpretations, the demystification of legitimations, and the expansion of spaces for public discussion. This social evolutionary perspective provides Habermas with a new vantage point from which to critically analyze modernity. In the final section of this overview, I consider this broader view of Western social development.

Capitalism, Democracy, and the State: Analyzing Contemporary Western Societies

Habermas's rethinking of the Marxian tradition has extended beyond reconstructing the basic premises and assumptions of historical materialism. He has revised the Marxian analysis of modern society. To the extent that the Marxian categorical framework is seriously defective, its empirical description of modernity will be flawed as well. For example, the failure to develop categories to explain dynamics centered on identity formation, social integration, or the development of world views suggests that Marxian explanations of social development will be inadequate. However brilliant *Capital* is as an analysis of modern social structure, it is a flawed portrait.

Capital and the various efforts at theoretical elaboration in the twentieth century (e.g., Hilferding, Baran and Sweezy, or Ernest Mandel) are in need of reformulation for another reason. History has rendered some of the basic premises of *Capital* obsolete. For example, the base-superstructure model that informs *Capital* or the assumption of the primacy of the economy allowed Marx to believe that by uncovering the economic laws of motion he could explain the dynamics of the whole social system. Recent social developments have made this assumption less and less credible. The state has become a principle agency in the production and distribution of wealth and cannot be described as superstructural. Similarly, the role of science in the political, economic, and cultural spheres suggests a different relation between culture and society than was salient in the nineteenth century. In short, to grasp contemporary modernity requires that the relationship between economy, culture, and the state be reconceived to give more analytical autonomy to each sphere and to frame their interaction in an explicitly multicausal, cybernetic way.

Recent social developments point, moreover, to a new configuration of thematic concerns that press well beyond the classical Marxian project of a political economic analyis of capitalism. The major threat to a rational society today is not the irrationality of capitalism exhibited, for example, in economic crises or worker insecurity. Habermas does not deny the seriousness of continued social inequities or class divisions, but he contends that these socioeconomic dynamics are not today the chief sites of social crisis or conflict. Social crises in contemporary Western societies are more likely to occur in noneconomic realms. In Habermas's view, it is concerns centered on the cultural underpinnings of the institutional order and problems revolving around maintaining a vigorous democratic public realm—problems of legitimation, social integration, democratization—that are the major issues in the current debate over social rationalization. As the site of potential social crises shifts, the focus of social conflict changes and the principal oppositional movements likewise are different from those in the Marxian synthesis. Social conflict centers around "quality of life" issues, for example, the protection of the natural environment, the preservation of the integrity of communities, the social inclusion of hitherto marginal or discredited groups, or the control over local education and health decisions. Political opposition arises less from the working class than from the new social movements, e.g., the movements for civil rights, liberation movements, or the peace and antinuclear movements.[21]

The task confronting a critical theory of contemporary capitalist societies is not that of revising *Capital* but of producing a new *Capital* for the post-World War II period. Although Habermas cannot claim to have accomplished this, we find successive efforts to at least outline what such an analysis might look like.

Habermas's pre-1970 writings are important primarily because they show his break from a more orthodox Marxian perspective on modernity. He introduces thematic concerns that go beyond the theorization of capitalism. Specifically, he highlights the retreat in Western industrial societies from a democratic culture with its norms of civic participation, ideological debate, and political accountability. For example, in *The Structural Transformation of the Public Realm* he describes the appearance in the eighteenth century of a democratic public realm (e.g., cafés, newspapers, journals) involving general discussion on public moral and political issues.[22] He details its enfeeblement in the nineteenth century under the impact of capitalism, party politics, and the commercialization of the media. In the twentieth century the public realm is depoliticized as practical-moral questions about a good and just society are marginal or entirely suppressed. The essays collected in *Towards a Rational Society* relate a similar story of the decline of a democratic political culture.[23] In "Technology and Science as 'Ideology'" (reprinted here as chapter 11), Habermas argues that the shift in the twentieth century to an interventionist state has been accompanied by efforts to redefine politics in a technocratic way. State regulation of the economy and its involvement in a range of social concerns (e.g., education, family matters, health) is justified by reference to nonideological reasons, e.g., economic growth, social stability, the maintenance of standards of living, or national security. Habermas alludes to the possibility of technocratic modes of legitimation assuming social dominance and precipitating a potential crisis of meaning and identity. The repression of a democratic moral and political culture by science, capitalism, and bureaucracy is seen as the chief threat to a good society.

These early writings are programmatic in nature and sustain the Frankfurt School vision of a totally administered society under the dominance of instrumental reason. With the publication of *Legitimation Crisis* Habermas offers a much more systematic analysis of late capitalism and one less unidimensional in its understanding and assessment.[24] The text proceeds from the claim that the major site of social crisis and conflict has shifted from the economic to the political and cultural spheres. The irrationality of capitalism continues to be exhibited in episodic cycles of economic growth and recession. However, state policies aimed at averting economic crises have minimized their social impact. Habermas is convinced that economic crises no longer have the potential of generating a societal crisis but can be addressed as a local social disturbance.

Although the state manages to avoid major economic crises, its very intervention creates new potential for crisis at the political level. Habermas speaks of a rationality crisis when the state is unable to reconcile the need for planning that is essential for safeguarding economic growth with the private control over resources that is definitive of capitalism. Rationality crises are manifested, then, in the failure of crisis management policies due to conflicting interests between capitalists or because of the private character of capital investment decisions.

Habermas speaks of a legitimation crisis when the state is faced with the contradictory demands of ensuring capital accumulation while needing to maintain mass loyalty. The former imperative requires that the state act to promote the particular interests of those strata (e.g., property owners, high-level management, administrative-technical elites) who most benefit from capitalism. The latter imperative demands that the state promote the general welfare of society. In other words, the class interests of the state that are revealed in its social and economic policies must be concealed in order to maintain its legitimacy. The latter rests on its claim to represent the general interest of society. To the extent that the state is perceived as a "capitalist state" or as a class-based state, it experiences legitimation problems. The withdrawal of mass loyalty may be manifested in citizen apathy, mass social disobedience, or proposals for social reform. Legitimation crises, then, hold out the potential of becoming a major social crisis.

In response to these legitimation problems, the state is best served by a depoliticized citizenry. Various policies seem designed or at least have the consequence of minimizing citizen political involvement. Habermas mentions, for example, material compensations in the form of state-funded support services and social welfare programs. To the extent that citizens give their loyalty in exchange for material rewards, the state avoids legitimation problems. Central to averting legitimation problems is the restriction of democracy to a formal parliamentary type. Confining citizen political involvement to periodic voting confers legitimacy on the state while providing state officials with substantial freedom from public accountability. Finally, elite, technocratic, or systems theories depoliticize citizens by redefining politics as a series of technical-administrative problems appropriately under the charge of specialized experts.

Although problems of legitimation appear to be endemic to late capitalist society, it is only when they are joined to a "motivation crisis" that a full-blown societal crisis may occur. Motivation crises can be interpreted as a type of legitimation crisis. In such a crisis, mass support for social institutions is withdrawn because individual motives and orientations do not lead to behavior supportive of late capitalist society. Habermas suggests that a motivation crisis could precipitate a general societal crisis. In such a condition, the crisis can be resolved by either "uncoupling" dynamics of identity formation from system integration or by transforming the system. The former response points in the direction of a technocratic solution; the latter holds out that potential for a social order anchored in a revitalized democratic culture.

To grasp this argument we need to understand an elementary point: societal reproduction presupposes the development of individual identities that are complementary to the social roles required for institutional order. Formation of these identities presupposes the vitality of those cultural traditions whose beliefs, values, and norms are internalized as part of the dynamic of personality development. Habermas's claim is that recent social developments are undermining the cultural traditions which are today functionally indispensable. Specifically, late capitalist societies require individuals whose highest values revolve around building a career and achieving a fulfilling private life. This value pattern is a product of the Judeo-Christian heritage and liberal ideological traditions. Under the impact of long-term processes of secularization, bureaucratization, scientism, and statism, these traditions and their capacity to shape identities are weakened. In short, the cultural underpinnings of late capitalist society are being eroded by its core social structural dynamics.

Without the right psycho-social attitudes the requisite level of identification with institutional roles is lacking. This poses a social danger since it threatens institutional reproduction. Habermas alludes to two possible outcomes. The first is that institutional order will be reestablished on a strictly technocratic basis. Individuals would, in effect, accept role demands in exchange for instrumental rewards without requiring that institutional norms and ends be justified by reference to any other substantive values or ideals. A second possibility is that capitalism will be transformed in a direction that more fully realizes the rationality embedded in social institutions. Habermas believes that there are structures of rationality embodied in science, postrepresentational art, and moral and juridical codes that are antagonistic to late capitalist societies. Specifically, these cultural developments embody, to varying degrees, a "communicative" ethical or moral consciousness whose chief feature is the demand for discursive justification of social conventions. This condition of social legitimacy can be satisfied only in a situation of relative social equality and a democratized political culture. It is Habermas's contention, moreover, that this utopian potential of late capitalism has been concretized in the demands of the new social movements, e.g., the women's, gay, black, ecological, and peace movements. Despite the heterogeneity of their political agenda, these groups represent, in Habermas's view, carriers of a communicative ethic and of the demand for a more rational society.

Between *Towards a Rational Society* and *The Theory of Communicative Action* Habermas has maintained the thesis that the basic contradictions of late capitalist society surface in disturbances in the cultural sphere. In "Technology and Science as 'Ideology'" he emphasizes how the devitalization of ideology under the impact of a technocratic consciousness may avert legitimation problems but threatens to disrupt social integration. In *Legitimation Crisis* Habermas describes how the culture of capitalism is eroded under the weight of capitalism, scientism, and a bureaucratic state. This creates the possibility that citizens may withdraw their support from the state (legitimation crisis) or from social institutions in general (motivation crisis). The analysis of crisis potential in *Legitimation Crisis* is at the core of Habermas's view of contemporary modernity in his subsequent work.

In *The Theory of Communicative Action* the crisis theory is reformulated in terms of the thesis of the "colonization of the lifeworld." In addition, Habermas situates his analysis of late capitalism within an encompassing theory of sociocultural rationalization.

As we have seen, Habermas criticizes the perspectives on modernization developed by Marx, Weber, Lukács, and the Frankfurt School. Although these theorists differ significantly in the details of their account of social evolution, they share the view that modernization is a rationalization process that leads to the dominance of instrumental modes of action and social order. Emancipation entails either an extension of instrumental rationalization (e.g., Marx) or an epochal transformation to a postmodern society (Frankfurt School) or the ideal itself is repudiated as an illusion (Weber). According to Habermas, this perspective on modernity is flawed. It implies a teleological model of action that fails to maintain the distinctiveness of communicative modes of action and order. It therefore fails to conceptualize the rationalization of the lifeworld as an analytically autonomous process. Furthermore, this theory of modernization fails to acknowledge the achievements of modernity and its continued potential for yielding a more rational society.

Habermas proposes an alternative model that conceives of modernization as involving social and cultural rationalization. The former relates to the progressive differentiation and complexity of social systems and involves enhanced levels of instrumental reason. The latter pertains to changes in the lifeworld: it involves the differentiation of the value spheres of truth, goodness, and beauty and their corresponding modes of knowledge (science, moral theory, aesthetic criticism), as well as the increasing secularization of beliefs and the institutionalization of the norms of reflexivity and criticism. In general, Habermas believes that this two-sided rationalization process creates the conditions of a good society, e.g., material abundance, enhanced organizational control over the environment, reflexivity, the criticizability of beliefs and norms. Social progress, then, requires that rationalization occur at both a system and lifeworld level and that a balance be maintained between them.

Habermas contends, however, that under the dominance of capitalism, rationalization has occurred in an abridged and uneven way.[25] He highlights three major limitations of rationalization processes in modern societies. First, scientific-technological knowledge and interests have been overdeveloped in comparison to moral and aesthetic knowledge and concerns. Devaluing moral-practical knowledge contributes to depoliticization and to a nondemocratic polity. In a fully rational society, each value sphere would be fully developed as rationality would be identified as covering scientific truth as well as moral and aesthetic knowledge. Second, there is a tendency for these expert cultures of science, morality, and art to become isolated from daily life. Although some degree of autonomous development of these value/knowledge spheres is necessary and progressive—it enhances reflexivity and critical discourse—daily life becomes impoverished as these expert cultures become wholly autonomous. In a fully rational society, the rationality developed in each value sphere would enrich everyday life through the institutionalization of regular interchanges between expert cultures and daily life. Third, Habermas believes that the balance between the rationalization of system and the lifeworld has been disrupted. Capitalism has promoted the rationalization of the social system at the expense of the lifeworld. Specifically, in late capitalism the instrumental modes of organizing and coordinating action characteristic of social systems (economy and the state) expand into the lifeworld. The attempt by the system, with its instrumental logic, to replace communicative action as the coordinating agency of the lifeworld is what Habermas calls the "colonization of the lifeworld." Although the lifeworld can be reproduced only through communicative action, these system incursions amount to an assault on the communicative infrastructure of the lifeworld. System penetration into the lifeworld destroys traditional forms of life and contributes to the appearance of unique problems associated with identity formation, anomie, psychopathologies, and the loss of meaning. These disturbances can evolve into major system problems to the extent that societal reproduction—both at the system and lifeworld level—continues to require stable identities and specific patterns of motivation and value orientation. In a fully rational society, the rationalization of system and lifeworld would occur in a balanced way; mutual interdependence would be maintained without either dimension overextending its proper place.

Habermas believes that his perspective on modernity and its current discontents allows him to explain the new politics of the 1970s and 1980s. The main political struggles of the last two decades have centered on the new social movements. The issues they define as basic revolve around concerns of equality, self-realization, issues of identity and community, the preservation of the environment, and peace issues. Habermas interprets these movements as reactions to system assaults on the lifeworld. Despite the diversity of interests and political projects of these heterogeneous groups, they have resisted the colonization of the lifeworld. In this regard, we can see a parallel between Marx and Habermas. Marx wrote *Capital* to clarify for the working class the conditions that sustain their social oppression and the possibilities of transforming these conditions. Habermas reformulates critical theory in order to clarify the conditions that make the new social movements possible and to identify major sites of contemporary social crises and change. In this regard, Habermas can correctly be described as a major contemporary heir to the tradition of Marxism and critical theory.

Part One
ON CRITICAL THEORY

Chapter One
DOGMATISM, REASON, AND DECISION: ON THEORY AND PRACTICE IN A SCIENTIFIC CIVILIZATION

In the classical tradition of philosophy, the relationship between theory and practice always referred to the good and proper life, the "true" life, both individual and collective, of individuals and citizens. In the eighteenth century this concept of a life guided by theory expanded to include the perspective provided by the philosophy of history. Since that time theory, which is both directed toward practice and dependent on it, has ceased to concern itself with the natural, true, or proper actions and institutions of a humanity whose essential nature remains constant, but has rather focused on the objective developmental context of a species which produces itself and which remains destined to attain its essence, i.e., humanity. Theory continues to claim to provide orientation for right action, but the realization of the good, happy, and rational life has been stretched out along the vertical axis of world history; practice has been extended to cover stages of emancipation. Rational practice is now interpreted as liberation from external compulsion, just as theory guided by an interest in this liberation is interpreted as enlightenment. The cognitive interest of this theory of enlightenment is expressly critical. It presupposes a specific experience, one reflected in Hegel's *Phenomenology of Mind* as much as in Freud's psychoanalysis: the experience of emancipation through critical insight into relationships of power, which derive their objectiveness solely from the fact that they have not been recognized for what they are. It is through analysis that critical reason gains power over dogmatic constraint.[1]

Reason takes a partisan position in the controversy between critique and dogmatism, and it gains ground with each new stage of emancipation. With practical reason of this kind, insight converges with an express interest in liberation by means of reflection. A higher level of reflection is equivalent to a step forward in realizing the autonomy of the individual, to the elimination of suffering and the furthering of genuine happiness. Reason, engaged in the struggle against dogmatism, has resolutely adopted this interest; moreover, reason does not consider itself separate from the moment of decision. Rather, the individual's decisions can be judged rationally, by the standard of the one objective decision demanded in the interest of reason itself. Reason has not yet renounced the will to the rational.

This constellation of dogmatism, reason, and decision has changed profoundly since the eighteenth century in direct proportion to the degree that the sciences have become productive forces in social development. For to the extent to which our civilization has become scientific, the aspect of theory that was once directed to practice has become constricted. The laws of self-reproduction require an advanced industrial society to maintain itself through the continually expanding technical control of nature and through the continually refined regulation, through social organization, of human beings and their relations to one another. In this system, science, technology, industry, and regulation interlock in a circular process. The relationship of theory and practice can come into play only as the purposive-rational application of techniques guaranteed by empirical science. The social potency of the sciences is reduced to the power of technical control—their potential for enlightened action becomes a moot point. The empirical-analytic sciences produce technical recommendations, but they do not provide answers to practical questions. The claim on which theory's former relation to practice was founded has become apocryphal. Emancipation through enlightenment is replaced by instruction in the control of objective, or objectified, processes. Socially efficacious theory is now concerned not with the consciousness of human beings who live together and communicate with one another but rather with the behavior of those who are engaged in manipulation. As a productive force in industrial development, theory changes the basis of human life, but it no longer extends critically beyond this basis to raise life to another level, purely for the sake of life itself.

But of course the real difficulty in the relation of theory to practice arises not from science's new function as a technical force but rather from the fact that we are no longer able to distinguish between technical and practical power.[2] Even a scientific civilization is not excused from practical questions; a peculiar danger arises, consequently, when the process of making civilization scientific goes beyond technical questions without freeing itself from the level of reflection of a rationality restricted to technology. For then no attempt at all is made to attain a rational consensus of citizens regarding the practical control of their destiny. Instead, an attempt is made to attain control over history technically, in the form of a perfected administration of society, an attempt that is as impractical as it is unhistorical. When theory still had a genuine relation to practice, it conceived society as a dynamic complex of communicating human beings who have to bring social intercourse into the context of conscious communication and within that context form themselves into a collective subject capable of action; otherwise, the fortunes of a society whose individual parts are increasingly rationalized would slip from the grasp of the rational cultivation that thus becomes all the more necessary. A theory that confuses action with control, on the other hand, is no longer capable of such a perspective. It conceives society as a nexus of modes of behavior in which rationality is supplied only by the understanding of sociotechnical controls, not by a coherent collective consciousness, that is, not by the interested reason that can attain practical power only through the minds of politically enlightened citizens.

In advanced industrial society, research, technology, production, and administration have converged to form an obscure but functionally interlocked system. This system has literally become the basis of our life. Our relationship to this system is peculiar—intimate and at the same time alienated. On the one hand we are tied to it externally, through a network of organizations and a chain of consumer goods; on the other hand, it remains remote from our knowledge and even more from our reflection. Only a theory directed toward practice can recognize the paradox in this state of affairs, a paradox which is nevertheless obvious: the more the growth and transformation of society are determined by the extreme rationality of research conducted through a division of labor, the less this civilization, which has now become scientific, is anchored in the knowledge and conscience of its citizens. With this disparity, techniques that are directed by social science and selected in accordance with decision theory, ultimately even cybernetically controlled techniques encounter a limitation they cannot overcome; the disparity can be altered only through a change in the state of consciousness itself, that is, through the practical working of a theory that is not merely efficient in manipulating things and reifications but rather advances reasons's interest in autonomy and responsibility [*Mündigkeit*][3] in autonomy of action and liberation from dogmatism, through the penetrating ideas of a persistent critique.

Committed Reason and the Interest in Enlightenment: Holbach, Fichte, and Marx

These categories, like the constellation of dogmatism, reason, and decision on which the unity of theory and practice is founded, date from the eighteenth century. In the preface to his *System of Nature*, Paul Thiry d'Holbach speaks of the contamination of the mind by prejudices: the mind becomes so encumbered by opinions accumulated since childhood that it can extricate itself only with the greatest difficulty.[4] Here dogmatism still goes by the name of prejudice; it is confronted by a reason guided by experience. That kind of reason urges individuals to study nature; in contrast, the misfortune of dogmatism arises from attempts to transcend the visible world. Critical reason will restrict human beings to the role of physicist; they become entangled in the chimeras of their prejudices because they try to be metaphysicians before being physicists. Here, then, the distinction for which the principles of positivism are merely a refrain has already been made with utmost clarity. And yet the Enlightenment's intention in opposing reason to dogmatism was not positivistic.

The term prejudice, in fact, encompassed more than the quintessence of subjective opinion. Dogmatic constraint is not a simple error, to be readily dispelled by means of analysis. The error with which the Enlightenment was concerned was rather the false consciousness of an age, anchored in the institutions of a false society, and helping in turn to solidify dominant interests. The massive objectivity of prejudice, which can be more aptly compared to prison walls than to a web or cocoon, became tangible in the repressions and denials of a withheld autonomy: "To error we owe the oppressive chains which despots and priests everywhere forge for the people. To error we owe the slavery in which the people languish in almost all countries. To error we owe the religious terrors which freeze human beings in fear and make them slaughter each other for the sake of figments of the mind. To error we owe deep-rooted enmity, barbarous persecutions, continual bloodshed and horrifying tragedies. . . ."[5] Ignorance is equivalent to suffering and frustrated happiness; uncertainty is equivalent to slavery and the inability to act rightly.

But because prejudices derive their peculiar objectivity from this link between withheld autonomy and the denial of freedom and satisfaction, the critical dissolution of existing untruth, of error as substance, requires, conversely, something beyond rational insight. It requires above all the cardinal virtue of courage; more precisely, reason itself draws its life from this courage to be rational, Kant's motto *sapre aude,* which was his answer to the question, What is enlightenment? Critical reason attains power over an embodied dogmatism only because it has made the will to reason part of its own interest. It cannot, therefore, address itself to corrupted human beings. Of this Holbach is convinced: "[The] voice [of reason] can only be heard by generous souls accustomed to reflection, whose sensibilities make them lament the numberless calamities showered on the earth by political and religious tyranny—whose enlightened minds contemplate with horror the immensity, the ponderousness of that series of misfortunes with which error has in all ages overwhelmed mankind." [6] Reason is equated unquestioningly with the talent for autonomy and responsibility and with a sensitivity to the evils of this world. It has long since made its decision in favor of justice, welfare, and peace; the reason that resists dogmatism is a committed reason.

It was possible to consider this commitment the undisputed basis of all rational endeavors because things that were precisely distinguished by a later enlightenment were at that time conceived as one, under the category of nature. Holbach's preface begins with the classical avowal: "Man is unhappy because he has an erroneous view of nature." It was thought that insight into the laws of nature could also provide instruction on how to live in the right way. It is no accident that in the subtitle of Holbach's *System* the laws of the physical and the moral world are reduced to a common denominator. As was the case with Hobbes, both knowledge of nature and guidance on how human beings are to conduct themselves in accordance with nature seemed to proceed from the study of nature. When nature was objectified in the empirical sciences, however, the hope of acquiring certainty about normative laws from a knowledge of causal laws had to be abandoned. The positivistic Enlightenment, which called itself radical for that reason, saw through the equivocations within the concept of nature, dissolved the convergence of truth and happiness, error and suffering, and reduced reason to a potential for knowledge that thereby loses its commitment and hence its critical acuity and becomes alienated from decision.

This result could still have been avoided, and reason could have been salvaged as a category of enlightenment and turned even more pointedly against dogmatism, when Fichte replaced the system of nature with a transcendental theory of knowledge at the end of the eighteenth century. Kant had already removed the source of the laws governing both the causally determined realm of phenomena and the realm of freedom determined by the self's own norms from nature and located it in the synthetic achievements of the subject. Fichte made practical reason autonomous and reduced nature to the material of action, a material produced by freedom. Under the new presuppositions of Idealism, dogmatism could no longer be overcome by a reason that studied nature and was verified by sense experience. In fact, dogmatism itself gained in power and impenetrability; it became penetrating and universal, because the prejudice institutionalized by tyrants and priests was no longer seen as the form in which dogmatic constraint was first established. Rather, a consciousness that conceives itself as the product of the things around us, as a product of nature, is already dogmatic: "The principle of the dogmatists is represented by faith in things for their own sake: thus an indirect faith in their own self which is dispersed and borne only by objects." [7] Fichte understands dogmatism in a more elementary way than Holbach. In German Idealism the "prejudice" of the French Encyclopedists appears under the term "dispersal," a fixation of the weak ego and immature consciousness on the external props provided by existing things; in other words, the reification of the subject.

But when reason is constituted through a critique of reified consciousness, its point of view, namely Idealism, cannot be compelled through arguments based on the rules of logic alone. In order to use reason to strip off the limitations of dogmatism, one must first have made reason's interest one's own: "The ultimate basis of the difference between the idealist and the dogmatist is thus the difference of interest." [8] Both the need for emancipation and an original act of freedom are presupposed here, so that humanity can eventually achieve a standpoint of autonomy, the standpoint from which critical insight into the hidden mechanism of the genesis of the world and consciousness becomes possible. The young Schelling expressed Fichte's idea by saying that we can begin to become rational only "through an anticipation of practical decision." [9] Reason is by no means conceived as knowledge detached from volition; in fact, it is reason itself that creates the level from which it can then recognize a consciousness adhering to objects as a false consciousness. The developed system of reason is "necessarily either an artifice, a game played in thought . . . or reality must be *conferred* on it, not by means of a theoretical capacity, but by a practical one; not by a cognitive capacity, but by a *productive one which actualizes* not by knowledge but by action."[10] Fichte's famous dictum must also be understood in precisely this sense: the kind of philosophy one chooses depends on the kind of person one is.[11] Just as for Holbach the preconditions of the capacity for critical insight were the rationality of the subject, a certain degree of autonomy, and a certain kind of sensibility, so for Fichte reason is even more closely intertwined with the complexity of the human spirit at an advanced stage in its historical development. The freedom to take the interest of reason as one's own, a freedom achieved in the world-historical formative process of the species, distinguishes those individuals who have overcome dogmatism; their merit is not primarily theoretical, but practical:

Some, who have not yet raised themselves to the full feeling of their freedom and absolute independence, find themselves only in the conceiving of things; they have only that dispersed self-consciousness that adheres to objects and can be reconstructed from the multiplicity of objects. Their image is reflected to them only by things, as by a mirror; for their own sake they cannot give up the belief in the independence of these things: for they themselves subsist only with them. . . . But whoever becomes conscious of his autonomy and his independence of all that is external to him—and this one can become only by making oneself into something independent of all things, through one's own self—that person does not need things as a support for his self, and can have no use for them, because they abolish that independence and turn it into empty semblance.[12]

The price Fichte paid for the unity of reason and decision in order to have a critical concept of reason was of course too high, as is especially evident in the last sentence of the passage above. Schelling and Hegel soon discovered that the spontaneity of an absolute "I" that posits the world and itself remains abstract; they showed that nature cannot be reduced to an indeterminate material for acting subjects, lest a human world itself divested of qualities shrink to a blind point of action for action's sake alone.[13] Thus on a level of discussion for which Hegel had paved the way, Marx, who after Holbach and Fichte represented a third generation of committed spokesmen of enlightenment, showed how both the inner content of reason and the partisan position of thought in opposition to dogmatism emerge only through a historical developmental process. In their confrontation with, and on the basis of, a nature that is structured in itself, laboring subjects strive for a form of social intercourse finally emancipated from the compulsion of nature and from domination—and in doing so they strive for political autonomy and responsibility. In opposition to Fichte, Marx shows that reified consciousness must be criticized in practical terms—through things, as it were—rather than merely epistemologically, through a withdrawal into the self-active subject, a renunciation of the realism of sound common sense. Just as Fichte made dogmatism more rigid than it was for Holbach, so Marx made it more rigid than it was for Fichte; once again the impenetrability of dogmatism's substance, the quasi-natural character of its objective delusion, was increased. The two "main subspecies of humanity," whom Fichte characterized as dogmatists and idealists, are divested of both the opposition between their interests and the purely subjective form of a moral definition. Instead, as material interests, the interests that subjugate consciousness to the authority of things and reified contexts are anchored in a specific socio-historical basis of alienated labor, frustrated satisfaction, and suppressed freedom; the interest that seeks to bring about, via the real contradictions of a disrupted world, the unity of life processes as the rationality that is immanent in social conditions is anchored in precisely the same historical matrix. Having been seen as institutionalized prejudice, and then mediated by its interpretation as transcendental dispersion, dogmatism now assumes the form of ideology. From now on, a reason committed to the opposition to dogmatism will operate as the critique of ideology. But it will claim the same objectivity for its partisan position as is attributed to the illusion it criticizes. Its cognitive interest is legitimized by the objective context in which it is embedded.

In the concept of a reason whose activity consists in the critique of ideology, the moments of knowledge and decision stand in a dialectical relationship to one another. On the one hand the dogmatism of an ossified society can be recognized for what it is only to the extent to which knowledge is resolutely guided by the anticipation of an emancipated society and the realization of the autonomy and responsibility of all human beings; but at the same time, conversely, this interest requires the attainment of insight into processes of social development, because it is only in these processes that the interest in emancipation is constituted as an objective interest. At the level of the historical self-reflection of science with critical intent, Marx identifies reason one last time with a decision in favor of rationality in its thrust against dogmatism.

In the second half of the nineteenth century, as science was reduced to a productive force in industrial society, positivism, historicism, and pragmatism each appropriated a part of this inclusive concept of rationality.[14] From that point onward the hitherto undisputed attempt of the great theories to reflect the context of life as a whole was discredited as dogmatic. Once particularized, reason was relegated to the level of subjective consciousness, whether as the capacity for the empirical testing of hypotheses, the capacity for historical understanding, or the capacity for the pragmatic control of behavior. At the same time, interest and inclination were expelled from the arena of knowledge as subjective factors. The spontaneity of hope, the taking of a position and particularly the experience of relevance or neutrality, sensitivity to suffering and oppression, the desire for autonomy and responsibility, the will to achieve emancipation, and the joy of discovering one's identity—all these were dismissed from reason's binding interest. A disinfected reason had been purged of the elements of enlightened volition; already alienated from itself, it divested itself of its life. And life deprived of spirit—in the guise of "decision"—is capricious and spectral indeed.

The Positivistic Isolation of Reason and Decision

Up to that point, critical knowledge had been connected with a scientific orientation in action. Even knowledge of nature (physics in the classical sense) had significance for practice (for ethics and politics). But after the new empirical sciences which had flourished since the time of Galileo had attained self-consciousness in positivism and pragmatism, and after analytic philosophy, inspired by the Vienna Circle as well as by Peirce and Dewey, had, in the work of Carnap, Popper, and Morris,[15] given a very precise explication of this self-understanding in terms of the philosophy of science, two cognitive functions came to be clearly distinguished—and both were deprived of their power to provide orientation for action.

The *affirmative activity* of the modern sciences consists in making statements about empirical uniformities. Lawlike hypotheses, derived from deductively linked propositions and tested in controlled experiments, are applied to regular covariances of empirical quantities in all domains accessible to intersubjective experience. Under given individual initial conditions, universal laws of this kind serve as explanations. The same theoretical statements that permit the causal explanation of effects make it possible to predict effects, given the causes. This predictive application of the theories of empirical science reveals the cognitive interest that guides the generalizing sciences. Just as artisans, in working with their materials, were once guided by rules of experience established through tradition, so today engineers in all fields rely on this kind of scientifically tested prediction in their choice of methods and materials, instruments and operations. The reliability of the rules, of course, distinguishes the exercise of technique in the old sense from what we call technique, or technology, today. Consequently, the cognitive function of the modern sciences must be understood in connection with the system of social labor: they extend and rationalize our power of technical control over objective or (what amounts to the same thing) objectified processes of nature and society.

The other function of knowledge that has been reduced to empirical science, namely, its critical activity, is derived from this affirmative achievement. For when that kind of science monopolizes the guidance of rational conduct, all competing claims to provide a scientific orientation for action must be rejected. That activity is now reserved for a positivistically curtailed critique of ideology, which is directed against a dogmatism that takes a new form. Any theory that relates to practice in any way other than by strengthening and perfecting the possibilities for purposive-rational action must now appear dogmatic. Because a technical cognitive interest that excludes all other interests is tacitly but surely rooted in the methodology of the empirical sciences, all other ways of relating to the practice of life can be blocked out in the name of value-freedom. Economy in the choice of purposive-rational means, guaranteed by conditional predictions in the form of technical recommendations, is the only admissible "value," [16] yet it is not explicitly presented as a value, since it is seen as equivalent to rationality as such. What we really have here is the formalization of a single relationship to life, namely, the experience of feedback control through results that is built into systems of social labor and that is already operative in every elementary act of labor.

According to the principles of analytic philosophy of science, empirical questions that cannot be posed and resolved in the form of technical tasks can expect no cogent theoretical answer. All practical questions that cannot be adequately answered through technical recommendations, but also require a self-understanding within a concrete situation, go beyond the cognitive interest invested in the empirical sciences. The only type of science that the positivistic approach admits is incapable of rationally examining such questions. By these criteria, theories that offer solutions are guilty of dogmatism. The goal of a critique of ideology that has been truncated in this way is to respond to every dogmatic assertion with the decisionistic thesis that practical questions (in our sense) cannot be discussed cogently and must in the final analysis simply be *decided*. The magic word for release from the spell of dogmatism is "decision," a decision that has been painfully isolated from reason: practical questions no longer "admit of truth."

At this point in the positivistic confrontation with the new forms of dogmatism,[17] the reverse side of this kind of critique of ideology is revealed. It is correct in unmasking, in the kind of value ethics put forth by Scheler and Hartmann, a false rationalization of what has been derationalized, and in relegating ideal objects back to the subjectivity of needs and inclinations, evaluations and decisions. But the result of its labor is monstrous enough: the impurities, the waste water of emotionality, are filtered out of the mainstream of empirical-scientific rationality and hygienically contained in a reservoir—an imposing mass of subjective values. Every individual value appears as a senseless agglomeration of meaning, but branded with the stigma of irrationality, so that the priority of one value over another, its authority for guiding action, simply cannot be rationally justified. On this level, then, the critique of ideology involuntarily furnishes the proof that the progress of a rationalization restricted in empirical scientific terms to technical control is bought at the price of the corresponding growth of a mass of irrationality in the domain of practice itself. For action requires an orientation and always has. But now that orientation is divided into the rational provision of techniques and strategies on the one hand and an irrational choice among so-called value systems on the other. The price of economy in the choice of means is an unrestricted decisionism in the selection of higher-level goals.

The clearcut boundary that positivism establishes between knowledge and values represents, however, less a result than a problem. For the separate domain of values, norms, and decisions is now once again seized upon by philosophical interpretations, precisely on the basis of a division of labor between philosophy and science in its reduced form.

The *subjective philosophy of value* is already not so certain of meanings that have been detached from the real context of life and hypostasized as was objective value ethics, which made of those meanings a realm of ideal being that transcended sense experience. Subjective value philosophy too proclaims the existence of orders of value (Max Weber) and "gods and demons," i.e., the forces of belief (Jaspers), in a sphere removed from history. Philosophical belief, which remains midway between pure decision and rational comprehension, must subscribe to one of the competing orders, without, however, being able to overcome the pluralism of these orders and dissolve the dogmatic core that is the source of its own life. In this realm of practical questions, responsible but in principle undecidable polemic among philosophers, the intellectually honest and existentially committed representatives of spiritual forces, seems to be the only form of confrontation allowed. Having become a worldview, decisionism no longer hesitates to reduce norms to decisions. In the analytic-philosophical form of a noncognitive ethics, the decisionistic complement to a positivistically restricted science is itself conceived positivistically (R. M. Hare). Once one has posited certain fundamental value judgments as axioms, one can produce, analytically, a logically coherent string of propositions regarding each one. Such principles, however, are not accessible to rational comprehension; acceptance of them is based solely on decision. Such decisions may then be interpreted in an existential-personal sense (Sartre), in a public political sense (Carl Schmitt), or institutionally, on the basis of anthropological presuppositions (Gehlen), but the thesis remains the same: that decisions relevant to the practice of life, whether they consist in the acceptance of values, in the choice of a life-historical project, or in the choice of an enemy, are not accessible to rational deliberation and are not capable of a rationally motivated consensus. But when practical questions, having been eliminated from a knowledge reduced to empirical science, are thus completely dismissed from the control of rational deliberation, when decisions on questions of the practice of life have to be pronounced beyond the jurisdiction of any authority committed in any way to rationality—then we cannot be surprised even at a last desperate attempt to secure socially binding prior decisions on practical questions institutionally, through a return to the closed world of mythical images and forces (Walter Brocker). As Adorno and Horkheimer have shown, this attempt to supplement positivism through *mythology* is not without its own logical force, the abysmal irony of which only dialectic can turn into laughter.

Honest positivists, in whom such prospects do not excite laughter, that is, positivists who recoil before the undertone of metaphysics in objective value ethics and the subjective philosophy of value as they recoil before the open irrationality of decisionism and even a return to mythology, seek a foothold in an autonomous critique of ideology, as it has been developed from Feuerbach to Pareto in the simple form of a deflating of projections; this itself, however, has solidified into the program of a worldview. For the one thing in the critique of ideology that has not been clarified, despite all its radicalism, is its root: the motivation for the critique of ideology itself. If its goal consists only in differentiating in principle the scientifically rationalized shaping of reality from the "value- and worldview-laden forms of humans' interpretation of themselves and the world" [18]—where such attempts at the "illumination of consciousness" can make no claim to compelling rationality—then the critique of ideology abandons the possibility of justifying its own enterprise in theoretical terms. As critique, it is itself attempting to illuminate consciousness and not to shape reality; it does not produce new techniques, although it may prevent existing techniques from being misused in the name of a theory that merely claims to be one. But from what source does this critique draw its power, if reason, separated from decision, must dispense with any interest whatsoever in the emancipation of consciousness from dogmatic constraint?

Certainly science must be allowed to exercise its affirmative cognitive function; it has been acknowledged, so to speak, as a value. The separation of knowledge from decision through the critique of ideology serves this function, and if the separation had been carried out to the end it would have meant an end to dogmatism. But even so, science in its critical cognitive function, the combating of dogmatism at the positivistic level, remains possible only in the form of a science that reflects on itself and wills itself as a goal, that is, in the form once again of a committed reason. But the very possibility of *justifying* this is precisely what the critique of ideology denies. Conversely, when it renounces rational justification, reason's battle with dogmatism itself remains a matter of dogmatism, and the indissolubility of dogmatism would have to be conceded from the start. What is behind this dilemma, it seems to me, is the fact that the critique of ideology must tacitly presuppose as its own motivation the very thing that it combats as dogmatic, namely, the convergence of reason and decision—and thus an inclusive concept of rationality. To be sure, this hidden concept of a substantive rationality is conceived differently depending on whether the motivating reflection is convinced solely of the value of scientific techniques or also of the significance of scientific emancipation in the service of autonomy and responsibility; thus, depending on whether the critique of ideology is motivated on the level of the understanding, by an interest in an empirical-scientific increase in technical knowledge, or on the level of reason, by an interest in enlightenment as such. Positivism is no more capable of distinguishing between these two concepts of rationality than it is capable of recognizing that it itself implies the very thing that it opposes outside itself: committed reason. It is on the distinction between these two forms of reason, however, that the relationship of theory and practice in a scientific civilization depends.

The Critique of Ideology's Partisan Support of Technological Rationality

No matter how much it insists on the separation of theory and decision in its opposition to dogmatism, positivism's critique of ideology is itself a form of committed reason; whether it will or not it takes a position in favor of progressive rationalization. In the case we will analyze here, it is concerned, without reservation, with the extension and dissemination of technical knowledge. In its battle against dogmatism as it understands it, the critique of ideology is engaged in removing traditionalist barriers, and ideological barriers of any sort, that could hinder the progress of the empirical-analytic sciences and the unimpeded process of their utilization. This critique is not a value-free analysis; it does not make a hypothetical assumption concerning the value of empirical-scientific theories but rather, in its very first analytical step, makes the normative presupposition that behavior that is in accordance with technical recommendations is not only desirable but also "rational." Even though it expresses positivism's intentions, however, this implicit concept of reason cannot be clarified using the conceptual means of positivism itself. According to positivistic criteria the rationality of behavior is a value that we decide to either accept or reject. At the same time, one can demonstrate conclusively by the same criteria that rationality is a means to the realization of values and to that extent cannot be placed on the same level as the other values. Indeed, the critique of ideology, as a preparation for rational conduct, recommends rationality as an excellent means of realizing values, if not the only means, because it guarantees the "efficiency" or the "economy" of the procedure. These two expressions reveal the cognitive interest of the empirical sciences as a technical one. They betray the fact that rationalization has from the outset been located within the boundaries of the system of social labor, and that its intention is precisely to enable control of objective and objectified processes. In that process the power of technical control is neutral with regard to the possible systems of value in the service of which it can be exercised. Efficiency and economy of behavior, the defining characteristics of this rationality, cannot themselves be conceived as values, and yet within the framework of positivism's self-understanding they can be justified only as if they were values. A critique of ideology whose only goal is to ensure the success of technological rationality cannot escape this dilemma: it desires rationality as a value because rationality has the advantage of being implicit in rational procedures themselves. Because this value can be legitimated through reference to research and its technical application and does not need to be justified on the basis of pure decision, it has a privileged status with respect to all other values. The experience of the controlled success of rational behavior exercises a rationally certified pressure to accept such norms of behavior: even this limited rationality implies a decision in favor of rationality. In the critique of ideology, where this is at least tacitly recognized, a bit of committed reason thus survives—in contradiction to the criteria in terms of which it criticizes dogmatism. Because, however, perverted, it remains of a piece with committed reason, it also entails consequences that violate its alleged neutrality toward any and all value systems whatsoever. The concept of rationality that it so resolutely promotes ultimately implies a whole organization of society in which, in the name of value-freedom, an autonomous technology would dictate even the value system—namely, its own—of the domains of practice it has usurped.

I would like to distinguish here between four levels of rationalization on which qualitatively we extend our technical powers of control. On the first two levels, technologies require the exclusion of normative elements from the process of scientific argumentation, but on the two subsequent levels this elimination changes to a subordination of values that were initially only categorized as irrational to technological procedures which then establish themselves as a value system.

The *first* level of rationalization is dependent on the methodological situation of the empirical sciences. The body of established lawlike hypotheses determines the scope of possible rational behavior. Technological rationality in the strict sense is involved here: in realizing goals, we employ techniques made available by science. When, however, there is a choice between actions of equal technical appropriateness, a rationalization of the *second* level is needed. The translation of technical recommendations into practice, hence the technical utilization of empirical scientific theories, must also be subject to the conditions of technological rationality. That can no longer be a task for the empirical sciences. Empirical scientific information does not suffice for a rational choice between functionally equivalent means, given concrete goals to be realized within the framework of a given value system. Instead, it is decision theory that clarifies the relationship between alternative techniques and given goals, on the one hand, and the value system and maxims for decision on the other.[19] Decision theory analyzes the possible decision normatively, using as its standard a rationality of choice defined as "economical" or "efficient." Here, rationality refers solely to the form of the decision, not, however, to the objective context and the actual result.[20]

On the first two levels, the rationality of behavior compels an isolation of values, which are withdrawn from all cogent discussion and can be related to given techniques and concrete goals only in the form of imperatives entertained hypothetically. These relationships are accessible to rational calculation because they remain external to values as such, which have been irrationalized. "What is designated as a value system here is thus a system of rules which prescribe how the consequences described by the information system are to be evaluated *on the basis of the value sentiments* of the actor."[21] The subjectivistic reduction of interests that are decisive for orientation in action to "sentiments" which are not susceptible of further rationalization is a precise expression of the fact that the value-freedom of the technological concept of rationality functions within the system of social labor and that all the other interests in the practice of life are mediatized for the sake of the single interest in effective performance and economic utilization of means. Hypostatized as values, the competing interests are excluded from discussion. Significantly, by the criteria of technological rationality, agreement on a collective value system can never be achieved by means of enlightened discussion within the political public sphere, that is, through a consensus arrived at rationally, but only additively or through compromise—values are in principle not subject to discussion.[22] Naturally, decision theory's assumption of "independent" value systems is not tenable in practice. The adoption of a formal rationality of choice, hence the extension of technological thinking to include the selection of scientific techniques, changes the previously existing value systems themselves. By this I mean not only the systematizing of notions of value, which every decision-theoretical analysis requires, but especially the reformulating or even devaluing of traditional norms, which break down as principles of orientation in the attempt to realize concrete goals technically. The dialectical relationship between values originating in specific interest positions and techniques for the satisfaction of value-oriented needs is obvious: just as values become discredited as ideological and die out when they have lost their connection with a technically adequate satisfaction of real needs over a long period, so, conversely, with the emergence of new techniques, new value systems can be formed on the basis of changed interest positions. We know that Dewey was able to link the connection between values and technical knowledge to the expectation that the deployment of continually increased and improved techniques would not simply remain tied to existing values, but that values themselves would be indirectly subjected to a pragmatic confirmation process. It is only because this connection between traditional values and scientific techniques exists, a connection that decision theory ignores, that Dewey can pose the provocative question: "How shall we employ what we know to . . . direct our practical behavior so as to test these beliefs and make possible better ones? The question is seen to be just what it has always been empirically: What shall we *do* to make objects having value more secure in existence?"[23] This question can be answered in the sense of a reason with an interest in enlightenment; in any case, that is the sense in which Dewey posed it. We will deal first, however, with the alternative answer, which subjects even the formation of value systems to the criteria of technological rationality. With this, we reach the *third* level of rationalization, which deals with strategic situations in which rational behavior in the face of an opponent who also acts rationally must be calculated. The two partners pursue competing interests; in the case of a strictly competitive situation, they evaluate the same consequences in terms of an opposite scale of preferences, whether their value systems are in agreement or not. Such a situation requires extensive rationalization. The actor is not trying to gain technical control over a field of events defined by scientific predictions, but to gain the same control over situations of rational indeterminacy; he cannot inform himself about his opponent's behavior empirically, through lawlike hypotheses, as he would inform himself about natural processes; he remains incompletely informed, not to a degree but in principle, because his opponent is also capable of a choice among alternative strategies and thus of reactions that are not unambiguously determined. What concerns us here, however, is not the game-theoretical solution of this problem, but the peculiar technical pressure that such strategic situations exert on value systems as well. A fundamental value, namely, successful self-assertion against the opponent and thus the ensuring of survival, enters into the technical task itself. The values originally invested, that is, the value systems with which alone decision theory is initially concerned, are relativized in terms of this strategic value, to which the game or the conflict itself is oriented.

Once the game-theoretical assumption of strategic positions has been generalized to all situations that call for decisions, decision-making processes can be analyzed in political terms (I use the word "political" here in the sense of an existential self-assertion, a sense developed in the tradition that runs from Hobbes to Carl Schmitt). Eventually it becomes sufficient to reduce value systems to one quasi-biological fundamental value and to pose the decision problem in a general form: How must the systems that make the decisions—individuals or groups, specific institutions or whole societies—be organized so as to satisfy the basic value of survival and avoid risks in a given situation? The functional goals that, together with the values actually invested, determined the program, disappear here and are replaced by formalized quantitative goals such as stability or adaptive capacity, which are tied solely to the system's fundamental, quasi-biological need to reproduce its life. This self-programming of feedback-controlled systems, however, is possible only on the *fourth* level of rationalization, once it becomes possible to transfer the decision-making effort to a machine. Even though there exists today a large class of problems for which machines are being successfully utilized to simulate extreme situations, this final stage of rationalization naturally remains largely a fiction. Nevertheless, it reveals for the first time in its entirety the intention to extend technological rationality over all domains of practice, and with it the substantive concept of rationality that a positivistic critique both presupposes and conceals. Learning machines as cybernetic mechanisms for social organization can in principle take over such decision-making processes under political conditions. Once this threshold has been crossed, the value systems excluded from the process of rationalization at a lower level would be rendered interchangeable in terms of the criteria of rational behavior; indeed, these values can enter into the adaptive processes of a homeostatic and self-programming machine in the form of a liquid mass, only because they have already been rendered irrational as values.[24]

In a manuscript on the scientific and political significance of decision theory, Horst Rittel draws unambiguous conclusions for the fourth stage of rationalization:

Value systems can no longer be regarded as stable over long periods. What can be desired depends on what can be made possible, and what can be made possible depends on what one desires. Goals and functional utility are not independent variables. They are in reciprocal interaction with the scope of decision-making. Within broad limits, conceptions of value can be directed. In the face of the uncertainty which marks the alternatives for future development, it is pointless to set up rigid modes of decision-making which provide long-range strategies. . . . It is more meaningful to view the problem of decision-making in more general terms and to consider the suitability of decision-making systems. How must an organization be constituted to be able to meet the uncertainties that arise through innovation and the vicissitudes of politics? . . . Instead of assuming a specific decision-making system and a value system as definitely given, the suitability of this system for fulfilling its tasks must be investigated. What mechanisms for providing feedback to the object system are necessary? What data about the object system are needed, and to what degree of precision? What provisions for the preparation of this data are necessary? What value systems are consistent with the system and guarantee chances for adaptation and thus "survival"?[25]

The negative utopia of technical control of history would indeed be fulfilled if one were to set up as a central system for social control an automaton that could answer these questions cybernetically, that is, by "itself."

The critique of ideology, which stubbornly separates reason from decision for the sake of the dissolution of dogmatism and the promotion of technologically rational behavior, ultimately automatizes decisions according to the laws of the rationality thus made dominant. Because critique cannot maintain the required separation but finds its own reason only in its partisan support of rationality, no matter how restricted that rationality might be, the rationalization developed on these four levels shows no tolerance or neutrality toward values. In fact, the ultimate decisions about the acceptance or rejection of norms have not been excluded from this concept of rationality at all. Even these decisions ultimately fall within the self-regulating adaptive process of learning automatons that function in accordance with laws of rational behavior—and they are thus not detached from a cognitive process oriented to technical control. In the anticipated concept of a cybernetically regulated self-organization of society, the substantive rationality suppressed within the ingenuous partisan support of formal rationality reveals a tacit philosophy of history. It rests on the questionable thesis that human beings control their destinies rationally to the degree to which social techniques are applied, and that human destiny is capable of being guided rationally to the extent to which even the application of these techniques is cybernetically regulated. This kind of rational administration of the world, however, cannot simply be identified with the solution of the practical questions posed by history. There is no basis for the assumption of a continuum of rationality extending from the capacity for technical control of objectified processes to a practical mastery of historical processes. The irrationality of history is rooted in the fact that we "make" it without hitherto having been able to make it consciously. The rationalization of history can thus be furthered not by an extension of the power to control on the part of human beings engaged in manipulation but only through a higher level of reflection, a consciousness on the part of acting human beings that advances toward emancipation.

On the Self-Reflection of Rationalist "Faith"

Only a reason that is fully aware of the interest ineradicably at work in every rational discussion, the interest in the progress of reflection toward autonomy and responsibility, can gain transcendent power from the consciousness of its own materialistic involvement. Only this kind of reason can subject to reflection the positivistic domination of the technical cognitive interest in the context of an industrial society which integrates science as a productive force and thus protects itself as a whole from critical knowledge. This reason alone can refrain from sacrificing the dialectical rationality of language that has already been attained to the profoundly irrational standards of a technologically restricted rationality of labor. It alone can seriously intervene in the coercive complex that is history, a context that remains dialectical only as long as it has not been opened to the dialogue of autonomous and responsible human beings. Today the convergence of reason and decision, which the philosophy of the great tradition considered to be unmediated, must be regained and reasserted in reflective terms on the level of the sciences, which means via the separation of reason and decision, that is necessarily and properly made on the level of technological rationality. The effect of science as a productive force is just as salutary when it flows into science as a force for emancipation as it is disastrous when it tries to subject the domain of practice, which lies outside the sphere of technical disposition, to its *exclusive* control. Demythologization that does not break the mythic spell but merely seeks to evade it only brings forth new witch doctors. Enlightenment that does not break the spell dialectically but only winds the veil on a half-completed rationalization more tightly around us turns the secularized world itself into a myth.

Schelling's romantic dictum about reason as controlled insanity acquires an oppressively acute significance under technology's domination of a practice that has only been separated from theory for the sake of that domination. If, in insanity, the central motivation of reason, the motivation that was decisive in myth, religion, and philosophy, lives on in perverted form— to create the unity and coherence of a world in the multiplicity of formless phenomena—then the sciences, which wrest empirical uniformities from contingency in a stream of phenomena that is in principle world-less, have been positivistically purged of insanity. They control, but they no longer control any insanity; and consequently insanity must remain uncontrolled. Reason would exist only in both at the same time, but this way it falls between them. The corresponding danger of an exclusively technical civilization that dispenses with the connection between theory and practice can be seen clearly: it is threatened by the splitting of consciousness and the division of human beings into two categories: the social engineers and the inmates of closed institutions.

Chapter Two
BETWEEN PHILOSOPHY AND SCIENCE: MARXISM AS CRITIQUE

Critique and Crisis: Mythological Origins and Scientific Structure of an Empirical Philosophy of History with Practical Intent

To say that Marxism lies "between" philosophy and science is to give it a merely formal designation; it does not establish anything about the particular type of scientific theory that Marxism represents. My purpose here is to confirm the structure of Marxism as a philosophy of history that is expressly designed with a political intent but is at the same time scientifically falsifiable. In demonstrating this, I will not hesitate to avail myself of the opportunity that falls to those who come afterward: to understand Marx better than he understood himself.

Marx gave his theory the name of critique—not a striking name, if one understands the critique of political economy as the completion of an undertaking that began with the philological criticism of the humanists, continued in the aesthetic criticism of the literati, and finally came to be understood *as* critique in the theoretical and practical criticism of the eighteenth-century philosophers. At that time critique became practically synonymous with reason; it signified good taste and clever judgment. It was the medium for ascertaining what was correct, which the laws of nature harmonized with what was just—and it was also the energy that drove the activity of reason restlessly forward and around and about until it finally turned against itself. "Les philosophes"—that was the name given to those who participated in this great undertaking, and Kant proudly called himself a philosopher, in the practical pedagogical sense of a "free teacher of the law" as well. In view of this it appears strange that Marx thought of his critique not as philosophy but rather as the dialectical overcoming of philosophy. In fact, it was only in the nineteenth century (although there are some allusions in the work of Rousseau) that critique expressly reassumed its relationship to crisis, both words deriving from the same root, and not only in an etymological sense.[1]

1. In Greek usage, critical judgment was associated with crisis as a legal conflict that pressed for decision; critique itself was an element in the objective context of the crisis. In Latin the word was limited to medical usage. The Gospel of Saint John, finally, transferred crisis to the process of salvation, as the process in which good is separated from evil. The critical decision between condemnation and acquittal thereby entered the dimension of damnation and salvation, a theological anticipation of the categories within which the eighteenth century outlined its philosophy of history. When, at that time, critique took on scientific form, it emancipated itself not only from application in pragmatic disciplines like jurisprudence and medicine but also from the objective context of crisis, which was retained in the notion of *Heilsgeschichte,* history as the process of salvation; critique became a subjective faculty. Even in the discipline which undertook to subject mankind's world-historical development to critique, the philosophy of history, critique no longer understood itself as corresponding to crisis. The process of civilization was thought of not as a self-critical process but, at best, as progress toward critique.

The material of world history, viewed from the perspective of a developing bourgeois society, appeared to offer so little resistance to the goal of emancipation from the quasi-natural character of feudal society that it seemed sufficient for critique to dissolve theoretically what had long been dissolving in practice; the separation of the new from the old, of bourgeois freedoms from feudal bonds, of the capitalist mode of production from feudal relations of production, was at that time borne forward by such powerful forces that the process did not need to be understood as a crisis. There seemed to be no need for a critical decision regarding uncertain or ambiguous consequences; Condorcet and his contemporaries understood history not as the critical process of separating ambivalent forces but as linear progress. The first shock this consciousness suffered, a shock felt by Voltaire, Lessing, and Goethe, came with the Lisbon earthquake, a natural event. But only when such events began to emerge from the soil of society itself, when the woes of industrial capitalism—e.g., the economic crises of the nineteenth century—caused the Lisbon earthquake to be forgotten did a subjectivized critique once again encounter crisis as an objective context; now, to be sure, one that emerged from history. The eschatological consciousness of itself.

Critique is now set in motion by practical interest in a favorable resolution of the crisis process. Consequently, it cannot find its theoretical foundations within itself. Indeed, because the crisis context, universalized to become the world as crisis, leaves no transmundane standpoint outside itself for pure knowledge, because on the contrary the judge is just as entangled in this legal dispute as the doctor is afflicted by this disease, critique becomes conscious of its own peculiar involvement in the object of its criticism. Given the rigidity of the objective context which critique, though included within it, reflects as a totality, attempting thereby to bring the crisis to completion, all efforts remain doomed to fruitlessness if they do not go beyond critique to intervene in the crisis with the means of crisis, that is, practically: *nemo contra Deum nisi Deus ipse*. Because the crisis, having become world-historical, defeats all merely subjective critique, decision is shifted into the dimension of practice, so that it is only with the success of practice that critique itself can become true.

2. In certain traditions, especially those of Jewish and Protestant mysticism (represented by Isaac Luria and Jakob Böhme), the weight of a radicalized theodicy problem led to a gnostically inspired version of *Heilsgeschichte*—namely, the remarkable version of theogony and cosmogony in which the original God, a quite sincere and playful God, becomes external to himself not by stepping outside himself, expressing himself, relinquishing himself, alienating himself, but rather by going into exile within himself, encapsulating himself egoistically, emigrating, so to speak, into the darkness of his own groundless ground and, in the most extreme intensification of self, becoming other—becoming nature: nature in God. Through this confinement within himself, an initial self-dethronement, God surrenders and loses himself to such an extent that, at the end of his tortured and creaturely process of restitution, Adam can dethrone him a second time. Thus, under this mythical repetition compulsion, man, left alone in history with the work of his own redemption and the redemption of nature along with it, must also manage the redemption of the fallen God: he becomes a Christ in the Promethean role of Lucifer. In man, God, while still God, has nevertheless ceased to be divine in the strict sense. He has given himself over completely to the risk of an irretrievable catastrophe; it is only at this price that he has initiated the world process as history.[2]

We will let the origins of this sophisticated myth stand without comment; it is mentioned here only because Hegel took from the dialectical metaphor of self-abasement a metaphysical calculus with which to compute the whole of world history as a crisis complex. At every stage of development, what is evil, contrary, and destructive unfolds a distinctive brittleness, obstinacy, and power; what is negative—indeed, negativity itself—acquires a positiveness that only the God within the Anti-godly could bring about. In each phase the outcome of the crisis is genuinely open once again only if the forces that come to be separated are of equal primacy and of equal stature in their struggle with one another—in Schelling's term, "equipollent." God's unreserved surrender of himself to history renders the crisis complex perfect as a totality. Yet a transcendence is preserved within this immanence because the lost God after all once *was* God, and consequently with his dead past he is still prior to the remnants of him that are submerged in the historical present. In the crisis he is prior to the crisis; he is the one who, at first returning to himself as a stranger, then recovers himself and recognizes himself. This is how Hegel rationalizes the mythical schema to turn it into a dialectical logic of world history as a crisis; indeed, the supple course of the crisis is the nimble movement of the dialectic itself. But in the end the

God in the absolute spirit, liberated by humanity to become himself, knows that he already knew everything beforehand and retained his mastery *over* history even while *in* history. Thus in Hegel's science of logic philosophy ruins the idea it stole from myth, the notion of the atheistic god who dies into history and genuinely risks being born within history through the hand of humanity, a birth which cannot therefore be merely a *re*birth.

In its dialectic this philosophy of the world as crisis retains enough of the contemplative substance of the mythical that it does not see itself as subject to that crisis and delivered over to it; rather, philosophy conceives itself as the resolution of the crisis. The philosophical god who, all appearances to the contrary, never completely sacrificed himself to history is restored to himself in the philosophical reflection of absolute spirit which, unaffected by the crisis and superior to it, thus does not need to understand itself as critique, as judgment in a life and death struggle—nor as a prologue to life which must itself be confirmed by life. Instead, philosophy makes itself into its own totality and is not critique but synthesis.

It is precisely this that Marx holds up against the Hegelian system, as early as in his dissertation, when he says of it that "philosophy has closed itself off to form a complete and total world." To that totality another totality stands opposed as existing evidence against the resolution claimed by philosophy—the unresolved character of a world torn apart. In the relationship between philosophy and the world, "the system is reduced to an abstract totality. . . . Enthusiastic in its drive to realize itself, it enters into tension with everything else. . . . The consequence, hence, is that the world's becoming philosophical is at the same time philosophy's becoming worldly, that its realization is at the same time its loss." [3]

And yet such a critique still presupposes the logic of this philosophy, that is, Hegel's dialectic. As we know, Lenin recommended reading Hegel's *Logic* as an aid to the study of *Capital*. Marxism's presupposition of Hegelian logic, moreover, is a frequent topic in recent critiques of Marxism. In fact, Marx systematically links his work to the categories of objective spirit; he posits Hegel's ideal of "ethical life" [Sittlichkeit] as the concept of society as a totality, so that the very reality of society is measured by that idea, and the reality of society can be recognized as the unethical relationship of a world torn asunder. As far as the objective spirit of Hegelian philosophy is concerned, Marxist sociology demonstrates that, as the deceptive reflection of an anticipated reconciliation, it can be attained only through determinate negation of the existing contradictions of established society—but precisely in determinate negation. Only if the dialectic is presupposed as a dialectic of social conditions themselves can these conditions be recognized. What "allows" Marx to do this? How can he justify his supposition without secretly adopting the idealist presuppositions he has explicitly rejected? The initial interest in the resolution of the crisis, by which critical knowledge is guided, is only a form of "subjective spirit" to begin with. The urgent experience of evil and the passionate urge to engage it Hegel calls a "practical feeling" for the "incommensurability between what is and what ought to be." [4] Marx must therefore show his practical interest to be an objective one; he must show that his critical impulse is rooted in the objective tendencies of the crisis itself. And because the crisis manifests itself in economic crisis, Marx attempts to furnish this proof through an analysis of social labor, precisely that labor which became alienated during the first phase of industrialization under the conditions of private ownership of the means of production. In our context it is particularly important that he begins his analysis without presupposing Hegelian logic. Only while carrying out his analysis does he discover in the relationship between wage labor and capital the peculiar domination of living labor by dead labor that can be decoded materialistically as the "rational core" of the idealist dialectic. Marx formulated this insight in a now famous sentence in the Paris manuscripts. What is great in Hegel's *Phenomenology of Mind,* he says, "is that Hegel conceives the self-creation of man as a process, conceives objectification as loss of the object, as alienation and as transcendence of this alienation; that he thus grasps the essence of *labor* and comprehends objective man—true, because real man—as the outcome of man's *own* labor." [5]

Marx goes to the root of a motif which in Hegel's dialectic, though stripped of its mythological form, is still distorted by the idealist self-understanding of philosophy—the motif of the god who debases himself and confines himself within himself: in their manifold efforts to preserve their lives through the work of their own hands, humans make themselves the authors of their own historical development, without, however, recognizing themselves as the subject of that development. The experience of alienated labor is the materialist verification of dialectical empiricism: what befalls men and women puts them on the tract of their own history; in the forces they draw down upon themselves they encounter their own generative powers; and in appropriating objects they are only taking back the objectification of their own inherent capacities. But when the field of social labor has thus been shown to be the experiential basis of the historical dialectic, then a guarantee still retained in the idealist version no longer holds good—the guarantee that at every stage humanity, in experiencing what befalls it, will also experience itself rationally, and will in fact overcome alienation. It remains uncertain whether critical insight into the dialectic of alienated labor not only emerges precisely from the objective context of crisis but also develops to the point of practical efficacy. The point of the myth of the atheistic god, which Hegel's idealist dialectic had ruined, shows the materialist dialectic to be in the right, in that the materialist dialectic makes atheism something true and recognizes that humanity had only encoded in the image of God its intimation of its own power over history, which kept slipping away from it. For a god who has truly become historical not only cannot be a god any longer but could not in seriousness have ever been one. Humanity is left alone with the task of its salvation; and only so long as it has not yet freed itself from its state of immaturity must it perceive as salvation what it alone can produce rationally through its self-generation. It is only against this background that the effect on Marx and Engels of Feuerbach's not especially profound critique of religion, an effect that is difficult to empathize with today, can be understood.[6]

3. Marx understands the crisis complex materialistically, in terms of the dialectic of social labor. The categories of that dialectic had been developed in the political economy of his time but had not been recognized as being thoroughly historical. Consequently, Marx gave his investigation of the capitalist system the form of a critique of political economy. In this unpretentious title, "critique" means first a critical examination of existing literature; but beyond this it also takes on the background meaning of a theory developed with the practical intent of overcoming the crisis: the critique of political economy is a theory of crisis in the genuine sense. The analysis of alienated labor has the propaedeutic character of an introduction to the materialist dialectic; the critique itself can then be conducted from the standpoint of this dialectic: it demonstrates to human beings, who make their own history without explicitly knowing that they do so, that the apparent overwhelming power of quasi-natural conditions is actually the product of the work of their own hands. Marx begins with a demonstration of the fetish character of commodities:

Thus the mystery of the commodity form is simply this, that it mirrors for men the social character of their own labor, mirrors it as an objective character attaching to the labor products themselves, mirrors it as the social natural property of these things. Consequently the social relation of the producers to the sum total of their own labor presents itself to them as a social relation, not between themselves, but between the products of their labor. Thanks to this transference of qualities, the labor products become commodities, sensuously transcendental or social things. . . . Inasmuch as the producers do not come into social contact until they exchange their labor products, the specifically social character of their individual labor does not manifest itself until exchange takes place. . . . That is why the social relations connecting the labor of one private individual (or group) with the labor of another seem to the producers not direct social relations between individuals, but what they really are: material relations between persons and social relations between things.[7]

But it is not only those who participate directly in the processes of production and distribution to whom social relations seem, with objective irony, to be what they are but in truth are not. Even the science that takes these relationships as its object falls victim to the illusion that reality itself produces: "Man's thought about the forms of social life, his scientific analysis of these forms, runs counter to the actual course of social evolution. He begins with an examination of the finished product, the extant result of the evolutionary process. The characters which stamp labor products as commodities, the characters which they must possess before they can circulate as commodities, have already acquired the fixity of the natural forms of social life, when economists begin to study, not indeed their history (for they are regarded as immutable), but their meaning."[8] It is for this reason that Marx can carry out his critique of the objective context of the crisis in the form of a critique of political economy.

Of course the commodity form can be generalized to all possible products of labor only when labor itself has assumed the form of a commodity, when the mode of production has become capitalistic. It is only with the figure of the free wage laborer, who sells his labor power as his sole commodity, that the historical condition is established under which the labor process comes to confront humanity in its independence as a process of valorization, so that the production of use-values seems to disappear in a kind of autonomous dynamic of capital. The critique of this objective illusion—as the theoretical presupposition for a practical appropriation of the essential powers that have been alienated through the capitalist process—identifies wage labor as the source of surplus value.

The theory of surplus value takes as its point of departure a simple reflection. If the transformation of money into capital is to be possible under the conditions of the exchange of equivalents, then the possessor of money must purchase commodities at their value, sell them at their value, and nevertheless be able to take out more value at the end of the process than he has put into it. There must, therefore, be a specific commodity that is exchanged, like all the others, at its value, but whose use-value is such that the consumption of this commodity creates value: "But if value is to be derived from the consumption of a commodity, our possessor of money must be lucky enough to find somewhere within the sphere of circulation, on the market, a commodity whose use-value has the peculiar quality of being a source of value; a commodity whose actual consumption is the process whereby labor is embodied [*Vergegenständlichung*], and whereby therefore value is created. Our friend does actually find it in the capacity for labor, or labor power." [9] The value of labor power is measured by the socially necessary labor time required for the production of the means for its subsistence; but labor power that is sold is in turn used by the capitalist for a longer time than the labor time that would be required for its reproduction. This surplus labor Marx holds to be the source of surplus value.

The analysis of this relationship does not, as the term "exploitation" might suggest, have the character of a moral judgment. (The behavior of capitalists is not in any way to be attributed to individual persons, but rather is objectively determined by their position in the production process.) Instead, Marx is interested in the opposition between wage labor and capital from a critical point of view, with a view to the practical resolution of the existing crisis complex, because he believes that he has discovered in this opposition the origin of the dialectic of self-concealment that prevents human beings from recognizing themselves as the subjects of their history and setting themselves right within it.

Marx asserts that the crises of the capitalist system arise of necessity from the valorization process of capital, thus from the fundamental relationship that is established with the appropriation of surplus value. This thesis presupposes another one, the thesis that the world as a crisis complex is grounded exclusively in economics, that it is thus inextricably entangled in those crises and is resolvable together with them. In political economy the first thesis is developed into a theory of crisis; in historical materialism the second is developed into a theory of ideology.

Chapter Three
SELF-REFLECTION AS SCIENCE: FREUD'S PSYCHOANALYTIC CRITIQUE OF MEANING

The end of the nineteenth century saw a discipline emerge, primarily as the work of a single man, that from the beginning moved in the element of self-reflection and at the same time could credibly claim legitimation as a scientific procedure in a rigorous sense. Freud was not, like Peirce and Dilthey, a philosopher of science who deals reflectively with his own experience in an established scientific discipline. To the contrary, it was by developing a new discipline that he reflected upon its presuppositions. Freud was no philosopher. Attempting to create a medical doctrine of neurosis led him to a theory of a new kind. He became involved in methodological discussions to the extent that the foundation of a science necessitates reflection about the new beginning. It was in this sense that Galileo not only created modern physics but also discussed it methodologically. Psychoanalysis is relevant to us as the only tangible example of a science incorporating methodical self-reflection. The birth of psychoanalysis opens up the possibility of arriving at the dimension that positivism closed off, and of doing so in a methodological manner that arises out of the logic of inquiry. This possibility has remained unrealized. For the scientific self-misunderstanding of psychoanalysis inaugurated by Freud himself, as the physiologist that he originally was, sealed off this possibility. However, this misunderstanding is not entirely unfounded. For psychoanalysis joins hermeneutics with operations that genuinely seemed to be reserved to the natural sciences.[1]

Initially psychoanalysis appears only as a special form of interpretation. It provides theoretical perspectives and technical rules for the interpretation of symbolic structures. Freud always patterned the interpretation of dreams after the hermeneutic model of philological research. Occasionally he compares it to the translation of a foreign author: of a text by Livy, for example.[2] But the interpretive effort of the analyst distinguishes itself from that of the philologist not only through the crystallization of a special object domain. It requires a specifically expanded hermeneutics, one that, in contrast to the usual method of interpretation in the cultural sciences, takes into account a *new dimension*. It was no accident that Dilthey took biography as the starting point of his analysis of understanding. The reconstruction of the structure of a life history that can be remembered is the model for the interpretation of symbolic structures in general. Dilthey chose biography as a model because life history seemed to have the merit of transparency. It does not resist memory through opacity. Here, in the focus of remembering life history, historical life is concentrated as "that which is known from within; it is the place of last resort." [3] For Freud, in contrast, biography is the object of analysis only as what is both known and unknown from inside, so that it is necessary to take resort to what is behind manifest memory. Dilthey directs hermeneutics toward subjective consciousness, whose meaning can be guaranteed by immediate recollection:

Life is historical insofar as it is comprehended in its course of movement in time and the casual nexus that originates in this way. This is possible owing to the representation of this sequence in a memory that reproduces not the individual but the nexus itself in its various stages. What memory achieves in the apprehension of a life process is attained in history by establishing the connection between the objectivations of life encompassed by objective mind in its movement and effects. [4]

Of course Dilthey knows that beyond the horizon of life history that is present to us we cannot count on the subjective guarantee of immediate memory. That is why understanding is directed at symbolic forms and texts in which meaning structures are objectivated. In this way hermeneutics can help out the faulty memory of mankind through the critical reconstruction of these texts.

The first condition of the construction of the historical world is thus the regeneration of mankind's confused and in many ways corrupted memories of itself through critique correlated with interpretation. Therefore the basic historical science is philology in the formal sense of the scientific study of languages, in which tradition has been sedimented; the collection of the heritage of earlier men; the elimination of errors contained therein; and the chronological order and combination that put these documents in internal relation with each other. In this philology is not the historian's aid but the basis of his procedure. [5]

Like Freud, Dilthey takes account of the unreliability and the confusion of subjective memory. Both see the necessity of a critique that sets right the mutilated text of tradition. But philological criticism differs from the psychoanalytic in that it takes the intentional structure of subjective consciousness as the ultimate experiential basis in the process of appropriating objective mind. It is true that Dilthey abandoned the psychological understanding of expression in favor of the hermeneutic understanding of meaning: "the understanding of mental forms has replaced psychological subtlety." [6] But even philology, in its concern with symbolic structures, remains restricted to a language in which conscious intentions are expressed. By rendering objectivations understandable, philology actualizes their intentional content in the medium of the everyday life experience. To this extent philology only supplements the ability of life-historical memory as it would function under normal conditions. What it eliminates through the labor of criticism, in preparing texts, are only accidental flaws. The omissions and distortions removed by philological criticism have no systematic role. For the meaning structure of the texts studied by hermeneutics is always threatened only by the impact of *external conditions*. Meaning can be destroyed through the capacity and efficiency limitations of the channels of transmission, whether of memory or cultural tradition.

Psychoanalytic interpretation, in contrast, is not directed at meaning structures in the dimension of what is consciously intended. The flaws eliminated by its critical labor are not accidental. The omissions and distortions that it rectifies have a systematic role and function. For the symbolic structures that psychoanalysis seeks to comprehend are corrupted by the impact of *internal conditions*. The mutilations have meaning as such. The meaning of a corrupt text of this sort can be adequately comprehended only after it has become possible to illuminate the meaning of the corruption itself. This distinguishes the peculiar task of a hermeneutics that cannot be confined to the procedures of philology but rather *unites linguistic analysis with the psychological investigation of causal connections*. In such cases an incomplete or distorted manifestation of meaning does not result from faulty transmission. For it is always a matter of the meaning of a biographical connection that has become inaccessible to the subject itself. Within the horizon of that measure of life history that can be made present, memory fails to such an extent that the disturbance of memory function as such calls hermeneutics to the scene and demands to be understood in the context of an objective meaning structure.

Dilthey had conceived life-historical memory as the condition of possible hermeneutic understanding, thus tying understanding to conscious intentions. Freud comes upon systematic disturbances of memory which, for their part, do express intentions. But the latter must then transcend the realm of what is subjectively thought. With his analysis of ordinary language, Dilthey only mentioned the limiting case of discrepancy between sentences, actions, and experiential expressions. For the psychoanalyst, however, this is the normal case.

The grammar of ordinary language governs not only the connection of symbols but also the interweaving of linguistic elements, action patterns, and expressions. In the normal case, these three categories of expressions are complementary, so that linguistic expressions "fit" interactions and both language and action "fit" experiential expressions, of course, their integration is imperfect, which makes possible the latitude necessary for indirect communications. In the limiting case, however, a language game can disintegrate to the point where the three categories of expressions no longer agree. Then actions and nonverbal expressions belie what is expressly stated. But the acting subject belies himself only for others who interact with him and observe his deviation from the grammatical rules of the language game. The acting subject himself cannot observe the discrepancy; or, if he observes it, he cannot understand it, because he both expresses and misunderstands himself in this discrepancy. His self-understanding must keep to what is consciously intended, to linguistic expression—or at least to what can be verbalized. Nonetheless, the intentional content that comes into view in discrepant actions and expressions is as much a part of the subject's life-historical structure as are subjectively intended meanings. The subject must deceive itself about these nonverbal expressions that are not coordinated with linguistic expression. And since it objectivates itself in them, it also deceives itself about itself.

Psychoanalytic interpretation is concerned with those connections of symbols in which a subject deceives itself about itself. The *depth hermeneutics* that Freud contraposes to Dilthey's philological hermeneutics deals with texts indicating *self-deceptions of the author*. Beside the manifest content (and the associated indirect but intended communication), such texts document the latent content of a portion of the author's orientations that has become inaccessible to him and alienated from him and yet belongs to him nevertheless. Freud coins the phrase "internal foreign territory"[7] to capture the character of the alienation of something that is still the subject's very own. Symbolic expressions belonging to this class of "texts" can be known according to characteristics that emerge only in the broad context of the interplay of linguistic expressions with the other forms of objectivation:

I am certainly going beyond the conventional meaning of the word in postulating an interest in psychoanalysis on the part of the *linguist*. For language must be understood here to mean not merely the expression of thoughts in words, but also the language of gestures and every other mode of expression of psychic activity, such as writing. Then it may be pointed out that the interpretations of psychoanalysis are primarily translations from a mode of expression that is alien to us into one with which our thought is familiar.[8]

The ongoing text of our everyday language games (speech and actions) is disturbed by apparently contingent mistakes: by omissions and distortions that can be discounted as accidents and ignored, as long as they fall within the conventional limits of tolerance. These *parapraxes* (errors), under which Freud includes cases of forgetting, slips of the tongue and of the pen, misreading, bungled actions, and so-called chance actions, indicate that the faulty text both expresses and conceals self-deceptions of the author.[9] If the mistakes in the text are more obtrusive and situated in the pathological realm, we speak of symptoms. They can be neither ignored nor understood. Nevertheless, the symptoms are part of intentional structures: the ongoing text of everyday language games is broken through not by external influences but by internal disturbances. Neuroses distort symbolic structures in all three dimensions: linguistic expression (obsessive thoughts), actions (repetition compulsions), and bodily experiential expression (hysterical body symptoms). In the case of psychosomatic disturbances, the symptom is so far removed from the original text that its symbolic character first has to be demonstrated by the work of interpretation. Neurotic symptoms in the narrower sense are located as it were between the parapraxes and psychosomatic illnesses. They cannot be belittled as accidents; at the same time their symbolic character, which identifies them as split-off parts of a symbolic structure, cannot be permanently denied. They are the scars of a corrupt text that confronts the author as incomprehensible.

The object domain of depth hermeneutics comprises all the places where, owing to internal disturbances, the text of our everyday language games are interrupted by incomprehensible symbols. These symbols cannot be understood because they do not obey the grammatical rules of ordinary language, norms of action, and culturally learned patterns of expression. They are either ignored and glossed over, rationalized through secondary elaboration (if they are not already the product of rationalizations), or reduced to external, somatic disturbances. Freud uses the medical term "symptom" to cover such deviant symbol formations, which he studied in the dream as an exemplar. Symptoms are persistent and normally disappear only if replaced by functional equivalents. The persistence of symptoms expresses a fixation of ideas and modes of behavior in constant and compelling patterns. They restrict the flexibility margin of speech and communicative action. They can depreciate the reality content of perceptions and thought processes, unbalance the emotional economy, ritualize behavior, and immediately impair bodily functions. Symptoms can be regarded as the result of a compromise between repressed wishes of infantile origin and socially imposed prohibitions of wish-fulfillment. That is why they mainly display both elements, although in varying quantities. For they have the character of substitute formations for a denied gratification and also express the sanction with which the defensive agency threatens the unconscious wish. Finally, symptoms are signs of a specific self-alienation of the subject who has them. The breaks in the text are places where an interpretation has forcibly prevailed that is ego-alien even though it is produced by the self. Because the symbols that interpret suppressed needs are excluded from public communication, *the speaking and acting subject's communication with himself is interrupted.* The privatized language of unconscious motives is rendered inaccessible to the ego, even though internally it has considerable repercussions upon the use of language and those motivations of action that the ego controls. The result is that the ego necessarily deceives itself about its identity in the symbolic structures that it consciously produces.

Usually an interpreter has the task of mediating communication between two partners speaking different languages. He translates from one language into the other, brings about the intersubjectivity of the validity of linguistic symbols and rules, and overcomes difficulties of mutual understanding between partners who are separated by historical, social, or cultural boundaries. This model of hermeneutics from the cultural sciences does not hold for the work of psychoanalytic interpretation. For, even in the pathological limiting case of neurosis, the patient's ability to maintain mutual understanding with his role or conversational partners is not restricted directly, but only indirectly through the repercussions of the symptoms. What happens is that the neurotic, even under conditions of repression, takes care to maintain the intersubjectivity of mutual understanding in everyday life and accords with sanctioned expectations. But for this undisturbed communication under conditions of denial, he pays the price of *communication disturbance within himself.* The institution of power relations necessarily restricts public communication. If this restriction is not to affect the appearance of intersubjectivity, then the limits to communication must be established in the interior of subjects themselves. Thus *the privatized portion of excommunicated language,* along with the undesired motives of action, are silenced in the neurotic and made inaccessible to him. This disturbance of communication does not require an interpreter who mediates between partners of divergent languages but rather one who teaches one and the same subject to comprehend his own language. The analyst instructs the patient in reading his own texts, which he himself has mutilated and distorted, and in translating symbols from a mode of expression deformed as a private language into the mode of expression of public communication. This translation reveals the genetically important phases of life history to a memory that was previously blocked, and brings to consciousness the person's own self-formative process. Thus psychoanalytic hermeneutics, unlike the cultural sciences, aims not at the understanding of symbolic structures in general. Rather, *the act of understanding* to which it leads is *self-reflection.*

The thesis that psychoanalytic knowledge belongs to the category of self-reflection can be easily demonstrated on the basis of Freud's papers on analytic technique.[10] For analytic treatment cannot be defined without recourse to the experience of reflection. Hermeneutics derives its function in the process of the genesis of self-consciousness. It does not suffice to talk of the translation of a text; the translation itself is reflection: "the translation of what is unconscious into what is conscious."[11] Repressions can be eliminated only by virtue of reflection:

The task which the psycho-analytic method seeks to perform may be formulated in different ways, which are, however, in their essence equivalent. It may, for instance, be stated thus: the task of the treatment is to remove the amnesias. When all gaps in memory have been filled in, all the enigmatic products of mental life elucidated, the continuance and even a renewal of the morbid condition are made possible. Or the formula may be expressed in this fashion: all repressions must be undone. The mental condition is then the same as one in which all amnesias have been removed. Another formulation reaches further: the task consists in making the unconscious accessible to consciousness, which is done by overcoming the resistances.[12]

The starting point of psychoanalytic theory is the experience of resistance, that is the blocking force that stands in the way of the free and public communication of repressed contents. The analytic process of making conscious reveals itself as a process of reflection in that it is not only a process on the cognitive level but also dissolves resistances on the affective level.

The dogmatic limitation of false consciousness consists not only in the lack of specific information but in its specific inaccessibility. It is not only a cognitive deficiency; for the deficiency is fixated by habitualized standards on the basis of affective attitudes. That is why the mere communication of information and the labelling of resistances have no therapeutic effect:

> It is a long superseded idea, and one derived from superficial appearances, that the patient suffers from a sort of ignorance, and that if one removes this ignorance by giving him information (about the causal connection of his illness with his life, about his experiences in childhood, and so on) he is bound to recover. The pathological factor is not his ignorance in itself, but the root of this ignorance in his *inner resistances;* it was they that first called this ignorance into being, and they still maintain it now. The task of the treatment lies in combating these resistances. Informing the patient of what he does not know because he has repressed it is only one of the necessary preliminaries to the treatment. If knowledge about the unconscious were as important for the patient as people inexperienced in psychoanalysis imagine, listening to lectures or reading books would be enough to cure him. Such measures, however, have as much influence on the symptoms of nervous illness as a distribution of menu-cards in a time of famine has upon hunger. The analogy goes even further than its immediate application; for informing the patient of his unconscious regularly results in an intensification of the conflict in him and an exacerbation of his troubles.[13]

At first glance the work of the analyst seems to coincide with that of the historian or, better, with that of the archaeologist. For it consists in reconstructing the patient's early history. At the end of analysis it should be possible to present narratively those events of the forgotten years of life that are relevant to the patient's case history and that neither the physician nor patient knew at the beginning of the analysis. The intellectual work is shared by physician and patient in the following way: the former *reconstructs* what has been forgotten from the faulty texts of the latter, from his dreams, associations, and repetitions, while the latter, animated by the constructions suggested by the physician as hypotheses, *remembers.* The interpreting analyst's work of construction accords considerably with the method of reconstruction used by the archaeologist with regard to the sites of archaeological finds. But whereas the goal of the archaeologist is the historical representation of a forgotten process or a "history," the "path that starts from the analyst's construction ought to end in the patient's [present] recollection."[14] Only the patient's recollection decides the accuracy of the construction. If it applies, then it must also "restore" to the patient a portion of lost life history: that is it must be able to elicit a self-reflection.

At the beginning of a step of analytic work, the knowledge of the physician making the construction does not differ from that of the patient who is putting up resistance. The construction being entertained as a hypothesis takes the scattered elements of a mutilated and distorted text and fills them out to make a comprehensible pattern. Seen from the analyst's perspective, it remains mere knowledge "for us," until its communication turns into enlightenment—that is, into knowledge "for it," for the patient's consciousness: "On that particular matter *our* knowledge will then have become *his* knowledge as well." [15] Freud calls the common endeavor that overcomes this gap between communication and enlightenment "working-through." Working-through designates the dynamic component of a cognitive activity that leads to recognition only against resistances.

The analyst can initiate the process of enlightenment to the degree that he succeeds in altering the function of the dynamic of repression in such a way that it works toward the critical dissolution of resistance instead of its stabilization:

> The unconscious impulses do not want to be remembered in the way the treatment desires them to be, but endeavour to reproduce themselves in accordance with the timelessness of the unconscious and its capacity for hallucination. Just as happens in dreams, the patient regards the products of the awakening of his unconscious impulses as contemporaneous and real; he seeks to put his passions into action without taking any account of the real situation. The doctor tries to compel him to fit these emotional impulses into the nexus of the treatment and of his life-history, to submit them to intellectual consideration and to understand them in the light of their psychical value. This struggle between the doctor and the patient, between intellect and instinctual life, between understanding and seeking to act, is played out almost exclusively in the phenomena of transference. [16]

The patient is subject to the compulsion to repeat his original conflict under the conditions of censorship. He acts within the constraints of the pathological attitudes and substitute formations that became fixed in childhood as compromises between wish-fulfillment and defense. The physician confronts the process that he is to reconstruct not as a historical matter but as a power operating in the present. The analytic situation, as the design of an experiment, has two main components. First, it weakens defense mechanisms through the reduction of conscious controls (by relaxation, free association, and unreserved communication), thus reinforcing the need to act. At the same time, however, it makes these repetitive reactions run idle in the presence of a reserved partner who suspends the pressure of life. Thus these reactions react back upon the patient himself. In this way the common neurosis is transformed into a *transference neurosis*. Under the controlled conditions of an artificial illness, the pathological repetition compulsion can be refashioned into a "motive to remember." The physician uses the opportunity to provide the symptoms with a new transference meaning and to "bring it about that something that the patient wishes to discharge in action is disposed of through the work of remembering." [17] The as it were experimental control of "repetition" under the conditions of the analytic situation offers the physician the opportunity for both knowledge and treatment. Acting in the transference situation (and in comparable situations in everyday life during the period of treatment) leads to scenes that offer clues to the reconstruction of the original scene of childhood conflict. But the physician's constructions can be changed into actual recollections of the patient only to the degree that the latter, confronted with the results of his action in transference with its suspension of the pressure of life, sees himself through the eyes of another and learns to reflect on his symptoms as off-shoots of his own actions.

We started with the assertion that the process of knowledge induced in the patient by the physician is to be comprehended as self-reflection. This assertion is supported by the logic of the transference situation and the division of labor in communication between the physician, who elaborates constructions, and the patient, who transforms action into recollection. Analytic insight complements a miscarried self-formative process, owing to a *compensatory learning process, which undoes processes of splitting-off.* These processes detach symbols from public linguistic usage and distort the prevailing rules of communication through private language in order to render harmless the motives of action connected with the excluded symbols. The virtual totality that is sundered by splitting-off is represented by the model of pure communicative action. According to this model all habitual interactions and all interpretations relevant to life conduct are accessible at all times. This is possible on the basis of internalizing the apparatus of unrestricted ordinary language of uncompelled and public communication, so that the transparency of recollected life history is preserved. Self-formative processes that deviate from this model (and Freud leaves no doubt that, under the conditions of a sexual development with two peaks and a forced latency period, *all* such socialization processes must take an *anomalous* course) are the result of suppression by social institutions. This external impact is replaced by the intrapsychic defense of an internally established agency and made permanent. It leads to long-term compromises with the demands of the split-off portion of the self, which come into being at the price of pathological compulsion and self-deception. This is the foundation of symptom formation, through which the text of everyday language games is characteristically affected and thus is made into the object of possible analytic treatment.

Analysis has immediate therapeutic results because the critical overcoming of blocks to consciousness and the penetration of false objectivations initiates the appropriation of a lost portion of life history; it thus reverses the process of splitting-off. That is why analytic knowledge is self-reflection. And that is why Freud rejects the comparison of psychoanalysis with chemical analysis. The analysis and decomposition of complexes into their simple components do not yield a manifold of elements which could then be recombined syntactically. Freud calls the expression "psychosynthesis" an intellectually empty phrase, because it misses the specific achievement of self-reflection, in which analytic decomposition *as such* is synthesis, the re-establishment of a corrupted unity:

In actual fact, indeed, the neurotic patient presents us with a torn mind, divided by resistances. As we analyze it and remove the resistances, it grows together; the great unity which we call his ego fits into itself all the instinctual impulses which before had been split off and held apart from it.[18]

Three additional peculiarities demonstrate that analytic knowledge is self-reflection. First, it includes two moments equally: the cognitive, and the affective and motivational. It is critique in the sense that the analytic power to dissolve dogmatic attitudes inheres in analytic insight. Critique terminates in a transformation of the affective-motivational basis, just as it begins with the need for practical transformation. Critique would not have the power to break up false consciousness if it were not impelled by a *passion for critique*. At the beginning there is the experience of suffering and desperation and the interest in overcoming this burdensome condition. The patient seeks out the physician because he suffers from his symptoms and would like to recover from them; psychoanalysis can rely on this just like medicine in general. But in distinction from usual medical treatment, the pressure of suffering and the interest in gaining health are not only the *occasion* for the inauguration of therapy but the *presupposition* of the success of the therapy itself.

It is possible to observe during the treatment that every improvement in his condition reduces the rate at which he recovers and diminishes the instinctual force impelling him towards recovery. But this instinctual force is indispensable; reduction of it endangers our aim—the patient's restoration to health. What, then, is the conclusion that forces itself inevitably upon us? Cruel though it may sound, we must see to it that the patient's suffering, to a degree that is in some way or other effective, does not come to an end prematurely. If, owing to the symptoms having been taken apart and having lost their value, his suffering becomes mitigated, we must re-instate it elsewhere in the form of some appreciable privation; otherwise we run the danger of never achieving any improvements except quite insignificant and transitory ones.[19]

Freud demands that analytic cure be carried out under conditions of abstinence. He would like to prevent the patient from prematurely replacing his symptoms with painless substitute-gratification during the course of treatment. In customary medical practice this demand would appear absurd. It is meaningful in psychoanalytic therapy because the latter's success depends not on the physician's technically successful influence on a sick organism but rather on the course of the sick person's self-reflection. And the latter proceeds only as long as analytic knowledge is impelled onward against motivational resistances by the *interest in self-knowledge*.

A second peculiarity is connected with this. Freud always emphasized that a patient who enters analytic treatment may not relate to his illness as to a somatic disease. He must be brought to regard the phenomena of his illness as part of his self. Instead of treating his symptoms and their causes as external, the patient must be prepared, so to speak, to assume responsibility for his illness. Freud discussed this problem in respect to the analogous case of responsibility for the content of dreams:

Obviously one must hold oneself responsible for the evil impulses of one's dreams. What else is one to do with them? Unless the content of the dream (rightly understood) is inspired by alien spirits, it is a part of my own being. If I seek to classify the impulses that are present in me according to social standards into good and bad, I must assume responsibility for both sorts; and if, in defence, I say that what is unknown, unconscious and repressed in me is not my "ego," then I shall not be basing my position upon psycho-analysis, I shall not have accepted its conclusions—and I shall perhaps be taught better by the criticisms of my fellow-men, by the disturbances in my actions and the confusion of my feelings. I shall perhaps learn that what I am disavowing not only "is" in me but sometimes "acts" from out of me as well.[20]

Because analysis expects the patient to undergo the experience of self-reflection, it demands "moral responsibility for the content" of the illness. For the insight to which analysis is to lead is indeed only this: that the ego[21] of the patient recognize itself in its other, represented by its illness, as in *its own* alienated *self* and identify with it. As in Hegel's dialectic of the moral life, the criminal recognizes in his victim his own annihilated essence; in this self-reflection the abstractly divorced parties recognize the destroyed moral totality as their common basis *and thereby* return to it. Analytic knowledge is also moral insight, because in the movement of self-reflection the unity of theoretical and practical reason has not yet been undone.

The work of Alfred Lorenzer, which conceives the analysis of processes of instinctual dynamics as linguistic analysis in the sense of depth hermeneutics,[22] has rendered us capable of grasping more precisely the crucial mechanisms of linguistic pathology, the deformation of internal structures of language and action, and their analytic elimination. Linguistic analysis takes symptoms and deciphers unconscious motives present in them just as a meaning suppressed by censorship can be reconstructed from corrupt passages and gaps in a text. In so doing, it transcends the dimension of the subjectively intended meaning of intentional action. It steps back from language as a means of communication and penetrates the symbolic level in which subjects *deceive themselves* about themselves through language and simultaneously give themselves away in it. As soon as language is excluded from public communication by repression, it reacts with a complementary compulsion, to which consciousness and communicative action bend as to the force of a second nature. Analysis attends to causal connections that come into being in this way. The terms of this relation are usually traumatic experiences of a childhood scene on the one hand and falsifications of reality and abnormal modes of behavior, both perpetuated owing to the repetition compulsion, on the other. The original defensive process takes place in a childhood conflict situation as flight from a superior partner. It removes from public communication the linguistic interpretation of the motive of action that is being defended against. In this way the grammatical structure of public language remains intact, but portions of its semantic content are privatized. Symptom formation is a substitute for a symbol whose function has been altered. The split-off symbol has not simply lost all connection with public language. But this grammatical connection has as it were gone underground. It derives its force from confusing the logic of the public usage of language by means of semantically false identifications. At the level of the public text, the suppressed symbol is objectively understandable through rules *resulting* from contingent circumstances of the individual's life history, but not connected with it according to intersubjectively *recognized* rules. That is why the symptomatic concealment of meaning and corresponding disturbance of interaction cannot at first be understood either by others or by the subject himself. They can only become understandable at the level of an intersubjectivity that must be created between the subject as ego and the subject as id. This occurs as physician and patient together reflectively break through the barrier to communication. This is facilitated by the transference situation; for the analyst does not participate in the patient's unconscious actions. The repeated conflict returns upon the patient and, with the interpretive assistance of the analyst, can be recognized in its compulsiveness, brought into connection with repetitive scenes outside the analysis, and ultimately be traced back to the scene in which it originated. This reconstruction undoes false identifications of common linguistic expressions with their meanings in private language and renders comprehensible the hidden grammatical connection between the split-off symbol and the symptomatically distorted public text. The essentially *grammatical* connection between linguistic symbols appears as a *causal* connection between empirical events and rigidified personality traits.[23] Self-reflection dissolves this connection, bringing about the disappearance of the deformation of private language as well as the symptomatic substitute-gratification of repressed motives of action, which have now become accessible to conscious control.

The model of the three mental agencies, id, ego, and superego, permits a systematic presentation of the structure of language deformation and behavioral pathology. Metahermeneutic statements can be organized in terms of it. They elucidate the methodological framework in which empirically substantive interpretations of self-formative processes can be developed. These general interpretations, however, must be distinguished from the metapsychological framework. They are interpretations of early childhood development (the origins of basic motivational patterns and the parallel formation of ego functions) and serve as narrative forms that must be used in each case as an interpretive scheme for an individual's life history in order to find the original scene of his unmastered conflict. The learning mechanisms described by Freud (object choice, identification with an ideal, introjection of abandoned love objects) make understandable the dynamics of the genesis of ego structures at the level of symbolic interaction. The defense mechanisms intervene in this process when and where social norms, incorporated in the expectations of primary reference persons, confront the infantile ego with an unbearable force, requiring it to take flight from itself and objectivate itself in the id. The child's development is defined by problems whose solution determines whether and to what extent further socialization is burdened with the weight of unsolved conflicts and restricted ego functions, creating the predisposition to an accumulation of disillusionments, compulsions, and denials (as well as failure)—or whether the socialization process makes possible a relative development of ego identity.

Freud's general interpretations contain assumptions about interaction patterns of the child and his primary reference persons, about corresponding conflicts and forms of conflict mastery, and about the personality structures that result at the end of the process of early childhood socialization, with their potential for subsequent life history. These personality structures even make possible conditional predictions. Since learning processes take place in the course of communicative action, theory can take the form of a narrative that depicts the psychodynamic development of the child as a course of action: with typical role assignments, successively appearing basic conflicts, recurrent patterns of interaction, dangers, crises, solutions, triumphs, and defeats. On the other hand, conflicts are comprehended metapsychologically from the viewpoint of defense, as are personality structures in terms of the relations between ego, id, and superego. Consequently this history is represented schematically as a self-formative process that goes through various stages of self-objectivation and that has its telos in the self-consciousness of a reflectively appropriated life history.

Only the metapsychology that is presupposed allows the *systematic generalization* of what otherwise would remain pure *history*. It provides a set of categories and basic assumptions that apply to the connections between language deformation and behavioral pathology in general. The general interpretations developed in this framework are the result of numerous and repeated clinical experiences. They have been derived according to the elastic procedure of hermeneutic anticipations. (*Vorgriffe*),[24] with their circular corroboration. But these experiences were already subject to the *general anticipation of the schema of disturbed self-formative processes*. In addition, an interpretation, once it claims the status of "generality," is removed from the hermeneutic procedure of continually correcting one's preunderstanding on the basis of the text. In contrast to the hermeneutic anticipation of the philologist, general interpretation is "fixed" and, like a general theory, must prove itself through predictions deduced from it. If psychoanalysis offers a narrative background against which interrupted self-formative processes can be filled out and become a complete history, the predictions that have been obtained with its help serve the reconstruction of the past. But they, too, are hypotheses that can prove wrong.

A general interpretation defines self-formative processes as lawlike successions of states of a system: Each succession varies in accordance with its initial conditions. Therefore the relevant variables of developmental history can be analyzed in their dependence on the system as a whole. However, the objective-intentional structure of life history, which is accessible only through self-reflection, is not functionalistic in the normal sense of this term. The elementary events are processes in a drama, they do not appear within the instrumentalist viewpoint of the purposive-rational organization of means or of adaptive behavior. The functional structure is interpreted in accordance with a dramatic model. That is, the elementary processes appear as parts of a structure of interactions through which a "meaning" is realized. We cannot equate this meaning with ends that are realized through means, on the model of the craftsman. What is at issue is not a category of meaning that is taken from the behavioral system of instrumental action, such as the maintenance of the state of a system under changing external conditions. It is a question, rather, of a meaning that, even if it is not intended as such, takes form in the course of communicative action and articulates itself reflectively as the experience of life history. This is the way in which "meaning" discloses itself in the course of a drama. But in our own self-formative process, we are at once both actor and critic. In the final instance, the meaning of the process itself must be capable of becoming part of our consciousness in a critical manner, entangled as we are in the drama of life history. The subject must be able to relate his own history and have comprehended the inhibitions that blocked the path of self-reflection. For the final state of a self-formative process is attained only if the subject remembers its identifications and alienations, the objectivations forced upon it and the reflections it arrived at, as the path upon which it constituted itself.

Only the *metapsychologically founded and systematically generalized history* of infantile development with its typical developmental variants puts the physician in the position of so combining the fragmentary information obtained in analytic dialogue that he can reconstruct the gaps of memory and hypothetically anticipate the experience of reflection of which the patient is at first incapable. He makes interpretive suggestions for a story that the patient cannot tell. Yet they can be verified in fact only if the patient adopts them and tells his own story with their aid. The interpretation of the case is corroborated only by the successful continuation of an interrupted self-formative process.

General interpretations occupy a singular position between the inquiring subject and the object domain being investigated. Whereas in other areas theories contain statements about an object domain to which they remain external as statements, the validity of general interpretations depends directly on statements about the object domain being applied by the "objects," that is the persons concerned, to *themselves*. Information in the empirical sciences usually has meaning only for participants in the process of inquiry and, subsequently, for those who use this information. In both cases, the validity of information is measured only by the standards of cogency and empirical accuracy. This information represents cognitions that have been tested on objects through application to reality; but it is valid only for subjects. To the contrary, analytic insights possess validity for the analyst only after they have been accepted as knowledge by the analysand himself. For the empirical accuracy of general interpretations depends not on controlled observation and subsequent communication among investigators but rather on the accomplishment of self-reflection and subsequent communication between the investigator and his "object."

It may be objected that, just as with general theories, the empirical validity of general interpretations is determined by repeated applications to real initial conditions and that, once demonstrated, it is binding for all subjects who have any access to knowledge. Although correct in its way, this formulation conceals the specific difference between general theories and general interpretations. In the case of testing theories through observation (that is in the behavioral system of instrumental action), the application of assumptions to reality is a matter for the inquiring subject. In the case of testing general interpretations through self-reflection (that is in the framework of communication between physician and patient), this application becomes *self-application* by the object of inquiry, who participates in the process of inquiry. The process of inquiry can lead to valid information only via a transformation in the patient's self-inquiry. When valid, theories hold for all who can adopt the position of the inquiring subject. When valid, general interpretations hold for the inquiring subject and all who can adopt its position only to the degree that those who are made the object of individual interpretations *know and recognize themselves* in these interpretations. The subject cannot obtain knowledge of the object unless it becomes knowledge for the object—and unless the latter thereby emancipates itself by becoming a subject.

This is not as odd as it may sound. Every accurate interpretation, including those in the cultural sciences, is possible only in a language *common* to the interpreter and his object, owing to the fact that interpretation restores an intersubjectivity of mutual understanding that had been disturbed. Therefore it must hold likewise for both subject and object. But this function of thought has consequences for general interpretations of self-formative processes that do not occur in the case of interpretations in the cultural sciences. For general interpretations share with general theories the additional claim of allowing causal explanations and conditional predictions. In distinction from the strict empirical sciences, however, psychoanalysis cannot make good this claim on the basis of a methodologically clear separation of the object domain from the level of theoretical statements. This has implications (1) for the construction of the language of interpretation, (2) for the conditions of empirical verification, and (3) for the logic of explanation itself.

Like all interpretations, (1) general interpretations also remain rooted in the dimension of ordinary language. Although they are systematically generalized narratives, they remain historical. Historical representation makes use of narrative statements. They are narrative because they represent events as elements of histories.[25] We explain an event narratively if we show

how a subject is involved in a history. In every history, individual names appear, because a history is always concerned with changes in the state of a subject or of a group of subjects who consider themselves as belonging together. The unity of the history is provided by the identity of the horizon of expectations that can be ascribed to them. The narrative tells of the influence of subjectively experienced events that change the state of the subject or group of subjects by intervening in a lifeworld and attaining significance for acting subjects. In such histories, the subjects must be able to understand both themselves and their world. The historical significance of events always refers implicitly to the meaning structure of a life history unified by ego identity or of a collective history defined by group identity. That is why narrative representation is tied to ordinary language. For only the peculiar reflexivity of ordinary language makes possible communicating what is individual in inevitably general expressions.

By representing an individuated temporal structure, every history is a particular history. Every historical representation implies the claim of *uniqueness*. A *general* interpretation, on the contrary, must break this spell of the historical without departing from the level of narrative representation. It has the form of a narrative, because it is to aid subjects in reconstructing their own life history in narrative form. But it can serve as the background of *many* such narrations only because it does not hold merely for an individual case. It is a *systematically generalized history*, because it provides a scheme for many histories with foreseeable alternative courses. Yet, at the same time, each of these histories must then be able to appear with the claim of being the autobiographical narrative of something individuated. How is such a generalization possible? In every history, no matter how contingent, there is something general, for someone else can find something exemplary in it. Histories are understood as examples in direct proportion to the typicality of their content. Here the concept of type designates a quality of translatability: a history or story is typical in a given situation and for a specific public, if the "action" can be easily taken out of its context and transferred to other life situations that are just as individuated. We can apply the "typical" case to our own. It is we ourselves who undertake the application, abstract the comparable from the differences, and concretize the derived model under the specific life circumstances of our own case.

So the physician, too, proceeds when reconstructing the life history of a patient on the basis of given material. So the patient proceeds himself when, on the basis of the scheme offered him, he recounts his life history even in its previously forgotten phases. Both physician and patient orient themselves not toward an *example* but, indeed, toward a *scheme*. In a general interpretation, the individual features of an example are missing; the step of abstraction has already been taken. Physician and patient have only to take the further step of application. What characterizes systematic generalization, therefore, is that in hermeneutic experiences, which are relatively a priori to application, the abstraction from many typical histories with regard to many individual cases has already taken place. A general interpretation contains no names of individuals but only anonymous roles. It contains no contingent circumstances, but recurring configurations and patterns of action. It contains no idiomatic use of language, but only a standardized vocabulary. It does not represent a typical process, but describes in type-concepts the scheme of an action with conditional variants. This is how Freud presents the Oedipal conflict and its solutions: by means of structural concepts such as ego, id, and superego (derived from the experience of analytic dialogue); by means of roles, persons, and patterns of interaction (arising from the structure of family); and by means of mechanisms of action and communication (such as object-choice, identification, and internalization). The terminological use of ordinary language is not just an attribute of an accidental stage in the development of psychoanalysis. Rather, all attempts to provide metapsychology with a more rigorous form have failed, because the conditions of the application of general interpretations exclude the formalization of ordinary language. For the terms used in it serve the structuring of narratives. It is their presence in the patient's ordinary language which the analyst and the patient make use of in completing an analytic narrative scheme by making it into a history. By putting individual names in the place of anonymous roles and filling out interaction patterns as experienced scenes, they develop ad hoc a new language, in which the language of general interpretation is brought into accord with the patient's own language.

This step reveals application to be a translation. This remains concealed as long as, owing to the common social background of bourgeois origins and college education, the terminological ordinary language of the theory meets the patient's language halfway. The problem of translation becomes explicit as such when the linguistic distance increases on account of social distance. Freud is aware of this. This is shown in his discussion of the possibility that in the future psychoanalysis might be propagated on a mass basis:

We shall then be faced by the task of adapting our technique to the new conditions. I have no doubt that the validity of our psychological assumptions will make its impression on the uneducated too, but we shall need to look for the simplest and most easily intelligible ways of expressing our theoretical doctrines.[26]

The problems of application that arise with theories in the empirical sciences only seem to be analogous. In the application of lawlike hypotheses to initial conditions, it is true that the singular events expressed in existential statements ("this stone") have to be brought into relation to the universal expressions of theoretical statements. But this subsumption is unproblematic, since the singular events only come to consideration insofar as they satisfy the criteria of general predicates ("this stone" is considered, for example, as "mass"). Thus it suffices to establish whether the singular event corresponds to the operational definition through which the theoretical expression is determined. This operational application necessarily proceeds within the framework of instrumental action. Consequently it does not suffice for the application of the theoretical expressions of general interpretations. The material to which the latter are applied consists not of singular events but of symbolic expressions of a fragmentary life history, that is of components of a structure that is individuated in a specific way. In this case it depends on the hermeneutic understanding of the person providing the material whether an element of his life history is adequately interpreted by a suggested theoretical expression. This hermeneutic application necessarily proceeds in the framework of communication in ordinary language. It does not do the same job as operational application. In the latter case, the deciding factor is whether given empirical conditions may count as a case for the application of the theory, leaving untouched the theoretical deductions as such. In contrast, hermeneutic application is concerned with *completing* the narrative background of a general interpretation by creating a narrative, that is the narrative presentation of an individual history. The conditions of application define a *realization* of the interpretation, which was precluded on the level of general interpretation itself. Although theoretical deductions are mediated by communication with the physician, they must be made by the patient himself.

This is the context of (2) the methodological peculiarity that general interpretations do not obey the same criteria of refutation as general theories. If a conditional prediction deduced from a lawlike hypothesis and initial conditions is falsified, then the hypothesis may be considered refuted. A general interpretation can be tested analogously if we derive a construction from one of its implications and the communications of a patient. We can give this construction the form of a conditional prediction. If it is correct, the patient will be moved to produce certain memories, reflect on a specific portion of forgotten life history, and overcome disturbances of both communication and behavior. But here the method of falsification is not the same as for general theories. For if the patient rejects a construction, the interpretation from which it has been derived cannot yet be considered refuted at all. For psychoanalytic assumptions refer to conditions in which the very experience in which they must corroborate themselves is suspended: the experience of reflection is the only criterion for the corroboration or failure of hypotheses. If it does not come about, there is still an alternative: either the interpretation is false (that is, the theory or its application to a given case) or, to the contrary, the resistances, which have been correctly diagnosed, are too strong. The criterion in virtue of which false constructions fail does not coincide with either controlled observation or communicative experience. The interpretation of a case is corroborated only by the successful *continuation of a self-formative process,* that is by the completion of self-reflection, and not in any unmistakable way by what the patient says or how he *behaves.* Here success and failure cannot be intersubjectively established, as is possible in the framework of instrumental action or that of communicative action, each in its way. Even the disappearance of symptoms does not allow a compelling conclusion. For they may have been replaced by other symptoms that at first are inaccessible to observation or the experience of interaction. For the symptom, too, is bound in principle to the meaning that it has *for* the subject engaged in defense. It is incorporated in the structure of self-objectivation and self-reflection and has no falsifying or verifying power independent of it. Freud is conscious of this methodological difficulty. He knows that the "no" of the analysand rejecting a suggested construction is ambiguous:

In some rare cases it turns out to be the expression of a legitimate dissent. Far more frequently it expresses a resistance which may have been evoked by the subject-matter of the construction that has been put forward but which may just as easily have arisen from some other factor in the complex analytic situation. Thus, a patient's "No" is no evidence of the correctness of a construction, though it is perfectly compatible with it. Since every such construction is an incomplete one, since it covers only a small fragment of the forgotten events, we are free to suppose that the patient is not in fact disputing what has been said to him but is basing his contradiction upon the part that has not yet been uncovered. As a rule he will not give his assent until he has learnt the whole truth—which often covers a very great deal of ground. So that the only safe interpretation of his "No" is that it points to incompleteness; there can be no doubt that the construction has not told him everything.
It appears, therefore, that the direct utterances of the patient after he has been offered a construction afford very little evidence upon the question whether we have been right or wrong. It is of all the greater interest that there are indirect forms of confirmation which are in every respect trustworthy.[27]

Freud is thinking of the confirming associations of the dreamer, who brings up previously forgotten text fragments or produces new dreams. On the other hand, doubt then arises whether the dreams have not been influenced by suggestion on the part of the physician:

If a dream brings up situations that can be interpreted as referring to scenes from the dreamer's past, it seems especially important to ask whether the physician's influence can also play a part in such contents of the dream as these. And this question is most urgent of all in the case of what are called "corroborative" dreams, dreams which, as it were, "tag along behind" the analysis. With some patients these are the only dreams that one obtains. Such patients reproduce the forgotten experiences of their childhood only after one has constructed them from their symptoms, associations and other signs and has propounded these constructions to them. Then follow the corroborative dreams, concerning which, however, the doubt arises whether they may not be entirely without evidential value, since they may have been imagined in compliance with the physician's words instead of having been brought to light from the dreamer's unconscious. This ambiguous position cannot be escaped in the analysis, since with these patients unless one interprets, constructs and propounds, one never obtains access to what is repressed in them.[28]

Freud is convinced that the physician's suggestion finds its limit in the mechanism of dream formation, which cannot be influenced. Still, the analytic situation attributes a special significance not only to the patients "no" but to his "yes" as well. For even the patient's confirmations cannot be taken at

face value. Some critics charge that the analyst merely induces a modification of a previous interpretation of life history by talking the patient into a
new terminology.[29] Freud counters that the patient's confirmation does not
have a different implication for the verification of a construction than for
its denial:

It is true that we do not accept the "No" of a person under analysis at its face value;
but neither do we allow his "Yes" to pass. There is no justification for accusing us
of invariably twisting his remarks into a confirmation. In reality things are not so
simple and we do not make it so easy for ourselves to come to a conclusion.

A plain "Yes" from a patient is by no means unambiguous. It can indeed signify
that he recognizes the correctness of the construction that has been presented to
him; but it can also be meaningless, or can even deserve to be described as "hypo-
critical," since it may be convenient for his resistance to make use of an assent in
such circumstances in order to prolong the concealment of a truth that has not been
discovered. The "Yes" has no value unless it is followed by indirect confirmations,
unless the patient, immediately after his "Yes," produces new memories which complete and extend the construction. Only in such an event do we consider that the
"Yes" has dealt completely with the subject under discussion.[30]

Even indirect confirmation by association only has a relative value when
considered in isolation. Freud is right in insisting that only the further
course of analysis can decide a construction's usefulness or lack of it. Only
the context of the self-formative process as a whole has confirming and
falsifying power.[31]

As with the other forms of knowledge, the testing of hypotheses in the
case of general interpretations can follow only those rules that are appropriate to the test situation. Only they guarantee the rigorous objectivity of
validity. Whoever demands, to the contrary, that general interpretations be
treated like the philological interpretation of texts or like general theories
and subjected to externally imposed standards, whether of a functioning
language game or of controlled observation, places himself from the very
beginning outside the dimension of self-reflection, which is the only context
in which psychoanalytic statements can have meaning.

A final peculiarity of the logic of general interpretations results (3) from
the combination of hermeneutic understanding with causal explanation:
understanding itself obtains explanatory power. The fact that, with regard
to symptoms, constructions can assume the form of explanatory hypotheses, shows their affinity with the causal-analytic method. At the same time,
the fact that a construction is itself an interpretation and that the standard
of verification is the patient's act of recollection and agreement demonstrates its difference from the causal-analytic procedure and a certain kinship with the hermeneutic-interpretive method. Freud takes up this question
in a medical form by inquiring whether psychoanalysis may seriously be
called a causal therapy. His answer is conflicting; the question itself seems
to be wrongly posed:

In so far as analytic therapy does not make it its first task to remove the symptoms,
it is behaving like a causal therapy. In another respect, you may say, it is not. For

we long ago traced the causal chain back through the repressions to the instinctual dispositions, their relative intensities in the constitution and the deviations in the course of their development. Supposing, now, that it was possible, by some chemical means, perhaps, to interfere in this mechanism, to increase or diminish the quantity of libido present at a given time or to strengthen one instinct at the cost of another—this then would be a causal therapy in the true sense of the word, for which our analysis would have carried out the indispensable preliminary work of reconnaissance. At present, as you know, there is no question of any such method of influencing libidinal processes; with our psychical therapy we attack at a different point in the combination—not exactly at what we know are the roots of the phenomena, but nevertheless far enough away from the symptoms, at a point which has been made accessible to us by some very remarkable circumstances.[32]

The comparison of psychoanalysis with biochemical analysis shows that its hypotheses do not extend to causal connections between observable empirical events. For if they did, then scientific information would put us in a position, as in biochemistry, to manipulatively transform a given situation. Psychoanalysis does not grant us a power of technical control over the sick psyche comparable to that of biochemistry over a sick organism. And yet it achieves more than a mere treatment of symptoms, because it certainly does grasp causal connections, although not at the level of physical events—at a point "which has been made accessible to us by some very remarkable circumstances." This is precisely the point where language and behavior are pathologically deformed by the causality of split-off symbols and repressed motives. Following Hegel we can call this the causality of fate, in contrast to the causality of nature. For the causal connection between the original scene, defense, and symptom is not anchored in the invariance of nature according to natural laws but only in the spontaneously generated invariance of life history, represented by the repetition compulsion, which can nevertheless be dissolved by the power of reflection.

The hypotheses we derive from general interpretations do not, like general theories, refer to nature, but rather to the sphere that has become second nature through self-objectivation: the "unconscious." This term designates the class of all motivational compulsions that have become independent of their context, that proceed from need dispositions that are not sanctioned by society, and that are demonstrable in the causal connection between the situation of original denial on the one hand and abnormal modes of speech and behavior on the other. The importance of causal motivations of action having this origin is a measure of the disturbance and deviance of the self-formative process. In technical control over nature we get nature to work for us through our knowledge of causal connections. Analytic insight, however, affects the causality of the unconscious as such. Psychoanalytic therapy is not based, like somatic medicine, which is "causal" in the narrower sense, on making use of known causal connections. Rather, its owes its efficacy to overcoming causal connections themselves. Metapsychology does, indeed, contain assumptions about the mechanisms of defense, the splitting-off of symbols, the suppression of motives, and about the complementary mode of operation of self-reflection: assumptions that thus "explain" the origin and elimination of the causality of fate. The analogue to the lawlike hypotheses of general theories would thus be these metapsychological basic assumptions about linguistic structure and action. But they are elaborated on the metatheoretical level and therefore do not have the status of normal lawlike hypotheses.

The concept of a causality of the unconscious also renders comprehensible the therapeutic effect of "analysis," a word in which critique as knowledge and critique as transformation are not accidentally combined. The immediate practical consequences of critique are obtained by causal analysis only because the *empirical* structure that it penetrates is at the same time an *intentional* structure that can be reconstructed and understood according to grammatical rules. We can at first view a construction offered to the patient by the physician as an explanatory hypothesis derived from a general interpretation and supplementary conditions. For the assumed causal connection exists between a past conflict situation and compulsively repeated reactions in the present (symptoms). Substantively, however, the hypothesis refers to a meaning structure determined by the conflict, the defense against the wish that sets off the conflict, the splitting-off of the wish symbol, the substitute gratification of the censored wish, symptom formation, and secondary defense. A causal connection is formulated hypothetically as a hermeneutically understandable meaning structure. This formulation satisfies simultaneously the conditions of a causal hypothesis and of an interpretation (with regard to a text distorted by symptoms). Depth-hermeneutic understanding takes over the function of explanation. It proves its explanatory power in self-reflection, in which an objectivation that is both understood and explained is also overcome. This is the critical accomplishment of what Hegel had called comprehending (*Begreifen*).

In its logical form, however, explanatory understanding differs in one decisive way from explanation rigorously formulated in terms of the empirical sciences. Both of them have recourse to causal statements that can be derived from universal propositions by means of supplementary conditions: that is, from derivative interpretations (conditional variants) or lawlike hypotheses. Now the content of theoretical propositions remains unaffected by operational application to reality. In this case we can base explanations on context-free laws. In the case of hermeneutic application, however, theoretical propositions are translated into the narrative presentation of an individual history in such a way that a causal statement does not come into being without this context. General interpretations can abstractly assert their claim to universal validity because their derivatives are additionally determined by context. Narrative explanations differ from strictly deductive ones in that the events or states of which they assert a causal relation is further defined by their application. Therefore general interpretations do not make possible context-free explanations.[33]

Chapter Four
THE TASKS OF A CRITICAL THEORY
OF SOCIETY

In respects a theory of capitalist modernization developed by some means of a theory of communicative action does follow the Marxian model. It is *critical* both of contemporary social sciences and of the social reality they are supposed to grasp. It is critical of the reality of developed societies inasmuch as they do not make full use of the learning potential culturally available to them, but deliver themselves over to an uncontrolled growth of complexity. As we have seen, this increasing system complexity encroaches upon nonrenewable supplies like a quasinatural force; not only does it outflank traditional forms of life, it attacks the communicative infrastructure of largely rationalized lifeworlds. But the theory is also critical of social-scientific approaches that are incapable of deciphering the paradoxes of societal rationalization because they make complex social systems their object only from one or another abstract point of view, without accounting for the historical constitution of their object domain (in the sense of a reflexive sociology).[1] Critical social theory does not relate to established lines of research as a competitor; starting from its concept of the rise of modern societies, it attempts to explain the specific limitations and the relative rights of those approaches.

If we leave to one side the insufficiently complex approach of behaviorism, there are today three main lines of inquiry occupied with the phenomenon of modern societies. We cannot even say that they are in competition, for they scarcely have anything to say to one another. Efforts at theory comparison do not issue in reciprocal critique; fruitful critique that might foster a common undertaking can hardly be developed across these distances, but at most within one or another camp.[2] There is a good reason for this mutual incomprehension: the object domains of the competing approaches do not come into contact, for they are the result of one-sided abstractions that unconsciously cut the ties between system and lifeworld constitutive for modern societies.

Taking as its point of departure the work of Max Weber, and also in part Marxist historiography, an approach—sometimes referred to as the history of society [*Gesellschaftsgeschichte*]—has been developed that is comparative in outlook, typological in procedure, and, above all, well informed about social history. The dynamics of class struggle are given greater or lesser weight according to the positions of such different authors as Reinhard Bendix, R. Lepsius, C. Wright Mills, Barrington Moore, and Hans-Ulrich Wehler; however, the theoretical core is always formed by assumptions about the structural differentiation of society in functionally specified systems of action. Close contact with historical research prevents the *theory of structural differentiation* from issuing in a more strongly theoretical program, for instance, in some form of systems functionalism. Rather, analysis proceeds in such a way that modernization processes are referred to the level of institutional differentiation. The functionalist mode of investigation is not so widely separated from the structuralist mode that the potential competition between the two conceptual strategies could develop. The modernization of society is, to be sure, analyzed in its various ramifications, but a one-dimensional idea of the whole process of structural differentiation predominates. It is not conceived as a second-order differentiation process, as an uncoupling of system and lifeworld that, when sufficiently advanced, makes it possible for media-steered subsystems to react back on structurally differentiated lifeworlds. As a result, the pathologies of modernity do not come into view as such from this research perspective; it lacks the conceptual tools to distinguish adequately between (a) the structural differentiation of the lifeworld, particularly of its societal components, (b) the growing autonomy of action systems that are differentiated out via steering media, as well as the internal differentiation of these subsystems, and finally (c) those differentiation processes that simultaneously dedifferentiate socially integrated domains of action in the sense of colonizing the lifeworld.

Taking as its point of departure neoclassical economic theory, on the one hand, and social-scientific functionalism, on the other, a *systems-theoretical approach* has established itself above all in economics and in the sciences of administration. These system sciences have, so to speak, grown up in the wake of the two media-steered subsystems. As long as they were occupied chiefly with the internal complexity of the economic and administrative systems, they could rest content with sharply idealized models. To the extent that they had to bring the restrictions of the relevant social environments into their analyses, however, there arose a need for an integrated theory that would also cover the interaction between the two functionally intermeshed subsystems of state and economy.

It is only with the next step in abstraction, which brought society as a whole under systems-theoretical concepts, that the system sciences overdrew their account. The systems theory of society first developed by Parsons and consistently carried further by Luhmann views the rise and development of modern society solely in the functionalist perspective of growing system complexity. Once systems functionalism is cleansed of the dross of the sociological tradition, it becomes insensitive to social pathologies that can be discerned chiefly in the structural features of socially integrated domains of action. It hoists the vicissitudes of communicatively structured lifeworlds up to the level of media dynamics; by assimilating them, from the observer perspective, to disequilibria in intersystemic exchange relations, it robs them of the significance of identity-threatening deformations, which is how they are experienced from the participant perspective.

Finally, from phenomenology, hermeneutics, and symbolic interactionism there has developed an *action-theoretical approach*. To the extent that the different lines of *interpretive sociology* proceed in a generalizing manner at all, they share an interest in illuminating structures of worldviews and forms of life. The essential part is a theory of everyday life, which can also be linked up with historical research, as it is in the work of E. P. Thompson. To the extent that this is done, modernization processes can be presented from the viewpoint of the lifeworlds specific to different strata and groups; the everyday life of the subcultures dragged into these processes are disclosed with the tools of anthropological research. Occasionally these studies condense to fragments of history written from the point of view of its victims. Then modernization appears as the sufferings of those who had to pay for the establishment of the new mode of production and the new system of states in the coin of disintegrating traditions and forms of life. Research of this type sharpens our perception of historical asynchronicities; they provide a stimulus to critical recollection in Benjamin's sense. But it has as little place for the internal systemic dynamics of economic development, of nation and state building, as it does for the structural logics of rationalized lifeworlds. As a result, the subcultural mirrorings in which the sociopathologies of modernity are refracted and reflected retain the subjective and accidental character of *uncomprehended* events.

Whereas the theory of structural differentiation does not sufficiently separate systemic and lifeworld aspects, systems theory and action theory, each isolates and overgeneralizes one of the two aspects. The methodological abstractions have the same result in all three cases. The theories of modernity made possible by these approaches remain insensitive to what Marx called "real abstractions"; the latter can be gotten at through an analysis that at once traces the rationalization of lifeworlds *and* the growth in complexity of media-steered subsystems, and that keeps the paradoxical nature of their interference in sight. As we have seen, it is possible to speak in a nonmetaphorical sense of paradoxical conditions of life if the structural differentiation of lifeworlds is described as rationalization. Social pathologies are not to be measured against "biological" goal states but in relation to the contradictions in which communicatively intermeshed interaction can get caught because deception and self-deception can gain objective power in an everyday practice reliant on the facticity of validity claims.

By "real abstractions" Marx was referring not only to paradoxes experienced by those involved as deformations of their lifeworld, but above all to paradoxes that could be gotten at only through an analysis of reification (or of rationalization). It is in this latter sense that we call "paradoxical" those situations in which systemic relief mechanisms made possible by the rationalization of the lifeworld turns around and overburden the communicative infrastructure of the lifeworld. After attempting to render a fourth approach to inquiry—the *genetic structuralism* of developmental psychology—fruitful for appropriating Weber's sociology of religion, Mead's theory of communication, and Durkheim's theory of social integration,[3] I proposed that we read the Weberian rationalization thesis in that way. The basic conceptual framework I developed by these means was, naturally, not meant to be an end in itself; rather, it has to prove itself against the task of explaining those pathologies of modernity that other approaches pass right by for methodological reasons.

It is just this that critical theory took as its task before it increasingly distanced itself from social research in the early 1940s. In what follows I will (A) recall the complex of themes that originally occupied critical theory, and (B) show how some of these intentions can be taken up without the philosophy of history to which they were tied. In the process, I shall (C) go into one topic at somewhat greater length: the altered significance of the critique of positivism in a postpositivist age.

A.—The work of the Institute for Social Research was essentially dominated by six themes until the early 1940s when the circle of collaborators that had gathered in New York began to break up. These research interests are reflected in the lead theoretical articles that appeared in the main part of the *Zeitschrift für Sozialforschung*. They have to do with (a) the forms of integration in postliberal societies, (b) family socialization and ego development, (c) mass media and mass culture, (d) the social psychology behind the cessation of protest, (e) the theory of art, and (f) the critique of positivism and science.[4] This spectrum of themes reflects Horkheimer's conception of an interdisciplinary social science.[5] In this phase the central line of inquiry, which I characterized with the catchphrase "rationalization as reification," was to be worked out with the differentiated means of various disciplines.[6] Before the "critique of instrumental reason" contracted the process of reification into a topic for the philosophy of history again, Horkheimer and his circle had made "real abstractions" the object of empirical inquiry. From this theoretical standpoint it is not difficult to see the unity in the multiplicity of themes enumerated above.

(a) To begin with, after the far-reaching changes in liberal capitalism the concept of reification needed to be specified.[7] National Socialism, above all, provided an incentive to examine the altered relationship between the economy and the state, to tackle the question of whether a new principle of social organization had arisen with the transition from the Weimar Republic to the authoritarian state, of whether fascism evinced stronger similarities to the capitalist societies of the West or, given the totalitarian features of its political system, had more in common with Stalinism. Pollock and

Horkheimer were inclined to the view that the Nazi regime was like the Soviet regime, in that a state-capitalist order had been established in which private ownership of the means of production retained only a formal character, while the steering of general economic processes passed from the market to planning bureaucracies; in the process the management of large concerns seemed to merge with party and administrative elites. In this view, corresponding to the authoritarian state we have a totally administered society. The form of societal integration is determined by a purposive rational—at least in intention—exercise of centrally steered, administrative domination.

Neumann and Kirchheimer opposed to this theory the thesis that the authoritarian state represented only the totalitarian husk of a monopoly capitalism that remained intact, in that the market mechanism functioned the same as before. On this view, even a developed fascism did not displace the primacy of economic imperatives in relation to the state. The compromises among the elites of economy, party, and administration came about *on the basis* of an economic system of private capitalism. From this standpoint, the structural analogies between developed capitalist societies—whether in the political form of a totalitarian regime or a mass democracy—stood out clearly. Since the totalitarian state was not seen as the center of power, societal integration did not take place exclusively in the forms of technocratically generalized, administrative rationality.[8]

(*b and c*) The relation between the economic and administrative systems of action determined how society was integrated, which forms of rationality the life-contexts of individuals were subjected to. However, the subsumption of sociated individuals under the dominant pattern of social control, the process of reification itself, had to be studied elsewhere: in the family, which, as the agency of socialization, prepared coming generations for the imperatives of the occupational system; and in the political-cultural public sphere, where, via the mass media, mass culture produced compliance in relation to political institutions. The theory of state capitalism could only explain the *type* of societal integration. The analytical social psychology that Fromm,[9] in the tradition of left Freudianism,[10] linked with questions from Marxist social theory was supposed, on the other hand, to explain the *processes* through which individual consciousness was adjusted to the functional requirements of the system, in which a monopolistic economy and an authoritarian state had coalesced.

Institute co-workers investigated the structural change of the bourgeois nuclear family, which had led to a loss of function and a weakening of the authoritarian position of the father, and which had at the same time mediatized the familial haven and left coming generations more and more in the socializing grip of extrafamilial forces. They also investigated the development of a culture industry that desublimated culture, robbed it of its rational content, and functionalized it for purposes of the manipulative control of consciousness. Meanwhile, reification remained, as it was Lukács, a category of the philosophy of consciousness; it was discerned in the attitudes and modes of behavior of individuals. The phenomena of reified consciousness were to be explained empirically, with the help of psychoanalytic personality theory. The authoritarian, easily manipulable character with a weak ego appeared in forms typical of the times; the corresponding superego formations were traced back to a complicated interplay of social structure and instinctual vicissitudes.

Again there were two lines of interpretation. Horkheimer, Adorno, and Marcuse held on to Freudian instinct theory and invoked the dynamics of an inner nature that, while it did react to societal pressure, nevertheless remained in its core resistant to the violence of socialization.[11] Fromm, on the other hand, took up ideas from ego psychology and shifted the process of ego development into the medium of social interaction, which permeated and structured the natural substratum of instinctual impulses.[12] Another front formed around the question of the ideological character of mass culture, with Adorno on one side and Benjamin on the other. Whereas Adorno (along with Löwenthal and Marcuse) implacably opposed the experiential content of authentic art to consumerized culture, Benjamin steadfastly placed his hopes in the secular illuminations that were to come from a mass art stripped of its aura.

(d) Thus in the course of the 1930s the narrower circle of members of the institute developed a consistent position in regard to all these themes. A monolithic picture of a totally administered society emerged; corresponding to it was a repressive mode of socialization that shut out inner nature and an omnipresent social control exercised through the channels of mass communication. Over against this, the positions of Neumann and Kirchheimer, Fromm and Benjamin are not easily reduced to a common denominator. They share a more differentiated assessment of the complex and contradictory character both of forms of integration in postliberal societies and of family socialization and mass culture. These competing approaches might have provided starting points for an analysis of potentials still resistant to the reification of consciousness. But the experiences of the German émigrés in the contemporary horizon of the 1930s motivated them rather to investigate the mechanisms that might explain the suspension of protest potentials. This was also the direction of their studies of the political consciousness of workers and employees, and especially of the studies of anti-Semitism begun by the institute in Germany and continued in America up to the late 1940s.[13]

(e and f) Processes of the reification of consciousness could be made the object of a wide-ranging program of empirical research only after the theory of value had lost its foundational role. With this, of course, also went the normative content of rational natural law theory that was preserved in value theory.[14] As we have seen, its place was then occupied by the theory of societal rationalization stemming from Lukács. The normative content of the concept of reification now had to be gotten from the rational potential of modern culture. For this reason, in its classical period critical theory maintained an emphatically affirmative relation to the art and philosophy of the bourgeois era. The arts—for Löwenthal and Marcuse, classical German literature above all; for Benjamin and Adorno, the literary and musical avant-garde—were the preferred object of an ideology critique aimed at separating the transcendent contents of authentic art—whether utopian or critical—from the affirmative, ideologically worn-out components of bourgeois ideals. As a result, philosophy retained central importance as the keeper of those bourgeois ideas. "Reason," Marcuse wrote in the essay that complemented Horkheimer's programmatic demarcation of critical theory from traditional theory, "is the fundamental category of philosophical thought, the only one by means of which it has bound itself to human destiny." [15] And further on: "Reason, mind, morality, knowledge, and happiness are not only categories of bourgeois philosophy, but concerns of mankind. As such they must be preserved, if not derived anew. When critical theory examines the philosophical doctrines in which it was still possible to speak of man, it deals first with the camouflage and misinterpretation that characterized the discussion of man in the bourgeois period." [16]

This confrontation with the tradition through the critique of ideology could aim at the truth content of philosophical concepts and problems, at appropriating their systematic content, only because critique was guided by theoretical assumptions. At that time critical theory was still based on the Marxist philosophy of history, that is, on the conviction that the forces of production were developing an objectively explosive power. Only on this presupposition could critique be restricted to "bringing to consciousness potentialities that have emerged within the maturing historical situation itself." [17] Without a *theory* of history there could be no immanent critique that applied to the manifestations of objective spirit and distinguished what things and human beings could be from what they actually were.[18] Critique would be delivered up to the reigning standards in any given historical epoch. The research program of the 1930s stood and fell with its historical-philosophical trust in the rational potential of bourgeois culture—a potential that would be released in social movements under the pressure of developed forces of production. Ironically, however, the critiques of ideology carried out by Horkheimer, Marcuse, and Adorno confirmed them in the belief that culture was losing its autonomy in postliberal societies and was being incorporated into the machinery of the economic-administrative system. The development of productive forces, and even critical thought itself, was moving more and more into a perspective of bleak assimilation to their opposites. In the totally administered society only instrumental reason, expanded into a totality, found embodiment; everything that existed was transformed into a real abstraction. In that case, however, what was taken hold of and deformed by these abstractions escaped the grasp of empirical inquiry.

The fragility of the Marxist philosophy of history that implicitly serves as the foundation of this attempt to develop critical theory in interdisciplinary form makes it clear why it had to fail and why Horkheimer and

Adorno scaled down this program to the speculative observations of the *Dialectic of Enlightenment*. Historical-materialist assumptions regarding the dialectical relation between productive forces and productive relations had been transformed into pseudonormative propositions concerning an objective teleology in history. This was the motor force behind the realization of a reason that had been given ambiguous expression in bourgeois ideals. Critical theory could secure its normative foundations only in a philosophy of history. But this foundation was not able to support an empirical research program.

This was also evident in the lack of a clearly demarcated object domain like the communicative practice of the everyday lifeworld in which rationality structures are embodied and processes of reification can be traced. The basic concepts of critical theory placed the consciousness of individuals directly vis-à-vis economic and administrative mechanisms of integration, which were only extended inward, intrapsychically. In contrast to this, the theory of communicative action can ascertain for itself the rational content of anthropologically deep-seated structures by means of an analysis that, *to begin with*, proceeds reconstructively, that is, unhistorically. It describes structures of action and structures of mutual understanding that are found in the intuitive knowledge of competent members of modern societies. There is no way back from them to a theory of history that does not distinguish between problems of developmental logic and problems of developmental dynamics.

In this way I have attempted to free historical materialism from its philosophical ballast.[19] Two abstractions are required for this: (i) abstracting the development of cognitive structures from the historical dynamic of events, and (ii) abstracting the evolution of society from the historical concretion of forms of life. Both help in getting beyond the confusion of basic categories to which the philosophy of history owes its existence.

A theory developed in this way can no longer start by examining concrete ideals immanent in traditional forms of life. It must orient itself to the range of learning processes that is opened up at a given time by a historically attained level of learning. It must refrain from critically evaluating and normatively ordering totalities, forms of life and cultures, and life-contexts and epochs *as a whole*. And yet it can take up some of the intentions for which the interdisciplinary research program of earlier critical theory remains instructive.

B.—Coming at the end of a complicated study of the main features of a theory of communicative action, this suggestion cannot count even as a "promissory note." It is less a promise than a conjecture. So as not to leave it entirely ungrounded, in what follows I will comment briefly on the theses mentioned above, and in the same order. With these illustrative remarks I also intend to emphasize the fully open character and the flexibility of an approach to social theory whose fruitfulness can be confirmed only in the ramifications of social and philosophical research. As to what social theory can accomplish in and of itself—it resembles the focusing power of a magnifying glass. Only when the social sciences no longer sparked a single thought would the time for social theory be past.

(a) *On the forms of integration in postliberal societies.* Occidental rationalism arose within the framework of bourgeois capitalist societies. For this reason, following Marx and Weber I have examined the initial conditions of modernization in connection with societies of this type and have traced the capitalist path of development. In postliberal societies there is a fork in this path: modernization pushes forward in one direction through endogenously produced problems of economic accumulation, in the other through problems arising from the state's efforts at rationalization. Along the developmental path of organized capitalism, a political order of welfare-state mass democracy took shape. In some places, however, under the pressure of economic crises, the mode of production, threatened by social disintegration, could be maintained for a time only in the political form of authoritarian or fascist orders. Along the developmental path of bureaucratic socialism a political order of dictatorship by state parties took shape. In recent years Stalinist domination by force has given way to more moderate, post-Stalinist regimes; the beginnings of a democratic workers' movement and of democratic decision-making processes within the Party are for the time visible only in Poland. Both the fascist and the democratic deviations from the two dominant patterns depend rather strongly, it seems, on national peculiarities, particularly on the political culture of the countries in question. At any rate, these branchings make historical specifications necessary even at the most general level of types of societal integration and of corresponding social pathologies. If we permit ourselves to simplify in an ideal-typical manner and limit ourselves to the two dominant variants of postliberal societies, and if we start from the assumption that alienation phenomena arise as systemically induced deformations of the lifeworld, then we can take a few steps toward a comparative analysis of principles of societal organizations, kinds of crisis tendencies, and forms of social pathology.

On our assumption, a considerably rationalized lifeworld is one of the initial conditions for modernization processes. It must be possible to anchor money and power in the lifeworld as media, that is, to institutionalize them by means of positive law. If these conditions are met, economic and administrative systems can be differentiated out, systems that have a complementary relation to one another and enter into interchanges with their environments via steering media. At this level of system differentiation modern societies arise, first capitalist societies, and later—setting themselves off from those—bureaucratic-socialist societies. A capitalist path of modernization opens up as soon as the economic system develops its own intrinsic dynamic of growth and, with its endogenously produced problems, takes the lead, that is, the evolutionary primacy, for society as a whole. The path of modernization runs in another direction when, on the basis of state ownership of most of the means of production and an institutionalized one-party rule, the administrative action system gains a like autonomy in relation to the economic system.

To the extent that these organizational principles are established, there arise interchange relations between the two functionally interlocked subsystems and the societal components of the lifeworld in locked subsystems and the societal components of the lifeworld in which the media are anchored. The lifeworld, more or less relieved of tasks of material reproduction, can in turn become more differentiated in its symbolic structures and can set free the inner logic of development of cultural modernity. At the same time, the private and public spheres are now set off as the environments of the system. According to whether the economic system or the state apparatus attains evolutionary primacy, either private households or politically relevant memberships are the points of entry for crises that are shifted from the subsystems to the lifeworld. In modernized societies disturbances in the material reproduction of the lifeworld take the form of stubborn systemic disequilibria; the latter either take effect directly as *crises* or they call forth *pathologies* in the lifeworld.

Steering crises were first studied in connection with the business cycle of market economies. In bureaucratic socialism, crisis tendencies spring from self-blocking mechanisms in planning administrations, as they do on the other side from endogenous interruptions of accumulation processes. Like the paradoxes of exchange rationality, the paradoxes of planning rationality can be explained by the fact that rational action orientations come into contradiction with themselves through unintended systemic effects. These crisis tendencies are worked through not only in the subsystem in which they arise, but also in the complementary action system into which they can be shifted. Just as the capitalist economy relies on organizational performances of the state, the socialist planning bureaucracy has to rely on self-steering performances of the economy. Developed capitalism swings between the contrary policies of "the market's self-healing powers" and state interventionism.[20] The structural dilemma is even clearer on the other side, where policy oscillates hopelessly between increased central planning and decentralization, between orienting economic programs toward investment and toward consumption.

These *systemic disequilibria* become *crises* only when the performances of economy and state remain manifestly below an established level of aspiration and harm the symbolic reproduction of the lifeworld by calling forth conflicts and reactions of resistance there. It is the societal components of the lifeworld that are directly affected by this. Before such conflicts threaten core domains of social integration, they are pushed to the periphery—before anomic conditions arise there are appearances of withdrawal of legitimation or motivation. But when steering crises—that is, perceived disturbances of material reproduction—are successfully intercepted by having recourse to lifeworld resources, pathologies arise in the lifeworld. These resources appear as contributions to cultural reproduction, social integration, and socialization. For the continued existence of the economy and the state, it is the resources that contribute to the maintenance of society that are relevant, for it is here, in the institutional orders of the lifeworld, that subsystems are anchored.

We can represent the replacement of steering crises with lifeworld pathologies as follows: anomic conditions are avoided, and legitimations and motivations important for maintaining institutional orders are secured, at the expense of, and through the ruthless exploitation of, other resources. Culture and personality come under attack for the sake of warding off crises and stabilizing society. Instead of manifestations of anomie (and instead of the withdrawal of legitimation and motivation in place of anomie), phenomena of alienation and the unsettling of collective identity emerge. I have traced such phenomena back to a colonization of the lifeworld and characterized them as a reification of the communicative practice of everyday life.

However, deformations of the lifeworld take the form of a reification of communicative relations only in capitalist societies, that is, only where the private household is the point of incursion for the displacement of crises into the lifeworld. This is not a question of the overextension of a single medium but of the monetarization and bureaucratization of the sphere of action of employees and of consumers, of citizens and of clients of state bureaucracies. Deformations of the lifeworld take a different form in societies in which the points of incursion for the penetration of crises into the lifeworld are politically relevant memberships. There too, in bureaucratic-socialist societies, domains of action that are dependent on social integration are switched over to mechanisms of system integration. But instead of the reification of communicative relations we find the shamming of communicative relations in bureaucratically desiccated, forcibly "humanized" domains of pseudopolitical intercourse in an overextended and administered public sphere. This pseudopoliticization is symmetrical to reifying privatization in certain respects. The lifeworld is not directly assimilated to the system, that is, to legally regulated, formally organized domains of action; rather, systemically self-sufficient organizations are fictively put back into a simulated horizon of the lifeworld. While the system is draped out as the lifeworld, the lifeworld is absorbed by the system.[21]

(*b*) *Family socialization and ego development.* The diagnosis of an uncoupling of system and lifeworld also offers a different perspective for judging the structural change in family, education, and personality development. For a psychoanalysis viewed from a Marxist standpoint, the theory of the Oedipus complex, interpreted sociologically, was pivotal for explaining how the functional imperatives of the economic system could establish themselves in the superego structures of the dominant social character. Thus, for example, Löwenthal's studies of drama and fiction in the nineteenth century served to show in detail that the constraints of the economic system—concentrated in status hierarchies, occupational roles, and gender stereotypes—penetrated into the innermost aspects of life history via intra-familial dependencies and patterns of socialization.[22] The intimacy of highly personalized relations merely concealed the blind force of economic inter-dependencies that had become autonomous in relation to the private sphere—a force that was experienced as "fate."

Thus the family was viewed as the agency through which systemic imper-atives influenced our instinctual vicissitudes; its communicative internal structure was not taken seriously. Because the family was always viewed only from functionalist standpoints and was never given its own weight from structuralist points of view, the epochal changes in the bourgeois fam-ily could be misunderstood; in particular, the results of the leveling out of paternal authority could be interpreted wrongly. It seemed as if systemic imperatives now had the chance—by way of a mediatized family—to take hold directly of intrapsychic events, a process that the soft medium of mass culture could at most slow down. If, by contrast, we *also* recognize in the structural transformation of the bourgeois family the inherent rationaliza-tion of the lifeworld; if we see that, in egalitarian patterns of relationship, in individuated forms of intercourse, and in liberalized child-rearing prac-tices, some of the potential for rationality ingrained in communicative ac-tion is *also* released; then the changed conditions of socialization in the middle-class nuclear family appear in a different light.

Empirical indicators suggest the growing autonomy of a nuclear family in which socialization processes take place through the medium of largely deinstitutionalized communicative action. Communicative infrastructures are developing that have freed themselves from latent entanglements in sys-temic dependencies. The contrast between the *homme* who is educated to freedom and humanity in the intimate sphere and the *citoyen* who obeys functional necessities in the sphere of social labor was always an ideology. But it has now taken on a different meaning. Familial lifeworlds see the imperatives of the economic and administrative systems coming at them from outside, instead of being mediatized by them from behind. In the fam-ilies and their environments we can observe a polarization between com-municatively structured and formally organized domains of action; this places socialization processes under different conditions and exposes them to a different type of danger. This view is supported by two rough sociopsy-chological clues: the diminishing significance of the Oedipal problematic and the growing significance of adolescent crises.

For some time now, psychoanalytically trained physicians have observed a symptomatic change in the typical manifestations of illness. Classical hys-terias have almost died out; the number of compulsion neuroses is drasti-cally reduced; on the other hand, narcissistic disturbances are on the in-crease.[23] Christopher Lasch has taken this symptomatic change as the occasion for a diagnosis of the times that goes beyond the clinical domain.[24]

It confirms the fact that the significant changes in the present escape socio-psychological explanations that start from the Oedipal problematic, from an internalization of societal repression which is simply masked by parental authority. The better explanations start from the premise that the communication structures that have been set free in the family provide conditions for socialization that are as demanding as they are vulnerable. The potential for irritability grows, and with it the probability that instabilities in parental behavior will have a comparatively strong effect—a subtle neglect.

The other phenomenon, a sharpening of the adolescence problematic, also speaks for the socializatory significance of the uncoupling of system and lifeworld.[25] Systemic imperatives do not so much insinuate themselves into the family, establish themselves in systematically distorted communication, and inconspicuously intervene in the formation of the self as, rather, openly come at the family from outside. As a result, there is a tendency toward disparities between competences, attitudes, and motives, on the one hand, and the functional requirements of adult roles on the other. The problem of detaching oneself from the family and forming one's own identity have in any case turned adolescent development (which is scarcely safeguarded by institutions anymore) into a critical test for the ability of the coming generation to connect up with the preceding one. When the conditions of socialization in the family are no longer functionally in tune with the organizational membership conditions that the growing child will one day have to meet, the problems that young people have to solve in their adolescence become insoluble for more and more of them. One indication of this is the social and even political significance that youth protest and withdrawal cultures have gained since the end of the 1960s.[26]

This new problem situation cannot be handled with the old theoretical means. If we connect the epochal changes in family socialization with the rationalization of the lifeworld, socializatory interaction becomes the point of reference for the analysis of ego development, and systematically distorted communication—the reification of interpersonal relations—the point of reference for investigating pathogenesis. The theory of communicative action provides a framework within which the structural model of ego, id, and superego can be recast.[27] Instead of an instinct theory that represents the relation of ego to inner nature in terms of a philosophy of consciousness—on the model of relations between subject and object—we have a theory of socialization that connects Freud with Mead, gives structures of intersubjectivity their due, and replaces hypotheses about instinctual vicissitudes with assumptions about identity information.[28] This approach can (i) appropriate more recent developments in psychoanalytic research, particularly the theory of object relations[29] and ego psychology,[30] (ii) take up the theory of defense mechanisms[31] in such a way that the interconnections between intrapsychic communication barriers and communication disturbances at the interpersonal level become comprehensible,[32] and (iii) use the assumptions about mechanisms of conscious and unconscious mastery to establish a connection between orthogenesis and pathogenesis. The cognitive and sociomoral development studied in the Piagetian tradition[33] takes place in accord with structural patterns that provide a reliable foil for intuitively recorded clinical deviations.

(c) *Mass media and mass culture.* With its distinction between system and lifeworld, the theory of communicative action brings out the independent logic of socializatory interaction; the corresponding distinction between two contrary types of communication media makes us sensitive to the ambivalent potential of mass communications. The theory makes us skeptical of the thesis that the essence of the public sphere has been liquidated in postliberal societies. According to Horkheimer and Adorno, the communication flows steered via mass media *take the place of* those communication structures that had once made possible public discussion and self-understanding by citizens and private individuals. With the shift from writing to images and sounds, the electronic media—first film and radio, later television—present themselves as an apparatus that completely permeates and dominates the language of everyday communication. On the one hand, it transforms the authentic content of modern culture into the sterilized and ideologically effective stereotypes of a mass culture that merely replicates what exists; on the other hand, it uses up a culture cleansed of all subversive and transcending elements for an encompassing system of social controls, which is spread over individuals, in part reinforcing their weakened internal behavioral controls, in part replacing them. The mode of functioning of the culture industry is said to be a mirror image of the psychic apparatus, which, as long as the internalization of paternal authority was still functioning, had subjected instinctual nature to the control of the superego in the way that technology had subjected outer nature to its domination.

Against this theory we can raise the empirical objections that can always be brought against stylizing oversimplifications—that it proceeds ahistorically and does not take into consideration the structural change in the bourgeois public sphere; that it is not complex enough to take account of the marked national differences—from differences between private, public-legal, and state-controlled organizational structures of broadcasting agencies, to differences in programming, viewing practices, political culture, and so forth. But there is an even more serious objection, and objection in principle, that can be derived from the dualism of media discussed above.[34]

I distinguished two sorts of media that can ease the burden of the (risky and demanding) coordinating mechanism of reaching understanding: on the one hand, steering media, via which subsystems are differentiated out of the lifeworld; on the other hand, generalized forms of communication, which do not replace reaching agreement in language but merely condense it, and thus remain tied to lifeworld contexts. Steering media uncouple the coordination of action from building consensus in language altogether and neutralize it in regard to the alternative of coming to an agreement or failing to do so. In the other case we are dealing with a specialization of linguistic processes of consensus formation that remains dependent on recourse to the resources of the lifeworld background. The mass media belong to these generalized forms of communication. They free communication processes from the provinciality of spatiotemporally restricted contexts and permit public spheres to emerge, through establishing the abstract simultaneity of a virtually present network of communication contents far removed in space and time and through keeping messages available for manifold contexts.

These media publics hierarchize and at the same time remove restrictions on the horizon of possible communication. The one aspect cannot be separated from the other—and therein lies their ambivalent potential. Insofar as mass media one-sidedly channel communication flows in a centralized network—from the center to the periphery or from above to below—they considerably strengthen the efficacy of social controls. But tapping this authoritarian potential is always precarious because there is a counterweight of emancipatory potential built into communication structures themselves. Mass media can simultaneously contextualize and concentrate processes of reaching understanding, but it is only in the first instance that they relieve interaction from yes/no responses to criticizable validity claims. Abstracted and clustered though they are, these communications cannot be reliably shielded from the possibility of opposition by responsible actors.

When communications research is not abridged in an empiricist manner and allows for dimensions of reification in communicative everyday practice,[35] it confirms this ambivalence. Again and again reception research and program analysis have provided illustrations of the theses in culture criticism that Adorno, above all, developed with a certain overstatement. In the meantime, the same energy has been put into working out the contradictions resulting from the facts that

- the broadcasting networks are exposed to competing interests; they are not able to smoothly integrate economic, political and ideological, professional and aesthetic viewpoints;[36]
- normally the mass media cannot, without generating conflict, avoid the obligations that accrue to them from their journalistic mission and the professional code of journalism;[37]
- the programs do not only, or even for the most part, reflect the standards of mass culture;[38] even when they take the trivial forms of popular entertainment, they may contain critical messages—"popular culture as popular revenge";[39]
- ideological messages miss their audience because the intended meaning is turned into its opposite under conditions of being received against a certain subcultural background;[40]
- the inner logic of everyday communicative practice sets up defenses against the direct manipulative intervention of the mass media;[41] and
- the technical development of electronic media does not necessarily move in the direction of centralizing networks, even though "video pluralism"

and "television democracy" are at the moment not much more than anarchist visions.[42]

(d) *Potentials for protest.* My thesis concerning the colonization of the lifeworld, for which Weber's theory of societal rationalization served as a point of departure, is based on a critique of functionalist reason, which agrees with the critique of instrumental reason only in its intention and in its ironic use of the word reason. One major difference is that the theory of communicative action conceives of the lifeworld as a sphere in which processes of reification do not appear as mere reflexes—as manifestations of a repressive integration emanating from an oligopolistic economy and an authoritarian state. In this respect, the earlier critical theory merely repeated the errors of Marxist functionalism.[43] My references to the socializatory relevance of the uncoupling of system and lifeworld and my remarks on the ambivalent potentials of mass media and mass culture show the private and public spheres in the light of a rationalized lifeworld in which system imperatives *clash with* independent communication structures. The transposition of communicative action to media-steered interactions and the deformation of the structures of a damaged intersubjectivity are by no means predecided processes that might be distilled from a few global concepts. The analysis of lifeworld pathologies calls for an (unbiased) investigation of tendencies *and* contradictions. The fact that in welfare-state mass democracies class conflict has been institutionalized and thereby pacified does not mean that protest potential has been altogether laid to rest. But the potentials for protest emerge now along different lines of conflict—just where we would expect them to emerge if the thesis of the colonization of the lifeworld were correct.

In the past decade or two, conflicts have developed in advanced Western societies that deviate in various ways from the welfare-state pattern of institutionalized conflict over distribution. They no longer flare up in domains of material reproduction; they are no longer channeled through parties and associations; and they can no longer be allayed by compensations. Rather, these new conflicts arise in domains of cultural reproduction, social integration, and socialization; they are carried out in subinstitutional—or at least extraparliamentary—forms of protest; and the underlying deficits reflect a reification of communicatively structured domains of action that will not respond to the media of money and power. The issue is not primarily one of compensations that the welfare state can provide, but of defending and restoring endangered ways of life. In short, the new conflicts are not ignited by distribution problems but by questions having to do with the grammar of forms of life.

This new type of conflict is an expression of the "silent revolution" in values and attitudes that R. Inglehart has observed in entire populations.[44] Studies by Hildebrandt and Dalton, and by Barnes Kaase, confirm the change in themes from the "old politics" (which turns on questions of economic and social security, internal and military security) to a "new politics." [45] The new problems have to do with quality of life, equal rights, individual self-realization, participation, and human rights. In terms of social statistics, the "old politics" is more strongly supported by employers, workers, and middle-class tradesmen, whereas the new politics finds stronger support in the new middle classes, among the younger generation, and in groups with more formal education. These phenomena tally with my thesis regarding internal colonization.

If we take the view that the growth of the economic-administrative complex sets off processes of erosion in the lifeworld, then we would expect old conflicts to be overlaid with new ones. A line of conflict forms between, on the one hand, a center composed of strata *directly* involved in the production process and interested in maintaining capitalist growth as the basis of the welfare-state compromise, and, on the other hand, a periphery composed of a variegated array of groups that are lumped together. Among the latter are those groups that are further removed from the "productivist core of performance" in late capitalist societies,[46] that have been more strongly sensitized to the self-destructive consequences of the growth in complexity or have been more strongly affected by them.[47] The bond that unites these heterogeneous groups is the critique of growth. Neither the bourgeois emancipation movements nor the struggles of the organized labor movement can serve as a model for this protest. Historical parallels are more likely to be found in the social-romantic movements of the early industrial period, which were supported by craftsmen, plebians, and workers, in the defensive movements of the populist middle class, in the escapist movements (nourished by bourgeois critiques of civilization) undertaken by reformers, the *Wandervögel,* and the like.

The current potentials for protest are very difficult to classify, because scenes, grouping, and topics change very rapidly. To the extent that organizational nuclei are formed at the level of parties or associations, members are recruited from the same diffuse reservoir.[48] The following catchphrases serve at the moment to identify the various currents in the Federal Republic of Germany: the antinuclear and environmental movements; the peace movement (including the theme of north-south conflict); single-issue and local movements; the alternative movement (which encompasses the urban "scene," with its squatters and alternative projects, as well as the rural communes); the minorities (the elderly, gays, handicapped, and so forth); the psychoscene, with support groups and youth sects; religious fundamentalism; the tax-protest movement, school protest by parents' associations, resistance to "modernist" reforms; and, finally, the women's movement. Of international significance are the autonomy movements struggling for regional, linguistic, cultural, and also religious independence.

In this spectrum I will differentiate emancipatory potentials from potentials for resistance and withdrawal. After the American civil rights movement—which has since issued in a particularistic self-affirmation of black subcultures—only the feminist movement stands in the tradition of bourgeois-socialist liberation movements. The struggle against patriarchal oppression and for the redemption of a promise that has long been anchored in the acknowledged universalistic foundations of morality and law gives feminism the impetus of an offensive movement, whereas the other movements have a more defensive character. The resistance and withdrawal movements aim at stemming formally organized domains of action for the sake of communicatively structured domains, and not at conquering new territory. There is an element of particularism that connects feminism with these movements; the emancipation of women means not only establishing formal equality and eliminating male privilege, but overturning concrete forms of life marked by male monopolies. Furthermore, the historical legacy of the sexual division of labor to which women were subjected in the bourgeois nuclear family has given them access to contrasting virtues, to a register of values complementary to those of the male world and opposed to a one-sidedly rationalized everyday practice.

Within resistance movements we can distinguish further between the defense of traditional and social rank (based on property) and a defense that already operates on the basis of a rationalized lifeworld and tries out new ways of cooperating and living together. This criterion makes it possible to demarcate the protest of the traditional middle classes against threats to neighborhoods by large technical projects, the protest of parents against comprehensive schools, the protest against taxes (patterned after the movement in support of Proposition 13 in California), and most of the movements for autonomy, on the one side, from the core of a new conflict potential, on the other: youth and alternative movements for which a critique of growth sparked by themes of ecology and peace is the common focus. It is possible to conceive of these conflicts in terms of resistance to tendencies toward a colonization of the lifeworld, as I hope now to indicate, at least in a cursory way.[49] The objectives, attitudes, and ways of acting prevalent in youth protest groups can be understood, to begin with, as reactions to certain problem situations that are perceived with great sensitivity.

"Green" problems. The intervention of large-scale industry into ecological balances, the growing scarcity of nonrenewable natural resources, as well as demographic developments present industrially developed societies with major problems; but these challenges are abstract at first and call for technical and economic solutions, which must in turn be globally planned and implemented by administrative means. What sets off the protest is rather the tangible destruction of the urban environment; the despoliation of the countryside through housing developments, industrialization, and pollution; the impairment of health through the ravages of civilization, pharmaceutical side-effects, and the like—that is, developments that noticeably affect the organic foundations of the lifeworld and make us drastically aware of standards of livability, of inflexible limits to the deprivation of sensual-aesthetic background needs.

Problems of excessive complexity. There are certainly good reasons to fear military potentials for destruction, nuclear power plants, atomic waste, genetic engineering, the storage and central utilization of private data, and the like. These real anxieties are combined, however, with the terror of a new category of risks that are literally invisible and are comprehensible only from the perspective of the system. These risks invade the lifeworld and at the same time burst its dimensions. The anxieties function as catalysts for a feeling of being overwhelmed in view of the possible consequences of processes for which we are morally accountable—since we do set them in motion technically and politically—and yet for which we can no longer take moral responsibility—since their scale has put them beyond our control. Here resistance is directed against abstractions that are forced upon the lifeworld, although they go beyond the spatial, temporal, and social limits of complexity of even highly differentiated lifeworlds, centered as these are around the senses.

Overburdening the communicative infrastructure. Something that is expressed rather blatantly in the manifestations of the psychomovement and renewed religious fundamentalism is also a motivating force behind most alternative projects and many citizens' action groups—the painful manifestations of deprivation in a culturally impoverished and one-sidedly rationalized practice of everyday life. For this reason, ascriptive characteristics such as gender, age, skin color, neighborhood or locality, and religious affiliation serve to build up and separate off communities, to establish subculturally protected communities supportive of the search for personal and collective identity. The revaluation of the particular, the natural, the provincial, of social spaces that are small enough to be familiar, of decentralized forms of commerce and despecialized activities, of segmented pubs, simple interactions and dedifferentiated public spheres—all this is meant to foster the revitalization of possibilities for expression and communication that have been buried alive. Resistance to reformist interventions that turn into their opposite, because the means by which they are implemented run counter to the declared aims of social integration, also belongs in this context.

The new conflicts arise along the seams between system and life-world. Earlier I described how the interchange between the private and public spheres, on the one hand, and the economic and administrative action systems, on the other, takes place via the media of money and power, and how it is institutionalized in the roles of employees and consumers, citizens and clients of the state. It is just these roles that are the targets of protest. Alternative practice is directed against the profit-dependent instrumentalization of work in one's vocation, the market-dependent mobilization of labor power, against the extension of pressures of competition and performance all the way down into elementary school. It also takes aim at the monetarization of services, relationships, and time, at the consumerist redefinition of private spheres of life and personal life-styles. Furthermore, the relation of clients to public service agencies is to be opened up and reorganized in a participatory mode, along the lines of self-help organizations. It is above all in the domains of social policy and health policy (e.g., in connection with psychiatric care) that models of reform point in this direction. Finally, certain forms of protest negate the definitions of the role of citizen and the routines for pursuing interests in a purposive-rational manner—forms ranging from the undirected explosion of disturbances by youth ("Zurich is burning!"), through calculated or surrealistic violations of rules (after the pattern of the American civil rights movement and student protests), to violent provocation and intimidation.

According to the programmatic conceptions of some theoreticians, a partial disintegration of the social roles of employees and consumers, of clients and citizens of the state, is supposed to clear the way for counterinstitutions that develop from within the lifeworld in order to set limits to the inner dynamics of the economic and political-administrative action systems. These institutions are supposed, on the one hand, to divert out of the economic system a second, informal sector that is no longer oriented to profit and, on the other hand, to oppose to the party system new forms of a "politics in the first person," a politics that is expressive and at the same time has a democratic base.[50] Such institutions would reverse just those abstractions and neutralizations by which in modern societies labor and political will-formation have been tied to media-steered interaction. The capitalist enterprise and the mass party (as an "ideology-neutral organization for acquiring power") generalize their points of social entry via labor markets and manufactured public spheres; they treat their employees and voters as abstract labor power and voting subjects; and they keep at a distance—as environments of the system—those spheres in which personal and collective identities can alone take shape. By contrast, the counterinstitutions are intended to dedifferentiate some parts of the formally organized domains of action, remove them from the clutches of the steering media, and return these "liberated areas" to the action-coordinating mechanism of reaching understanding.

However unrealistic these ideas may be, they are important for the polemical significance of the new resistance and withdrawal movements reacting to the colonization of the lifeworld. This significance is obscured, both in the self-understanding of those involved and in the ideological imputations of their opponents, if the communicative rationality of cultural modernity is rashly equated with the functionalist rationality of self-maintaining economic and administrative action systems—that is, whenever the rationalization of the lifeworld is not carefully distinguished from the increasing complexity of the social system. This confusion explains the fronts—which are out of place and obscure the real political oppositions— between the antimodernism of the Young Conservatives[51] and the neoconservative defense of postmodernity[52] that robs a modernity at variance with itself of its rational content and its perspectives on the future.[53]

C.—In this work I have tried to introduce a theory of communicative action that clarifies the normative foundations of a critical theory of society. The theory of communicative action is meant to provide an alternative to the philosophy of history on which earlier critical theory still relied, but which is no longer tenable. It is intended as a framework within which interdisciplinary research on the selective pattern of capitalist modernization can be taken up once again. The illustrative observations (*a*) through (*d*) were meant to make this claim plausible. The two additional themes (*e*) and (*f*) are a reminder that the investigation of what Marx called "real abstraction" has to do with the social-scientific tasks of a theory of modernity, not the philosophical. Social theory need no longer ascertain the normative contents of bourgeois culture, of art and of philosophical thought, in an indirect way, that is, by way of a critique of ideology. With the concept of a communicative reason ingrained in the use of language oriented to reaching understanding, it again expects from philosophy that it take on systematic tasks. The social sciences can enter into a cooperative relation with a philosophy that has taken up the task of working on a theory of rationality.

It is no different with modern culture as a whole than it was with the physics of Newton and his heirs: modern culture is as little in need of a philosophical grounding as science. As we have seen, in the modern period culture gave rise of itself to those structures of rationality that Weber then discovered and described as value spheres. With modern science, with positive law and principled secular ethics, with autonomous art and institutionalized art criticism, three moments of reason crystallized without help from philosophy. Even without the guidance of the critiques of pure and practical reason, the sons and daughters of modernity learned how to divide up and develop further the cultural tradition under these different aspects of rationality—as questions of truth, justice, or taste. More and more the sciences dropped the elements of worldviews and do without an interpretation of nature and history as a whole. Cognitive ethics separates off problems of the good life and concentrates on strictly deontological, universalizable aspects, so that what remains from the Good is only the Just. And an art that has become autonomous pushes toward an ever purer expression of the basic aesthetic experiences of a subjectivity that is decentered and removed from the spatiotemporal structures of everyday life. Subjectivity frees itself here from the conventions of daily perception and of purposive activity, from the imperatives of work and of what is merely useful.

These magnificent "one-sidednesses," which are the signature of modernity, need no foundation and no justification in the sense of a transcendental grounding, but they do call for a self-understanding regarding the character of this knowledge. Two questions must be answered: (i) whether a reason that has objectively split up into its moments can still preserve its unity, and (ii) how expert cultures can be mediated with everyday practice. The reflections offered in the first and third chapters of volume 1 of *The Theory of Communicative Action* are intended as a provisional account of how formal pragmatics can deal with these questions. With that as a basis, the theory of science, the theory of law and morality, and aesthetics, in cooperation with the corresponding historical disciplines, can then reconstruct both the emergence and the internal history of those modern complexes of knowledge that have been differentiated out, each under a different single aspect of validity—truth, normative rightness, or authenticity.

The mediation of the moments of reason is no less a problem than the separation of the aspects of rationality under which questions of truth, justice, and taste were differentiated from one another. The only protection against an empiricist abridgement of the rationality problematic is a steadfast pursuit of the tortuous routes along which science, morality, and art communicate with one another. In each of these spheres, differentiation processes are accompanied by countermovements that, under the primacy of one dominant aspect of validity, bring back in again the two aspects that were at first excluded. Thus nonobjectivist approaches to research within the human sciences bring viewpoints of moral and aesthetic critique to bear[54]—without threatening the primacy of questions of truth; only in this way is critical social theory made possible. Within universalistic ethics the discussion of the ethics of responsibility and the stronger consideration given to hedonistic motives bring the calculation of consequences and the interpretation of needs into play[55]—and they lie in the domains of the cognitive and the expressive; in this way materialist ideas can come in without threatening the autonomy of the moral.[56] Finally, post-avant-garde art is characterized by the coexistence of tendencies toward realism and engagement with those authentic contributions of classical modern art that distilled out the independent logic of the aesthetic;[57] in realist art and *l'art engagé,* moments of the cognitive and of the moral-practical come into play again in art itself, and at the level of the wealth of forms that the avant-garde set free. It seems as if the radically differentiated moments of reason want in such countermovements to point toward a unity—not a unity that could be had at the level of worldviews, but one that might be established *this side* of expert cultures, in a nonreified communicative everyday practice.

How does this sort of affirmative role for philosophy square with the reserve that critical theory always maintained in regard to both the established scientific enterprise and the systematic pretensions of philosophy? Is not such a theory of rationality open to the same objections that pragmatism and hermeneutics have brought against every kind of foundationalism?[58] Do not investigations that employ the concept of communicative reason without blushing bespeak universalistic justificatory claims that will have to fall to those—only too well grounded—metaphilosophical doubts about theories of absolute origins and ultimate grounds? Have not both the historicist enlightenment and materialism forced philosophy into a self-modesty for which the tasks of a theory of rationality must already appear extravagant? The theory of communicative action aims at the moment of unconditionality that, with criticizable validity claims, is built into the conditions of processes of consensus formation. *As claims* they transcend all limitations of space and time, all the provincial limitations of the given context. Rather than answer these questions here with arguments already set out in the introductory chapter to volume 1 of *The Theory of Communicative Action,* I shall close by adding two methodological arguments that speak against the suspicion that the theory of communicative action is guilty of foundationalist claims.

First we must see how philosophy changes its role when it enters into cooperation with the sciences. As the "feeder" [*Zubringer*] for a theory of rationality, it finds itself in a division of labor with reconstructive sciences; these sciences take up the pretheoretical knowledge of compentently judging, acting, and speaking subjects, as well as the collective knowledge of traditions, in order to get at the most general features of the rationality of experience and judgment, action and mutual understanding in language. In this context, reconstructions undertaken with philosophical means also retain a hypothetical character; precisely because of their strong universalistic claims, they are open to further, indirect testing. This can take place in such a way that the reconstructions of universal and necessary presuppositions of communicative action, of argumentative speech, of experience and of objectivating thought, of moral judgments and of aesthetic critique, enter into empirical theories that are supposed to explain *other* phenomena—for example, the ontogenesis of language and of communicative abilities, of moral judgment and social competence; the structural transformation of religious-metaphysical worldviews; the development of legal systems or of forms of social integration generally.

From the perspective of the history of theory, I have taken up the work of Mead, Weber, and Durkheim and tried to show how in their approaches, which are simultaneously empirical and reconstructive, the operations of empirical science and of philosophical conceptual analysis intermesh. The best example of this cooperative division of labor is Piaget's genetic theory of knowledge.[59]

A philosophy that opens its results to indirect testing in this way is guided by the fallibilistic consciousness that the theory of rationality it once wanted to develop on its own can now be sought only in the felicitous coherence of different theoretical fragments. Coherence is the sole criterion of considered choice at the level on which mutually fitting theories stand to one another in relations of supplementing and reciprocally presupposing, for it is only the individual propositions derivable from theories that are true or false. Once we have dropped foundationalist claims, we can no longer expect a hierarchy of sciences; theories—whether social-scientific or philosophical in origin—have to fit with one another, unless one puts the other in a problematic light and we have to see whether it suffices to revise the one or the other.

The test case for a theory of rationality with which the modern understanding of the world is to ascertain its own universality would certainly include throwing light on the opaque figures of mythical thought, clarifying the bizarre expressions of alien cultures, and indeed in such a way that we not only comprehend the learning processes that separate "us" from "them," but also become aware of what we have *unlearned* in the course of this learning. A theory of society that does not close itself off a priori to this possibility of unlearning has to be critical also in relation to the preunderstanding that accrues to it from its own social setting, that is, it has to be open to self-criticism. Processes of unlearning can be gotten at through a critique of deformations that are rooted in the selective exploitation of a potential for rationality and mutual understanding that was once available but is now buried over.

There is also another reason why the theory of society based on the theory of communicative action cannot stray into foundationalist byways. Insofar as it refers to structures of the lifeworld, it has to explicate a background knowledge over which no one can dispose at will. The lifeworld is at first "given" to the theoretician (as it is to the layperson) as his or her own, and in a paradoxical manner. The mode of preunderstanding or of intuitive knowledge of the lifeworld from within which we live together, act and speak with one another, stands in peculiar contrast, as we have seen, to the explicit knowledge of something. The horizontal knowledge that communicative everyday practice *tacitly* carries with it is paradigmatic for the *certainty* with which the lifeworld background is present; yet it does not satisfy the criterion of knowledge that stands in internal relation to validity claims and can therefore be criticized. That which stands beyond all doubt seems as if it could never become problematic; as what is simply unproblematic, a lifeworld can at most fall apart. It is only under the pressure of approaching problems that relevant components of such background knowledge are torn out of their unquestioned familiarity and brought to consciousness as something in need of being ascertained. It takes an earthquake to make us aware that we had regarded the ground on which we stand everyday as unshakable. Even in situations of this sort, only a small segment of our background knowledge becomes uncertain and is set loose after having been enclosed in complex traditions, in solidaric relations, in competences. If the objective occasion arises for us to arrive at some understanding about a situation that has become problematic, background knowledge is transformed into explicit knowledge only in a piecemeal manner.

This has an important methodological implication for sciences that have to do with cultural tradition, social integration, and the socialization of individuals—an implication that became clear to pragmatism and to hermeneutic philosophy, each in its own way, as they came to doubt the possibility of Cartesian doubt. Alfred Schutz, who so convincingly depicted the lifeworld's mode of unquestioned familiarity, nevertheless missed just this problem; whether a lifeworld, in its opaque take-for-grantedness, eludes the phenomenologist's inquiring gaze or is opened up to it does not depend on just *choosing* to adopt a theoretical attitude. The totality of the background knowledge constitutive for the construction of the lifeworld is no more at his disposition than at that of any social scientist—unless an objective challenge arises, in the face of which the lifeworld as a whole becomes problematic. Thus a theory that wants to ascertain the general structures of the lifeworld cannot adopt a transcendental approach; it can only hope to be equal to the *ratio essendi* of its object when there are grounds for assuming that the objective context of life in which the theoretician finds himself is opening up to him its *ratio cognoscendi*.

This implication accords with the point behind Horkheimer's critique of science in his programmatic essay "Traditional and Critical Theory": "The traditional idea of theory is abstracted from scientific activity as it is carried on within the division of labor at a particular stage in the latter's development. It corresponds to the activity of the scholar which takes place alongside all the other activities of a society, but in no immediately clear connection with them. In this view of theory, therefore, the real social function of science is not made manifest; it conveys not what theory means in human life, but only what it means in the isolated sphere in which, for historical reasons, it comes into existence." [60] As opposed to this, critical social theory is to become conscious of the self-referentiality of its calling; it knows that in and through the very act of knowing it belongs to the objective context of life that it strives to grasp. The context of its emergence does not remain external to the theory; rather, the theory takes this reflectively up into itself: "In this intellectual activity the needs and goals, the experiences and skills, the customs and tendencies of the contemporary form of human existence have all played their part." [61] The same holds true for the context of application: "As the influence of the subject matter on the theory, so also the application of the theory to the subject matter is not only an instrascientific process but a social one as well." [62]

In his famous methodological introduction to his critique of political economy of 1857, Marx applied the type of reflection called for by Horkheimer to one of his central concepts. He explained there why the basic assumptions of political economy rest on a seemingly simple abstraction, which is in fact quite difficult:

It was an immense step forward for Adam Smith to throw out every limiting specification of wealth-creating activity—not only manufacturing, or commercial, or agricultural labor, but one as well as the others, labor in general. With the abstract universality of wealth-creating activity we now have the universality of the object defined as wealth, the product as such or again labor as such, but labor as past objectified labor. How difficult and great this transition was may be seen from how

Adam Smith himself from time to time still falls back into the Physiocratic system. Now it might seem that all that had been achieved thereby was to discover the abstract expression for the simplest and most ancient relation in which human beings—in whatever form of society—play the role of producers. This is correct in one respect. Not in another. . . . Indifference toward specific labors corresponds to a form of society in which individuals can with ease transfer from one labor to another, and where the specific kind is a matter of chance for them, hence of indifference. Not only the category 'labor,' but labor in reality has here become the means of creating wealth in general, and has ceased to be organically linked with particular individuals in any specific form. Such a state of affairs is at its most developed in the modern form of existence of bourgeois society—in the United States. Here, then, for the first time, the point of departure of modern economics, namely the abstraction of the category 'labor,' 'labor as such,' labor pure and simple, becomes true in practice.[63]

Smith was able to lay the foundations of modern economics only after a mode of production arose that, like the capitalist mode with its differentiation of an economic system steered via exchange value, forced a transformation of concrete activities into abstract performances, intruded into the world of work with this real abstraction, and thereby created a problem for the workers themselves: "Thus the simplest abstraction which modern economics places at the head of its discussions and which expresses an immeasurably ancient relation valid in all forms of society, nevertheless achieves practical truth as an abstraction only as a category of the most modern society." [64]

A theory of society that claims universality for its basic concepts, without being allowed simply to bring them to bear upon their object in a conventional manner, remains caught up in the self-referentiality that Marx demonstrated in connection with the concept of abstract labor. As I have argued above, when labor is rendered abstract and indifferent, we have a special case of the transference of communicatively structured domains of action over to media-steered interaction. This interpretation decodes the deformations of the lifeworld with the help of another category, namely, "communicative action." What Marx showed to be the case in regard to the category of labor holds true for this as well: "how even the most abstract categories, despite their validity—precisely because of their abstractness— for all epochs, are nevertheless, in the specific character of this abstraction, themselves likewise a product of historical relations, and possess their full validity only for and within these relations." [65] The theory of communicative action can explain why this is so: the development of society must *itself* give rise to the problem situations that *objectively* afford contemporaries a privileged access to the general structures of the lifeworld.

The theory of modernity that I have here sketched in broad strokes permits us to recognize the following: In modern societies there is such an expansion of the scope of contingency for interaction loosed from normative contexts that the inner logic of communicative action "becomes practically true" in the deinstitutionalized forms of intercourse of the familial private sphere as well as in a public sphere stamped by the mass media. At the same time, the systemic imperatives of autonomous subsystems penetrate into the lifeworld and, through monetarization and bureaucratization, force an assimilation of communicative action to formally organized domains of action—even in areas where the action-coordinating mechanism of reaching understanding is functionally necessary. It may be that this provocative threat, this challenge that places the symbolic structures of the lifeworld as a whole in question, can account for why they have become accessible to us.

Part Two
RECONSTRUCTING HISTORICAL MATERIALISM

Chapter Five
PSYCHOANALYSIS AND SOCIAL THEORY: NIETZSCHE'S REDUCTION OF COGNITIVE INTERESTS

Freud conceived of sociology as applied psychology.[1] In his writings on the theory of civilization (*Kultur*)[2] he tried his hand at sociology, led to the area of social theory by problems of psychoanalysis.

The analyst makes use of a preliminary conception of normality and deviance when he regards certain disturbances of communication, behavior, and organic function as "symptoms." But this conception is obviously culturally determined and cannot be defined in terms of a clearly established matter of fact: "We have seen that it is not scientifically feasible to draw a line of demarcation between what is psychically normal and abnormal; so that that distinction, in spite of its practical importance, possesses only a conventional value."[3] If, however, what counts as a normal or deviant self-formative process can be defined only in accordance with the institutional framework of a society, then this society as a whole could itself be in a pathological state when compared with other cultures, even though it sets the standard of normality for the individual cases it subsumes:

In an individual neurosis we take as our starting point the contrast that distinguishes the patient from his environment, which is assumed to be "normal." For a group all of whose members are affected by one and the same disorder no such background could exist; it would have to be found elsewhere.[4]

What Freud calls the diagnosis of communal neuroses requires an investigation that goes beyond the criteria of a given institutional framework and takes into account the history of the cultural evolution of the human species, the "process of civilization." This evolutionary perspective is suggested as well by another consideration arising from psychoanalysis.

The central fact of defense against undesirable instinctual impulses points to a fundamental conflict between functions of self-preservation, which must be secured under the constraint of external nature through the collective effort of societal individuals, and the transcending potential of internal nature of libidinal and aggressive needs. Furthermore the superego, constructed on the basis of substitutive identifications with the expectations of primary reference persons, ensures that there is no immediate confrontation between an ego governed by wishes and the reality of external nature. The reality which the ego comes up against and which makes the instinctual impulses leading to conflict appear as a source of danger is the system of self-preservation, that is, society, whose institutional demands upon the emergent individual are represented by the parents. Consequently, the external authority whose intrapsychic extension is the superego has an *economic* foundation:

The motive of human society is in the last resort an economic one; since it does not possess enough provisions to keep its members alive unless they work, it must restrict the number of its members and divert their energies from sexual activity to work. It is faced, in short, by the eternal, primaeval exigencies of life, which are with us to this day.[5]

But if the basic conflict is defined by the conditions of material labor and economic scarcity, i.e., the shortage of goods, then the renunciations it imposes are a historically variable factor. The pressure of reality and the corresponding degree of societal repression then depend on the degree of technical control over natural forces as well as on the organization of their exploitation and the distribution of the goods produced. The more the power of technical control is extended and the pressure of reality decreased, the weaker becomes the prohibition of instincts compelled by the system of self-preservation: The organization of the ego becomes correspondingly stronger, along with the capacity to master denial rationally. This suggests a comparison of the world-historical process of social organization with the socialization process of the individual. As long as the pressure of reality is overpowering and ego organization is weak, so that instinctual renunciation can only be brought about by the forces of affect, the species finds collective solutions for the problem of defense, which resemble neurotic solutions at the individual level. The same configurations that drive the individual to neurosis move society to establish institutions. What characterizes institutions is at the same time what constitutes their similarity with pathological forms. Like the repetition compulsion from within, institutional compulsion from without brings about a relatively rigid reproduction of uniform behavior that is removed from criticism:

Knowledge of the neurotic afflictions of individuals has well served the understanding of the major social institutions, for the neuroses ultimately reveal themselves as attempts to solve on an individual basis the problems of wish compensation that ought to be solved socially by institutions.[6]

This also provides a perspective for the deciphering of cultural tradition. In tradition, the projective contents of wish fantasies expressing defended-against intentions have been deposited. They can be viewed as sublimations that represent suspended gratifications and guarantee publicly sanctioned compensation for necessary cultural renunciation. "All of the history of civilization shows only the paths men have taken to bind their unsatisfied wishes under the varying conditions of fulfillment and denial by reality, which are changed by technical progress."[7]

This is the psychoanalytic key to a social theory that converges in a surprising manner with Marx's reconstruction of the history of the species while in another regard advancing specifically new perspectives. Freud comprehends "civilization," as Marx does society, as the means by which the human species elevates itself above animal conditions of existence. It is a system of self-preservation that serves two functions in particular: self-assertion against nature and the organization of men's interrelations.[8] Like Marx, although in different terms, Freud distinguishes the forces of production, which indicate the level of technical control over natural processes, from the relations of production:

Human civilization, by which I mean all those respects in which human life has raised itself above its animal status and differs from the life of beasts—and I scorn to distinguish between culture and civilization—presents, as we know, two aspects to the observer. It includes on the one hand all the knowledge and capacity that men have acquired in order to control the forces of nature and extract its wealth for the satisfaction of human needs, and, on the other hand, all the regulations necessary in order to adjust the relations of men to one another and especially the distribution of the available wealth. The two trends of civilization are not independent of each other: firstly, because the mutual relations of men are profoundly influenced by the amount of instinctual satisfaction which the existing wealth makes possible; secondly, because an individual man can himself come to function as wealth in relation to another one, in so far as the other person makes use of his capacity for work, or chooses him as a sexual object; and thirdly, moreover, because every individual is virtually an enemy of civilization, though civilization is supposed to be an object of universal human interest.[9]

The last assertion, that *everyone* is virtually an enemy of civilization, already points up the difference between Freud and Marx. Marx conceives the institutional framework as an ordering of interests that are immediate functions of the system of social labor according to the relation of social rewards and imposed obligations. Institutions derive their force from perpetuating a distribution of rewards and obligations that is rooted in force and distorted according to class structure. Freud, on the contrary, conceives the institutional framework in connection with the repression of instinctual impulses. In the system of self-preservation this repression must be universally imposed, independent of a class-specific distribution of goods and misfortune (as long as an economy of scarcity stamps every satisfaction with the compulsory character of a reward):

It is remarkable that, little as men are able to exist in isolation, they should nevertheless feel as a heavy burden the sacrifices which civilization expects of them in order to make a communal life possible. Thus civilization has to be defended against the individual, and its regulations, institutions and commands are directed to that task. They aim not only at effecting a certain distribution of wealth but at maintaining that distribution; indeed, they have to protect everything that contributes to the conquest of nature and the production of wealth against men's hostile impulses.

Human creations are easily destroyed, and science and technology, which have built them up, can also be used for their annihilation.[10]

Freud defines institutions in a different context than that of instrumental action. What requires ordering is not labor but the compulsion of *socially divided* labor:

With the recognition that every civilization rests on a compulsion to work and a renunciation of instinct and therefore inevitably provokes opposition from those affected by these demands, it has become clear that civilization cannot consist principally or solely in wealth itself and the means of acquiring it and the arrangements for its distribution; for these things are threatened by the rebelliousness and destructive mania of the participants in civilization. Alongside of wealth we now come upon the means by which civilization can be defended—measures of coercion and other measures that are intended to reconcile men to it and to recompense them for their sacrifices. These latter may be described as the mental assets of civilization.[11]

The institutional framework of the system of social labor serves the organization of labor in cooperation and the division of labor and in the distribution of goods, that is in *embedding purposive-rational action in an interaction structure.* Although this web of communicative action also serves functional needs of the system of social labor, at the same time it must be institutionally stabilized. For, under the pressure of reality, not all interpreted needs find gratification, and socially transcendent motives of action cannot all be defended against with consciousness, but only with the aid of affective forces. Thus the institutional framework consists of compulsory norms, which not only sanction linguistically interpreted needs but also redirect, transform, and suppress them.

The power of social norms is based on a defense which enforces substitute-gratifications and produces symptoms as long as it is a result of unconscious mechanisms and not of conscious control. These norms obtain their institutionally fixed and opaque character precisely from the collective neurotic, hidden compulsion that replaces the manifest compulsion of open sanctions. At the same time, a part of the substitute-gratifications can be refashioned into legitimations for prevailing norms. Collective fantasies compensate for the renunciations imposed by civilization. Since they are not private, but instead, on the level of public communication itself, lead a split-off existence that is removed from criticism, they are elaborated into interpretations of the world and taken into service as rationalizations of authority. Freud calls this the "mental assets of civilization": religious worldviews and rites, ideals and value systems, styles and products of art, the world of projective formations and objective appearances—in short, "illusions."

Nevertheless, Freud is not so careless as to reduce the cultural superstructure to pathological phenomena. An illusion that has taken objective form at the level of cultural tradition, such as the Judaeo-Christian religion, is not a delusion:

What is characteristic of illusions is that they are derived from human wishes. In this respect they come near to psychiatric delusions. But they differ from them, too, apart from the more complicated structure of delusions. In the case of delusions, we emphasize as essential their being in contradiction with reality. Illusions need not necessarily be false—that is to say, unrealizable or in contradiction of reality.[12]

For the individual, the institutional framework of the established society is an immovable reality. Wishes that are incompatible with this reality cannot be realized. Therefore they retain the character of fantasies, after being transformed into symptoms by the defensive process and shunted into the path of substitute-gratification. But for the species as a whole, the boundaries of reality are in fact movable. The degree of socially necessary repression can be measured by the variable extent of the power of technical control over natural processes. With the development of technology, the institutional framework, which regulates the distribution of obligations and rewards and stabilizes a power structure that maintains cultural renunciation, can be loosened. Increasingly, parts of cultural tradition that at first have only projective content can be changed into reality. That is, virtual gratification can be transposed into institutionally recognized gratification. "Illusions" are *not merely* false consciousness. Like what Marx called ideology, they too harbor utopia. If technical progress opens up the objective possibility of reducing socially necessary repression below the level of institutionally demanded repression, this utopian content can be freed from its fusion with the delusory, ideological components of culture that have been fashioned into legitimations of authority and be converted into a critique of power structures that have become historically obsolete.

It is in this context that class struggle has its place. The system of power maintains general repressions, which are imposed likewise on all members of society. As long as it is administered by a social class, then *class-specific* privations and denials are linked to the general ones. The traditions that legitimate authority also must compensate the mass of the population for these specific renunciations that go beyond the general privations. That is why the oppressed masses are the first to be incapable of integration by legitimations that have become fragile. It is they who first critically turn the utopian content of tradition against the established civilization:

If we turn to those restrictions that apply only to certain classes of society, we meet with a state of things which is flagrant and which has always been recognized. It is to be expected that these underprivileged classes will envy the favoured ones their privileges and will do all they can to free themselves from their own surplus of privation. Where this is not possible, a permanent measure of discontent will persist within the culture concerned and this can lead to dangerous revolts. If, however, a culture has not got beyond a point at which the satisfaction of one portion of its participants depends upon the suppression of another, and perhaps larger, portion—and this is the case in all present-day cultures—it is understandable that the suppressed people should develop an intense hostility towards a culture whose existence they make possible by their work, but in whose wealth they have too small a share. . . . It goes without saying that a civilization which leaves so large a number of its participants unsatisfied and drives them into revolt neither has nor deserves the prospect of a lasting existence.[13]

Marx had developed the idea of the self-constitution of the human species in natural history in two dimensions: as a process of self-production, which is impelled forward by the productive activity of those who perform social labor and stored in the forces of production, and as a self-formative process, which is impelled forward by the critical-revolutionary activity of classes and which is stored in experiences of reflection. On the other hand, Marx was not able to provide an account of the status of the science that, as critique, was supposed to reconstruct the self-constitution of the species; for his materialist concept of the synthesis of man and nature remained restricted to the categorial framework of instrumental action. This framework could account for productive knowledge but not reflective knowledge. Nor was the model of productive activity suited for the reconstruction of power and ideology. In contrast, Freud has acquired in metapsychology a framework for distorted communicative action that allows the conceptualization of the origins of institutions and the role and function of illusions, that is of power and ideology. Freud's theory can represent a structure that Marx did not fathom.

Freud comprehends institutions as a power that has exchanged acute external force for the permanent internal compulsion of distorted and self-limiting communication. Correspondingly he understands cultural tradition as the collective unconscious, censored in varying measure and turned outwards, where motives that have been split off from communication are driven incessantly about and are directed by the excluded symbols into channels of substitute gratification. These motives, rather than external danger and immediate sanction, are now the forces that hold sway over consciousness by legitimating power. These are the same forces from which ideologically imprisoned consciousness can free itself through self-reflection when a new potential for the mastery of nature makes old legitimations lack credibility.

Marx was not able to see that power and ideology are distorted communication, because he made the assumption that men distinguished themselves from animals when they began to produce their means of subsistence. Marx was convinced that at one time the human species elevated itself above animal conditions of existence by transcending the limits of animal intelligence and being able to transform adaptive behavior into instrumental action. Thus what interests him as the natural basis of history is the physical organization specific to the human species under the category of possible labor: the tool-making animal. Freud's focus, in contrast, was not the system of social labor but the family. He made the assumption that men distinguished themselves from animals when they succeeded in inventing an agency of socialization for their biologically endangered offspring subject to extended childhood dependency. Freud was convinced that at one time the human species elevated itself above animal conditions of existence by transcending the limits of animal society and being able to transform instinct-governed behavior into communicative action. Thus what interests him as the natural basis of history is the physical organization specific to the human species under the category of surplus impulses and their canalization: the drive-inhibited and at the same time fantasizing animal. The two-stage development of human sexuality, which is interrupted by a latency period owing to Oedipal repression, and the role of aggression in the establishment of the superego make man's basic problem not the organization of labor but the evolution of institutions that permanently solve the conflict between surplus impulses and the constraint of reality. Hence Freud does not investigate primarily those ego functions that develop on the cognitive level within the framework of instrumental action. He concentrates on the origins of the motivational foundation of communicative action. What interests him is the destiny of the primary impulse potentials in the course of the growing child's interaction with an environment, determined by his family structure, on which he remains dependent during a long period of upbringing.

But if the natural basis of the human species is essentially determined by surplus impulses and extended childhood dependency, and if the emergence of institutions from structures of distorted communication can be comprehended on this basis, then power and ideology acquire a different and more substantial role than they do for Marx. In this way the logic of the movement of reflection directed against power and ideology, which derives its thrust from developments in the system of social labor (technology and science), becomes graspable. It is the logic of trial and error, but transposed to the level of world history. Within the premises of Freudian theory, the natural basis neither offers a promise that the development of the productive forces will ever create the objective possibility for completely freeing the institutional framework from repressiveness, nor can it discourage such a hope. Freud clearly set out the direction of the history of the species, determined simultaneously by a process of self-production under categories of work and a self-formative process under conditions of distorted communication. At every stage, development of the forces of production produces the objective possibility of mitigating the force of the institutional framework and "[replacing] the affective basis of [man's] obedience to civilization by a rational one."[14] Every step on the road to realizing an idea beset by the contradiction of violently distorted communication is marked by a transformation of the institutional framework and the destruction of an ideology. The goal is "providing a rational basis for the precepts of civilization": in other words, an organization of social relations according to the principle that the validity of every norm of political consequence be made dependent on a consensus arrived at in communication free from domination.[15] But Freud insists that every effort to incorporate this idea into action and to promote enlightenment in a critical-revolutionary way be strictly committed to the determinate negation of unequivocally identifiable suffering—and committed equally to the practical-hypothetical consciousness of carrying out an experiment that can *fail*.

Chapter Six
TOWARD A RECONSTRUCTION OF
HISTORICAL MATERIALISM

Only twice did Marx express himself connectedly and fundamentally on the materialist conception of history,[1] otherwise he used this theoretical framework, in the role of historian, to interpret particular historical situations or developments—unsurpassedly in *The Eighteenth Brumaire of Louis Bonaparte*. Engels characterized historical materialism as a guide and a method.[2] This could create the impression that Marx and Engels saw this doctrine as no more than a heuristic that helped to structure a (now-as-before) narrative presentation of history with systematic intent. But historical materialism was not understood in this way—either by Marx and Engels or by Marxist theoreticians or in the history of the labor movement. I shall not, therefore, treat it as a heuristic but as a theory, indeed as a theory of social evolution that, owing to its reflective status, is also informative for purposes of political action and can under certain circumstances be connected with the theory and strategy of revolution. The theory of capitalist development that Marx worked out in the *Grundrisse* and in *Capital* fits into historical materialism as a *subtheory*.

In 1938 Stalin codified historical materialism in a way that has proven of great consequence,[3] the historical-materialist research since undertaken has remained largely bound to this theoretical framework.[4] The version set down by Stalin needs to be reconstructed. My attempt to do so is also intended to further the critical appropriation of competing approaches—above all of neoevolutionism and of structuralism. Of course, I shall be able to make plausible only a few viewpoints from which such a reconstruction might be attempted with some hope of success.

I would like first to introduce and consider critically some basic concepts and assumptions of historical materialism; I shall then point out certain difficulties that arise in applying its hypotheses and advance and illustrate an (abstract) proposal for resolving them; finally, I shall see what can be learned from competing approaches.

1

To begin I shall examine the concepts of *social labor* and *history of the species,* as well as three fundamental assumptions of historical materialism.

1. *Socially organized labor* is the specific way in which humans, in contradistinction to animals, reproduce their lives.

Man can be distinguished from the animal by consciousness, religion, or anything else you please. He begins to distinguish himself from the animal the moment he begins to *produce* his means of subsistence, a step required by his physical organization. By producing food, man indirectly produces his material life itself.[5]

At a level of description that is unspecific in regard to the human mode of life, the exchange between the organism and its environment can be investigated in the physiological terms of material-exchange processes. But to grasp what is specific to the human mode of life, one must describe the relation between organism and environment at the level of labor processes. From the physical aspect the latter signify the expenditure of human energy and the transfer of energies in the economy of external nature; but what is decisive is the sociological aspect of the goal-directed transformation of material according to *rules of instrumental action.*[6]

Of course, under "production" Marx understands not only the instrumental actions of a single individual, but also the *social cooperation* of different individuals:

The production of life, of one's own life in labor, and of another in procreation, now appears as a double relationship: on the one hand as a natural relationship, on the other as a social one. The latter is social in the sense that individuals co-operate, no matter under what conditions, in what manner, and for what purpose. Consequently a certain mode of production or industrial stage is always combined with a certain mode of co-operation or social stage, and this mode of co-operation is itself a "productive force." We observe in addition that the multitude of productive forces accessible to men determines the nature of society and that the "history of mankind" must always be studied and treated in relation to the history of industry and exchange.[7]

The instrumental actions of different individuals are coordinated in a purposive-rational way, that is, with a view to the goal of production. The *rules of strategic action,* in accord with which cooperation comes about, are a necessary component of the labor process.

Means of subsistence are produced only to be consumed. The distribution of the product of labor is, like the labor itself, socially organized. In the case of rules of distribution, the concern is not with processing material or with the suitably coordinated application of means, but with the systematic connection of reciprocal expectations or interests. Thus the distribution of products requires rules of interaction that can be set intersubjectively at the level of linguistic understanding, detached from the individual case, and made permanent as recognized norms or *rules of communicative action.*

We call a system that socially regulates labor and distribution an *economy*. According to Marx, then, the economic form of reproducing life is characteristic of the human stage of development.

The concept of social labor as the *form of reproduction of human life* has a number of connotations. It is critical of the most basic assumptions of the modern philosophy of the subject or reflection. The statement—"As individuals express their life, so they are. What they are, therefore, coincides with *what* they produce and *how* they produce"[8]—can be understood, according to the first of the *Theses on Feuerbach,* in the sense of an epistemologically oriented *pragmatism,* that is, as a critique of a phenomenalism of any sort, empiricist or rationalist, which understands the knowing subject as a passive, self-contained consciousness. The same statement has *materialist* connotations as well; it is directed equally against theoretical and practical idealism, which assert the primacy of the spirit over nature and that of the idea over the interest. Or consider the statement: "But the essence of man is no abstraction inhering in each single individual. In its actuality it is the ensemble of social relationships."[9] Here Marx, schooled in the Hegelian concept of objective spirit, declares war on the methodological individualism of the bourgeois social sciences and on the practical individualism of English and French moral philosophy; both set forth the acting subject as an isolated monad.

In the present context we are naturally interested in the question, whether the concept of social labor adequately characterizes the form of reproduction of human life. Thus we must specify more exactly what we wish to understand by "human mode of life." In the last generation anthropology has gained new knowledge about the long (more than four million years) phase during which the development from primates to humans, that is, the process of hominization, took place; beginning with a postulated common ancestor of chimpanzees and humans, the evolution proceeded through *Homo erectus* to *Homo sapiens.* This hominization was determined by the *cooperation of organic and cultural mechanisms of development.* On the one hand, during this period of anthropogenesis, there were changes—based on a long series of mutations—in the size of the brain and in important morphological features. On the other hand, the environments from which the pressure for selection proceeded were no longer determined solely by natural ecology, but through the active, adaptive accomplishments of hunting bands of hominids. Only at the threshold to *Homo sapiens* did this mixed organic-cultural form of evolution give way to an exclusively *social evolution.* The natural mechanism of evolution came to a standstill. No new species arose. Instead, the exogamy that was the basis for the societization of *Homo sapiens* resulted in a broad, intraspecific dispersion and mixture of the genetic inheritance. This internal differentiation was the natural basis for a cultural diversification evidenced in a multiplicity of social learning processes. It is therefore advisable to demarcate the sociocultural stage of development—at which alone social evolution takes place (i.e., society is caught up in evolution)—from not only the primate stage—at which there is a still exclusively natural evolution (i.e., the species are caught up in evolution)—but also from the hominid stage—at which the two evolutionary mechanisms are working together, the evolution of the brain being the most important single variable.[10]

2. If we examine the concept of social labor in the light of more recent anthropological findings, it becomes evident that it cuts too deeply into the evolutionary scale; not only humans but hominids too were distinguished from the anthropoid apes in that they converted to reproduction through social labor and developed an economy. The adult males formed hunting bands, which (a) made use of weapons and tools (technology), (b) cooperated through a division of labor (cooperative organization), and (c) distributed the prey within the collective (rules of distribution). The making of the means of production and the social organization of labor, as well as of the distribution of its products, fulfilled the conditions for an economic form of reproducing life.

The society of hominids is more difficult to reconstruct than their mode of production. It is not clear how far beyond interactions mediated by gestures—already found among primates—their system of communication progressed. The conjecture is that they possessed a *language* of gestures and a system of *signal calls.*[11] In any event, cooperative big-game hunting requires reaching understanding about experiences, so that we have to assume a protolanguage, which at least paved the way for the systematic connection of cognitive accomplishments, affective expressions, and interpersonal relations that was so important for hominization. The division of labor in the hominid groups presumably led to a development of two subsystems: on the one hand, the adult males, who were together in egalitarian hunting bands and occupied, on the whole, a dominant position; on the other hand, the females, who gathered fruit and lived together with their young, for whom they cared. In comparison to primate societies, the strategic forms of cooperation and the rules of distribution were new; both innovations were directly connected with the establishment of the *first mode of production,* the cooperative hunt.

Thus the Marxian concept of social labor is suitable for delimiting the mode of life of the hominids from that of the primates; but it does not capture the specifically human reproduction of life. Not hominids, but humans were the first to break up the social structure that arose with the vertebrates—the one-dimensional rank ordering in which every animal was transitively assigned one and only one status. Among chimpanzees and baboons this status system controlled the rather aggressive relations between adult males, sexual relations between male and female, and social relations between the old and the young. A familylike relationship existed only between the mother and her young, and between siblings. Incest between mothers and growing sons was not permitted;[12] there was no corresponding incest barrier between fathers and daughters, because the father role did not exist. Even hominid societies converted to the basis of social labor did not yet know a family structure. We can, of course, imagine how the family might have emerged. The mode of production of the socially organized hunt created a system problem that was resolved by the familialization of the male (Count),[13] that is, by the introduction of a kinship system based on exogamy. The male society of the hunting band became independent of the plant-gathering females and the young, both of whom remained behind during hunting expeditions. With this differentiation, linked to the division of labor, there arose a new need for integration, namely, the need for a controlled exchange between the two subsystems. But the hominids apparently had at their disposal only the pattern of status-dependent sexual relations. This pattern was not equal to the new need for integration, the less so, the more the status order of the primates was further undermined by forces pushing in the direction of egalitarian relations within the hunting band. Only a family system based on marriage and regulated descent permitted the adult male member to link—via the father role—a status in the male system of the hunting band with a status in the female and child system, and thus (1) integrate functions of social labor with functions of nurture of the young, and, moreover, (2) coordinate functions of male hunting with those of female gathering.

3. We can speak of the reproduction of *human* life, with *Homo sapiens*, only when the economy of the hunt is supplemented by a familial social structure. This process lasted several million years; it represented an important replacement of the animal status system, which among the anthropoid apes was already based on symbolically mediated interaction (in Mead's sense) by a system of social norms that presupposed *language*. The rank order of the primates was one-dimensional; every individual could occupy one and only one—that is, in all functional domains the same—status. Only when the same individual could unify various status positions and different individuals could occupy the same status was a socially regulated exchange between functionally specified subsystems possible. The animal status system was based on the status occupant's capacity to threaten, that is, on power as an attribute of personality. By contrast, social role systems are based on the intersubjective recognition of normed expectations of behavior and not on respect for the possibilities of sanction situationally available to a role occupant because of peculiarities of his personality structure. This change means a *moralization of motives for action*. Social roles can conditionally link two different behavioral expectations in such a way that a system of reciprocal motivation is formed. Alter can count on ego fulfilling his (alter's) expectations because ego is counting on alter fulfilling his (ego's) expectations. Through social roles social influence on the motives of the other can be made independent of accidental, situational contexts, and motive formation can be brought into the symbolic world of interaction. For this to occur, however, three conditions must be met:

a. Social roles presuppose not only that participants in interaction can assume the perspective of other participants (which is already the case in symbolically mediated interaction), but that they can also exchange the perspective of the participant for that of the observer. Participants must be able to adopt, in regard to themselves and others, the perspective of an observer, from which they view the system of their expectations and actions from the outside, as it were. Otherwise they could not conditionally link their reciprocal expectations and make them, as a system, the basis of their own action.[14]

b. Social roles can be constituted only if the participants in interaction possess a *temporal horizon* that extends beyond the immediately actual consequences of action. Otherwise spatially, temporally, and materially differentiated expectations of behavior could not be linked with one another in a single social role. Burial rites are a sign that living together as a family induced a categorically expanded consciousness of time.[15]

c. Social roles have to be connected with mechanisms of sanction if they are to control the action motives of participants. Since [in the first human societies] the possibility of sanction was no longer (as in primate societies) covered by the accidental qualities of concrete reference persons and was not yet (as in civilizations) covered by the means of power of political domination, it could consist only in ambivalently cathected interpretations of established norms. As can be seen in the way that taboos function, interpretive patterns tied to social roles reworked the feeling ambivalence, which must have resulted from dedifferentiating the drive system, into the consciousness of normative validity, that is, into readiness to respect established norms.[16]

For a number of reasons these three conditions could not be met before language was fully developed. We can assume that the developments that led to the specifically human form of reproducing life—and thus to the initial state of social evolution—first took place in the structures of labor and language. *Labor and language are older than man and society.* For the basic anthropological concepts of historical materialism this might imply the following:

a. The concept of social labor is fundamental, because the evolutionary achievement of socially organized labor and distribution obviously precedes the emergence of developed linguistic communication, and this in turn precedes the development of social role systems.

b. The specifically human mode of life, however, can be adequately described only if we combine the concept of social labor with that of the familial principle of organization.

c. The structures of role behavior mark a new stage of development in relation to the structures of social labor; rules of communicative action, that is, intersubjectively valid and ritually secured norms of action, cannot be reduced to rules of instrumental or strategic action.

d. Production and socialization, social labor and care for the young, are equally important for the reproduction of the species; thus the familial social structure, which controls both—the integration of external as well as of internal nature—is fundamental.[17]

2

Marx links the concept of social labor with that of the *history of the species*. This phrase is intended in the first place to signal the materialist message that in the case of a single species natural evolution was continued by other means, namely, through the productive activity of the socialized individuals themselves. In sustaining their lives through social labor, men produce at the same time the material relations of life; they produce their society and the historical process in which individuals change along with their societies. The key to the reconstruction of the history of the species is provided by the concept of a *mode of production*. Marx conceives of history as a discrete series of modes of production, which, in its developmental-logical order, reveals the direction of social evolution. Let us recall the most important definitions.

A *mode of production* is characterized by a specific state of development of productive forces and by specific forms of social intercourse, that is, relations of production. The *forces of production* consist of (1) the labor power of those engaged in production, the producers; (2) technically useful knowledge insofar as it can be converted into instruments of labor that heighten productivity, that is, into technologies of production; (3) organizational knowledge insofar as it is applied to set labor power efficiently into motion, to qualify labor power, and to effectively coordinate the cooperation of laborers in accord with the division of labor (mobilization, qualification, and organization of labor power). Productive forces determine the degree of possible control over natural processes. On the other hand, the *relations of production* are those institutions and social mechanisms that determine the way in which (at a given stage of productive forces) labor power is combined with the available means of production. Regulation of access to the means of production, the way in which socially employed labor power is controlled, also determines indirectly the distribution of socially produced wealth. The relations of production express the distribution of social power; with the distributional pattern of socially recognized opportunities for need satisfaction, they prejudge the *interest structure* of a society. Historical materialism proceeds from the assumption that productive forces and productive relations do not vary independently, but form structures that (a) correspond with one another and (b) yield a finite number of structurally analogous stages of development, so that (c) there results a series of modes of production that are to be ordered in a developmental logic. (The handmill produces a society of feudal lords, the steam mill a society of industrial capitalists.)[18]

In the orthodox version, five modes of production are distinguished: (1) the primitive communal mode of bands and tribes prior to civilization; (2) the ancient mode based on slaveholding; (3) the feudal; (4) the capitalist; and finally (5) the socialist modes of production. The discussion of how the ancient Orient and the ancient Americas were to be ordered in this historical development led to the insertion of (6) an Asiatic mode of production.[19] These six modes of production are supposed to mark universal stages of social evolution. From an evolutionary standpoint, every particular *economic structure* can be analyzed in terms of the various modes of production that have entered into a hierarchical combination in a historically concrete society. (A good example of this is Godelier's analysis of the Inca culture at the time of the Spanish colonization.)[20]

The *dogmatic version* of the concept of a history of the species shares a number of weaknesses with eighteenth-century designs for a philosophy of history. The course of previous world history, which evidences a sequence of five or six modes of production, sets down the *unilinear, necessary, uninterrupted, and progressive development of a macrosubject.* I should like to oppose to this model of species history a weaker version, which is not open to the familiar criticisms of the objectivism of philosophy of history.[21]

a. Historical materialism does not need to assume a *species-subject* that undergoes evolution. The bearers of evolution are rather societies and the acting subjects integrated into them; social evolution can be discerned in those structures that are replaced by more comprehensive structures in accord with a pattern that is to be rationally reconstructed. In the course of. this structure-forming process, societies and individuals, together with their ego and group identities, undergo change. Even if social evolution should point in the direction of unified individuals consciously influencing the course of their own evolution, there would not arise any large-scale subjects, but at most self-established, higher-level, intersubjective commonalities. (The specification of the concept of development is another question: in what sense can one conceive the rise of new structures as a movement?— only the empirical substrates are in motion.)[22]

b. If we separate the logic from the dynamics of development—that is, the rationally reconstructible *pattern* of a hierarchy of more and more comprehensive structures from the *processes* through which the empirical substrates develop—then we need require of history neither unilinearity nor necessity, neither continuity nor irreversibility. We certainly do reckon with anthropologically deep-seated general structures, which were formed in the phase of hominization and which lay down the initial state of social evolution; these structures presumably arose to the extent that the cognitive and motivational potential of the anthropoid apes were transformed and reorganized under conditions of linguistic communication. These basic structures correspond, possibly, to the structures of consciousness that children today normally master between their fourth and seventh years, as soon as their cognitive, linguistic, and interactive abilities are integrated with one another.

Such structures describe the logical space in which more comprehensive structural formations can take shape; whether new structural formations arise at all, and if so, when, depends on *contingent* boundary conditions and on learning processes that can be investigated empirically. The genetic explanation of why a certain society has attained a certain level of development is independent of the structural explanation of how a system behaves—a system that conforms at every given stage to the logic of its acquired structures. Many paths can lead to the same level of development; *unilinear* developments are all the less probable, the more numerous the evolutionary units. Moreover, there is no guarantee of uninterrupted development; rather, it depends on accidental constellations whether a society remains unproductively stuck at the threshold of development or whether it solves its system problems by developing new structures. Finally, *retrogressions* in evolution are possible and in many cases empirically corroborated; of course, a society will not fall back behind a level of development, once it is established, without accompanying phenomena of forced regression; this can be seen, for example, in the case of Fascist Germany. It is not evolutionary processes that are *irreversible* but the structural sequences that a society must run through *if* and *to the extent that* it is involved in evolution.

3. Naturally the most controversial point in the *teleology* that, according to historical materialism, is supposed to be inherent in history. When we speak of evolution, we do in fact mean cumulative processes that exhibit a direction. Neoevolutionism regards *increasing complexity* as an acceptable directional criterion. The more states a system can assume, the more complex the environment with which it can cope and against which it can maintain itself. Marx too attributed great significance to the category of the "social division of labor"; by this he meant processes of system differentiation and of integration of functionally specified subsystems at a higher level, that is, processes that increase the internal complexity—and thereby the adaptive capacity—of a society. However, as a social-evolutionary directional criterion, complexity has a number of disadvantages:

a. Complexity is a multidimensional concept. A society can be complex with respect to size, interdependence, and variability, with respect to achievements of generalization, integration, and respecification. As a result, complexity comparisons can become blurred, and questions of global classification from the viewpoint of complexity undecidable.[23]

b. Moreover, there is no clear relation between complexity and self-maintenance. There are increases in complexity that turn out to be evolutionary dead ends. But without this connection, increases in complexity are unsuitable as directional signs; system complexity is equally ill-suited to be the basis for evolutionary stages of development.

c. The connection between complexity and self-maintenance becomes problematic because societies, unlike organisms, do not have clear-cut boundaries and objectively decidable problems of self-maintenance. The reproduction of societies is not measured in terms of rates of reproduction, that is, possibilities of the physical survival of their members, but in terms of securing a normatively prescribed societal identity, a culturally interpreted "good" or "tolerable" life.[24]

Marx judged social development not by increases in complexity but by the stage of development of productive forces and by the maturity of the forms of social intercourse.[25] The development of productive forces depends on the application of technically useful knowledge; and the basic institutions of a society embody moral-practical knowledge. Progress in these two dimensions is measured against the two universal validity claims we also use to measure the progress of empirical knowledge and of moral-practical insight, namely, the truth of propositions and the rightness of norms. I would like, therefore, to defend the thesis that the criteria of social progress singled out by historical materialism as the development of productive forces and the maturity of forms of social intercourse can be systematically justified. I shall come back to this.

3

Having elucidated the concepts of *social labor* and *history of the species*, I want to look briefly at two basic assumptions of historical materialism: the superstructure theorem and the dialectic of the forces and relations of production.

1. The best-known formulation of the superstructure theorem runs as follows:

In the social production of their existence, men inevitably enter into definite relations of production appropriate to a given stage in the development of their material forces of production. The totality of these relations of production constitutes the economic structure of society, the real foundation, on which arises a legal and political superstructure and to which correspond definite forms of social consciousness. The mode of production of material life conditions the general process of social, political and intellectual life. It is not the consciousness of men that determines their existence, but their social existence that determines their consciousness.[26]

In every society the forces and relations of production form—in accordance with the dominant mode of production—and economic structure by which all other subsystems of society are determined. For a long time an *economistic version* of this theorem was dominant. On this interpretation every society is divided—in accord with its degree of complexity—into subsystems that can be hierarchically placed in the order: economic sphere, administrative-political sphere, social sphere, cultural sphere. The theorem then states that processes in any higher subsystems are determined, in the sense of causal dependency, by processes in the subsystems below it. A weaker version of this thesis states that lower subsystems place structural limits on developments in systems higher than themselves. Thus the economic system determines "in the final analysis," as Engels puts it, the scope of the developments possible in other subsystems. In Plekhanov we find formulations that support the first interpretation; in Labriola and Max Adler, passages that support the second. Among Hegelian Marxists like Lukács, Korsch, and Adorno, the concept of the social totality excludes a model of levels. The superstructure theorem here posits a kind of concentric dependency of all social appearances on the economic structure, the latter being conceived dialectically as the essence that comes to existence in the observable appearances.

The context in which Marx put forth his theorem makes it clear, however, that the dependency of the superstructure on the base was intended in the first instance only for the critical phase in which a society passes into a new developmental level. It is not some ontological interpretation of society that is intended but the leading role that the economic structure assumes in social evolution. Interestingly, Karl Kautsky saw this:

Only in the final analysis is the whole legal, political, ideological apparatus to be regarded as a superstructure over an economic infrastructure. This in no way holds for its individual appearance in history. The latter—whether of an economic, ideological, or some other type—will act in many respects as infrastructure, in others as superstructure. The Marxian statement about infrastructure and superstructure is unconditionally valid *only for new appearances in history*.[27]

Marx introduced the concept of *base* in order to delimit a domain of problems to which an explanation of evolutionary innovations must make reference. The theorem states that evolutionary innovations only solve those problems that arise in the basic domain of society.

The equation of *base* and *economic structure* could lead to the view that the basic domain always coincides with the economic system. But this is true only of capitalist societies. We have specified the relations of production by means of their function of regulating access to the means of production and thereby indirectly regulating the distribution of social wealth. In primitive societies this function was performed by kinship systems, and in civilizations, by systems of domination. Only in capitalism, when the market, along with its steering function, also assumed the function of stabilizing class relationships, did the relations of production come forth as such and take on an economic form. The theories of postindustrial society even envision a state in which evolutionary primacy would pass from the economic system to the educational and scientific system.[28] Be that as it may, the relations of production can make use of different institutions.[29]

The institutional core around which the relations of production crystallize lays down a specific form of social integration. By *social integration*, I understand, with Durkheim, securing the unity of a social lifeworld through values and norms. If system problems cannot be solved in accord with the dominant form of social integration, if the latter must itself be revolutionized in order to create latitude for new problem solutions, the identity of society is in danger.

2. Marx sees the mechanism of crisis as follows:

At a certain stage of development, the material productive forces of society come into conflict with the existing relations of production or—this merely expresses the same thing in legal terms—with the property relations within the framework of which they have operated hitherto. From forms of development of the productive forces, these relations turn into their fetters. Then begins an era of social revolution. The changes in the economic foundation lead sooner or later to the transformation of the whole immense superstructure.[30]

The dialectic of forces and relations of production has often been understood in a *technologistic sense.* The theorem then states that techniques of production necessitate not only certain forms of organizing and mobilizing labor power, but also, through the social organization of labor, the relations of production appropriate to it. The production process is conceived as so unified that relations of production are set up in the very process of deploying the forces of production. In the young Marx, precisely the idealist conceptual apparatus ("the objectification of essential powers in labor") lends support to this idea; in Engels, Plekhanov, Stalin, and others the concept of productive relations "issuing" from productive forces is borne instead by instrumentalist models of action.[31]

We must however separate the level of communicative action from that of the instrumental and strategic action combined in social cooperation. If we take this into account, the theorem can be understood to state that (a) there exists an endogenous learning mechanism that provides for spontaneous growth of technically and organizationally useful knowledge and for its conversion into forces of production; (b) a mode of production is in a state of equilibrium only if there is a structural correspondence between the stages of development of the forces and relations of production; (c) the endogeneously caused development of productive forces makes it possible for structural incompatibilities between the two orders to arise, which (d) bring forth disequilibriums in the given mode of production and must lead to an overthrow of existing relations of production. (Godelier, for example, appropriated the theorem in this *structuralist sense.*)[32]

In this formulation too it remains unclear what mechanism could help to explain evolutionary innovations. The postulated learning mechanism explains the growth of a cognitive potential and perhaps also its conversion into technologies and strategies that heighten productivity. It can explain the emergence of system problems that, when the structural dissimilarities between forces and relations of production become too great, threaten the continued existence of the mode of production. But this learning mechanism does not explain how the problems that arise can be solved. The introduction of new forms of social integration—for example, the replacement of the kinship system with the state—requires knowledge of a moral-practical sort and not technically useful knowledge that can be implemented in rules of instrumental and strategic action. It requires not an expansion of our control over external nature but knowledge that can be embodied in structures of interaction—in a word, an extension of the autonomy of society in relation to our own, internal nature.

This can be shown in the example of industrially developed societies. The progress of productive forces has led to a highly differentiated division of labor processes and to a differentiation of the organization of labor within industries. But the cognitive potential that has gone into this "socialization of production" has no structural similarity to the moral-practical consciousness that can support social movements pressing for a revolutionizing of bourgeois society. Thus the advance of industry does not, as the *Communist Manifesto* claims, "replace the isolation of the laborers by their revolutionary combination,"[33] rather, it replaces an old organization of labor with a new one.

The development of productive forces can then be understood as a problem-generating mechanism that *triggers but does not bring about* the overthrow of relations of production and an evolutionary renewal of the mode of production. But even in this formulation the theorem can hardly be defended. To be sure, we know of a few instances in which system problems arose as a result of an increase in productive forces, overloading the adaptive capacity of societies organized on kinship lines and shattering the primitive communal order—this was apparently the case in Polynesia and South Africa.[34] But the great endogenous, evolutionary advances that led to the first civilizations or to the rise of European capitalism were not conditioned but followed by significant development of productive forces. In these cases the development of productive forces could not have led to an evolutionary challenge.

It is advisable to distinguish between the potential of available knowledge and the implementation of this knowledge. It seems to be the case that the mechanism of not-being-able-not-to-learn (for which Moscovici has supplied intuitive support) again and again provides surpluses that harbor a potential of technical-organizational knowledge utilized only marginally or not at all. When this cognitive potential is drawn upon, it becomes the foundation of structure-forming social divisions of labor (between hunters and gatherers, tillers and breeders, agriculture and city craftsmen, crafts and industry, and so on).[35] The endogenous growth of knowledge is thus a necessary condition of social evolution. But only when a new institutional framework has emerged can the as-yet unresolved system problems be treated with the help of the accumulated cognitive potential; from this there *results* an increase in productive forces. Only in this sense can one defend the statement that a social formation is never destroyed and that new, superior relations of production never replace older ones "before the material conditions for their existence have matured within the framework of the old society."[36]

Our discussion has led to the following, provisional results:

a. The system problems that cannot be solved without evolutionary innovations arise in the basic domain of a society.

b. Each new mode of production means a new form of social integration, which crystallizes around a new institutional core.

c. An endogenous learning mechanism provides for the accumulation of a cognitive potential that can be used for solving crisis-inducing system problems.

d. This knowledge, however, can be implemented to develop the forces of production only when the evolutionary step to a new institutional framework and a new form of social integration has been taken.

It remains an open question, *how* this step is taken. The *descriptive* answer of historical materialism is: through social conflict, struggle, social movements, and political confrontations (which, when they take place under the conditions of a class structure, can be analyzed as class struggles). But only an analytic answer can explain *why* a society takes an evolutionary step and how we are to understand that social struggles under certain conditions lead to a new level of social development. I would like to propose the following answer: the species learns not only in the dimension of technically useful knowledge decisive for the development of productive forces but also in the dimension of moral-practical consciousness decisive for structures of interaction. The rules of communicative action do develop in reaction to changes in the domain of instrumental and strategic action; but in doing so they follow *their own logic*.

4

The historical-materialist concept of the history of the species calls for reconstructing social development in terms of a *developmental sequence of modes of production*. I would like to indicate a few advantages and difficulties that arise in applying this concept and then put up for discussion a proposed resolution of the problem.

1. The advantages can be seen through comparison with competing attempts to find viewpoints from which the historical material can be ordered in a developmental logic. Thus there are proposals for periodization based on the principal materials being worked (from stone, bronze, and iron, up to the synthetic products of today) or on the most important energy sources being exploited (from fire, water, and wind, up to atomic and solar energy). But the attempt to discover a developmental pattern in these sequences soon leads to the techniques for making natural resources accessible and for working them. There does, in fact, seem to be a pattern of development to the history of technology.[37] At any rate, technological development accommodates itself to being interpreted *as if* mankind had successively projected the elementary components of the behavioral system of purposive-rational action (which is attached in the first instance to the human organism) onto the level of technical means, and relieved itself of the corresponding functions—at first of the functions of the motor apparatus (legs and hands), then of the functions of the sensory apparatus (eyes, ears, skin) and of the brain.

We can, of course, go beyond the level of the history of technology. In the ontogenetic dimension, Piaget has pointed out a *universal developmental sequence* for cognitive development—from preoperational through concrete-operational to formal-operational thought. The history or technology is probably connected with the great evolutionary advances of society through the *evolution of world views;* and this development might, in turn, be explicable through formal structures of thought for which cognitive psychology has provided a well-examined ontogenetic model, a model that enables us to place these structures in a developmental-logical order.[38]

In any case, since the "neolithic revolution" the great technical discoveries have not brought about new epochs but here merely accompanied them. A history of technology, no matter how rationally reconstructible, is not suited for delimiting social formations. The concept of a mode of production takes into account the fact that the development of productive forces, while certainly an important dimension of social development, *is not decisive* for periodization. Other proposals for periodization are guided by a classification of *forms of cooperation;* and certainly the development from household industries, through their coordination in cottage industry, through factories, national enterprises involving division of labor, up to multinational concerns, does play an important role. But this line of development can be traced only within a single social formation, namely the capitalist; this shows that social evolution cannot be reconstructed in terms of the organization of labor power. The same holds for the development of the *market* (from the household economy, through town and national economies, up to the world economy), or for the *social division of labor* (between hunting and gathering, cultivating and breeding, city crafts and agriculture, agriculture and industry, and so on). These developments increase the complexity of social organization; but it is not written on the face of any of these phenomena, when a new form of organization, a new medium of communication, or a new functional specification means development of productive forces (increased power to dispose of external nature) and when it serves the repression of internal nature and has to be understood as a component of productive relations. For this reason it is more informative to determine the different modes of production directly through relations of production and to analyze changes in the complexity of a society in dependence on its mode of production.[39]

2. There are, of course, also *difficulties* in employing this concept. The decisive point of view here is how access to the means of production is regulated. The state of discussion within historical materialism today is marked by the acceptance of *six* universal, developmental-logically consecutive *modes of production.*[40] In primitive societies, labor and distribution were organized by means of kinship relations. There was no private access to nature and to the means of production (primitive communal mode of production). In the early civilizations of Mesopotamia, Egypt, Ancient China, Ancient India, and pre-Columbian America, land was owned by the state and administered by the priesthood, the military, and the bureaucracy; this arrangement was superimposed upon the remains of village communal property (the so-called Asiatic mode of production). In Greece, Rome, and

other Mediterranean societies, the private landowner combined the position of despotic master of slaves and day laborers in the framework of the household economy with that of a free citizen in the political community of city or state (ancient mode of production). In medieval Europe, feudalism was based on large private estates allotted to individual holders who stood in various relations of dependence (including serfdom) to the feudal lord; these relations were defined in terms that were at once political and economic (feudal mode of production). Finally, in capitalism, labor power became a commodity, so that the dependency of the immediate producers on the owners of the means of production was secured legally through the institution of the labor contract, and economically through the labor market.

The application of this schema runs into difficulties in anthropological and historical research. These are in part problems of mixed and transitional forms—there are only a few instances in which the economic structure of a specific society coincides with a single mode of production; both intercultural diffusion and temporal overlay permit complex structures to arise that have to be deciphered as a combination of several modes of production. But the more important problems are those posed by the developmental-logical ordering of the modes of production themselves. If I am not mistaken, contemporary discussion revolves primarily around the following complexes:

a. It is not entirely clear how we can distinguish paleolithic from neolithic societies on the basis of the same primitive communal mode of production. The "neolithic revolution" signifies not only a new stage of development of productive forces but also a new mode of life.[41] For this reason, some have proposed distinguishing a stage of appropriative economy from a stage of producing economy. Whereas hunters and gatherers seized nature's treasures for their direct use, tillage and breeding already required means of production (earth and soil, livestock), which raised the question of ownership.[42] Other differences are related to the complexity of social organization (band, tribe, chiefdom).[43] Finally, it is possible to provide grounds for the conjecture that the technical innovations that marked the transition to neolithic society were dependent on the coherent development of mythological world views.[44]

b. The many-sided discussion of the so-called Asiatic mode of production has given rise to a whole series of systematic questions. Should this mode be understood as the last stage of the primitive communal order or as the first form of class society?[45] If the latter alternative can be made plausible—as I believe it can—does the Asiatic mode of production mark a universal stage of development or a special line of development of class societies *alongside of* the path of the ancient mode of production? Or is it a mixed form of the ancient and feudal modes of production?[46]

c. The classification of feudalism raises equally great difficulties.[47] Is this at all a clearly specifiable mode of production or merely a collective concept with no analytic pretensions? If there is an independent mode of production of this type, does it mark a universal stage of development? If so, did only the society of medieval Europe reach this stage; in other words, is feudalism a unique phenomenon, or did other civilizations also reach feudal stages of development?

d. This is connected with the further question, how can archaic civilizations be distinguished from developed civilizations? The differentiation of social subsystems and the increase in stratification took place within the framework of the same political class organization. In all evolutionarily successful civilizations there was a noteworthy structural change of world view—the change from a mythological-cosmogonic world view to a rationalized world view in the form of cosmological ethics. This change took place between the eighth and third centuries B.C. in China, India, Palestine, and Greece.[48] How can this be explained on materialist principles?

e. The controversy between theories of postindustrial society, on the one side, and theories of organized capitalism, on the other, also belongs in this context. It involves, among other things, the question of whether the capitalism regulated through state intervention in the developed industrial nations of the West marks the last phase of the old mode of production or the transition to a new one.

f. The classification of so-called socialist transitional societies is a special problem. Is bureaucratic socialism, compared to developed capitalism, in any sense an evolutionarily higher social formation; or are the two merely variants of the same stage of development?

These and similar problems have led as important a Marxist historian as Hobsbawm to cast doubt on the concept of *universal* stages of development (in his introduction to Marx's "Pre-Capitalist Economic Formations"). Of course, there remains the question of whether the aforementioned problems are merely lining the path of a normal scientific discussion or whether they are to be understood as signs of the unfruitfulness of a research program. I am of the opinion that the alternative should not be posed in this way at present. Perhaps the concept of a mode of production is not so much the wrong key to the logic of social development as a key that has not yet been sufficiently filed down.

5

The concept of a mode of production is not abstract enough to capture the universals of societal development. Modes of production can be compared at two levels: (a) regulation of access to the means of production, and (b) the structural compatibility of these rules with the stage of development of productive forces. On the first level, Marx differentiates according to whether property is communal or private. The viewpoint of exclusive disposition over the means of production leads, however, only to a demarcation of societies with and without class structures. Further differentiation according to the degree to which private property is established, and according to the forms of exploitation (the exploitation of village communities by the state, slavery, serfdom, wage labor), is as yet too imprecise to permit unambiguous comparisons.[49] To achieve greater precision, Finley recommends adopting the following points of view: claims to property versus power over things; power over human labor-force versus power over human movements; power to punish versus immunity from punishment; privileges and liabilities in judicial process; privileges in the area of the family; privileges of social mobility, horizontal and vertical; privileges versus duties in the sacral, political, and military spheres.[50] These general sociological points of view certainly permit a more concrete description of a given economic structure; but they broaden rather than deepen the analysis. The result of this procedure would be a pluralistic compartmentalization of modes of production and a weakening of their developmental logic. At the end of this inductivist path lies the surrender of the concept of the history of the species—and with it of historical materialism. The possibility that anthropological-historical research might one day force us to this cannot be excluded a priori. But in the meantime, the path leading in the opposite direction strikes me as not yet sufficiently explored.

It points in the direction of even stronger generalization, namely, the search for highly abstract principles of social organization. By principles of organization I understand innovations that become possible through developmental-logically reconstructible stages of learning, and which institutionalize new levels of societal learning.[51] The organizational principle of a society circumscribes ranges of possibility. It determines in particular: within which structures changes in the system of institutions are possible; to what extent the available capacities of productive forces are socially utilized and the development of new productive forces can be stimulated; to what extent system complexity and adaptive achievements can be heightened. A principle of organization consists of regulations so abstract that in the social formation which it determines a number of functionally equivalent modes of production are possible. Accordingly, the economic structure of a given society would have to be examined at two analytic levels: firstly in terms of the modes of production that have been concretely combined in it; and then in terms of that social formation to which the dominant mode of production belongs. A postulate of this sort is easier to put forward than to satisfy. I can only try to elucidate the research program and to make it plausible.

Organizational principles of society can be characterized, in a first approximation, through the institutional core that determines the dominant form of social integration. These institutional cores—kinship as a total institution, the state as a general political order, the complementary relation between a functionally specified state and a differentiated economic system—have not yet been thoroughly analyzed into their formal components. But I shall not follow this path of analysis here, since the formal components of these basic institutions lie in so many different dimensions that they can hardly be brought into a developmental-logical sequence. A more promising attempt can be made directly to classify, according to evolutionary features, the forms of social integration determined by principles of social organization.

Developmental-logical connections for the ontogenesis of action competence, particularly of moral consciousness, have already been rendered plausible. Of course, we ought not draw from ontogenesis over-hasty conclusions about the developmental levels of societies. It is the personality system that is the bearer of the ontogenetic learning process; and in a certain way, only social subjects can learn. But social systems, by drawing on the learning capacities of social subjects, can form new structures in order to solve steering problems that threaten their continued existence. To this extent the evolutionary learning process of societies is dependent on the competences of the individuals that belong to them. The latter in turn acquire their competences not as isolated monads but by growing into the symbolic structures of their lifeworlds. This development passes through three stages of communication, which I would like to characterize now in a very rough way.

At the stage of *symbolically mediated interaction,* speaking and acting are still enmeshed in the framework of a single, imperativist mode of communication. With the help of a communicative symbol, A expresses a behavioral expectation, to which B reacts with an action, in the intention of fulfilling A's expectation. The meaning of the communicative symbol and of the action are reciprocally defined. The participants suppose that in interpersonal relations they could in principle exchange places; but they remain bound to their performative attitudes.

At the stage of *propositionally differentiated speech,* speaking and acting separate for the first time. A and B can connect the performative attitude of the participant with the propositional attitude of an observer; each can not only adopt the perspective of the other but can exchange the perspective of participant for that of observer. Thus two reciprocal behavioral expectations can be coordinated in such a way that they constitute a system of reciprocal motivation or, as we can also say, a social role. At this stage actions are separated from norms.

At the third stage, that of *argumentative speech,* the validity claims we connect with speech acts can be made thematic. In grounding assertions or justifying actions in discourse, we treat statements or norms (underlying the actions) hypothetically, that is, in such a way that they might or might not be the case, that they might be legitimate or illegitimate. Norms and roles appear as in need of justification; their validity can be contested or grounded with reference to principles.

I shall not deal with the cognitive aspects of this communicative development, but merely point out the step-by-step differentiation of a social reality graduated in itself. At first actions, motives (or behavioral expectations), and acting subjects are perceived on a single plane of reality. At the next stage actions and norms separate; norms draw together with actors and their motives on a plane that lies behind, so to speak, the reality plane of actions. At the last stage, principles with which norms of action can be generated are distinguished from these norms themselves; the principles, together with actors and their motives, are placed behind even the line of norms, that is, the existing system of action.

In this way we can obtain basic concepts for a genetic theory of action. These concepts can be read in two ways: either as concepts of the competences—acquired in stages—of speaking and acting subjects who grow into a symbolic universe or as concepts of the infrastructure of the action system itself. I would like to use them in this latter sense to characterize different forms of social integration. In doing so I shall distinguish the institutions that regulate the normal case from those special institutions, which, in cases of conflict, re-establish the endangered intersubjectivity of understanding (law and morality).

To the extent that action conflicts are not regulated through force or strategic means but on a consensual basis, there come into play structures that mark the moral consciousness of the individual and the legal and moral system of society. They comprise the core domain of the aforementioned general action structures—the representations of justice crystallizing around the reciprocity relation that underlies all interaction. In the Piagetian research tradition, developmental stages of moral consciousness have been uncovered which correspond to the stages of interactive competence.[52] At the *preconventional stage,* at which actions, motives, and acting subjects are still perceived on a single plane of reality, only the consequences of action are evaluated in cases of conflict. At the *conventional stage,* motives can be assessed independently of concrete action consequences; conformity with a certain social role or with an existing system of norms is the standard. At the *postconventional stage,* these systems of norms lose their quasi-natural validity; they require justification from universalistic points of view.

I have distinguished between general structures of action underlying the normal state (with little conflict) and those core structures that underlie the consensual regulation of conflicts. These structures of moral consciousness can find expression either in simply judging action conflicts or in actively resolving them. If at the same time we keep in mind the stages of development according to which these structures can be ordered, we can make intuitively plausible why there are often structural differences between these action domains; that is, (a) between the ability to master normal action situations and the ability to bring conflict situations under moral-legal points of view; and (b) between moral judgment and moral action. As in the behavior of the individual, stage differences also appear on the level of social systems. For example, in neolithic societies the moral and legal systems are at the preconventional stage of arbitration and feuding law; while normal situations (with little conflict) are regulated within the framework of the kinship system, that is, at the conventional stage. The situation is similar with structures of consciousness that are already clearly established in interpretive systems but have not yet found institutional embodiment in action systems. Thus in many myths of primitive societies there are already narratively constructed models of conflicts and their resolutions that correspond to the conventional stage of development of moral consciousness; at the same time the institutionalized law satisfies the criteria of the preconventional stage of moral consciousness.

In our (very tentative) attempt to distinguish *levels of social integration,* it is therefore advisable to keep separate (a) general structures of action, (b) structures of world views insofar as they are determinant for morality and law, and (c) structures of *institutionalized* law and of *binding* moral representations.

Neolithic societies: (a) conventionally structured system of action (symbolic reality is graduated into the level of actions and that of norms); (b) mythological world views still immediately enmeshed with the system of action (with conventional patterns of resolving moral conflicts of action); (c) legal regulation of conflict from preconventional points of view (assessment of action consequences, compensation for resultant damages, restoration of status quo ante).

Early civilizations: (a) conventionally structured system of action; (b) mythological world views, set off from the system of action, which take on legitimating functions for the occupants of positions of authority; (c) conflict regulation from the point of view of a conventional morality tied to the figure of the ruler who administers or represents justice (evaluation according to action intentions, transition from retaliation to punishment, from joint liability to individual liability).

Developed civilizations: (a) conventionally structured system of action; (b) break with mythological thought, development of rationalized world views (with postconventional legal and moral representations); (c) conflict regulation from the point of view of a conventional morality detached from the reference person of the ruler (developed system of administering justice, tradition-dependent but systematized law).

The modern age: (a) postconventionally structured domains of action—differentiation of a universalistically regulated domain of strategic action (capitalist enterprise, bourgeois civil law), approaches to a political will-formation grounded in principles (formal democracy); (b) universalistically developed doctrines of legitimation (rational natural law); (c) conflict regulation from the point of view of a strict separation of legality and morality; general, formal, and rationalized law, private morality guided by principles.

6

I would like now to illustrate how this approach can be made fruitful for the theory of social evolution. I shall choose the example of the emergence of class societies, since I can rely here on the aforementioned study by Klaus Eder.[53]

1. Class societies develop within the framework of a political order; social integration no longer needs to proceed through the kinship system; it can be taken over by the state. There have been a number of theories of the origin of the state, which I would like briefly to mention and to criticize.[54]

a. The *superimposition theory*[55] explains the emergence of a political ruling class and the establishment of a political order by nomadic tribes of herdsmen who subjugated sedentary farmers and set up a rule of conquerors. Today this theory is regarded as empirically refuted since nomadism appeared later than the first civilization.[56] The emergence of the state must have had endogenous causes.

b. The *division of labor theory*[57] is usually advanced in a complex version. Agricultural production achieved a surplus and led (in combination with demographic growth) to the freeing of labor forces. This made a social division of labor possible. The various social groups which thereby emerged appropriated social wealth differently and formed social classes, one (at least) of which assumed the functions of rule. Despite its suggestive power, this theory is not coherent. Social division of labor means functional specification within the vocational system; but vocational groups differentiated by knowledge and skill need not per se develop opposing interests that result in differential access to the means of production. There is no argument showing why functions of domination had to emerge from the contrast of interests rooted in vocational specialization. There was a social division of labor within the politically ruling class (the priesthood, military, and bureaucracy) as well as within the working population (e.g., between farmers and craftsmen).

c. The *inequality theory*[58] traces the emergence of the state directly to problems of distribution. With the productivity of labor there arose a surplus of goods and means of production. The growing differences in wealth resulted in social differences that a relatively egalitarian kinship system could not manage. The distribution problems required a different organization of social intercourse. If this thesis were correct, it could explain the emergence of system problems that could be solved by organization in a state; but this new form of social integration itself remains unexplained. Furthermore, the assumption of an automatic growth of productive forces is incorrect, at least for agricultural production. The Indians of the Amazon, for example, possessed all the technical means for producing a surplus in foodstuffs; but only contact with European settlers provided the impetus to use the available potential.[59] Among stock farmers there were, it is true, considerable inequalities, since herds can be enlarged rather easily.

d. The *irrigation hypothesis*[60] explains the merger of several village communities into a political unity by the desire to master the aridity of the land through large-scale irrigation systems. An administration was a functional requirement for the construction of such systems, and this administration became the institutional core of the state. This assumption has been empirically refuted since in Mesopotamia, China, and Mexico the formation of the state preceded the irrigation projects. Moreover, this theory would explain only the emergence of system problems and not the way in which they were resolved.

e. The *theory of population density*[61] explains the emergence of the state chiefly through ecological and demographic factors. One can assume an endogenous population growth that led normally to spatial expansion of segmentary societies, that is, to emigration to new areas. When, however, the ecological situation, adjoining mountains, the sea or the desert, barren tracts of land, or the like, hindered emigration or flight, conflicts were triggered by population density and the scarcity of land. This left no alternative but the subjugation of large segments of the population under the political domination of a victorious tribe. The complexity of densely populated settlements could be managed only through state organization. Even if population problems of this type could be demonstrated to have existed in *all* early civilizations, this theory, like the others, does not explain why and how these problems could be solved.

None of the above theories distinguishes between *system problems* that overload the adaptive capacity of the kinship system and the *evolutionary learning process* that explains the change to a new form of social integration. Only with the help of learning mechanisms can we explain why a few societies could find solutions to the steering problems that triggered their evolution, and why they could find precisely the solution of state organization. Thus I shall adopt the following orientations:

a. Developmental stages (in the sense of cognitive developmental psychology) can be distinguished in the ontogenesis of knowing and acting abilities. I understand these stages as learning levels that lay down the conditions for possible learning processes. Since the learning mechanisms belong to the equipment of the human organism (capable of speech), social evolution can rely on individual learning capacities only if the (in part phase-specific) boundary conditions are fulfilled.

b. The learning capacities first acquired by individual members of society or marginal social groups gain entrance into the interpretive system of the society through exemplary learning processes. Collectively shared structures of consciousness and stores of knowledge represent, in terms of empirical knowledge and moral-practical insight, a cognitive potential that can be used socially.

c. We may also speak of evolutionary learning processes on the part of societies insofar as they solve system problems that represent evolutionary challenges. These are problems that overload the adaptive capacities available within the limits of a given social formation. Societies can learn evolutionarily by utilizing the cognitive potential contained in world views for reorganizing action systems. This process can be represented as an institutional embodiment of rationality structures already developed in world views.

d. The introduction of a new principle of organization means the establishment of a new level of social integration. This in turn makes it possible to implement available (or to produce new) technical-organizational knowledge; it makes possible, that is, an increase in productive forces and an expansion of system complexity. Thus for social evolution, learning processes in the domain of moral-practical consciousness function as pacemakers.

2. With these as my points of orientation, I would like now to offer the following explanatory sketch of the origin of class societies.[62]

a. *The phenomenon to be explained* is the emergence of a political order that organized a society so that its members could belong to different lineages. The function of social integration passed from kinship relations to political relations. Collective identity was no longer represented in the figure of a common ancestor but in that of a common ruler.

b. *Theoretical explication of the phenomenon.* A ruling position gave the right to exercise legitimate power. The legitimacy of power could not be based solely on authorization through kinship status; for claims based on family position, or on legitimate kinship relations in general, were limited precisely by the political power of the ruler. Legitimate power crystallized around the function of administering justice and around the position of the judge after the law was recognized in such a way that it possessed the characteristics of conventional morality. This was the case when the judge, instead of being bound as a mere referee to the contingent constellations of power of the involved parties, could judge according to intersubjectively recognized legal norms sanctified by tradition, when he took the intention of the agent into account as well as the concrete consequences of action, and when he was no longer guided by the ideas of reprisal for damages caused and restoration of a status quo ante, but punished the guilty party's violation of a rule. Legitimate power had in the first instance the form of a power to dispose of the means of sanction in a conventional administration of justice. At the same time, mythological world views also took on—in addition to their explanatory function—justificatory functions, in the sense of legitimating domination.

c. *The goal of explanation follows from this.* The differentiation of ruling positions presupposed that the presumptive ruler built legitimate power by virtue of a conventional administration of justice. Thus the emergence of the state should be explained through successful stabilization of a judicial position that permitted consensual regulation of action conflicts at the level of conventional morality.

The explanation sketch runs as follows:

d. *The initial state.* I consider those neolithic societies in which the complexity of the kinship system had already led to a more strongly hierarchical organization to be the evolutionarily promising societies. They had already institutionalized temporally limited political roles. The chieftains, kings, or leaders were judged by their concrete actions; their actions were not legitimate per se. Such roles were only temporarily institutionalized (e.g., for warfare) or limited to special tasks (e.g., to provide for rain and a good harvest). Viewed sociostructurally, these roles had not yet moved to the center of social organization.[63]

e. *Particular system problems.* In the evolutionarily promising neolithic societies system problems arose which could not be managed with an adaptive capacity limited by the kinship principle of organization. These might have been, for example, ecologically conditioned problems of land scarcity and population density or problems having to do with an unequal distribution of social wealth. These problems, irresolvable within the given framework, became more and more visible the more frequently they led to conflicts that overloaded the archaic legal institutions (courts of arbitration, feuding law).

f. *The testing of new structures.* A few societies under the pressure of evolutionary challenges from such problems made use of the cognitive potential in their world views and institutionalized—at first on a trial basis—an administration of justice at a conventional level. Thus, for example, the war chief was empowered to adjudicate cases of conflict, no longer only according to the concrete distribution of power, but according to socially recognized norms grounded in tradition. Law was no longer only that on which the parties could agree.

g. *Stabilization through the formation of systems.* These judicial positions could become the pacemakers of social evolution. However, as the example of the African Barotse empire shows, not all promising experiments led via such judicial functions to the permanent institutionalization of a ruling position, that is, to evolutionary success. Only under suitable conditions—such as, for example, the military victory of a tribe or construction of an irrigation project—could such roles be permanently differentiated, that is, stabilized in such a way that they became the core of a political subsystem. This marked off the evolutionarily successful from the merely promising social systems.

h. *The emergence of class structures.* "On the basis of political domination the material production process could then be uncoupled from the limiting conditions of the kinship system and reorganized via relations of domination."[64] The ruler secured the loyalty of his officials, of the priest and warrior families by assuring them privileged access to the means of production (palace and temple economy).

i. *Development of productive forces.* "The forces of production which were already discovered in the neolithic revolution could now be utilized on a large scale: the intensification of cultivation and stock-farming, and the expansion of the crafts were the results of the enlarged organizational capacity of class society. Thus there emerged new forms of cooperation (e.g., in irrigational farming) or of exchange (e.g., in the market exchange between town and country)." [65]

3. If it holds up empirically, this argument could also explain how opposing developments are connected in social evolution; namely, the cumulative learning process without which history could not be interpreted as evolution (i.e., as a directional process) and, on the other hand, the exploitation of man by man, which is intensified in class societies. [66] Historical materialism marked off linear progress along the axis of development of productive forces and adopted dialectical figures of thought for the development of productive relations. When we assume learning processes not only in the dimension of technically useful knowledge but also in that of moral-practical consciousness, we are maintaining the existence of developmental stages both for productive forces and for the forms of social integration. But the extent of exploitation and repression by no means stands in inverse proportion to these levels of development. Social integration accomplished via kinship relations and secured in cases of conflict by preconventional legal institutions belongs, from a developmental-logical point of view, to a lower stage than social integration accomplished via relations of domination and secured in cases of conflict by conventional legal institutions. Despite this progress, the exploitation and oppression *necessarily* practiced in political class societies has to be considered retrogressive in comparison with the less significant social inequalities *permitted* by the kinship system. Because of this, class societies are structurally unable to satisfy the need for legitimation that they themselves generate. This is, of course, the key to the social dynamic of class struggle. How is this *dialectic* of progress to be explained?

I see an explanation in the fact that new levels of learning mean not only expanded ranges of options but also new problem situations. A higher stage of development of productive forces and of social integration does bring relief from problems of the superseded social formation. But the problems that arise at the new stage of development can—insofar as they are at all comparable with the old ones—increase in intensity. This seems to be the case, at least intuitively, with the burdens that arise in the transition to societies organized through a state. On the other hand, the perspective from which we make this comparison is distorted so long as we do not also take into account the specific burdens of prestate societies; societies organized along kinship lines have to come off better if we examine them in the light of the kinds of problem first typical of class societies. The socialist battle-concepts of exploitation and oppression do not adequately discriminate among evolutionarily different problem situations. In certain heretical traditions one can indeed find suggestions for differentiating not only the concept of progress but that of exploitation. It is possible to differentiate according to bodily harm (hunger, exhaustion, illness), personal injury (degradation, servitude, fear), and finally spiritual desperation (loneliness, emptiness)—to which in turn there correspond various hopes—for well-being and security, freedom and dignity, happiness and fulfillment.

Excursus on Progress and Exploitation

I have tried to bring the basic institutions with which we can (to begin with) circumscribe principles of social organization—family, state, differentiated economic system—into relation with historical progress via developmental stages of social integration. But evolutionarily important innovations mean not only a new level of learning but a new problem situation as well, that is, a new category of burdens that accompany the new social formation. The dialectic of progress can be seen in the fact that with the acquisition of problem-solving abilities new problem situations come to consciousness. For instance, as natural-scientific medicine brings a few diseases under control, there arises a consciousness of contingency in relation to all illness. This reflexive experience is captured in the concept of *quasi-nature [Naturwüchsigkeit]*—an area of life having been seen through in its pseudo-naturalness is quasi-natural. Suffering from the contingencies of an uncontrolled process gains a new quality to the extent that we believe ourselves capable of rationally intervening in it. This suffering is then the negative of a new need. Thus we can make an attempt to interpret social evolution taking as our guide those problems and needs that are first brought about by evolutionary advances. At every stage of development the social-evolutionary learning process itself generates new resources, which mean new dimensions of scarcity and thus new historical needs.

With the transition to the sociocultural form of life, that is, with the introduction of the family structure, there arose *the problem of demarcating society from external nature*. In neolithic societies, at the latest, harmonizing society with the natural environment became thematic. Power over nature came into consciousness as a scarce resource. The experience of powerlessness in relation to the contingencies of external nature had to be interpreted away in myth and magic. With the introduction of a collective political order, there arose *the problem of the self-regulation of the social system*. In developed civilizations, at the latest, the achievement of order by the state became a central need. Legal security came to consciousness as a scarce resource. The experience of social repression and arbitrariness had to be balanced with legitimations of domination. This was accomplished in the framework of rationalized world views (through which, moreover, the central problem of the previous stage—powerlessness—could be defused). In the modern age, with the autonomization of the economy (and complementarization of the state), there arose *the problem of a self-regulated exchange of the social system with external nature*. In industrial capitalism, at the latest, society consciously placed itself under the imperatives of economic growth and increasing wealth. Value came into consciousness as a scarce resource. The experience of social inequality called into being social movements and corresponding strategies of appeasement. These seemed to lead to their goal in social welfare state mass democracies (in which, moreover, the central problem of the preceding stage—legal insecurity—could be defused). Finally, if postmodern societies, as they are today envisioned from different angles, should be characterized by a primacy of the scientific and educational systems, one can speculate about the emergence of *the problem of a self-regulated exchange of society with internal nature*. Again a scarce resource would become thematic—not the supply of power, security, or value, but the supply of motivation and meaning. To the extent that the social integration of internal nature—the previously quasi-natural process of interpreting needs—was accomplished discursively, principles of participation could come to the fore in many areas of social life; whereas the simultaneously increasing dangers of *anomie* (and *acedie*) could call forth new administrations concerned with motivational control. Perhaps a new institutional core would then take shape around a new organizational principle, an institutional core in which there merge elements of public education, social welfare, liberalized punishment, and therapy for mental illness.

I mention this perspective—for which there exist clues at best—only to elucidate the *possibility* that a sociostructurally anchored pattern of differential exercise of social power could outlive even the *economic form* of class domination (whether exercised through private property rights or state bureaucracies occupied by elites). In a future form of class domination, softened and at the same time intensified, to sociopsychological coercion, "domination" (*Herrschaft*—the term calls to mind the open, person-bound, political form of exercising social force, especially that of European feudalism) would be refracted for a second time, not through bourgeois civil war, but through the educational system of the social welfare state. Whether this would *necessarily* give rise to a vicious circle between expanded participation and increasing social administration, between the process of motive formation becoming reflective and the increase in social control (i.e., in the manipulation of motives) is, in my opinion, a question that cannot be decided in advance (despite the confident judgment of revivified pessimistic anthropologies).

I have proposed a spectrum of problems connected with the self-constitution of society, ranging from demarcation in relation to the environment, through self-regulation and self-regulated exchange with external nature, to self-regulated exchange with internal nature. With each evolutionarily new problem situation there arise new scarcities, scarcities of technically feasible power, politically established security, economically produced value, and culturally supplied meaning; and thus new historical needs come to the fore. If this bold schema is plausible, it follows that the logical

space for evolutionarily new problem domains is exhausted with the reflexive turn of motive formation and the structural scarcity of meaning; the end
of the *first* run-through could mean a return, at a new level, to problems of
demarcation—namely, to the discovery of internal limits which the socialization process runs up against—and to *the outbreak of new contingencies
at these limits of social individuation.*

Chapter Seven
SOCIAL ACTION AND RATIONALITY

In what follows I shall no longer employ the Popperian terminology. My purpose in reviewing Jarvie's action-theoretic translation of Popper's three-world theory was only to prepare the way for the thesis that with the choice of a specific sociological concept of action we generally make specific "ontological" assumptions. And the aspects of possible rationality of an agent's actions depend, in turn, on the world relations that we thereby impute to him. The profusion of action concepts employed (for the most part, implicitly) in social-scientific theories can be reduced in essence to four basic, analytically distinguishable concepts.

Since Aristotle the concept of *teleological action* has been at the center of the philosophical theory of action.[1] The actor attains an end or brings about the occurrence of a desired state by choosing means that have promise of being successful in the given situation and applying them in a suitable manner. The central concept is that of a *decision* among alternative courses of action, with a view to the realization of an end, guided by maxims, and based on an interpretation of the situation.

The teleological model of action is expanded to a *strategic* model when there can enter into the agent's calculation of success the anticipation of decisions on the part of at least one additional goal-directed actor. This model is often interpreted in utilitarian terms; the actor is supposed to choose and calculate means and ends from the standpoint of maximizing utility or expectations of utility. It is this model of action that lies behind decision-theoretic and game-theoretic approaches in economics, sociology, and social psychology.[2]

The concept of *normatively regulated action* does not refer to the behavior of basically solitary actors who come upon other actors in their environment, but to members of a social group who orient their action to common values. The individual actor complies with (or violates) a norm when in a given situation the conditions are present to which the norm has application. Norms express an agreement that obtains in a social group. All members of a group for whom a given norm has validity may expect of one another that in certain situations they will carry out (or abstain from) the actions commanded (or proscribed). The central concept of *complying with a norm* means fulfilling a generalized expectation of behavior. The latter does not have the cognitive sense of expecting a predicted event, but the normative sense that members are *entitled* to expect a certain behavior. This normative model of action lies behind the role theory that is widespread in sociology.[3]

The concept of *dramaturgical action* refers primarily neither to the solitary actor nor to the member of a social group, but to participants in interaction constituting a public for one another, before whom they present themselves. The actor evokes in his public a certain image, an impression of himself, by more or less purposefully disclosing his subjectivity. Each agent can monitor public access to the system of his own intentions, thoughts, attitudes, desires, feelings, and the like, to which only he has privileged access. In dramaturgical action, participants make use of this and steer their interactions through regulating mutual access to their own subjectivities. Thus the central concept of *presentation of self* does not signify spontaneous expressive behavior by stylizing the expression of one's own experiences with a view to the audience. The dramaturgical model of action is used primarily in phenomenologically oriented descriptions of interaction; but it has not yet been developed into a theoretically generalizing approach.[4]

Finally the concept of *communicative action* refers to the interaction of at least two subjects capable of speech and action who establish interpersonal relations (whether by verbal or by extraverbal means). The actors seek to reach an understanding about the action situation and their plans of action in order to coordinate their actions by way of agreement. The central concept of *interpretation* refers in the first instance to negotiating definitions of the situation which admit of consensus. As we shall see, language is given a prominent place in this model.[5]

The teleological concept of action was first rendered fruitful for an economic theory of choice by the founders of neoclassical economics, and then for a theory of strategic games by von Neumann and Morgenstern. The concept of normatively regulated action gained paradigmatic significance for theory formation in the social sciences through Durkheim and Parsons, that of dramaturgical action through Goffman, that of communicative action through Mead and later Garfinkel. I cannot carry out a detailed explication of these concepts here. My concern is rather with the rationality implications of the corresponding conceptual strategies. At first glance, only the teleological concept of action seems to open up an aspect of the rationality of action. Action represented as purposeful activity can be viewed under the aspect of purposive rationality. This is a point of view from which actions can be more or less rationally planned and carried out, or can be judged by a third person to be more or less rational. In elementary cases of purposeful activity the plan of action can be represented in the form of a practical syllogism.[6] The other three models of action appear at first not to place action in the perspective of rationality and possible rationalization. That this appearance is deceiving becomes evident when we represent to ourselves the "ontological"—in the broad sense—presuppositions that are, as a matter of conceptual necessity, connected with these models of action. In the sequence teleological, normative, dramaturgical, the presuppositions not only become increasingly complex; they reveal at the same time stronger and stronger implications for rationality.

The concept of teleological action presupposes relations between an actor and a world of existing states of affairs. This objective world is defined as the totality of states of affairs that either obtain or could arise or could be brought about by purposeful intervention. The model equips the agent with a "cognitive-volitional complex," so that he can, on the one hand, form *beliefs* about existing states of affairs through the medium of perception, and can, on the other hand, develop *intentions* with the aim of bringing desired states of affairs into existence. At the semantic level such states of affairs are represented as propositional contents of sentences expressing beliefs or intentions. Through his beliefs and intentions the actor can take up basically two types of rational relation to the world. I call these relations rational because they are open to objective appraisal depending on the "direction of fit."[7] In one direction the question arises whether the actor has succeeded in bringing his perceptions and beliefs into agreement with what is the case in the world; in the other direction the question is whether he succeeds in bringing what is the case in the world into agreement with his desires and intentions. In both instances the actor can produce expressions susceptible of being judged by a third person in respect to "fit and misfit"; he can make assertions that are *true* or *false* and carry out goal-directed interventions that succeed or fail, that *achieve* or *fail to achieve* the intended effect in the world. These relations between actor and world allow then for expressions that can be judged according to criteria of *truth* and *efficacy*.

With regard to ontological presuppositions, we can classify *teleological* action as a concept that presupposes *one* world, namely the objective world. The same holds for the concept of *strategic action*. Here we start with at least two goal-directed acting subjects who achieve their ends by way of an orientation to, and influence on, the decisions of other actors.[8] Success in action is also dependent on other actors, each of whom is oriented to his own success and behaves cooperatively only to the degree that this fits with his egocentric calculus of utility.[9] Thus strategically acting subjects must be cognitively so equipped that for them not only physical objects but decision-making systems can appear in the world. They must expand their conceptual apparatus for what can be the case; but they do not need any richer *ontological presuppositions*. The concept of the objective world does not itself become more complex with the growing complexity of innerworldly entities. Even purposeful activity differentiated to include strategic action remains, as regards its ontological presuppositions, a *one-world concept*.

By contrast, the concept of normatively regulated action presupposes relations between an actor and exactly two worlds. Besides the objective world of existing states of affairs there is the social world to which the actor belongs as a role-playing subject, as do additional actors who can take up normatively regulated interactions among themselves. A social world consists of a normative context that lays down which interactions belong to the totality of legitimate interpersonal relations. And all actors for whom the corresponding norms have force (by whom they are accepted as valid) belong to the same social world. As the meaning of the objective world can be elucidated with reference to the existence [*Existieren*] of states of affairs, the meaning of the social world can be elucidated with reference to the "existence" [*Bestehen*] of norms. It is important here that we do *not* understand the "existence" of norms in the sense of existence sentences stating that there are social facts of the type: normative regulations. The sentence "It is the case that *q* is commanded" obviously has a different meaning than the sentence "It is commanded that *q*." The latter sentence expresses a norm or a specific command when it is uttered in suitable form with the claim to normative rightness, that is, such that it claims *validity* for a circle of addressees. And we say that a norm exists, is in force, or enjoys social currency [*Geltung*] when it is recognized as valid [*gültig*] or justified by those to whom it is addressed. Existing states of affairs are represented by true statements, "existing" norms by general ought-sentences or commands that count as justified among the addressees. That a norm is ideally *valid* means that it *deserves* the assent of all those affected because it regulates problems of action in their common interest. That a norm is *de facto established* means by contrast that the validity claim with which it appears is recognized by those affected, and this intersubjective recognition grounds the *social force or currency* of the norm.

We do not attach such a normative validity claim to cultural values; but values are candidates for embodiment in norms—they *can* attain a general binding force with respect to a matter requiring regulation. In the light of cultural values the needs [*Bedürfnisse*] of an individual appear as plausible to other individuals standing in the same tradition. However, plausibly interpreted needs are transformed into legitimate motives of action only when the corresponding values become, for a circle of those affected, normatively binding in regulating specific problem situations. Members can then expect of one another that in corresponding situations each of them will orient his action to values normatively prescribed for all concerned.

This consideration is meant to make comprehensible the fact that the normative model of action equips the agent not only with a "cognitive" but also with a "motivational complex" that makes norm-conformative behavior possible. Moreover this model of action is connected with a learning model of value internalization.[10] According to this model, existing norms gain action-motivating force to the degree that the values embodied in them represent the standards according to which, in the circle of addressees, needs are interpreted and developed through learning processes into need dispositions.

Under these presuppositions the actor can again take up relations to the world, here to the social world, which are open to objective evaluation according to the "direction of fit." In one direction the question is whether the motives and actions of an agent are in accord with existing norms or deviate from these. In the other direction the question is whether the existing norms themselves embody values that, in a particular problem situation, give expression to generalizable interests of those affected and thus deserve the assent of those to whom they are addressed. In the one case, actions are judged according to whether they are in accord with or deviate from an existing normative context, that is, whether or not they are right with respect to a normative context recognized as legitimate. In the other case, norms are judged according to whether they can be justified, that is, whether they deserve to be recognized as legitimate.[11]

With regard to its ontological—in the broad sense—presuppositions, we can classify *normatively regulated action* as a concept that presupposes *two worlds*, the objective world and a social world. Norm-conformative action presupposes that the agent can distinguish the factual from the normative elements of an action situation, that is, conditions and means from values. The point of departure for the normative model of action is that participants can simultaneously adopt both an objectivating attitude to something that is or is not the case, and a norm-conformative attitude to something that is commanded (whether rightly or not). But as in the teleological model, action is represented *primarily* as a relation between the actor and a world—there, as a relation to the objective world over against which the actor as knower stands and in which he can goal-directly intervene; here, as a relation to the social world to which the actor in his role as a norm-addressee belongs and in which he can take up legitimately regulated interpersonal relations. Neither here nor there is the actor *himself* presupposed as a world toward which he can behave reflexively. It is the concept of dramaturgical action that requires the additional presupposition of a subjective world to which the actor relates when in acting he puts himself "on stage."

The concept of dramaturgical action is less clearly developed in social-science literature than are those of teleological and normatively guided action. Goffman first explicitly introduced it in 1956 in his investigation of "the presentation of self in everyday life."[12] From the perspective of dramaturgical action we understand social action as an encounter in which participants form a visible public for each other and perform for one another. "Encounter" and "performance" are the key concepts. The performance of a troupe before the eyes of third persons is only a special case. A performance enables the actor to present himself to his audience in a certain way; in bringing something of his subjectivity to appearance, he would like to be seen by his public in a particular way.

The dramaturgical qualities of action are in a certain way parasitic; they rest on a structure of goal-directed action.

For certain purposes people control the style of their actions . . . and superimpose this upon other activities. For instance work may be done in a manner in accordance with the principles of dramatic performance in order to project a certain impression of the people working to an inspector or manager. . . . In fact what people are doing is rarely properly described as *just* eating, or *just* working, but has stylistic features which have certain conventional meanings associated with recognized types of per-sonae.[13]

Of course, there are special roles tailored to virtuoso self-staging: "The roles of prizefighters, surgeons, violinists, and policemen are cases in point. These activities allow so much dramatic self-expression that exemplary practitioners—whether real or fictional—become famous and are given special places in the commercially organized fantasies of the nation."[14] The trait that is here stylized into an element of the professional role, namely the reflexive character of self-presentation before others, is, however, con-stitutive for social interactions in general insofar as they are regarded only under the aspect of persons encountering one another.

In dramaturgical action the actor, in presenting a view of himself, has to behave toward his own subjective world. I have defined this as the totality of subjective experiences to which the actor has, in relation to others, a privileged access.[15] To be sure, this domain of subjectivity deserves to be called a "world" only if the significance of the subjective world can be ex-plicated in a way similar to that in which I explained the significance of the social world, through referring to an "existence" of norms analogous to the existence of states of affairs. Perhaps one can say that the subject is repre-sented by truthfully uttered experiential sentences in nearly the same way as are existing states of affairs by true statements and valid norms by justi-fied ought-sentences. We should not understand subjective experiences as mental states or inner episodes, for we would thereby assimilate them to entities, to elements of the objective world. We can comprehend having sub-jective experiences as something analogous to the existence of states of af-fairs without assimilating the one to the other. A subject capable of expres-sion does not "have" or "possess" desires and feelings in the same sense as an observable object has extension, weight, color, and similar properties. An actor has desires and feelings in the sense that he can at will express these experiences before a public, and indeed in such a way that this public, if it trusts the actor's expressive utterances, attributes to him, as something subjective, the desires and feelings expressed.

Desires and feelings have a paradigmatic status in this connection. Of course, cognitions, beliefs, and intentions also belong to the subjective world; but they stand in internal relation to the objective world. Beliefs and intentions come to consciousness *as* subjective only when there is in the objective world no corresponding state of affairs that exists or is brought to exist. It becomes a question of "mere," that is, "mistaken" belief as soon as the corresponding statement turns out to be untrue. It is a matter merely of "good," that is, of "ineffectual" intentions as soon as it turns out that the corresponding action was either left undone or failed. In a similar way, feelings of, say, obligation, shame, or guilt stand in internal relation to the social world. But in general feelings and desires can *only* be expressed as something subjective. They cannot be expressed *otherwise,* cannot enter into relation with the external world, whether the objective or the social. For this reason the expression of desires and feelings is measured only against the reflexive relation of the speaker to his inner world.

Desires and feelings are two aspects of a partiality rooted in needs.[16] Needs have two faces. They are differentiated on the volitional side into inclinations and desires; and on the other side, the intuitive, into feelings and moods. Desires are directed toward situations of need satisfaction; feelings "perceive" situations in the light of possible need satisfaction. Needs are, as it were, the background of a partiality that determines our subjective attitudes in relation to the external world. Such predilections express themselves both in the active striving for goods and in the affective perception of situations (so long as the latter are not objectivated into something in the world and thus lose their situational character). The partiality of desires and feelings is expressed at the level of language in the interpretation of needs, that is, in evaluations for which evaluative expressions are available. One can gain clarity about the meaning of value judgments by examining the dual, descriptive-prescriptive content of these evaluative, need-interpreting expressions. They serve to make predilection understandable. This component of justification[17] is the bridge between the subjectivity of experience and that intersubjective transparency that experience gains in being truthfully expressed and, on this basis, attributed to an actor by onlookers. For example, in characterizing an object or a situation as splendid, ample, elevating, auspicious, dangerous, forbidding, dreadful, and so forth, we are trying to express a predilection and at the same time to justify it, in the sense of making it plausible by appeal to general standards of evaluation that are widespread at least in our own culture. Evaluative expressions or standards of value have justificatory force when they characterize a need in such a way that addressees can, in the framework of a common cultural heritage, recognize in these interpretations their own needs. This explains why attributes of style, aesthetic expression, formal qualities in general, have such weight in dramaturgical action.

In the case of dramaturgical action the relation between actor and world is also open to objective appraisal. As the actor is oriented to his own subjective world in the presence of his public, there can be *one* direction of fit: In regard to a self-presentation, there is the question whether at the proper moment the actor is expressing the experiences he has, whether he *means* what he *says,* or whether he is merely feigning the experiences he expresses. So long as we are dealing here with beliefs or intentions, that is, with cognitive acts, the question of whether someone says what he means is clearly a question of truthfulness or sincerity. With desires and feelings this is not always the case. In situations in which accuracy of expression is important, it is sometimes difficult to separate questions of sincerity from those of authenticity. Often we lack the words to say what we feel; and this in turn places the feelings themselves in a questionable light.

According to the dramaturgical model of action, a participant can adopt an attitude to his own subjectivity in the role of an actor and to the expressive utterances of another in the role of a public, but only in the awareness that ego's inner world is bounded by an external world. In this external world the actor can certainly distinguish between normative and nonnormative elements of the action situation; but Goffman's model of action does not provide for his behaving toward the social world in a norm-conformative attitude. He takes legitimately regulated interpersonal relations into account only as social facts. Thus it seems to me correct also to classify *dramaturgical action* as a concept that presupposes *two worlds,* the internal world and the external. Expressive utterances present subjectivity in demarcation from the external world; the actor can in principle adopt only an objectivating attitude toward the latter. And in contrast to the case of normatively regulated action, this holds not only for physical but for social objects as well.

In virtue of this option, dramaturgical action can take on latently strategic qualities to the degree that the actor treats his audience as *opponents* rather than as a public. The scale of self-presentations ranges from sincere communication of one's own intentions, desires, moods, etc., to cynical management of the impressions the actor arouses in others.

At one extreme, one finds that the performer can be fully taken in by his own act; he can be sincerely convinced that the impression of reality which he stages is the real reality. When his audience is also convinced in this way about the show he puts on—and this seems to be the typical case—then for the moment at least, only the sociologist or the socially disgruntled will have doubts about the "realness" of what is presented. At the other extreme . . . the performer may be moved to guide the conviction of his audience only as a means to other ends, having no ultimate concern with the beliefs of his audience; we may call him cynical, reserving the term "sincere" for individuals who believe in the impression fostered by their own performance.[18]

The manipulative production of false impressions—Goffman investigates techniques of "impression management," from harmless segmentation to long-term information control—is by no means identical with strategic action. It too remains dependent on a public that takes itself to be present at a performance and fails to recognize its strategic character. Even a strategically intended self-presentation has to be capable of being understood as an expression that appears with the claim to subjective truthfulness. As soon as it is judged only according to criteria of success by the audience as well, it no longer falls under the description of dramaturgical action. We then have a case of strategic interaction in which participants have conceptually enriched their objective world in such a way that opponents can appear in it who are capable not only of purposive-rational action but of subjective expressions as well.

With the concept of communicative action there comes into play the additional presupposition of a *linguistic medium* that reflects the actor's world-relations as such. At this level of concept formation the rationality problematic, which until now has arisen only for the social scientist, moves into the perspective of the agent himself. We have to make clear in what sense achieving understanding in language is thereby introduced as a mechanism for coordinating action. Even the strategic model of action *can* be understood in such a way that participants' actions, directed through egocentric calculations of utility and coordinated through interest situations, are mediated through speech acts. In the cases of normatively regulated and dramaturgical action we even *have to* suppose a consensus formation among participants that is in principle of a linguistic nature. Nevertheless, in these three models of action language is conceived *one-sidedly* in different respects.

The teleological model of action takes language as one of several media through which speakers oriented to their own success can influence one another in order to bring opponents to form or to grasp beliefs and intentions that are in the speakers' own interest. This concept of language—developed from the limit case of indirect communication aimed at *getting* someone to form a belief, an intention, or the like—is, for instance, basic to intentionalist semantics. The normative model of action presupposes language as a medium that transmits cultural values and carries a consensus that is merely reproduced with each additional act of understanding. This culturalist concept of language is widespread in cultural anthropology and content-oriented linguistics.[19] The dramaturgical model of action presupposes language as a medium of self-presentation; the cognitive significance of the propositional components and the interpersonal significance of the illocutionary components are thereby played down in favor of the expressive functions of speech acts. Language is assimilated to stylistic and aesthetic forms of expression.[20] Only the communicative model of action presupposes language as a medium of uncurtailed communication whereby speakers and hearers, out of the context of their preinterpreted lifeworld, refer simultaneously to things in the objective, social, and subjective worlds in order to negotiate common definitions of the situation. This interpretive concept of language lies behind the various efforts to develop a formal pragmatics.[21]

The one-sidedness of the first three concepts of language can be seen in the fact that the corresponding types of communication singled out by them prove to be limit cases of communicative action: *first,* the indirect communication of those who have only the realization of their own ends in view;

second, the consensual action of those who simply actualize an already existing normative agreement; and *third,* presentation of self in relation to an audience. In each case only one function of language is thematized: the release of perlocutionary effects, the establishment of interpersonal relations, and the expression of subjective experiences. By contrast, the communicative model of action, which defines the traditions of social science connected with Mead's symbolic interactionism, Wittgenstein's concept of language games, Austin's theory of speech acts, and Gadamer's hermeneutics, takes all the functions of language equally into consideration. As can be seen in the ethnomethodological and hermeneutic approaches, there is a danger here of reducing social *action* to the interpretive accomplishments of participants in communication, of assimilating action to speech, interaction to conversation. In the present context I can introduce this concept of communicative action only in a provisional way. I shall restrict myself to remarks concerning: (a) the character of independent actions; and (b) the reflective relation to the world of actors in processes of understanding.

In order to avoid mislocating the concept of communicative action from the start, I would like to characterize the level of complexity of speech acts that simultaneously express a propositional content, the offer of an interpersonal relationship, and the intention of the speaker. In the course of the analysis it will become evident how much this concept owes to investigations in the philosophy of language stemming from Wittgenstein. Precisely for this reason it might be well to point out that the concept of following a rule with which analytic philosophy of language begins does not go far enough. If one grasps linguistic conventions only from the perspective of rule following, and explains them by means of a concept of intentions based on rule consciousness, one loses that aspect of the *threefold relation to the world* of communicative agents that is important to me.[22]

I shall use the term "action" only for those symbolic expressions with which the actor takes up a relation to at least one world (but always to the objective world *as well*)—as is the case in the previously examined models of teleological, normatively regulated, and dramaturgical action. I shall distinguish from actions the bodily movements and operations that are *concurrently executed* and can acquire the independence of actions only *secondarily,* through being *embedded, for instance, in play or teaching* practices. This can easily be shown through the example of bodily movements. Under the aspect of observable events in the world, actions appear as bodily movements of an organism. Controlled by the central nervous system, these movements are the substratum in which actions are carried out. With his actions the agent changes something in the world. We can, of course, distinguish the movements with which a subject intervenes in the world (acts instrumentally) from those with which a subject embodies a meaning (expresses himself communicatively). In both cases the bodily movements bring about a physical change in the world; in the one case this is of causal relevance, in the other of semantic relevance. Examples of causally relevant bodily movements are straightening the body, spreading the hand, lifting the arm, bending the leg, and so forth. Examples of semantically relevant bodily movements are movements of the larynx, tongue, lips, etc. in the generation of phonetic sounds; nodding the head; shrugging the shoulders; finger movements while playing the piano; hand movements while writing, drawing; and so on.

Arthur Danto has analyzed these movements as "basic actions." [23] This has given rise to a broad discussion which is biased by the idea that bodily movements do not represent the substratum through which actions enter into the world but are themselves primitive actions.[24] In this view, a complex action is characterized by the fact that it is performed "through" carrying out another action: "through" flicking the light switch I turn on the light; "through" raising my right arm I greet someone; "through" forcefully kicking a ball I score a goal. These are examples of actions performed "through" a basic action. A basic action is characterized in turn by the fact that it cannot be performed by means of an additional act. I regard this conceptual strategy as misleading. In a certain sense, actions are realized through movements of the body, but only in such a way that the actor, in following a technical or social rule, *concomitantly executes* these movements. Concomitant execution means that the actor intends an action but not the bodily movements with the help of which he realizes it.[25] *A bodily movement is an element of an action but not an action.*

As far as their status as nonindependent actions is concerned, *bodily* movements are similar to just those *operations* from which Wittgenstein developed his concepts of rules and rule following. Operations of thought and speech are always only executed concomitantly in *other* actions. If need be, they can be *rendered independent* within the framework of a training exercise—for instance, when a Latin teacher, in the course of a lesson, demonstrates the passive transformation with a sample sentence formed in the active voice. This explains the special heuristic utility of the model of social games. Wittgenstein preferred to elucidate operational rules with reference to chess. He did not see that this model has only limited value. We can certainly understand speaking or doing sums as practices constituted by the grammar of a particular language or the rules of arithmetic, in a way similar to that in which chess playing is constituted by the familiar rules of the game. But the two cases are as distinct as is the concomitantly executed arm movement from the gymnastic exercise that is carried out by means of the same movement. In applying arithmetical or grammatical rules we generate symbolic objects such as sums or sentences; but they do not lead an independent existence. We normally carry out *other* actions by means of sums and sentences—for example, schoolwork or commands. Operatively generated structures can, taken by themselves, be judged as more or less correct, in conformity with a rule, or wellformed; but they are not, as are actions, open to criticism from the standpoints of truth, efficacy, rightness, or sincerity, for they acquire relations to the world only as the infrastructure of other actions. *Operations do not concern the world.*

This can be seen in the fact that operational rules can serve to identify an operatively generated structure as more or less well formed, that is, to make it *comprehensible* but not to *explain* its appearance. They permit an answer to the question of whether certain scrawled-out symbols are sentences, measurements, computations, etc.; and if they are, say, a computation, just which one it is. To show that someone has calculated, and indeed correctly, does not, however, explain *why* he carried out this computation. If we wish to answer *this* question, we must have recourse to a rule of *action;* for example, to the fact that a pupil used this sheet of paper to solve a mathematical problem. With the help of arithmetic rules, we can, it is true, state the reason why he continues the number series 1, 3, 6, 10, 15 . . . with 21, 28, 36, and so forth; but we cannot *explain* why he writes this series on a piece of paper. We are explicating the meaning of a symbolic structure and not giving a rational explanation for its coming to be. Operational rules do not have explanatory power; following them does not mean, as does following rules of action, that the actor is relating to something in the world and is thereby oriented to validity claims connected with action-motivating reasons.

This should make clear why we cannot analyze communicative utterances in the same way as we do the grammatical sentences with the help of which we carry them out. For the communicative model of action, language is relevant only from the pragmatic viewpoint that speakers, in employing sentences with an orientation to reaching understanding, take up relations to the world, not only directly as in teleological, normatively regulated, or dramaturgical action, but in a reflective way. Speakers integrate the three formal world-concepts, which appear in the other models of action either singly or in pairs, into a system and presuppose this system in common as a framework of interpretation within which they can reach an understanding. They no longer relate *straightaway* to something in the objective, social, or subjective worlds; instead they relativize their utterances against the possibility that their validity will be contested by other actors. Reaching an understanding functions as a mechanism for coordinating actions only through the participants in interaction coming to an agreement concerning the claimed *validity* of their utterances, that is, through intersubjectively recognizing the *validity claims* they reciprocally raise. A speaker puts forward a criticizable claim in relating with his utterance to at least one "world"; he thereby uses the fact that this relation between actor and world is in principle open to objective appraisal in order to call upon his opposite number to take a rationally motivated position. The concept of communicative action presupposes language as the medium for a kind of reaching understanding, in the course of which participants, through relating to a world, reciprocally raise validity claims that can be accepted or contested.

With this model of action we are supposing that participants in interaction can now mobilize the rationality potential—which according to our previous analysis resides in the actor's three relations to the world—expressly for the cooperatively pursued goal of reaching understanding. If we leave to one side the well-formedness of the symbolic expressions employed, an actor who is oriented to understanding in this sense must raise at least three validity claims with his utterance, namely:

1. That the statement made is true (or that the existential presuppositions of the propositional content mentioned are in fact satisfied);
2. That the speech is right with respect to the existing normative context (or that the normative context that it is supposed to satisfy is itself legitimate); and
3. That the manifest intention of the speaker is meant as it is expressed.

Thus the speaker claims truth for statements or existential presuppositions, rightness for legitimately regulated actions and their normative context, and truthfulness or sincerity for the manifestation of subjective experience. We can easily recognize therein the three relations of actor to world presupposed *by the social scientist* in the previously analyzed concepts of action; but in the concept of communicative action they are ascribed to the perspective of *the speakers and hearers themselves.* It is the actors themselves who seek consensus and measure it against truth, rightness, and sincerity, that is, against the "fit" or "misfit" between the speech act, on the one hand, and the three worlds to which the actor takes up relations with his utterance, on the other. Such relations hold between an utterance and;

1. The objective world (as the totality of all entities about which true statements are possible);
2. The social world (as the totality of all legitimately regulated interpersonal relations);
3. The subjective world (as the totality of the experience of the speaker to which he has privileged access).

Every process of reaching understanding takes place against the background of a culturally ingrained preunderstanding. This background knowledge remains unproblematic as a whole; only that part of the stock of knowledge that participants make use of and thematize at a given time is put to the test. To the extent that definitions of situations are negotiated by participants *themselves,* this thematic segment of the lifeworld is at their disposal and the negotiation of each new definition of the situation.

A definition of the situation establishes an order. Through it, participants in communication assign the various elements of an action situation to one of the three worlds and thereby incorporate the actual action situation into their preinterpreted lifeworld. A definition of the situation by another party that prima facie diverges from one's own presents a problem of a peculiar sort; for in cooperative processes of interpretation no participant has a monopoly on correct interpretation. For both parties the interpretive task consists in incorporating the other's interpretation of the situation into one's own in such a way that in the revised version "his" external world and "my" external world can—against the background of "our" lifeworld—be relativized in relation to "the" world, and the divergent situation definitions can be brought to coincide sufficiently. Naturally this does not mean that interpretation must lead in every case to a stable and unambiguously differentiated assignment. Stability and absence of ambiguity are rather the exception in the communicative practice of everyday life. A more realistic picture is that drawn by ethnomethodologists—of a diffuse, fragile, continuously revised and only momentarily successful communication in which participants rely on problematic and unclarified presuppositions and feel their way from one occasional commonality to the next.

To avoid misunderstanding I would like to repeat that the communicative model of action does not equate action with communication. Language is a medium of communication that serves understanding, whereas actors, in coming to an understanding with one another so as to coordinate their actions, pursue their particular aims. In this respect the teleological structure is fundamental to *all* concepts of action.[26] Concepts of *social action* are distinguished, however, according to how they specify the *coordination* among the goal-directed actions of different participants: as the interlacing of egocentric calculations of utility (whereby the degree of conflict and cooperation varies with the given interest positions); as a socially integrating agreement about values and norms instilled through cultural tradition and socialization; as a consensual relation between players and their publics; or as reaching understanding in the sense of a cooperative process of interpretation. In all cases the teleological structure of action is presupposed, inasmuch as the capacity for goal-setting and goal-directed action is ascribed to actors, as well as an interest in carrying out their plans of action. But only the strategic model of action *rests content* with an explication of the features of action oriented directly to success; whereas the other models of action specify conditions under which the actor pursues his goals—conditions of legitimacy, of self-presentation, or of agreement arrived at in communication, under which alter can "link up" his actions with those of ego. In the case of communicative action the interpretive accomplishments on which cooperative processes of interpretation are based represent the mechanism for *coordinating action;* communicative action is *not exhausted* by the act of reaching understanding in an interpretive manner. If we take as our unit of analysis a simple speech act carried out by *S,* to which at least one participant in interaction can take up a yes or no position, we can clarify the conditions for the communicative coordination of action by stating what it means for a hearer to understand what is said. But communicative action designates a type of interaction that is *coordinated through* speech acts and does *not coincide with* them.

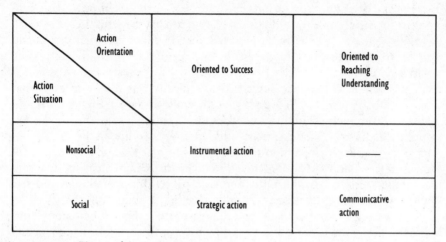

Action Orientation / Action Situation	Oriented to Success	Oriented to Reaching Understanding
Nonsocial	Instrumental action	————
Social	Strategic action	Communicative action

FIGURE I.   Types of Action

I would like to take up once again the concept of communicative action expounded in the introduction and, by drawing upon speech act theory, to pursue those aspects of the rationality of action neglected in Weber's official action theory. In this way I hope to capture in action-theoretic terms the complex concept of rationality that Weber did employ in his cultural analyses. I shall be starting from a typology that is modelled on the unofficial version of Weber's action theory, insofar as social actions are distinguished according to two action orientations—corresponding to the coordination of action through interest positions and through normative agreement (see figure 1).

The model of purposive-rational action takes as its point of departure the view that the actor is primarily oriented to attaining an end (which has been rendered sufficiently precise in terms of purposes), that he selects means that seem to him appropriate in the given situation, and that he calculates other foreseeable consequences of action as secondary conditions of success. Success is defined as the appearance in the world of a desired state, which can, in a given situation, be causally produced through goal-oriented action or omission. The effects of action comprise the results of action (which the actor foresaw and intended, or made allowance for) and the side effects (which the actor did not foresee). We call an action oriented to success *instrumental* when we consider it under the aspect of following technical rules of action and assess the efficiency of an intervention into a complex of circumstances and events. We call an action oriented to success *strategic* when we consider it under the aspect of following rules of rational choice and assess the efficacy of influencing the decisions of a rational opponent. Instrumental actions can be connected with and subordinated to social interactions of a different type—for example, as the "task elements" of social roles; strategic actions are social actions by themselves. By contrast, I shall speak of *communicative* action whenever the actions of the agents involved are coordinated not through egocentric calculations of success but through acts of reaching understanding. In communicative action participants are not primarily oriented to their own individual successes; they pursue their individual goals under the condition that they can harmonize their plans of action on the basis of common situation definitions. In this respect the negotiation of definitions of the situation is an essential element of the interpretive accomplishments required for communicative action.

Orientation to Success versus Orientation to Reaching Understanding. In identifying strategic action and communicative action as types, I am assuming that concrete actions can be classified from these points of view. I do not want to use the terms "strategic" and "communicative" only to designate two analytic aspects under which the same action could be described— on the one hand as a reciprocal influencing of one another by opponents acting in a purposive-rational manner and, on the other hand, as a process of reaching understanding among members of a lifeworld. Rather, social actions can be distinguished according to whether the participants adopt either a success-oriented attitude or one oriented to reaching understanding. And, under suitable conditions, these attitudes should be identifiable on the basis of the intuitive knowledge of the participants themselves.

In the framework of action theory, the conceptual analysis of the two attitudes cannot be understood as a psychological task. It is not my aim to characterize behavioral dispositions empirically, but to grasp structural properties of processes of reaching understanding, from which we can derive general pragmatic presuppositions of communicative action. To explain what I mean by "an attitude oriented to reaching understanding," I have to analyze the concept of "reaching understanding." This is not a question of the predicates an observer uses when describing processes of reaching understanding, but of the pretheoretical knowledge of competent speakers, who can themselves distinguish situations in which they are causally exerting an influence *upon* others from those in which they are coming to an understanding *with* them, and who know when their attempts have failed. Once we are able to specify the standards on which these distinctions are implicitly based, we will be in a position to explain the concept of reaching understanding.

Reaching understanding [*Verständigung*] is considered to be a process of reaching agreement [*Einigung*] among speaking and acting subjects. Naturally, a group of persons can feel at one in a mood which is so diffuse that it is difficult to identify the propositional content or the intentional object to which it is directed. Such a collective like-mindedness [*Gleichgestimmtheit*] does not satisfy the conditions for the type of agreement [*Einverständnis*] in which attempts at reaching understanding terminate when they are successful. A communicatively achieved agreement, or one that is mutually presupposed in communicative action, is propositionally differentiated. Owing to this linguistic structure, it cannot be merely induced through outside influence; it has to be accepted or presupposed as valid by the participants. To this extent it can be distinguished from merely de facto accord [*Übereinstimmung*]. Processes of reaching understanding aim at an agreement that meets the conditions of rationally motivated assent [*Zustimmung*] to the content of an utterance. A communicatively achieved agreement has a rational basis; it cannot be imposed by either party, whether instrumentally through intervention in the situation directly or strategically through influencing the decisions of opponents. Agreement can indeed be objectively obtained by force; but what comes to pass manifestly through outside influence or the use of violence cannot count subjectively as agreement. Agreement rests on common *convictions*. The speech act of one person succeeds only if the other accepts the offer contained in it by taking (however implicitly) a yes or no position on a validity claim that is in principle criticizable. Both ego, who raises a validity claim with his utterance, and alter, who recognizes or rejects it, base their decisions on potential grounds or reasons.

If we were not in a position to refer to the model of speech, we could not even begin to analyze what it means for two subjects to come to an understanding with one another. Reaching understanding is the inherent telos of human speech. Naturally, speech and understanding are not related to one another as means to end. But we can explain the concept of reaching understanding only if we specify what it means to use sentences with a communicative intent. The concepts of speech and understanding reciprocally interpret one another. Thus we can analyze the formal-pragmatic features of the attitude oriented to reaching understanding in connection with the model of the attitude of participants in communication, one of whom—in the simplest case—carries out a speech act, to which the other takes a yes or no position (even though utterances in the communicative practice of everyday life usually do not have a standard linguistic form and often have no verbal form at all).

If we approach the task of delimiting actions oriented to success from those oriented to reaching understanding by way of an analysis of speech acts, we encounter the following difficulty. On the one hand, we are regarding the communicative acts with the help of which speakers and hearers come to an understanding about something as a mechanism for coordinating actions. The concept of communicative action is presented in such a way that the acts of reaching understanding, which link the teleologically structured plans of action of different participants and thereby first combine individual acts into an interaction complex, cannot themselves be reduced to teleological actions. In this respect the paradigmatic concept of linguistically mediated interaction is compatible with a theory of meaning which, like intentionalist semantics, tries to conceptualize reaching understanding as the solution to a problem of coordination among subjects acting with an orientation to success. On the other hand, not every linguistically mediated interaction is an example of action oriented to reaching understanding. Without doubt, there are countless cases of indirect understanding, where one subject gives another something to understand through signals, indirectly gets him to form a certain opinion or to adopt certain intentions by way of inferentially working up perceptions of the situation; or where, on the basis of an already habitual communicative practice of everyday life, one subject inconspicuously harnesses another for his own purposes, that is, induces him to behave in a desired way by manipulatively employing linguistic means and thereby instrumentalizes him for his own success. Such examples of the use of language with an orientation to consequences seem to decrease the value of speech acts as the model for action oriented to reaching understanding.

This will turn out not to be the case only if it can be shown that the use of language with an orientation to reaching understanding is the *original mode* of language use, upon which indirect understanding, giving something to understand or letting something be understood, and the instrumental use of language in general, are parasitic. In my view, Austin's distinction between illocutions and perlocutions accomplishes just that.

As is well known, Austin distinguishes locutionary, illocutionary and perlocutionary acts.[27] He applies the term "locutionary" to the content of propositional sentences (p) or of nominalized propositional sentences (that p). Through *locutionary acts* the speaker expresses states of affairs; he says something. Through *illocutionary acts* the speaker performs an action in saying something. The illocutionary role establishes the mode of a sentence ("Mp") employed as a statement, promise, command, avowal, or the like. Under standard conditions, the mode is expressed by means of a performative verb in the first person present; the action meaning can be seen particularly in the fact that "hereby" can be added to the illocutionary component of the speech act: "I hereby promise you (command you, confess to you that p." Finally, through *perlocutionary acts* the speaker produces an effect upon the hearer. By carrying out a speech act he brings about something in the world. Thus the three acts that Austin distinguishes can be characterized in the following catchphrases: to say *something,* to act *in* saying something, to bring about something *through* acting in saying something.

Austin makes his conceptual incisions in such a way that the speech act ("Mp"), composed of an illocutionary and a propositional component, is presented as a self-sufficient act which the speaker always performs with a communicative intent, that is, so that a hearer may understand and accept his utterance.[28] The self-sufficiency of the speech act is to be understood in the sense that the communicative intent of the speaker and the illocutionary aim he is pursuing follow from the manifest meaning of what is said. It is otherwise with teleological actions. We identify their meaning only in connection with the intentions their authors are pursuing and the ends they want to realize. As *the meaning of what is said* is constitutive for illocution-ary acts, *the intention of the agent* is constitutive for teleological actions.

What Austin calls *perlocutionary effects* arise from the fact that illocu-tionary acts are embedded in contexts of interaction. Speech acts, like ac-tions in general, can produce side effects that the actor did not foresee; these are perlocutionary effects in a trivial sense, which I shall not consider any further. Less trivial are the perlocutionary effects which result from the fact that illocutionary acts sometimes take on roles in contexts of strategic in-teraction. These effects ensue whenever a speaker acts with an orientation to success and thereby instrumentalizes speech acts for purposes that are only contingently related to the meaning of what is said. This is what Austin has in mind:

There is a further sense in which to perform a locutionary act, and therein an illo-cutionary act, may also be to perform an act of another kind. Saying something will often, or even normally, produce certain consequential effects upon the feelings, thoughts, or actions of the audience, or of the speaker, or of other persons: and it may be done with the design, intention, or purpose of producing them; and we may then say, thinking of this, that the speaker has performed an act in the nomenclature of which reference is made either only obliquely, or even not at all, to the perfor-mance of the locutionary or illocutionary act. We shall call the performance of an act of this kind the performance of a *perlocutionary act* or *perlocution*.[29]

The demarcation between illocutionary and perlocutionary acts has given rise to an extended controversy.[30] From it have emerged four criteria of demarcation.

The illocutionary aim a speaker pursues with an utterance follows from the very meaning of what is said; speech acts are, in this sense, self-identifying.[31] By means of an illocutionary act a speaker lets a hearer know that he wants what he says to be understood as a greeting, command, warn-ing, explanation, and so forth. His communicative intent does not go be-yond wanting the hearer to understand the manifest content of the speech act. By contrast, the perlocutionary aim of a speaker, like the ends pursued with goal-directed actions generally, does not follow from the manifest con-tent of the speech act; this aim can be identified only through the agent's intention. For example, a hearer who understands a request directed to him can just as little know thereby what *else* the speaker has in view in uttering it as an observer who sees an acquaintance hurrying along the street can know why he is in a hurry. The addressee could at best infer the speaker's perlocutionary aims from the context.[32] The three remaining criteria have to do with this character of self-identification of speech acts.

From the description of a speech act, as in (1) and (2) below, we can infer the conditions for the corresponding illocutionary success of the speaker, but not the conditions for the perlocutionary results that a speaker acting with an orientation to success might want to achieve, or did achieve, in a given case by carrying out this speech act. Into the description of perlocu-tions, as in (3) and (4) below, there enter results that go beyond the meaning of what is said and thus beyond what an addressee could directly understand.

1. *S* asserted to *H* that he gave notice to his firm.

S will have achieved illocutionary success with the utterance represented by (1) if *H* understands his assertion and accepts it as true. The same holds for

2. *H* warned *S* not to give notice to his firm.

H will have achieved illocutionary success with the utterance represented by (2) if *S* understands his warning and accepts it as true or right—depending on whether in a given context it has more the sense of a prognosis or of a moral appeal. In any case, accepting the utterance described in (2) is grounds for certain obligations on the part of the addressee and for corresponding expectations on the part of the speaker. Whether the expected consequences actually come to pass or not has no effect on the illocutionary success of the speaker. If, for instance, *S* does not give notice, this is not a perlocutionarily achieved effect but the consequence of a communicatively achieved agreement and thus the fulfillment of an obligation the addressee took upon himself with his yes to a speech act offer. Consider now:

3. Through informing *H* that he had given notice to his firm, *S* gave *H* a fright (as he intended to do).

From this description it follows that the illocutionary success of the assertion described in (1) is not a sufficient condition for achieving a perlocutionary effect. In another context the hearer could just as well react to the same utterance with relief. The same holds for:

4. *H* upset *S* with the warning against giving notice to his firm.

In another context the same warning could just as well strengthen *S* in his resolve, for instance if *S* harbors a suspicion that *H* does not wish him well. The description of perlocutionary effects must therefore refer to a context of teleological action that *goes beyond* the speech act.[33]

From considerations of this kind Austin concluded that illocutionary results stand in a *conventionally* regulated or *internal* connection with speech acts, whereas perlocutionary effects remain external to the meaning of what is said. The possible perlocutionary effects of a speech act depend on fortuitous contexts and are not fixed by conventions, as are illocutionary results.[34] Of course, one might use (4) as a counterexample. Only if the addressee takes the warning seriously is being upset a plausible reaction, and only if he doesn't take it seriously is a feeling of being confirmed (in his decision) plausible. In some cases, the meaning conventions of the action predicates with which illocutionary acts are formed exclude certain classes of perlocutionary effects. At the same time, these effects are not connected with speech acts only in a conventional way. When a hearer accepts an assertion of S as true, a command as right, an admission as truthful, he therewith implicitly declares himself ready to tie his further action to certain conventional obligations. By contrast, the feeling of being upset which a friend arouses in S with a warning that the latter takes seriously is a state that may or may not ensue.

Similar considerations have motivated Strawson to replace the criterion of conventionality with another criterion of demarcation.[35] A speaker, if he wants to be successful, may not let his perlocutionary aims be known, whereas illocutionary aims can be achieved only through being expressed. Illocutions are expressed openly; perlocutions may not be "admitted" as such. This difference can also be seen in the fact that the predicates with which perlocutionary acts are described (to give a fright to, to cause to be upset, to plunge into doubt, to annoy, mislead, offend, infuriate, humiliate, and so forth) cannot appear among those predicates used to carry out the illocutionary acts by means of which the corresponding perlocutionary effects can be produced. Perlocutionary acts constitute a subclass of teleological actions which must be carried out by means of speech acts, under the condition that the actor does not declare or admit to his aims as such.

Whereas the sense of the division into locutionary and illocutionary acts is to separate the propositional content from the mode of speech acts as analytically different aspects, the distinction between these two types of acts, on the one side, and perlocutionary acts on the other, is by no means analytical in character. Perlocutionary effects can be achieved by way of speech acts only if the latter are *incorporated as means* into actions oriented to success. Perlocutionary acts are an indication of the integration of speech acts into contexts of strategic interaction. They belong to the intended consequences or results of a teleological action which an actor undertakes with the intention of influencing a hearer in a certain way by means of illocutionary successes. Naturally, speech acts can serve this *nonillocutionary aim of influencing hearers* only if they are suited to achieve illocutionary aims. If the hearer failed to understand what the speaker was saying, a strategically acting speaker would not be able to bring the hearer, by means of communicative acts, to behave in the desired way. To this extent, what we initially designated as "the use of language with an orientation to consequences" is not an original use of language but the subsumption of speech acts that serve illocutionary aims under conditions of action oriented to success.

As speech acts by no means always function in this way, however, it must also be possible to clarify the structure of linguistic communication without reference to structures of purposive activity. The teleological actor's orientation to success is not constitutive for the "success" of processes of reaching understanding, particularly not when these are incorporated into strategic actions. What we mean by reaching understanding has to be clarified *solely* in connection with illocutionary acts. From this it also follows that we cannot explain illocutionary success in terms of the conditions for the purposively achieved success of a teleological action. Illocutionary aims are different from those purposes that can be achieved *under the description* of something to be brought about in the world.

Perlocutionary effects, like the results of teleological actions generally, are intended under the description of states of affairs brought about through intervention in the world. By contrast, illocutionary results are achieved at the level of interpersonal relations on which participants in communication come to an understanding with one another about something in the world. In this sense, they are not innerworldly but extramundane. Illocutionary results appear in the lifeworld to which the participants belong and which forms the background for their processes of reaching understanding. They cannot be intended under the description of causally produced effects.

I would like to suggest that we conceive perlocutions as a special class of strategic interactions in which illocutions are employed as means in teleological contexts of action. As Strawson has shown, this employment is subject to certain provisos. A teleologically acting speaker has to achieve his illocutionary aim—that the hearer understand what is said and undertake the obligations connected with the acceptance of the offer contained in the speech act—without betraying his perlocutionary aim. This proviso lends to perlocutions the peculiarly asymmetrical character of concealed strategic actions. These are interactions in which at least one of the participants is acting strategically while he deceives other participants regarding the fact that he is *not* satisfying the presuppositions under which illocutionary aims can normally be achieved. For this reason as well, this type of interaction is not suitable as the model for an analysis that is supposed to explain the linguistic mechanism of coordinating action by way of the illocutionary binding (or bonding) effect of speech acts. It would be advisable to select for this purpose a type of interaction that is not burdened with the asymmetries and provisos of perlocutions. I have called the type of interaction in which *all* participants harmonize their individual plans of action with one another and thus pursue their illocutionary aims *without reservation* "communicative action."

Austin also analyzes speech acts in contexts of interaction. It is precisely the point of his approach to work out the performative character of linguistic utterances in connection with institutionally bound speech acts like baptizing, betting appointing, and the like, in which the obligations issuing from the performance of the speech act are unambiguously regulated by accompanying institutions or norms of action. However, Austin confuses the picture by not treating these interactions, in connection with which he analyzes the illocutionary binding effect of speech acts, as *different in type* from those interactions in which perlocutionary effects occur. Someone who makes a bet, appoints an officer as supreme commander, gives a command, admonishes or warns, makes a prediction, tells a story, makes a confession, reveals something, and so forth, is acting communicatively and cannot at all produce perlocutionary effects *at the same level of interaction.* A speaker can pursue perlocutionary aims only when he deceives his partner concerning the fact that he is acting strategically—when, for example, he gives the command to attack in order to get his troops to rush into a trap, or when he proposes a bet of $3,000 in order to embarrass others, or when he tells a story late in the evening in order to delay a guest's departure. It is certainly true that in communicative action unintended consequences may appear at any time; but as soon as there is a danger that these will be attributed to the speaker as intended results, the latter finds it necessary to offer explanations and denials, and if need be, apologies, in order to dispel the false impression that these side effects are perlocutionary effects. Otherwise, he has to expect that the other participants will feel deceived and adopt a strategic attitude in turn, steering away from action oriented to reaching understanding. Of course, in complex action contexts a speech act that is directly performed and accepted under the conditions of communicative action can at the same time have a strategic position at *other* levels of interaction, can have perlocutionary effects on *third parties*.

Thus I count as communicative action those linguistically mediated interactions in which all participants pursue illocutionary aims, and *only* illocutionary aims, with their mediating acts of communication. On the other hand, I regard as linguistically mediated strategic action those interactions in which at least one of the participants wants with his speech acts to produce perlocutionary effects on his opposite number. Austin did not keep these two cases separate as different types of interaction, because he was inclined to identify acts of communication, that is, acts of reaching understanding, with the interactions coordinated by speech acts. He didn't see that acts of communication or speech acts function as a coordinating mechanism for *other* actions. "Acts of communication" should not be confused with what I have introduced as "communicative action." Indeed, they have to be disengaged from contexts of communicative action before they can be incorporated into strategic interactions. And this is possible in turn only because speech acts have a certain independence in relation to communicative action, though the meaning of what is said always points to the interaction structures of communicative action. The difference between a speech act and the context of interaction that it constitutes through achieving a coordination of the plans of different actors can be recognized the more easily if one is not fixated on the model of institutionally bound speech acts, as Austin was.[36]

Chapter Eight
THE CONCEPT OF THE LIFEWORLD AND
THE HERMENEUTIC IDEALISM OF
INTERPRETIVE SOCIOLOGY

I would like to explicate the concept of the lifeworld, and to this end I shall pick up again the threads of our reflection on communication theory. It is not my intention to carry further our formal-pragmatic examination of speech acts and of communicative action; rather, I want to build upon these concepts so far as they have already been analyzed, and take up the question of how the lifeworld—as the horizon within which communicative actions are "always already" moving—is in turn limited and changed by the structural transformation of society as a whole.

I have previously introduced the concept of the lifeworld rather casually and only from a reconstructive research perspective. It is a concept complementary to that of communicative action. Like the phenomenological lifeworld analysis of the late Husserl,[1] or the late Wittgenstein's analysis of forms of life (which were not, to be sure, carried out with a systematic intent),[2] formal-pragmatic analysis aims at structures that, in contrast to the historical shapes of particular lifeworlds and life-forms, are put forward as invariant. With this first step we are taking into the bargain a separation of form and content. So long as we hold to a formal-pragmatic research perspective, we can take up questions that have previously been dealt with in the framework of transcendental philosophy—in the present context, we can focus our attention on structures of the lifeworld in general.

I should like to begin by making clear how the lifeworld is related to those three worlds on which subjects acting with an orientation to mutual understanding base their common definitions of situations. The concepts of the lifeworld normally employed in interpretive [verstehenden] sociology are linked with everyday concepts that are, to begin with, serviceable only for the narrative presentation of historical events and social circumstances. An investigation of the functions that communicative action takes on in maintaining a structurally differentiated world originates from within this horizon. In connection with these functions, we can clarify the necessary conditions for a rationalization of the lifeworld. This takes us to the limit of theoretical approaches that identify society with the lifeworld. I shall therefore propose that we conceive of society simultaneously as a system and as a lifeworld.

In examining the ontological presuppositions of teleological, normatively regulated, and dramaturgical action, I have distinguished three different actor-world relations that a subject can take up to something in a world—to something that either obtains or can be brought about in the one objective world, to something recognized as obligatory to the social world supposedly shared by all the members of a collective, or to something that other actors attribute to the speaker's own subjective world (to which he has privileged access). These actor-world relations turn up again in the pure types of action oriented to mutual understanding. By attending to the modes of language use, we can clarify what it means for a speaker, in performing one of the standard speech acts, to take up a pragmatic relation

· to something in the objective world (as the totality of entities about which true statements are possible); or
· to something in the social world (as the totality of legitimately regulated interpersonal relations); or
· to something in the subjective world (as the totality of experience to which a speaker has privileged access and which he can express before a public);

such that what the speech act refers to appears to the speaker as something objective, normative, or subjective. In introducing the concept of communicative action, I pointed out that the pure types of action oriented to mutual understanding are merely limit cases. In fact, communicative utterances are always embedded in various world relations at the same time. Communicative action relies on a cooperative process of interpretation in which participants relate simultaneously to something in the objective, the social, and the subjective worlds, even when they *thematically stress only one* of the three components in their utterances. Speaker and hearer use the reference system of the three worlds as an interpretive framework within which they work out their common situation definitions. They do not relate point blank to something in a world but relativize their utterances against the chance that their validity will be contested by another actor. Coming to an understanding [*Verständigung*] means that participants in communication reach an agreement [*Einigung*] concerning the validity of an utterance; agreement [*Einverständnis*] is the intersubjective recognition of the validity claim the speaker raises for it. Even when an utterance clearly belongs only to one mode of communication and sharply thematizes one corresponding validity claim, all three modes of communication and the validity claims corresponding to them are internally related to each other. Thus, it is a rule of communicative action that when a hearer assents to a thematized validity claim, he acknowledges the other two implicitly raised validity claims as well—otherwise, he is supposed to make known his dissent. Consensus does not come about when, for example, a hearer accepts the *truth of an assertion* but at the same time doubts the sincerity of the speaker or the normative appropriateness of his utterance; the same holds for the case in which a speaker accepts the *normative validity of a command* but suspects the seriousness of the intent thereby expressed or has his doubts about the existential presuppositions of the action commanded (and thus about the possibility of carrying it out). The example of a command that the addressee regards as unfeasible reminds us that participants are always expressing themselves in situations that they have to define in common so far as they are acting with an orientation to mutual understanding. An older construction worker who sends a younger and newly arrived co-worker to fetch some beer, telling him to hurry it up and be back in a few minutes, supposes that the situation is clear to everyone involved—here, the younger worker and any other workers within hearing distance. The *theme* is the upcoming midmorning snack; taking care of the drinks is a *goal* related to this theme; one of the older workers comes up with the *plan* to send the "new guy," who, given his status, cannot easily get around this request. The informal group hierarchy of the workers on the construction site is the *normative framework* in which the one is allowed to tell the other to do something. The action situation is defined *temporally* by the upcoming break and *spatially* by the distance from the site to the nearest store. If the situation were such that the nearest store could not be reached by foot in a few minutes, that is, that the plan of action of the older worker could—at least under the conditions specified—only be carried out with an automobile (or other means of transportation), the person addressed might answer with: "But I don't have a car."

The background of a communicative utterance is thus formed by situation definitions that, as measured against the actual need for mutual understanding, have to overlap to a sufficient extent. If this commonality cannot be presupposed, the actors have to draw upon the means of strategic action, with an orientation toward coming to a mutual understanding, so as to bring about a common definition of the situation or to negotiate one directly—which occurs in everyday communicative practice primarily in the form of "repair work." Even in cases where this is not necessary, every new utterance is a test: the definition of the situation implicitly proposed by the speaker is either confirmed, modified, partly suspended, or generally placed in question. This continual process of definition and redefinition involves correlating contents to worlds—according to what counts in a given instance as a consensually interpreted element of the objective world, as an intersubjectively recognized normative component of the social world, or as a private element of a subjective world to which someone has privileged access. At the same time, the actors demarcate themselves from these three worlds. With every common situation definition they are determining the boundary between external nature, society, and inner nature; at the same time, they are renewing the demarcation between themselves as interpreters, on the one side, and the external world and their own inner worlds, on the other.

So, for instance, the older worker, upon hearing the other's response, might realize that he has revised his implicit assumption that a nearby shop is open on Mondays. It would be different if the younger worker had answered: "I'm not thirsty." He would then learn from the astonished reaction that beer for the midmorning snack is a norm held to independent of the subjective state of mind of one of the parties involved. Perhaps the newcomer does not understand the normative context in which the older man is giving him an order, and asks whose turn to get the beer it will be tomorrow. Or perhaps he is missing the point because he is from another region where the local work rhythm, that is, the custom of midmorning snack, is not familiar, and thus responds with the question: "Why should I interrupt my work *now*?" We can imagine continuations of this conversation indicating that one or the other of the parties changes his initial definition of the situation and brings it into accord with the situation definitions of the others. In the first two cases described above, there would be a regrouping of the individual elements of the situation, a Gestalt-switch: the presumed fact that a nearby shop is open becomes a subjective belief that turned out to be false; what is presumed to be a desire to have beer with the midmorning snack turns out to be a collectively recognized norm. In the other two cases, the interpretation of the situation gets supplemented with respect to elements of the social world: the low man on the pole gets the beer; in this part of the world one has a midmorning snack at 9:00 A.M. These *redefinitions* are based on suppositions of commonality in respect to the objective, social, and each's own subjective world. With this reference system, participants in communication suppose that the situation definitions forming the background to an actual utterance hold intersubjectively.

Situations do not get "defined" in the sense of being sharply delimited. They always have a horizon that shifts with the theme. A *situation* is a segment of *lifeworld contexts of relevance* [*Verweisungszusammenhänge*] that is thrown into relief by themes and articulated through goals and plans of action; these contexts of relevance are concentrically ordered and become increasingly anonymous and diffused as the spatiotemporal and social distance grows. Thus, as regards our little scene with the construction workers, the construction site located on a specific street, the specific time—a Monday morning shortly before midmorning snack—and the reference group of co-workers who are at this site constitute the null point of a spatiotemporal and social reference system, of a world that is "within my actual reach." The city around the building site, the region, the country, the continent, and so on, constitute, as regards space, a "world within my potential reach"; corresponding to this, in respect to time, we have the daily routine, the life history, the epoch, and so forth; and in the social dimension, the reference groups from the family through the community, nation, and the like, to the "world society." Alfred Schultz again and again supplied us with illustrations of these spatiotemporal and social organizations of the lifeworld.[3]

The *theme* of an upcoming midmorning snack and the *plan* of fetching some beer, with regard to which the theme is broached, mark off a situation from the lifeworld of those directly involved. This action situation presents itself as a field of actual needs for mutual understanding and of actual options for action: the expectations the workers attach to midmorning snack, the status of a newly arrived younger co-worker, the distance of the store from the construction site, the availability of a car, and the like, belong to the elements of the situation. The facts that a single-family house is going up here, that the newcomer is a foreign "guest worker" with no social security, that another co-worker has three children, and that the new building is subject to Bavarian building codes are circumstances irrelevant to the given situation. There are, of course, shifting boundaries. That becomes evident as soon as the homeowner shows up with a case of beer to keep the workers in a good mood, or the guest worker falls from the ladder as he is getting ready to fetch the beer, or the theme of the new government regulations concerning child subsidies comes up, or the architect shows up with a local official to check the number of stories. In such cases, the theme shifts and with it the horizon of the situation, that is to say, the segment of the lifeworld relevant to the situation for which mutual understanding is required in view of the options for action that have been actualized. Situations have boundaries that can be overstepped at any time—thus Husserl introduced the image of the *horizon* that shifts according to one's position and that can expand and shrink as one moves through the rough countryside.[4]

For those involved, the action situation is the center of their lifeworld; it has a moveable horizon because it points to the complexity of the lifeworld. In a certain sense, the lifeworld to which participants in communication belong is always present, but only in such a way that it forms the background for an actual scene. As soon as a *context of relevance* of this sort is brought into a situation, becomes part of a situation, it loses its triviality and unquestioned solidity. If, for instance, the fact that the new worker is not insured against accidental injury suddenly enters the domain of relevance of a thematic field, it can be explicitly mentioned—and in various illocutionary roles: a speaker can state that *p;* he can deplore or conceal that *p;* he can blame someone for the fact that *p*, and so on. When it becomes part of the situation, this state of affairs can be known and problematized as a fact, as the content of a norm or of a feeling, desire, and so forth. Before it becomes relevant to the situation, the same circumstance is given only in the mode of something taken for granted in the lifeworld, something with which those involved are intuitively familiar without anticipating the possibility of its becoming problematic. It is not even "known," in any strict sense, if this entails that it can be justified and contested. Only the limited segments of the lifeworld brought into the horizon of a situation constitute a thematizable context of action oriented to mutual understanding; only they appear under the category of *knowledge*. From a perspective turned toward the situation, the lifeworld appears as a reservoir of taken-for-granteds, of unshaken convictions that participants in communication draw upon in cooperative processes of interpretation. Single elements, specific taken-for-granteds, are, however, mobilized in the form of consensual and yet problematizable knowledge only when they become relevant to a situation.

If we now relinquish the basic concepts of the philosophy of consciousness in which Husserl dealt with the problem of the lifeworld, we can think of the lifeworld as represented by a culturally transmitted and linguistically organized stock of interpretive patterns. Then the ideal of a "context of relevance" that connects the elements of the situation with one another, and the situation with the lifeworld, need no longer be explained in the framework of a phenomenology and psychology of perception.[5] Relevance structures can be conceived instead as interconnections of meaning holding between a given communicative utterance, the immediate context, and its connotative horizon of meanings. Contexts of relevance are based on *grammatically regulated* relations among the elements of a *linguistically organized* stock of knowledge.

If, as usual in the tradition stemming from Humboldt,[6] we assume that there is an internal connection between structures of lifeworlds and structures of linguistic worldviews, language and cultural tradition take on a certain transcendental status in relation to everything that can become an element of a situation. Language and culture neither coincide with the formal world concepts by means of which participants in communication together define their situations, nor do they appear as something inner-worldly. Language and culture are constitutive for the lifeworld itself. They are neither one of the formal frames, that is, the worlds to which participants assign elements of situations, nor do they appear as something in the objective, social, or subjective worlds. In performing or understanding a speech act, participants are very much moving within their language, so that they cannot bring a present utterance *before themselves* as "something intersubjective," in the way they experience an event as something objective, encounter a pattern of behavior as something normative, experience or ascribe a desire or feeling as something subjective. The very medium of mutual understanding abides in a peculiar *half-transcendence*. So long as participants maintain their performative attitudes, the language actually in use remains *at their backs*. Speakers cannot take up an extramundane position in relation to it. The same is true of culture—of those patterns of interpretation transmitted in language. From a semantic point of view, language does have a peculiar affinity to linguistically articulated worldviews. Natural languages conserve the contents of tradition, which persist only in symbolic forms, for the most part in linguistic embodiment. For the semantic capacity of a language has to be adequate to the complexity of the stored-up cultural contents, the patterns of interpretation, valuation, and expression.

This stock of knowledge supplies members with unproblematic, common, background convictions that are assumed to be guaranteed; it is from these that contexts for processes of reaching understanding get shaped, processes in which those involved use tried and true situation definitions or negotiate new ones. Participants find the relations between the objective, social, and subjective world already preinterpreted. When they go beyond the horizon of a given situation, they cannot step into a void; they find themselves right away in another, now actualized, yet *preinterpreted* domain of what is culturally taken for granted. In everyday communicative practice there are no completely unfamiliar situations. Every new situation appears in a lifeworld composed of a cultural stock of knowledge that is "always already" familiar. Communicative actors can no more take up an extramundane position in relation to their lifeworld than they can in relation to language as the medium for the processes of reaching understanding through which their lifeworld maintains itself. In drawing upon a cultural tradition, they also continue it.

The category of the lifeworld has, then, a different status than the normal world-concepts dealt with above. Together with criticizable validity claims, these latter concepts form the frame or categorial scaffolding that serves to order problematic situations—that is, situations that need to be agreed upon—in a lifeworld that is already substantively interpreted. With the formal world-concepts, speakers and hearers can qualify the possible referents of their speech acts so that they can relate to something objective, normative, or subjective. The lifeworld, by contrast, does not allow for analogous assignments; speakers and hearers cannot refer by means of it to something as "something intersubjective." Communicative actors are always moving *within* the horizon of their lifeworld; they cannot step outside of it. As interpreters, they themselves belong to the lifeworld, along with their speech acts, but they cannot refer to "something in the lifeworld" in the same way as they can to facts, norms, or experiences. The structures of the lifeworld lay down the forms of the intersubjectivity of possible understanding. It is to them that participants in communication owe their extramundane positions vis-à-vis the innerworldly items about which they can come to an understanding. The lifeworld is, so to speak, the transcendental site where speaker and hearer meet, where they can reciprocally raise claims that their utterances fit the world (objective, social, or subjective), and where they can criticize and confirm those validity claims, settle their disagreements, and arrive at agreements. In a sentence: participants cannot assume *in actu* the same distance in relation to language and culture as in relation to the totality of facts, norms, or experiences concerning which mutual understanding is possible.

While the communication-theoretic concept of the lifeworld we have been discussing gets us away from the philosophy of consciousness, it nevertheless still lies on the same analytical level as the transcendental lifeworld concept of phenomenology. It is obtained by reconstructing the pretheoretical knowledge of competent speakers: from the perspective of participants the lifeworld appears as a horizon-forming context of processes of reaching understanding; in delimiting the domain of relevance for a given situation, this context remains itself withdrawn from thematization within that situation. The communication-theoretic concept of the lifeworld developed from the participant's perspective is not directly serviceable for theoretical purposes; it is not suited for demarcating an object domain of social science, that is, the region within the objective world formed by the totality of hermeneutically accessible, in the broadest sense historical or sociocultural facts. The *everyday concept of the lifeworld* is better suited for this purpose; it is by this means that communicative actors locate and date their utterances in social spaces and historical times. In the communicative practice of everyday life, persons do not only encounter one another in the attitude of participants; they also give narrative presentations of events that take place in the context of their lifeworld. *Narration* is a specialized form of constative speech that serves to describe sociocultural events and objects. Actors base their narrative presentations on a lay concept of the "world," in the sense of the everyday world or lifeworld, which defines the totality of states of affairs that can be reported in true stories.

This everyday concept carves out of the objective world the region of narratable events or historical facts. Narrative practice not only serves trivial needs for mutual understanding among members trying to coordinate their common tasks; it also has a function in the self-understanding of persons. They have to objectivate their belonging to the lifeworld to which, in their actual roles as participants in communication, they do belong. For they can develop personal identities only if they recognize that the sequences of their own actions form narratively presentable life histories; they can develop social identities only if they recognize that they maintain their membership in social groups by way of participating in interactions, and thus that they are caught up in the narratively presentable histories of collectivities. Collectivities maintain their identities only to the extent that the ideas members have of their lifeworld overlap sufficiently and condense into unproblematic background convictions.

The lay concept of the lifeworld refers to the totality of sociocultural facts and thus provides a jumping-off point for social theory. In my view, one methodologically promising way to clarify this concept would be to analyze the form of narrative statements, as Arthur Danto was one of the first to do,[7] and to analyze the form of narrative texts. In the grammar of narratives we can see how we identify and *describe* states and events that appear in a lifeworld; how we *interlink* and *sequentially organize* into complex unities members' interactions in social spaces and historical times; how we explain the actions of the individuals and the events that befall them, the acts of collectivities and the fates they meet with, from the perspective of managing situations. In adopting the narrative form, we are choosing a perspective that "grammatically" forces us to base our descriptions on an everyday concept of the lifeworld as a *cognitive reference system*.

This intuitively accessible *concept of the sociocultural lifeworld* can be rendered theoretically fruitful if we can develop from it a reference system for descriptions and explanations relevant to the lifeworld as a whole and not merely to occurrences within it. Whereas narrative presentation refers to what is innerworldly, theoretical presentation is intended to explain the reproduction of the lifeworld itself. Individuals and groups maintain themselves by mastering situations; but how is the lifeworld, of which each situation forms only a segment, maintained? A narrator is already constrained grammatically, through the form of narrative presentation, to take an interest in the identity of the persons acting as well as in the integrity of their life-context. When we tell stories, we cannot avoid also saying indirectly how the subjects involved in them are faring, and what fate the collectivity they belong to is experiencing. Nevertheless, we can make harm to personal identity or threats to social integration visible only indirectly in narratives. While narrative presentations do point to higher-level reproduction processes—to the maintenance imperatives of lifeworlds—they cannot take as their theme the structures of a lifeworld the way they do with what happens in it. The everyday concept of the lifeworld that we bring to narrative presentation as a reference system has to be worked up for theoretical purposes in such a way as to make possible statements about the reproduction or self-maintenance of communicatively structured lifeworlds.

Whereas the lifeworld is given from the *perspective of participants* only as the horizon-forming context of an action situation, the everyday concept of the lifeworld presupposed in the *perspective of narrators* is already being used for cognitive purposes. To make it theoretically fruitful we have to start from those basic functions that, as we learned from Mead, the medium of language fulfills for the reproduction of the lifeworld. In coming to an understanding with one another about their situation, participants in interaction stand in a cultural tradition that they at once use and renew; in coordinating their actions by way of intersubjectively recognizing criticizable validity claims, they are at once relying on membership in social groups and strengthening the integration of those same groups; through participating in interactions with competently acting reference persons, the growing child internalizes the value orientations of his social group and acquires generalized capacities for action.

Under the functional aspect of *mutual understanding*, communicative action serves to transmit and renew cultural kowledge; under the aspect of *coordinating action,* it serves social integration and the establishment of solidarity; finally, under the aspect of *socialization,* communicative action serves the formation of personal identities. The symbolic structures of the lifeworld are reproduced by way of the continuation of valid knowledge, stabilization of group solidarity, and socialization of responsible actors. The process of reproduction connects up new situations with the existing conditions of the lifeworld; it does this in the *semantic* dimension of meanings or contents (of the cultural tradition), as well as in the dimensions of *social space* (of socially integrated groups), and *historical time* (of successive generations). Corresponding to these processes of *cultural reproduction, social integration,* and *socialization* are the structural components of the lifeworld: culture, society, person.

I use the term *culture* for the stock of knowledge from which participants in communication supply themselves with interpretations as they come to an understanding about something in the world. I use the term *society* for the legitimate orders through which participants regulate their memberships in social groups and thereby secure solidarity. By *personality* I understand the competence that make a subject capable of speaking and acting, that put him in a position to take part in processes of reaching understanding and thereby to assert his own identity. The dimensions in which communicative action extends comprise the semantic field of symbolic contents, social space, and historical time. The interactions woven into the fabric of every communicative practice constitute the medium through which culture, society, and person get reproduced. These reproduction processes cover the symbolic structures of the lifeworld. We have to distinguish from this the maintenance of the material substratum of the lifeworld.

Material reproduction takes place through the medium of the purposive activity with which sociated individuals intervene in the world to realize their aims. As Weber pointed out, the problems that actors have to deal with in a given situation can be divided into problems of "inner need" and problems of "outer need." To these categories of tasks as viewed from the perspective of action, there correspond, when the matter is viewed from the perspective of lifeworld maintenance, processes of symbolic and material reproduction.

I would like now to examine how different approaches to interpretative sociology conceive of society as a lifeworld. The structural complexity of a lifeworld, as it has revealed itself to our communication-theoretical analysis, does not come into view along this path. Whenever "the lifeworld" has been made a fundamental concept of social theory—whether under this name, as in Husserl and his followers, or under the title of "forms of life," "cultures," "language communities," or whatever—the approach has remained selective; the strategies of concept formation usually connect up with only one of the three structural components of the lifeworld.

Even the communication-theoretical reading I gave to Schutz's analysis suggests a concept of the lifeworld limited to aspects of mutual understanding and abridged in a culturalistic fashion. On this model, participants actualize on any given occasion some of the background convictions drawn from the cultural stock of knowledge; the process of reaching understanding serves the negotiation of common situation definitions, and these must in turn meet the critical conditions of an agreement accepted as reasonable. Cultural knowledge, insofar as it flows into situation definitions, is thus exposed to a test: it has to prove itself "against the world," that is, against facts, norms, experiences. Any revisions have an indirect effect on nonthematized elements of knowledge internally connected with the problematic contents. From this view, communicative action presents itself as an interpretive mechanism through which cultural knowledge is reproduced. The reproduction of the lifeworld consists essentially in a continuation and renewal of tradition, which moves between the extremes of a mere reduplication of and a break with tradition. In the phenomenological tradition stemming from Husserl and Schutz, the social theory based on such a culturalistically abridged concept of the lifeworld, when it is consistent, issues in a *sociology of knowledge*. This is the case, for instance, with Peter Berger and Thomas Luckmann, who state the thesis of *The Social Construction of Reality* as follows: "The basic contentions of the argument of this book are implicit in its title and subtitle, namely, that reality is socially constructed and that the sociology of knowledge must analyze the processes in which this occurs." [8]

The one-sidedness of the culturalistic concept of the lifeworld becomes clear when we consider that communicative actions is not only a process of reaching understanding; in coming to an understanding about something in the world, actors are at the same time taking part in interactions through which they develop, confirm, and renew their memberships in social groups and their own identities. Communicative actions are not only processes of interpretation in which cultural knowledge is "tested against the world"; they are at the same time processes of social integration and of socialization. The lifeworld is "tested" in quite a different manner in these latter dimensions: these tests are not measured directly against the criticizable validity claims or standards of rationality, but against standards for the solidarity of members and for the identity of socialized individuals. While participants in interaction, turned "toward the world," reproduce through their accomplishment of mutual understanding the cultural knowledge upon which they draw, they simultaneously reproduce their memberships in collectivities and their identities. When one of these other aspects shifts into the foreground, the concept of the lifeworld is again given a one-sided formulation: it is narrowed down either in an *institutionalistic* or in a *sociopsychological* fashion.

In the tradition stemming from Durkheim, social theory is based on a concept of the lifeworld reduced to the aspect of social integration. Parsons chooses for this expression "societal community"; he understands by it the lifeworld of a social group. It forms the core of every society, where "society" is understood as the structural component that determines the status— the rights and duties—of group members by way of legitimately ordered interpersonal relations. Culture and personality are represented only as functional supplements of the 'societal community': culture supplies society with values that can be institutionalized, and socialized individuals contribute motivations that are appropriate to normed expectations.

By contrast, in the tradition stemming from Mead, social theory is based on a concept of the lifeworld reduced to the aspect of the socialization of individuals. Representatives of symbolic interactionism, such as Herbert

Blumer, A. M. Rose, Anselm Strauss, or R. H. Turner, conceive of the life-world as the sociocultural milieu of communicative action represented as role playing, role taking, role defining, and the like. Culture and society enter into consideration only as media for the self-formative processes in which actors are involved their whole lives long. It is only consistent when the theory of society shrinks down then to *social psychology.*[9]

If, by contrast, we take the concept of symbolic interaction that Mead himself made central and work it out in the manner suggested above—as a concept of linguistically mediated, normatively guided interaction—and thereby gain access to phenomenological lifeworld analyses, then we are in a position to get at the complex interconnection of all three reproduction processes.

The cultural reproduction of the lifeworld ensures that newly arising situations are connected up with existing conditions in the world in the semantic dimension: it secures a *continuity* of tradition and *coherence* of knowledge sufficient for daily practice. Continuity and coherence are measured by the *rationality* of the knowledge accepted as valid. This can be seen in disturbances of cultural reproduction that get manifested in a loss of meaning and lead to corresponding legitimation and orientation crises. In such cases, the actors' cultural stock of knowledge can no longer cover the need for mutual understanding that arises with new situations. The interpretive schemes accepted as valid fail, and the resource "meaning" becomes scarce.

The social integration of the lifeworld ensures that newly arising situations are connected up with existing conditions in the world in the dimension of social space: it takes care of coordinating actions by way of legitimately regulated interpersonal relations and stabilizes the identity of groups to an extent sufficient for everyday practice. The coordination of actions and the *stabilization of group identities* are measured by the *solidarity* among members. This can be seen in disturbances of social integration, which manifest themselves in *anomie* and corresponding conflicts. In such cases, actors can no longer cover the need for coordination that arises with new situations from the inventory of legitimate orders. Legitimately regulated social memberships are no longer sufficient, and the resource "social solidarity" becomes scarce.

Finally the socialization of the members of a lifeworld ensures that newly arising situations are connected up with existing situations in the world in the dimension of historical time: it secures for succeeding generations the acquisition of *generalized competences for action* and sees to it that *individual life histories are in harmony with collective forms of life.* Interactive capacities and styles of life are measured by the *responsibility of persons.* This can be seen in disturbances of the socialization process, which are manifested in psychopathologies and corresponding phenomena of alienation. In such cases, actors' competences do not suffice to maintain the intersubjectivity of commonly defined action situations. The personality system can preserve its identity only by means of defensive strategies that are detrimental to participating in social interaction on a realistic basis, so that the resource "ego strength" becomes scarce.

Once one has drawn these distinctions, a question arises concerning the contribution of the individual reproduction processes to maintaining the structural components of the lifeworld. If culture provides sufficient valid knowledge to cover the given need for mutual understanding in a lifeworld, the contributions of cultural reproduction to maintaining *the two other* components consist, on the one hand, in *legitimations* for existing institutions and, on the other hand, in *socialization patterns* for the acquisition of generalized competences for action. If society is sufficiently integrated to cover the given need for coordination in a lifeworld, the contribution of the integration process to maintaining *the two other* components consist, on the one hand, in *legitimately regulated social memberships* of individuals and, on the other, in moral duties or *obligations:* the central stock of cultural values institutionalized in legitimate orders is incorporated into a normative reality that is, if not criticism-proof, at least resistant to criticism and to this extent beyond the reach of continuous testing by action oriented to reaching understanding. If, finally, personality systems have developed such strong identities that they can deal on a realistic basis with the situations that come up in their lifeworld, the contribution of socialization processes to maintaining *the other two* components consists, on the one hand, in *interpretive accomplishments* and, on the other, in *motivations for actions that conform to norms* (see figure 1).

The individual reproduction processes can be evaluated according to standards of the *rationality of knowledge,* the *solidarity of members,* and the *responsibility of the adult personality.* Naturally, the measurements within each of these dimensions vary according to the degree of structural differentiation of the lifeworld. The degree of differentiation also determines how great the need for consensual knowledge, legitimate orders, and personal autonomy is at any given time. Disturbances in reproduction are manifested in their own proper domains of culture, society, and personality as loss of meaning, anomie, and mental illness (psychopathology). There are corresponding manifestations of deprivation in the other domains (see figure 2).

On this basis we can specify the functions that communicative action takes on in the reproduction of the lifeworld (see figure 3). The highlighted areas along the diagonal in figure 3 contain the characterizations with which we first demarcated cultural reproduction, social integration, and socialization from one another. In the meantime we have seen that *each* of these reproduction processes contributes in maintaining *all* the components of the lifeworld. Thus we can attribute to the medium of language, through which the structures of the lifeworld are reproduced, the functions set forth in figure 3.

With these schematically summarized specifications, our communication-theoretical concept of the lifeworld has not yet attained the degree of explication of its phenomenological counterpart. Nonetheless, I shall leave it

Structural components / Reproduction processes	Culture	Society	Personality
Cultural reproduction	Interpretative schemes fit for consensus ("valid knowledge")	Legitimations	Socialization patterns Educational goals
Social integration	Obligations	Legitimately ordered interpersonal relations	Social memberships
Socialization	Interpretive accomplishments	Motivations for actions that conform to norms	Interactive capabilities ("personal identity")

FIGURE I.   Contributions of Reproduction Processes to Maintaining the Structural Components of the Lifeworld

with this outline to return to the question of whether the concept of the lifeworld proposed here is fit to serve as a basic concept of social theory. Despite his many reservations, Schutz continued to hold to the approach of transcendental phenomenology. If one considers the method developed by Husserl to be unobjectionable, the claim to universality of lifeworld analysis carried out phenomenologically goes without saying. However, once we introduce the concept of the lifeworld in communication-theoretical terms, the idea of approaching any society whatsoever by means of it is not at all trivial. The burden of truth for the universal validity of the lifeworld concept—a validity reaching across cultures and epochs—shifts then to the complementary concept of communication action.

Mead attempted to reconstruct a sequence of stages of forms of interaction for the transition from the animal to the human. According to this

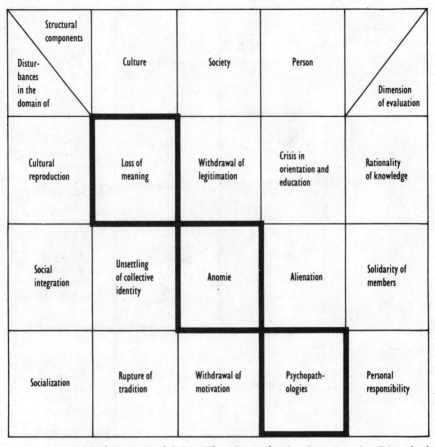

Structural components / Disturbances in the domain of	Culture	Society	Person	Dimension of evaluation
Cultural reproduction	Loss of meaning	Withdrawal of legitimation	Crisis in orientation and education	Rationality of knowledge
Social integration	Unsettling of collective identity	Anomie	Alienation	Solidarity of members
Socialization	Rupture of tradition	Withdrawal of motivation	Psychopath-ologies	Personal responsibility

FIGURE 2.   Manifestations of Crisis When Reproduction Processes Are Disturbed (Pathologies)

reconstruction, communicative action is anthropologically fundamental; there are empirical reasons—and not merely methodological prejudgements—for the view that the structures of linguistically mediated, normatively guided interaction determine the starting point of sociocultural development. This also determines the range within which historical lifeworlds can vary. Questions of *developmental dynamics* cannot, of course, be answered by identifying structural restrictions of this sort. They can be dealt with only if we take contingent boundary conditions into account and analyze the interdependence between sociocultural transformations and changes in material reproduction. Nevertheless, the fact that sociocultural developments are subject to the structural constraints of communicative action can have a systematic effect. We can speak of a developmental logic—in the sense of the tradition stemming from Piaget, a sense that calls for

Structural components / Reproduction processes	Culture	Society	Person
Cultural reproduction	Transmission, critique, acquisition of cultural knowledge	Renewal of knowledge effective for legitimation	Reproduction of knowledge relevant to child rearing, education
Social integration	Immunization of a central stock of value orientations	Coordination of actions via intersubjectively recognized validity claims	Reproduction of patterns of social membership
Socialization	Enculturation	Internalization of values	Formation of identity

FIGURE 3. Reproductive Functions of Action Oriented to Mutual Understanding

further clarification—if the structures of historical lifeworlds vary within the scope defined by the structural constraints of communicative action not accidentally but directionally, that is, in dependence on learning processes. For instance, there would be a *directional variation of lifeworld structures* if we could bring evolutionary changes under the description of a structural differentiation between cultures, society, and personality. One would have to postulate learning processes for such a structural differentiation of the lifeworld if one could show that this meant an increase in rationality.

The idea of the linguistification of the sacred has served us as a guiding thread for basing an interpretation of this sort on Mead and Durkheim. We can now reformulate this idea as follows: the further the structural components of the lifeworld and the processes that contribute the maintaining them get differentiated, the more interaction contexts come under conditions of rationally motivated mutual understanding, that is, of consensus formation that rests *in the end* on the authority of the better argument. Up to this point, we have considered Mead's utopian projection of a universal discourse in the special form of a communication community that allows for both self-realization and moral argumentation. Behind this, however, stands the more general idea of a situation in which the reproduction of the lifeworld is no longer merely routed *through* the medium of communicative action, but is saddled *upon* the interpretative accomplishments of the actors themselves. Universal discourse points to an idealized lifeworld reproduced through processes of mutual understanding that have been largely detached from normative contexts and transferred over to rationally motivated yes/no positions. This sort of growing autonomy can come to pass only to the extent that the constraints of material reproduction no longer hide behind the mask of a rationally impenetrable, basic, normative consensus, that is to say, behind the authority of the sacred. A lifeworld rationalized in this sense would by no means reproduce itself in conflict-free forms. But the conflicts would appear in their own names; they would no longer be concealed by convictions immune from discursive examination. Such a lifeworld would gain a singular transparence, inasmuch as it would allow only for situations in which adult actors distinguished between success-oriented and understanding-oriented actions just as clearly as between empirically motivated attitudes and rationally motivated yes/no positions.

The—rather rough—historical reference points that Mead and Durkheim cite in support of a rationalization of the lifeworld can be systematized under three perspectives: (*a*) structural differentiation of the lifeworld, (*b*) separation of form and content, and (*c*) growing reflexivity of symbolic reproduction.

(*ad a*) In the relation of culture to society, structural differentiation is to be found in the gradual uncoupling of the institutional system from worldviews; in the relation of personality to society, it is evinced in the extension of the scope of contingency for establishing interpersonal relationships; and in the relation of culture to personality, it is manifested in the fact that the renewal of traditions depends more and more on individuals' readiness to criticize and their ability to innovate. The vanishing point of these evolutionary trends are: for culture, a state in which traditions that have become reflective and then set aflow undergo continuous revision; for society, a state in which legitimate orders are dependent upon formal procedures for positing and justifying norms; and for personality, a state in which a highly abstract ego-identity is continuously stabilized through self-steering. These trends can establish themselves only insofar as the yes/no decisions that carry everyday communicative practice no longer go *back* to an ascribed normative consensus, but issue *from* the cooperative interpretation processes of participants themselves. Thus they signal a release of the rationality potential inherent in communicative action.

(*ad b*) Corresponding to the differentiation of culture, society, and personality, there is a differentiation of form and content. *On the cultural level,* the core, identity-securing traditions separate off from the concrete contents with which they are still tightly interwoven in mythical worldviews. They shrink to formal elements such as world-concepts, communication presuppositions, argumentation procedures, abstract basic values, and the like. *At the level of society*, general principles and procedures crystallize out of the particular contexts to which they are tied in primitive societies. In modern societies, principles of legal order and of morality are established which are less and less tailored to concrete forms of life. *On the level of the personality system*, the cognitive structures acquired in the socialization process are increasingly detached from the content of cultural knowledge with which they were at first integrated in "concrete thinking." The objects in connection with which formal competences can be exercised become increasingly variable.

(*ad c*) To the structural differentiation of the lifeworld, there corresponds finally a functional specification of various reproduction processes. In modern societies, action systems take shape in which specialized tasks of cultural transmission, social integration, and child rearing are dealt with professionally. Weber emphasized the evolutionary significance of *cultural systems of action* (for science, law, and art). Mead and Durkheim further stress the evolutionary significance of democracy: democratic forms of political will-formation are not only the result of a power shift in favor of the carrier strata of the capitalist economic system; *forms of discursive will-formation* are established in them. And these affect the quasi naturalness of traditionally legitimated domination in a similar way, even as modern natural science, jurisprudence with specialized training, and autonomous art break down the quasi naturalness of ecclesiastical traditions. But the rationalization of the lifeworld does not cover only the areas of cultural reproduction and social integration; among the classical thinkers we have considered, Durkheim occupied himself with parallel developments in the area of socialization. Since the eighteenth century, there has been an increasingly pedagogical approach to child-rearing processes, which has made possible a formal system of education free from the imperative mandates of church and family. Formal education today reaches into early childhood socialization. As in the case of cultural systems of action and political processes of will-formation that have been converted to discursive forms, the formalization of education means not only a professional treatment of the symbolic reproduction of the lifeworld, but its *reflective refraction* as well.

Naturally, the progressive rationalization of the lifeworld, as it is described under different aspects by Weber, Mead, and Durkheim, does not at all guarantee that processes of reproduction will be free of disturbances. It is only the level at which disturbances can appear that shifts with the degree of rationalization. As his theses concerning the loss of meaning and freedom indicate, Weber geared his theory of rationalization precisely to diagnosing negative developments. In Mead we find echoes of a critique of instrumental reason,[10] though his studies in the theory of communication are primarily concerned with the orthogenesis of contemporary societies. Their pathogenesis was the stated target of Durkheim's theory of the division of labor. However, he was not able to connect the changing forms of social integration with stages of system differentiation so clearly as to be able to explain the "anomic division of labor," that is, the modern forms of anomie. If we understand the conflicts that Durkheim attributed to social disintegration more generally than he did, that is, as disturbances of reproduction in structurally quite differentiated lifeworlds, "organic solidarity" represents the normal form of social integration in a rationalized lifeworld. It lies on the plane of the symbolic structures of the lifeworld, as do the "abnormal forms" to which Durkheim dedicated book 3 of *The Division of Labor in Society.*

The systemic mechanisms that Durkheim introduced under the rubric of "the division of labor" lie at another level. This raises the possibility of treating modern forms of anomie in connection with the question of how processes of system differentiation affect the lifeworld and possibly cause disturbances of its symbolic reproduction. In this way, phenomena of reification can also be analyzed along the lines of lifeworld deformations. The counter-Enlightenment that set in immediately after the French Revolution grounded a critique of modernity that has since branched off in different directions.[11] Their common denominator is the conviction that loss of meaning, anomie, and alienation—the pathologies of bourgeois society, indeed of posttraditional society generally—can be traced back to the rationalization of the lifeworld itself. This backward-looking critique is in essence a critique of bourgeois culture. By contrast, the Marxist critique of bourgeois society is aimed first at the relations of production, for it accepts the rationalization of the lifeworld and explains its deformation by the conditions of material reproduction. This materialist approach to disturbances in the symbolic reproduction of the lifeworld requires a theory that operates on a broader conceptual basis than that of "the lifeworld." It has to opt for a theoretical strategy that neither identifies the lifeworld with society as a whole, nor reduces it to a systemic nexus.

My guiding idea is that, on the one hand, the dynamics of development are steered by imperatives issuing from problems of self-maintenance, that is, problems of materially reproducing the lifeworld; but that, on the other hand, this societal development draws upon structural *possibilities* and is subject to structural *limitations* that, with the rationalization of the lifeworld, undergo systematic change in dependence upon corresponding learning processes. Thus the systems-theoretical perspective is relativized by the fact that the rationalization of the lifeworld leads to a directional variation of the structural patterns defining the maintenance of the system.

A *verstehende* sociology that allows society to be wholly absorbed into the lifeworld ties itself to the perspective of self-interpretation of the culture under investigation; this internal perspective screens out everything that inconspicuously affects a sociocultural lifeworld from the outside. In particular, theoretical approaches set out from a culturalistic concept of the lifeworld get entangled in the fallacies of "hermeneutic idealism," as Albrecht Wellmer has called it. The other side of this is a methodological descriptivism that denies itself the justified explanatory claims of theory formation in the social sciences.[12] This is true, about all, of the phenomenological, linguistic, and ethnomethodological variants of interpretive sociology, which as a rule do not get beyond reformulations of a more or less trivial everyday knowledge.

From the internal perspective of the lifeworld, society is represented as a network of communicatively mediated cooperation, with strategic relations and ruptures inserted into it. This is not to say that every contingency, every unintended consequence, every unsuccessful coordination, every conflict is expunged from this view. Nevertheless, what binds sociated individuals to one another and secures the integration of society is a web of communicative actions that thrives only in the light of cultural traditions, and not systemic mechanisms that are out of the reach of a member's intuitive knowledge. The lifeworld that members construct from common cultural traditions is coextensive with society. It draws all societal processes into the searchlight of cooperative processes of interpretation. It lends to everything that happens in society the transparency of something about which one can speak—even if one does not (yet) understand it. When we conceive of society in this way, we are accepting three fictions. We are presupposing (a) the autonomy of actors, (b) the independence of culture, and (c) the transparency of communication. These three fictions are built into the grammar of narratives and turn up again in a culturalistically one-sided, interpretive sociology.

(ad a) As members of a sociocultural lifeworld, actors satisfy in principle the presuppositions for responsible participation and communication. Responsibility means here that they can orient themselves to criticizable validity claims. It does not follow from this fiction that the web of interactions extending across social spaces and historical times can be explained solely by the intentions and decisions of those involved. Actors never have their action situations totally under control. They control neither the possibilities for mutual understanding and conflict, nor the consequences and side effects of their actions; they are, to borrow a phrase from W. Schapp, "entangled" in their (hi)stories.[13] A given setting presents a situation in which they orient themselves and which they seek to master, according to their insights and opinions. If society consists only of relations entered into by subjects acting autonomously, we get the picture of a process of sociation that takes place with the will and consciousness of adult members.

(ad b) The concept of the lifeworld also suggests that culture is independent from external constraints. The imperative force of culture rests on the convictions of the actors who draw upon, test, and further develop transmitted schemes of interpretation, valuation, and expression. From the perspective of subjects who are acting communicatively, no *alien* authority can be hiding behind cultural symbolism. In the situation of action, the lifeworld forms a horizon behind which we cannot go; it is a totality with no reverse side. Accordingly, it is strictly meaningless for members of a sociocultural lifeworld to inquire whether the culture in whose light they deal with external nature, society, and internal nature is empirically dependent on anything *else.*

(*ad c*) Finally, participants in communication encounter one another in a horizon of unrestricted possibilities of mutual understanding. What is represented at a methodological level as hermeneutics' claim to universality, merely reflects the self-understanding of lay persons who are acting with an orientation to mutual understanding. They have to assume that they could, in principle, arrive at an understanding about anything and everything.

As long as they maintain a performative attitude, communicative actors cannot reckon with a systematic distortion of their communication, that is, with resistances built into the linguistic structure itself and inconspicuously restricting the scope of communication. This does not exclude a fallibilistic consciousness. Members know that they can err, but even a consensus that *subsequently* proves to be deceptive rests to start with on uncoerced recognition of criticizable validity claims. From the internal perspective of participants of a sociocultural lifeworld, there can be no pseudoconsensus in the sense of convictions brought about by force; in a basically transparent process of reaching understanding—which is transparent for the participants themselves—no force can gain a footing.

These three fictions become apparent when we drop the identification of society with the lifeworld. They are convincing only so long as we assume that the integration of society can take place *only* on the premises of communicative action—leaving space, of course, for the alternative of acting strategically when consensus breaks down. This is the way things look to the members of a sociocultural lifeworld themselves. In fact, however, their goal-directed actions are coordinated not only through processes of reaching understanding, but also through functional interconnections that are not intended by them and are usually not even perceived within the horizon of everyday practice. In capitalist societies the market is the most important example of a norm-free regulation of cooperative contexts. The market is one of those systemic mechanisms that stabilize nonintended interconnections of action by way of functionally intermeshing action *consequences,* whereas the mechanism of mutual understanding harmonizes the action *orientations* of participants. Thus I have proposed that we distinguish between *social integration and system integration:* the former attaches to action orientations, while the latter reaches right through them. In one case the action system is integrated through consensus, whether normatively guaranteed or communicatively achieved; in the other case it is integrated through the nonnormative steering of individual decisions not subjectively coordinated.

If we understand the integration of society as exclusively *social integration,* we are opting for a conceptual strategy that, as we have seen, starts from communicative action and construes society as a lifeworld. It ties social-scientific analysis to the internal perspective of members of social groups and commits the investigator to hermeneutically connect up his own understanding with that of the participants. The reproduction of society then appears to be the maintenance of the symbolic structures of the lifeworld. Problems of material reproduction are not simply filtered out of this perspective; maintenance of the material substratum of the lifeworld is a necessary condition for maintaining its symbolic structures. But processes of material reproduction come into view only from the perspective of acting subjects who are dealing with situations in a goal-directed manner; what gets filtered out are all the counterintuitive aspects of the nexus of societal reproduction. This limitation suggests an immanent critique of the hermeneutic idealism of interpretive sociology.

If, on the other hand, we understand the integration of society exclusively as *system integration*, we are opting for a conceptual strategy that presents society after the model of a self-regulating system. It ties social-scientific analysis to the external perspective of an observer and poses the problem of interpreting the concept of a system in such a way that it can be applied to interconnections of action. For now I want only to note that action systems are considered to be a special case of living systems. Living systems are understood as open systems, which maintain themselves vis-à-vis an unstable and hypercomplex environment through interchange processes across their boundaries. States of the system are viewed as fulfilling functions with respect to its maintenance.[14]

However, the conceptualization of societies cannot be so smoothly linked with that of organic systems, for, unlike structural patterns in biology, the structural patterns of action systems are not accessible to purely external observation; they have to be gotten at hermeneutically, that is, from the internal perspective of participants. The entities that are to be subsumed under systems-theoretical concepts from the external perspective of an observer must be identified beforehand as the lifeworlds of social groups and understood in their symbolic structures. The inner logic of the symbolic reproduction of the lifeworld, which we discussed from the standpoints of cultural reproduction, social integration, and socialization, results in *internal limitations* on the reproduction of the societies we view from the outside as boundary-maintaining systems. Because they are structures of a lifeworld, the structures important for the maintenance of a social system, those with which the identity of a society stands or falls, are accessible only to a reconstructive analysis that begins with the members' intuitive knowledge.

The fundamental problem of social theory is how to connect in a satisfactory way the two conceptual strategies indicated by the notions of "system" and "lifeworld". I shall leave this to one side for now and take it up again in the context of discussing Parsons's work. Until then, we shall have to be content with a provisional concept of society as a system that has to fulfill conditions for the maintenance of sociocultural lifeworlds. The formula—societies are *systemically stabilized* complexes of action of *socially integrated* groups—certainly requires more detailed explanation; for the present, it may stand for the heuristic proposal that we view society as an entity that, in the course of social evolution, gets differentiated both as a system and as a lifeworld. Systemic evolution is measured by the increase in a society's steering capacity,[15] whereas the state of development of a symbolically structured lifeworld is indicated by the separation of culture, society, and personality.

Chapter Nine
THE UNCOUPLING OF SYSTEM AND LIFEWORLD

The provisional concept of society proposed here is radically different in one respect from the Parsonian concept: the mature Parsons reinterpreted the structural components of the lifeworld—culture, society, personality—as action systems constituting environments for one another. Without much ado, he subsumed the concept of the lifeworld gained from an action-theoretical perspective under systems-theoretical concepts. As we shall see below, the structural components of the lifeworld become subsystems of a general system of action, to which the physical substratum of the lifeworld is reckoned along with the "behavior system." The proposal I am advancing here, by contrast, attempts to take into account the methodological differences between the internalist and the externalist viewpoints connected with the two conceptual strategies.

From the participant perspective of members of a lifeworld it looks as if sociology with a systems-theoretical orientation considers only one of the three components of the lifeworld, namely, the institutional system, for which culture and personality merely constitute complementary environments. From the observer perspective of systems theory, on the other hand, it looks as if lifeworld analysis confines itself to one societal subsystem specialized in maintaining structural patterns (pattern maintenance); in this view, the components of the lifeworld are merely internal differentiations of this subsystem which specifies the parameters of societal self-maintenance. It is already evident on methodological grounds that a systems theory of society cannot be self-sufficient. The structures of the lifeworld, with their own inner logic placing internal constraints on system maintenance, have to be gotten at by a hermeneutic approach that picks up on members' pretheoretical knowledge. Furthermore, the objective conditions under which the systems-theoretical objectification of the lifeworld becomes necessary have themselves only arisen in the course of social evolution. And this calls for a type of explanation that does not already move within the system perspective.

I understand social evolution as a second-order process of differentiation: system and lifeworld are differentiated in the sense that the complexity of the one and the rationality of the other grow. But it is not only qua system and qua lifeworld that they are differentiated; they get differentiated from one another at the same time. It has become conventional for sociologists to distinguish the stages of social evolution as tribal societies, traditional societies, or societies organized around a state, and modern societies (where the economic system has been differentiated out). From the system perspective, these stages are marked by the appearance of new systemic mechanisms and corresponding levels of complexity. On this plane of analysis, the uncoupling of system and lifeworld is depicted in such a way that the lifeworld, which is at first coextensive with a scarcely differentiated social system, gets cut down more and more to one subsystem among others. In the process, system mechanisms get further and further detached from the social structures through which social integration takes place. As we shall see, modern societies attain a level of system differentiation at which increasingly autonomous organizations are connected with one another via delinguistified media of communication: these systemic mechanisms—for example, money—steer a social intercourse that has been largely disconnected from norms and values, above all in those subsystems of purposive rational economic and administrative action that, on Weber's diagnosis, have become independent of their moral-political foundations.

At the same time, the lifeworld remains the subsystem that defines the pattern of the social system as a whole. Thus, systemic mechanisms need to be anchored in the lifeworld: they have to be institutionalized. This institutionalization of new levels of system differentiation can also be perceived from the internal perspective of the lifeworld. Whereas system differentiation in tribal societies only leads to the increasing complexity of pregiven kinship systems, at higher levels of integration new social structures take shape, namely, the state and media-steered subsystems. In societies with a low degree of differentiation, systemic interconnections are tightly interwoven with mechanisms of social integration; in modern societies they are consolidated and objectified into norm-free structures. Members behave toward formally organized action systems, steered via processes of exchange and power, as toward a block of quasi-natural reality; within these media-steered subsystems society congeals into a second nature. Actors have always been able to sheer off from an orientation to mutual understanding, adopt a strategic attitude, and objectify normative contexts into something in the objective world, but in modern societies, economic and bureaucratic spheres emerge in which social relations are regulated only via money and power. Norm-conformative attitudes and identity-forming social memberships are neither necessary nor possible in these spheres; they are made peripheral instead.

Niklas Luhmann distinguishes three levels of integration or of system differentiation: the level of simple interactions between present actors; the level of organizations constituted through voluntary and disposable memberships; and finally the level of society in general, encompassing all the interactions reachable, or potentially accessible, in social spaces and historical times.[1] Simple interactions, organizations that have become autonomous and are linked via media, and society form an evolutionarily developed hierarchy of action systems nesting inside one another; this replaces Parsons' conception of a general system of action. It is interesting to note that Luhmann is here reacting to the phenomenon of the uncoupling of system and lifeworld as it presents itself from the perspective of the lifeworld. Systemic interconnections that have consolidated in modern societies into an organizational reality appear as an objectified segment of society, assimilated to external nature, which thrusts itself between given action situations and their lifeworld horizon. Luhmann hypostatizes this lifeworld—which is now pushed back behind media-steered subsystems and is no longer directly connected to action situations, but merely forms the background for formally organized interactions—into "society."

The uncoupling of system and lifeworld cannot be conceived as a *second-order* differentiation process so long as we stick either to the system perspective or to the lifeworld perspective instead of transforming each into the other. I will, therefore, analyze the connections that obtain between the increasing complexity of the system and the rationalization of the lifeworld. I will view tribal societies (A) first as sociocultural lifeworlds and then (B) as self-maintaining systems, in order to show that system integration and social integration are still tightly interwoven at this level of development. Then I will (C) describe four mechanisms that successively take the lead in social evolution, in each case bringing about a new level of differentiation or, in Durkheim's phrase, of the "division of labor." Every new level of system differentiation requires a change in the institutional basis; it is (D) the evolution of law and morality that plays the role of pacemaker in this transformation. The rationalization of the lifeworld can be understood (E) in terms of successive releases of the potential for rationality in communicative action. Action oriented to mutual understanding gains more and more independence from normative contexts. At the same time, ever greater demands are made upon this basic medium of everyday language; it gets overloaded in the end and replaced by delinguistified media. When this tendency toward an uncoupling of system and lifeworld is (F) depicted on the level of a systematic history of forms of mutual understanding, the irresistible irony of the world-historical process of enlightenment becomes evident: the rationalization of the lifeworld makes possible a heightening of systemic complexity, which becomes so hypertrophied that it unleashes system imperatives that burst the capacity of the lifeworld they instrumentalize.

A.—The lifeworld concept of society finds its strongest empirical foothold in archaic societies, where structures of linguistically mediated, normatively guided interaction immediately constitute the supporting social structures. The small, prestate societies, which have been studied above all by English social anthropologists in Africa, Southeast Asia, and Australia, differ from Durkheim's ideal type of an almost homogeneous, and nearly ultrastable, primitive society by their comparatively greater complexity and their surprising social dynamism.[2] Residual tribal societies do, however, resemble Durkheim's picture of *segmental* societies with a pronounced collective consciousness. This is why Thomas Luckmann can base his sociological generalizations concerning archaic societies on the concept of the lifeworld without doing violence to the empirical material. In the words of K. Gabriel, Luckmann's ideal-typical sketch "seeks to establish a high degree of congruence in the relations between institutions, worldviews, and persons. As socially objectivated, worldviews are at the same time close to persons. They integrate institutional orders into unities of meaning and at the same time furnish individual biographies with a situation-transcending context of meaning. There is a high degree of correspondence between socially objectivated structures of meaning and the relevance structures of personal biographies. Worldviews are spread over the social structure as a whole and yet are tightly bound up with daily routines. Institutionally stamped patterns of action and their interpretations . . . have their correlate in the construction of subjective relevance structures and their integration into the meaning contexts of personal identities. In turn, the institutionally stabilized worldviews gain in plausibility."[3]

Durkheim's stated views can be smoothly transposed into the model of the lifeworld so long as the supporting structures of society remain intuitively accessible in principle from the action perspectives of adult members of the tribe. This will be the case as long as the social structures do not transcend the horizon of simple interactions interwoven over comprehensible social spaces and relatively short periods (defined by a few generations). It must be possible, naturally, for various interactions to take place simultaneously in different places, with varying participants and themes. Nonetheless, all the interactions that are structurally possible in such a society are enacted within the context of a *commonly* experienced social world. Despite a differential distribution of cultural knowledge, which is already administered by specialists, the universe of possible events and initiatives is well circumscribed spatiotemporally and thematically; thus the collectively available situation interpretations are stored by all participants similarly and can be narratively called upon when needed. Tribal members can still orient their actions *simultaneously* to the present action situation and to expected communications with those not present. A society of this type, which in a certain sense merges into the dimension of the lifeworld, is omnipresent; to put this another way: it reproduces itself as a whole in every single interaction.

This sketch of a collectively shared, homogeneous lifeworld is certainly an idealization, but archaic societies more or less approximate this ideal type by virtue of the kinship structures of society and the mythical structures of consciousness. The *kinship system* is composed of families ordered according to relations of legitimate descent. As a rule, domestic groups form the core, that is, groups composed of parents and children living together in the same place. New families arise through marriage. Marriage has the function of securing for the newborn an identifiable place in the society, an unambiguous status, by way of assignment to socially recognized parents. Status means here one's position within a group formed along the lines of legitimate descent. How these lineages or descent groups get formed depends upon the principles according to which lines of descent are constructed. Descent groups constitute the reference system for the rules of marriage. These are basically exogamous, which is to say, they guarantee that women are exchanged between families of different descent. The rules of marriage vary on the common basis of a prohibition of incest, which covers sexual intercourse between parent and child as well as between siblings.

The system of kinship relations forms something like a total institution. *Social memberships* are defined via these relations, and role differentiations are possible only within the kinship dimensions of sex, generation, and descent. The calculus of kinship relations also defines the *boundary of the social unit*. It divides the lifeworld into areas of interaction with those who are kin and those who are not. This side of the boundary, one is obligated in one's behavior to honesty, loyalty, and mutual support—in short, to act with an orientation toward mutual understanding. The principle of "amity" that M. Fortes introduces in this context can be understood as a metanorm that obliges one to satisfy the presuppositions of communicative action in dealing with one's kin. This does not exclude rivalries, altercations, and latent hostilities, but it normally does exclude manifestly strategic action:

Two of the commonest discriminating indices are the locus of prohibited or prescribed marriage, and the control of strife that might cause bloodshed. Kinship, amity, the regulation of marriage and the restriction of serious fighting form a syndrome. Where kinship is demonstrable or assumed, regardless of its grounds, there amity must prevail and this posits prescription, more commonly proscription, of marriage and ban on serious strife. Conversely, where amity is the rule in the relations of clans or tribes or communities, there kinship or quasi-kinship by myth or ritual allegiance, or by such institutions as the East African joking relationships, is invoked and the kind of fighting that smacks of war is outlawed. By contrast, non-kin, whether or not they are territorially close or distant, and regardless of the social and cultural affinities of the parties, are very commonly identified as being outside the range of prescriptive altruism and therefore marriageable as well as potentially hostile to the point of serious fighting (or, nowadays, litigation) in a dispute. It is as if marriage and warfare are thought of as two aspects of a single constellation, the direct contrary of which is kinship and amity.[4]

On the other hand, the boundary generated by the calculus of kinship relations has to be porous, since small tribes can practice exogamy only under the condition that kinship relations can also be established with alien tribes—we marry those with whom we fight, say the Tallensi:[5] "Different communities, even those of different tribal or linguistic provenance, can exchange personnel by marriage, and can fuse for particular ceremonial occasions by, so to speak, intermeshing their kinship fields. It seems, therefore, that the view that an Australian *community* or *society* is a closed system is in part illusory. It is the kinship calculus that is closed—by its very nature, one might argue—not any community, as such. It is the kinship calculus which, by reason of its exact limitation of range, serves as the basic boundary-setting mechanism for the field of social relations that is at one and the same time the maximum kinship field and the maximum politico-jural field for a specified group." [6]

The lines of legitimate descent and the dictates of exogamy together ensure that there is a clear boundary, not necessarily tied to territories, and that this boundary remains flexible and porous. Boundaries marked out on the level of interaction can remain porous because *mythical worldviews* make it difficult to draw unambiguous social boundaries. As we have seen, mythical interpretive systems assimilate external and internal nature to the social order, natural phenomena to interpersonal relations, events to communicative utterances. On the one hand, the sociocultural lifeworld flows together with the world as a whole and takes on the form of an objective world order; on the other hand, no state, no event, no person is too alien to be drawn into the universal nexus of interactions and transformed into something familiar. In the framework of mythical worldviews, there is no categorical distinction between society and its natural surroundings. [7] Thus there can be no social groups so alien that they could not connect up with a given kinship system.

The norms of the kinship system draw their binding power from their religious foundations. The members of the tribe are thus always a *cultic community*. In tribal societies the validity of social norms has to be maintained without recourse to a state's power of sanction. Social control requires a cultically anchored, religious grounding: violations of central norms of the kinship system count as sacrilege. The place of the missing external sanctions is taken by a mythical worldview that immobilizes the potential of speech for negation and innovation, at least in the domain of the sacred.

I have already indicated how mythical worldviews blur the categorical distinctions between the objective, social, and subjective worlds, and how they do not even draw a clear line between interpretations and the interpreted reality. Internal relations among meanings are fused with external relations among things. There is no concept of the nonempirical validity that we ascribe to symbolic expressions. Concepts of validity such as morality and truth are merged with empirical concepts such as causality and health. To the extent that the mythical understanding of the world actually steers action orientation, action oriented to mutual understanding and action oriented to success cannot yet be separated, and a participant's no cannot yet signify the critical rejection of a validity claim. Myth binds the critical potential of communicative action, stops up, so to speak, the source of inner contingencies springing from communication itself. The scope for innovatively intervening in cultural tradition is relatively narrow; culture is orally transmitted and enters into habitual practices almost without much distance. It is still scarcely possible to distinguish between an identity-securing core of tradition and a periphery open to revision; nearly all of the elements of myth support the identity of the tribe and that of its members.

This pronounced homogeneity of the lifeworld should not blind us to the fact that the social structure of tribal societies already provides a relatively large scope for differentiation.[8] Sex, age, descent are the dimensions in which roles are differentiated. Naturally, these are not yet consolidated into professional roles. In small societies with a simple technology, or more generally with a low level of productive forces, the division of labor does not yet rest on specialized skills exercised over an entire lifetime. In general, men engage in activities that take them away from the home and call for physical strength—warfare, hunting, tending the livestock, deep-sea fishing, overseas trade, and the like—whereas women are responsible for working around the home and the garden, and often in the fields as well. There is a corresponding division of labor among the generations: as soon as they can walk, children are taught to do things around the house and yard, whereas the elderly—above all, the old men—take on the "political" (in the broadest sense) tasks. Incentives for differentiating the social structure come first and foremost from the domain of material reproduction.

Social systems regulate their exchanges with their social and natural environments by way of coordinated interventions into the external world. Looked at from *the member's perspective,* this is a matter of maintaining the material substratum of the lifeworld, that is, of producing and distributing goods, of performing military tasks, of settling internal conflicts, and so on. Performance of these tasks calls for cooperation; they can be dealt with more or less economically, more or less effectively. Even simple tasks like preparing for festivities or building a canoe require that the complex activities of different persons be expediently coordinated and that demands be made upon the goods and services of other people. To the extent that *economy of effort* and *efficacy of means* serve as intuitive standards for the successful resolution of such tasks, there are incentives for a *functional specification of activities* with a corresponding *differentiation of their results* or products. In other words, there is a premium on adapting simple action systems to the conditions of *cooperation based on a division of labor.* There are inducements to regulate interaction in such a way that specialized activities can be *authoritatively joined together* and their different results (or products) *exchanged.* The authoritative combination of specialized performances requires delegating the authority to direct, or *power,* to persons who take on the tasks of organization;[9] the functional exchange of products calls for the establishment of *exchange relations.* Thus a progressive division of labor is to be expected only in action systems that make provision for *institutionalizing organizational power and exchange relations.*

When we view a society's interchanges with its social and natural environments from the *system perspective,* we drop the action-theoretical presupposition that a combination of activities on the basis of a division of labor, which enhances the social system's capacity for adaptation and goal attainment, has to be *intended* by all or by some of those involved. What appears from the perspective of participants to be a task-induced division of labor, presents itself from the system perspective as an increase in societal complexity. The adaptive capacity of an action system is measured only by what the aggregate effects of actions contribute to maintaining a system in a given environment; it matters not whether the objective purposiveness of the action consequences can be traced back to purposes of the subjects involved or not. From systemic points of view as well, *power* and *exchange relations* are the dimensions in which action systems adapt themselves to the requirements of the functional specifications of social cooperation. These are, at any rate, the two dimensions we come across in looking for the mechanisms with which tribal societies can expand their complexity within the range for structural variation set by kinship relations.

B.—Relatively small family groups working with simple technologies can increase their complexity either by becoming internally differentiated or by combining themselves into larger social units. Since these groups have *similar structures* and produce *similar products,* exchange between them cannot be economically motivated in the first instance. Rather, there must be some normative constraint that prevents autarky, that is, self-satisfaction through the consumption of their own goods and services, and calls for exchanging even products whose use values would not make this necessary. Exogamous marriage satisfies this condition. Built into the principle of kinship organization, it can be understood as a norm that requires an exchange of marriageable women. The bilateral relations established by marriage create a network of lasting reciprocities that subsequently extends to objects of use and value, to services, immaterial forms of attention, and loyalties.

The exchange of women, normed by rules of marriage, makes possible a *segmental differentiation* of society. Society can gain in complexity when subgroups emerge within given social groups or when similar social units join together in larger units with the same structure. Segmental dynamics develops along the lines either of cell division or of the combination of cells into larger organisms. It can, of course, also react to demographic pressure and other ecological circumstances in an inverse manner, that is, not in the direction of greater complexity but in that of a dedifferentiating splintering off; kinship solidarity continues on and subgroups become self-sufficient.[10] With respect to the establishment of lasting reciprocities between initially alien groups, the ritual exchange of valuables is a functional equivalent for the exchange of women. In his classical study of the circulation exchange of valuable but not really useful gifts in the archipelago of eastern New Guinea,[11] Malinowski showed how the normatively required exchange of two sorts of symbolic objects (bracelets and necklaces not used as ornaments) brought about partnerships (in pairs) among several thousand members of tribes, scattered over a very large area. Like the potlatch observed by Boas among the Kwakiutl and the system of indebtedness observed by Leach among the Kachin, this exchange of valuables can be seen as an example of an *exchange mechanism* that transforms bellicose relations into reciprocal obligations. At any rate, the ritual exchange of valuable objects and the symbolic consumption of useful objects serve less to accumulate wealth than to foster sociation, that is, to stabilize friendly relations with the social environment and to incorporate foreign elements into their own system.[12]

Segmental differentiation via exchange relations increases the complexity of a society by way of horizontally stringing together similarly structured groups. This does not necessarily promote the functional specification of social cooperation. It is only with the *vertical stratification* of unilinear descent groups that power differentials arise that can be used for the authoritative combination of specialized activities, that is, for *organization*. Naturally, in tribal societies organizational power does not yet take the form of political power but that of generalized prestige. The dominant descent groups owe their status, as a rule, to a prestige grounded genealogically, through origins, divine descent, or the like. But, as Shapera observed in connection with the Australian Bushmen, even in small nomadic groups of freebooters (with fifty to one hundred members) a division of labor can develop under the leadership of the chief. "The chief is the leader, not in the sense that he can overrule the opinion of the other men (which would be impossible since he has no means of compelling them to accept his wishes), but in the sense that he is expected to organize the activities that have been decided upon; he tells the hunters where they are to go, when they bring back meat he divides it, he leads them in their moves from one water-hole to the next and in attacks on neighboring bands, and he conducts negotiations with other bands on such matters as permission to enter his territory, or the conclusion of a marriage with one of their members, or the organization of a joint ritual."[13]

Planning the cumulative effects of interdependent actions requires positions with the authority to direct; the decisions of a part have to be attributable to the whole. Collectivities secure their capacity to act through organization when they ensure that the decisions of someone authorized to issue directions are accepted by the other participants as premises for their own decisions. This can also be accomplished through *stratification*. In stratified tribal societies the members of the more distinguished, older descent groups lay claim to positions of leadership. A status system based on prestige allows for integrating tribes of considerable size. The best known example of this is the Nuer studied by Evans-Pritchard. The individual tribe is a unit of up to sixty thousand members which exercises territorial sovereignty. Every tribe identifies itself with a ruling "aristocratic" descent group. Evans-Pritchard emphasizes that while dominant groups enjoy a certain authority in relation to "ordinary" family groups, and while they have a corresponding power of organization at their disposal, they neither exercise political power nor enjoy material advantages. In other cases, tribal stratification also attaches to age-groups. Both in cultic matters and in the profane affairs of production, warfare, the administration of justice, and the like, stratification clears a considerable space for organization.

Just as segmental dynamics did not point only in the direction of growing size and increasing population density, the mechanism of stratification is not linked to any "safety-catch" effect. As Leach's studies in Burma show,[14] the process of hierarchizing descent groups is reversible. Reports reaching as far back as the beginning of the last century document the low level of stability in the size of the tribal groups in the Kachlin Hills area; they oscillate between small, autonomous units of some four households to large societies with forty-nine subgroups, some of which comprised in turn one hundred villages each. M. Gluckmann has compared the dynamics of such systems with the fluctuating expansion and contraction of African kingdoms before the European invasion.[15] Apparently, the complexity of these social systems adjusts to changing demographic, ecological, and social conditions in the environments; the processes of differentiation and dedifferentiation take place by way of both segmental differentiation and stratification.

In tribal societies the mechanism of exchange takes on economic functions only to a limited extent. In these societies, organized predominantly as subsistence economies, there are, to be sure, the beginnings of a market commerce in which goods are often exchanged across great distances. There is less trade with objects of daily use than with raw materials, implements, and jewelry. Certain categories of goods—such as livestock or articles of clothing—already serve on occasion as a primitive form of money; Karl Polanyi spoke of "special purpose money." But economic transactions in the narrower sense have no structure-forming effects in tribal societies. Like the mechanism of power formation, the mechanism of exchange gains system-differentiating strength only when it gets tied directly to religion and the kinship system. *Systemic mechanisms have not yet become detached from institutions effective for social integration.* Thus, an important part of the circulation of economic goods is dependent on kinship relations; services circulate primarily in the noneconomic form of normatively required, reciprocal measures of assistance. And as we have seen, the ritual exchange of valuable objects serves the purpose of social integration. In the non-monetarized economic activities of archaic societies, the mechanism of exchange has so little detached itself from normative contexts that a clear separation between economic and noneconomic values is hardly possible.[16] Only where the mechanism of exchange is at the same time an integral element of the kinship system can it develop its full, complexity-increasing dynamics.

In the exchange of women normed by the rules of marriage, social integration and system integration come together. The same holds for the mechanism of power formation. It operates within the dimensions set by the kinship system: sex, generation, descent. And it allows only for status differentiations based on prestige, not on the possession of political power. This interweaving of system integration and social integration, which is typical of tribal societies, is reflected at the level of methodology.

In archaic societies functional interconnections are peculiarly transparent. When they are not trivially accessible from the perspective of everyday practice, they are encoded in ritual actions. Fortes's account of the great festival of the Tallensi tribe of Talleland provides a nice illustration. In an elaborate arrangement of encounters and ritual agreements, the cooperation, based on a division of labor, among old established groups and immigrant descent groups from which religious and political leaders are recruited, is simultaneously made visible and affirmed.[17] Presumably, social-scientific functionalism was able to establish itself in cultural anthropology because in tribal societies systemic interdependencies are directly mirrored in normative structures.

However, since the social system is largely merged into the sociocultural lifeworld at this stage of development, anthropology is at the same time a hermeneutic science par excellence. Hermeneutic efforts are provoked by the fact that the interweaving of system integration and social integration not only keeps societal processes transparent but also makes them opaque in other respects. On the one hand, it draws all societal processes into the horizon of the lifeworld and gives them the appearance of intelligibility—tribal members know what they are doing when they perform their hunting, fertility, initiation, and marriage rites. On the other hand, the mythical structure of the stories with which they make their lifeworld and their own actions plausible is unintelligible *to us*. The anthropologist is faced with a paradox: the lifeworlds of archaic societies are in principle accessible via their members' intuitive knowledge; at the same time, they stubbornly escape our comprehension owing to our hermeneutic distance from mythical narratives. This situation explains why depth-hermeneutic procedures are popular in anthropology, in both psychoanalytic and structuralist variations. I regard the *hermeneutic paradox* that vexes cultural anthropology as the methodological reflex of a failure to differentiate coordination of action by systemic means from coordination in terms of social integration. It may be that society can be present in the lifeworld, along with its functional interconnections—that is, as a system—only so long as ritual practice, which reduces both purposive activity and communication to a common denominator, supports and shapes the social structure.

To the extent, then, that the structures of the lifeworld get differentiated, the mechanisms of systemic and social integration also get separated from each other. It is this revolutionary process that is the key to Weber's problematic of societal rationalization.

C.—The segmental differentiation of tribal societies via exchange relations and their stratification via power relations mark two different *levels of sys-*

tem differentiation. Social integration (in the sense of coordinating action *orientations*) is required for system maintenance only insofar as it fixes the boundary conditions for the functionally necessary correlation of action *effects*. But the mechanisms that serve to heighten system complexity are not a priori harmonized with the mechanisms that provide for the social cohesiveness of the collectivity via normative consensus and mutual understanding in language. Systemic mechanisms remain tightly intermeshed with mechanisms of social integration only so long as they attach to *pregiven* social structures, that is, to the kinship system. With the formation of genuinely political power that no longer derives its authority from the prestige of leading descent groups, but from disposition over judicial means of sanction, the power mechanism detaches itself from kinship structures. Organizational complexity constituted at the level of political domination becomes the crystallizing nucleus of a new institution: the state. For this reason I shall refer to the mechanism of *state organization;* it is incompatible with the social structure of societies organized along kinship lines; the social structure appropriate to it is a general political order, within which social strata are assigned their proper places, and to which they are subordinated.

In the framework of societies organized around a state, markets for goods arise that are steered by symbolically generalized relations of exchange, that is, by the medium of money. However, this medium has a structure-forming effect for the social system as a whole only when the economy is separated off from the political order. In Europe during the early modern period, there arose with the capitalist economy a subsystem differentiated out via the money medium—a subsystem that in turn necessitated a reorganization of the state. In the complementary relationship between the subsystems of the market economy and modern administration, the mechanism of steering media—which Parsons referred to as symbolically generalized media of communication—finds its appropriate social structure.

Figure 1 arranges the four mechanisms of system differentiation mentioned above in the order in which they appeared in the course of social evolution. As each mechanism takes the lead in evolution, it characterizes a higher level of interaction at which the preceding mechanisms are at once degraded, sublated, and refunctionalized. Each new level of system differentiation opens up space for further increases in complexity, that is, for additional functional specifications and a correspondingly more abstract integration of the ensuing subsystems. Mechanisms 1 and 4 operate through exchange relations, mechanisms 2 and 3 through power relations. Whereas mechanisms 1 and 2 remain tied to pregiven kinship structures, mechanisms 3 and 4 give rise to the formation of new social structures. In the process, exchange and power lose the concrete forms of the exchange of women according to marriage rules and the stratification of descent groups measured in differentials of prestige; they are transformed into abstract magnitudes: organizational power and steering media. Mechanisms 1 and 2 bring about the differentiation of kin groups, that is, of similarly structured units, whereas mechanisms 3 and 4 mean a differentiation of propertied classes

Coordination of action via — Differentiation and integration of	Exchange	Power
Similarly structured units	1. Segmentary differentiation	2. Stratification
Dissimilar, functionally specified units	4. Steering media	3. State organizations

FIGURE 1.   Mechanisms of System Differentiation

and organizations, that is, of units that are themselves already functionally specified. The structures that these units take on are already stamped in each case by the mechanisms of the preceding level. The four mechanisms characterize different levels of integration, with which different social formations are connected, as depicted in figure 2.

Of course, social formations cannot be distinguished by degrees of systemic complexity alone. They are, rather, defined by the *institutional complex* that anchors a newly emerging mechanism of system differentiation in the lifeworld. Thus, segmental differentiation is institutionalized in the form of kinship relations, stratification in that of rank ordering, state organization in forms of political domination, and the first steering medium in the form of relations between private legal persons. The corresponding institutions are sex and generation roles, the status of descent groups, political office, and bourgeois private law.

In archaic societies interactions are determined only by the kinship system's repertoire of roles. The concept of *role* can be unproblematically applied at this level because communicative action is almost entirely prejudiced by normative behavior patterns. When a status system arises in stratified tribal societies such that families are ordered hierachically by pres-

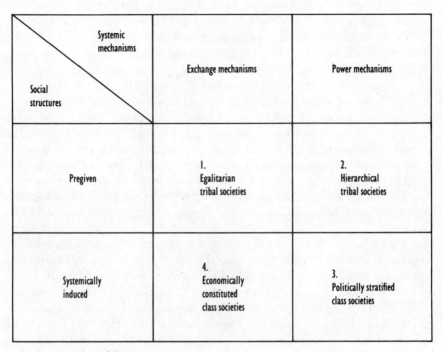

Systemic mechanisms	Exchange mechanisms	Power mechanisms
Social structures		
Pregiven	1. Egalitarian tribal societies	2. Hierarchical tribal societies
Systemically induced	4. Economically constituted class societies	3. Politically stratified class societies

FIGURE 2. Social Formations

tige, sex and generation roles get relativized; the rank of the family one belongs to is more important for one's social status than one's position within the family. The concept of *status* can be unambiguously applied at this level because society is stratified along one dimension: the prestige a family enjoys owing to its descent. In state-organized societies this status ordering is relativized. When the state rather than kinship determines the structure of society, social stratification is combined with features of participation in political domination and of place in the production process. The concept of the *authority of office* takes on a precise meaning only at this level. The ruler and the political estates vested with the privileges of domination enjoy authority by virtue of offices that still presuppose a unity of public and private spheres of life and thus are understood as their own personal rights. Finally, when money is legally institutionalized as a steering medium for depoliticized economic activity, the authority of the state, political domination in general, is relativized by the private legal order. At this level, *positive law* becomes the guarantor of the calculability of private business activity.[18]

If we take the institutionalization of levels of system differentiation as the mark of social formations, we get a parallel to the Marxist notions of base and superstructure. The impulses toward a differentiation of the social system emanate from the domain of material reproduction. Thus we can understand by "base" the institutional complex that, at a given stage, anchors the evolutionarily leading system mechanism in the lifeworld and that, therefore, defines the scope for possible increases in complexity in a given social formation. This is all the more plausible if, following Kautsky, we interpret the distinction between base and superstructure with reference to the theory of social evolution.[19] On this account, "base" designates the domain of emerging problems to which an explanation of the transition from one social formation to the next has to make reference. It is in the "basic" domain that we find those system problems that can be resolved only through evolutionary innovations, that is, only when a higher level of system differentiation is institutionalized. It is of course misleading to equate "base" with "economic structure," for not even in capitalist societies does the basic domain, as defined above, coincide with the economic system.

Marx describes the basic institutions of a society in terms of the mode of production; it has to be kept in mind, however, that every social formation allow for various modes of production (and combinations thereof). As is well known, Marx characterizes modes of production by the stage of development of productive forces and by certain forms of social intercourse— the relations of production. The *forces of production* comprise (*a*) the labor power of those active in production, the producers; (*b*) technically utilizable knowledge insofar as it is converted into productivity-enhancing tools of labor, into techniques of production; and (*c*) organizational knowledge insofar as it is used to set labor power efficiently into motion, to qualify labor power, and to coordinate effectively the cooperation of workers on the basis of a division of labor (mobilization, qualification, and organization of labor power). The forces of production determine the extent of a society's possible disposition over natural resources. The *relations of production* comprise those institutions and societal mechanisms that determine the ways in which labor power is combined with the available means of production at a given stage of the forces of production. Regulation of access to the means of production, the manner of controlling socially employed labor power, also indirectly determines the distribution of socially produced wealth. Relations of production express the distribution of social power; with their pattern of distribution of social rewards, that is, of socially recognized opportunities for need satisfaction, they determine the interest structure that obtains in a given society.

In tribal societies, whether stratified or not, the kinship system takes on the role of relations of production, as M. Godelier has rightly emphasized.[20] These societies consist of base and superstructure both in one; not even religion is sufficiently differentiated off from kinship institutions that it could be characterized as superstructural. In traditional societies the relations of production are incorporated into the general political order, while religious worldviews take on ideological functions. It is only with capitalism, where the market also serves the function of stabilizing class relations, that production relations assume an economic shape. There is a corresponding differentiation of base from superstructure: first the traditional political order is differentiated off from the religious worldviews that legitimate the state; then the complementary subsystems of an economy specialized in "adaptation" and a state administration specialized in "goal attainment" (to use Parsonian terms) are differentiated off from domains of action that primarily serve the needs of cultural reproduction, social integration, and socialization. Base and superstructure can separate off from one another only when the kinship system breaks down as the basic social structure, thus bursting apart the clamps that held systemic and socially integrative mechanisms tightly together. In what follows, I shall comment on the levels of system differentiation which politically stratified and economically constituted class societies attain by means of state organization and the monetary medium.

(*a*) In *hierarchized tribal societies,* functional specification increases along with organizational activities; special roles can be differentiated out for leadership functions in war and peace, for ritual actions and healing practices, for settling legal conflicts, and so on. But this specialization remains within the bounds of a kinship system whose units have basically similar structures. It is in *societies organized around a state* that functional specification first encroaches upon the very way of life of social groups. Under the conditions of political domination, social stratification detaches itself from the substratum of the kinship system. Social units can themselves become functionally specified via participation and exclusion from political power. The dominant-status groups—officials, military men, landowners—and the mass of the population—fishermen, farmers, mine workers, craftsmen, and so forth—change from classifications based on birth to politically guaranteed social classes based on possessions. The different strata are no longer differentiated only by the extent of their possessions, but by the way they acquire them, their position in the production process. Socioeconomic classes arise, even if they do not yet appear in economic form—that is, as classes based on source of income. They are stratified according to political power and criteria relating to particular modes of life. On the basis of an increasingly sharp dichotomy between high and popular culture,[21] classes develop their own milieus, lifeworlds, and value orientations specific to the various strata. In place of the stratification of similar social units, we find a political organization of dissimilar social units, in place of hierarchized descent groups, stratified classes.

As the large empires of antiquity impressively demonstrate, social systems with the mechanism of state organization can develop incomparably greater complexity than tribal societies. Anthropological field studies of the political systems in African tribal cultures show that societies at a precivilization (or preliterary) level, which acquire some form of state organization, are already more complex than the most complex of those societies organized along kinship lines.[22] Social anthropologists distinguish these social formations on the basis of the appearance of "governments"—that is, organizations for central rule, which have administrative staffs, however rudimentary, that are maintained by taxes and tribute, and have jurisdiction to ensure that the rulers' demands are followed. What is decisive from a systemic point of view is disposition over the power to sanction, for this makes binding decisions possible:

> In our judgment, the most significant characteristic distinguishing the centralized, pyramidal, state-like forms of government of the Ngwato, Bemba, etc., from the segmentary political systems of the Logoli, the Tallensi, and the Nuer is the incidence and function of organized force in the system. In the former group of societies, the principle sanction of a ruler's rights and prerogatives, and the authority exercised by his subordinate chief, is the command of organized force. This may enable an African to rule oppressively for a time, if he is inclined to do so, but a good ruler uses the armed forces under his control in the public interest, as an accepted instrument of government—that is, for the defense of the society as a whole or of any sections of it, for offense against a common enemy, and as a coercive sanction to enforce the law or respect for the constitution.[23]

Disposition over the means to sanction binding decisions provides the basis for an authority of office with which organizational power is institutionalized for the first time *as such*—and not merely as an appendix to, and filling out of, pregiven social structures. In the state, organizations that secure the collectivity's capacity to act as a whole take on a directly institutional shape. Society as a whole can now be understood as an organization. Social affiliation with the collectivity is interpreted through the fiction of a membership that is in principle contingent; it is interpreted, in short, as citizenship in a state. Whereas one is born into a family, citizenship is based on a legal act. One does not "have" it in the way that one has a family background; it can be acquired and lost. Citizenship in a state presupposes voluntary—at least in principle—recognition of the political order; for political rule means that citizens commit themselves, at least in principle, to a general willingness to obey those who hold office. In this way, the many cede to the few the competence to act on behalf of all. They relinquish the right that participants in simple interactions can claim for themselves: the right to orient their actions only by actual agreement with those present.

(*b*) In traditional societies the state is an organization in which is concentrated the collectivity's capacity for action—that is, the capacity for action of society as a whole; by contrast, modern societies do without the accumulation of steering functions within a single organization. Functions relevant to society as a whole are distributed among different subsystems. With an administration, military, and judiciary, the state specializes in attaining collective goals via binding decisions. Other functions are depoliticized and given over to nongovernmental subsystems. The capitalist economic system marks the breakthrough to this level of system differentiation; it owes its emergence to a new mechanism, the steering medium of money. This medium is specifically tailored to the economic function of society as a whole, a function relinquished by the state; it is the foundation of a subsystem that grows away from normative contexts. The capitalist economy can no longer be understood as an institutional order in the sense of the traditional state; it is the medium of exchange that is institutionalized, while the subsystem differentiated out via this medium is, as a whole, a block of more or less norm-free sociality.

Money is a special exchange mechanism that transforms use values into exchange values, the natural economic exchange of goods into commerce in commodities. Traditional societies already allow for internal and external markets; it is only with capitalism, however, that we have an economic system such that both the internal commerce among business enterprises and the interchange with noneconomic environments, private households, and the state are carried out through monetary channels. The institution-alization of wage labor, on the one hand, and of a state based on taxation,[24] on the other, is just as constitutive for the new mode of production as the emergence of the capitalist enterprise. Money has structure-forming effects only when it becomes an *intersystemic medium of interchange*. The econ-omy can be constituted as a monetarily steered subsystem only to the degree that it regulates its interchanges with its social environments via the me-dium of money. Complementary environments take shape as the production process is converted over to wage labor and the state apparatus is connected up with production via the yield from taxes on those employed. The state apparatus becomes dependent upon the media-steered subsystem of the economy; this forces it to reorganize and leads, among other things, to an assimilation of power to the structure of a steering medium: power becomes assimilated to money.

Within a subsystem that has been differentiated out for a single function relevant to society as a whole, the scope for organizational accomplish-ments expands once again. Now, the activities of different organizations for the same function and the activities of the same organization for different functions can be clustered together. Under these conditions, organizations are institutionalized as private enterprises and public institutions, that is, in such as way that what had to remain largely a fiction when applied to the state as a political organization of the whole, actually becomes true of them: private enterprises and public institutions actualize the principle of volun-tary membership, which is first made possible by autonomous forms of or-ganization. In Luhmann's words: "We shall designate as 'formally orga-nized' . . . those social systems which make recognizing certain expectations of behavior a condition of membership in the system. Only those who ac-cept certain specifically marked out expectations can become and remain members of formally organized social systems."[25] The traditional state is an organization that structures society as a whole; in defining its membership, shaping its program, and recruiting its personnel, it therefore has to link up with the established lifeworlds of a stratified class society and with the corresponding cultural traditions. By contrast, the capitalist enterprise and the modern administration are systemically independent units within norm-free subsystems. As Luhmann has shown, what distinguishes *autonomous organizations* is that, by means of membership conditions that have to be accepted all at once, they can make themselves independent from communicatively structured lifeworld relations, from the concrete value orientations and action dispositions—susceptible to conflict as they are—of persons who have been pushed out into the environment of the organization.[26]

D.—To this point I have been viewing social evolution from the perspective of increasing systemic complexity, but the institutionalization of new levels of system differentiation is also visible from the internal perspective of the lifeworld involved. In tribal societies, system differentiation is linked to existing structures of interaction through the exchange of spouses and the formation of prestige; for this reason it does not yet make itself noticeable by intervening in the structures of the lifeworld. In politically stratified class societies, a new level of functional interconnection, in the form of the state, rises above the level of simple interactions. This difference in levels is reflected in the relation of the whole to its parts—a relation that is at the heart of classical political theory from the time of Aristotle, although the corresponding images of society as polity that arise in the spectrum from popular to high culture are considerably different. The new level of system differentiation has the form of a general political order that needs to be legitimated; this order can be brought into the lifeworld only at the cost of an illusory interpretation of class society, that is, through religious worldviews taking on ideological functions. Finally, a third level of functional interconnection arises in modern societies with interchange processes that operate via media. These systemic interconnections, detached from normative contexts and rendered independent as subsystems, challenge the assimilative powers of an all-encompassing lifeworld. They congeal into the "second nature" of a norm-free sociality that can appear as something in the objective world, as an *objectified* context of life. The uncoupling of system and lifeworld is experienced in modern society as a particular kind of objectification: the social system definitively bursts out of the horizon of the lifeworld, escapes from the intuitive knowledge of everyday communicative practice, and is henceforth accessible only to the counterintuitive knowledge of the social sciences developing since the eighteenth century.

What we have already found in the system perspective seems to be confirmed from this internal perspective: the more complex social systems become, the more provincial lifeworlds become. In a differentiated social system the lifeworld seems to shrink to a subsystem. This should not be read causally, as if the structures of the lifeworld changed in dependence on increases in systemic complexity. The opposite is true: increases in complexity are dependent on the structural differentiation of the lifeworld. And however we may explain the dynamics of this structural transformation, it follows the inner logic of communicative rationalization. I have developed this thesis with reference to Mead and Durkheim and have carried it over to lifeworld analysis. Now I shall make systematic use of it.

As we have seen, the level of possible increases in complexity can be raised only by the introduction of a new system mechanism. Every new leading mechanism of system differentiation must, however, be anchored in the lifeworld; it must be *institutionalized* there via family status, the authority of office, or bourgeois private law. In the final analysis, social formations are distinguished by the institutional cores that define society's "base," in the Marxian sense. These basic institutions form a series of evolutionary innovations that can come about only if the lifeworld is sufficiently rationalized, above all only if law and morality have reached a corresponding stage of development. The institutionalization of a new level of system differentiation requires reconstruction in the core institutional domain of the moral-legal (i.e., consensual) regulation of conflicts.

Morality and law are specifically tailored to check open conflict in such a way that the basis of communicative action—and with it the social integration of the lifeworld—does not fall apart. They secure the next level of consensus to which we can have recourse when the mechanism of reaching understanding fails in the normatively regulated communication of everyday life, that is, when the coordination of actions anticipated in the moral case does not come to pass and the alternative of violent confrontation becomes a reality. Moral and legal norms are, in this sense, *second-order norms of action;* the different forms of social integration can be profitably studied in regard to them. As we have seen, Durkheim analyzed the transformation of social integration in connection with the development of law and morality; he noted a long-term trend toward heightened abstractness and universality in law and morality, with a simultaneous differentiation between the two. Taking our cue from ontogenesis, it is now possible to construct stages of development for morality and law, with the underlying sociocognitive concepts of 'expectation', 'norm' (= generalized expectation), and 'principle' (= higher-level norm) as our measure. Lawrence Kohlberg distinguishes three levels of moral consciousness:[27] the preconventional level, on which only the consequences of action are judged, the conventional level, on which the orientation to norms and the intentional violation of them are already judged, and finally the postconventional level, on which norms themselves are judged in the light of principles. Klaus Eder has shown that there are homologous structures of consciousness in the moral and legal developments of archaic, traditional, and modern societies.[28] Wolfgang Schluchter has interpreted Weber's historically supported typology of law from this point of view.[29] I shall confine myself here to the schematic presentation in figure 3.

In the first row, morality and law are not separated; in the second row, they are separated by a broken line to mark the processes of differentiation that will lead to a separation of law and morality at the postconventional level. At the level of principled moral consciousness, morality is deinstitu-

States of moral consciousness	Basic socio-cognitive concepts	Ethics	Types of law
Preconventional	Particular expectations of behavior	Magical ethics	Revealed law
Conventional	Norm	Ethics of the law	Traditional law
Postconventional	Principle	Ethics of conviction and responsibility	Formal law

FIGURE 3. Stages in the Development of Law

tionalized to such an extent that it is now anchored only in the personality system as an *internal* control on behavior. Likewise, law develops into an *external* force, imposed from without, to such an extent that modern compulsory law, sanctioned by the state, becomes an institution detached from the ethical motivations of the legal person and dependent upon abstract obedience to the law. This development is part of the structural differentiation of the lifeworld. It reflects both the growing independence of the societal component of the lifeworld—the system of institutions—in relation to culture and personality, and the trend toward the growing dependence of legitimate orders on formal procedures for positing and justifying norms.

My thesis is that higher levels of integration cannot be established in social evolution until legal institutions develop in which moral consciousness on the conventional, and then postconventional, levels is embodied.[30] So long as the kinship system represents some sort of total institution, which it does in tribal societies, there is no place for the administration of justice as a *meta*institution. The practices of administering justice are developed not as superordinate, but as coordinate institutions. This explains the continuing debate among anthropologists as to how the concept of law is appropriately defined. There are rights [*Rechte*] following from all socially recognized norms of action, but law [*das Recht*] refers only to the treatment of norm violations considered to be so serious that they can neither be made good directly nor tolerated without further ado. At the other end, the modern concept of compulsory law as a system of laws covered by the state's power to sanction is too narrow. Law in tribal societies is not yet compulsory law. The self-help of the disputing parties remains the *ultima ratio;* it cannot be replaced by judicial decisions in any obligatory fashion. There are not even institutions in all societies that specialize in the administration of justice (or the infliction of punishment). But even where there are no courts, there are routines for peacefully settling disputes that affect the interests of an individual and his family or the welfare of the collective as a whole.

Recent work done by anthropologists has concentrated on the careful recording of cases, as far as possible in the context of what is already known about the disputants, their relative status, and the events that led up to a "trouble case." P. H. Gulliver, a London anthropologist who has done much work of this kind in Tanzania, maintains what is implicit in Hoebel, that when we are studying law what we should really be looking for is *the process of dispute settlement.* By a dispute he means a quarrel that has reached the point where the man who thinks he is injured demands some kind of third party intervention to establish what his rights are and give him the satisfaction due to him. He reminds us that "settlement" does not necessarily dispose of the issue. But once a *quarrel* has been treated by either party as a *dispute* something has to be done.[31]

Durkheim's distinction between offenses or crimes that are avenged through penal law and crimes that require compensation for the injured party was picked up by Radcliffe-Brown, but it could not be sustained in relation to the empirical material in quite the way Durkheim had expected. For our purposes, what is important is that the idea of restoring an integral state or a normal order also has application to situations in which Durkheim's distinction between penal and civil laws holds. "There are two main ways of dealing with a complaint that somebody has broken the law. One is to persuade or compel him to make restitution to the person he has robbed. The other is to punish the law-breaker; if that method is chosen, it could be argued that he is making restitution to the community as a whole, being held by his action to have injured them all."[32] The facts of the case are judged from a preconventional perspective of restitution for harm done; it is the consequences of action that are morally relevant and not the intentions of the wrongdoer. Thus, for example, a violation of the incest prohibition counts as a crime that results in the spiritual contamination of society, a kind of pollution of the environment—and the punishment attached to it is not meant to avenge a norm violation for which an individual is accountable, but rather functions to ward off imminent harm to the collectivity. The validity of norms is directly rooted in the ritual action of the cultic community. It is not based on external sanctions under the exclusive control of some supreme legal authority. The punishment for trespasses against the sacred order has the character of an atonement that cannot, in the end, be forced by social authority.

The moment of accepting a punishment is even clearer in civil-law conflicts between opposing parties. Against the background of the right of self-

defense or other self-help routines (e.g., blood vengeance), the court of arbitration can at most exert pressure upon the disputants to come to some
agreement; it cannot impose its judgment upon them, that is, against the
will of one or the other party.

One cannot divide society neatly into those in which disputes are fought out, and
those in which they are argued out before an impartial authority which decides who
is right and what is to be done. The latter type indubitably have legal institutions;
some of the former might be said to go only part of the way. Thus, among the Luhya
of Western Kenya, the heads of descent groups were traditionally held to be responsible for the actions of their members, and if someone was involved in a dispute the
elders of the two groups got together and tried to agree on a solution. Except within
the narrowest descent group, no solution could be imposed unless the party agreed.
In the case of a dispute between members of a larger lineage, it was not considered
permissible to fight the matter out, but if no reconciliation could be attained the
weaker party numerically (who could not have won in a fight) moved away and
broke off relations with the rest of the lineage.[33]

Things work differently in societies organized around a state. The basis
of political authority is disposition over centralized means of sanction,
which gives to the decision of officeholders a binding character. The ruler
gets this authority not from a merely factual power to sanction, but from a
power of sanction recognized as legitimate by citizens. According to a hypothesis advanced by Klaus Eder, legitimate disposition over power, which
represents the core of political domination, can be traced back to the royal
judgeship. The latter could take shape only after the institutions for the
administration of justice had been cognitively changed over to another stage
of moral consciousness, namely, the conventional. From a conventional perspective, an offense appears as a violation of intersubjectively recognized
norms for which an individual is held accountable. Normative deviation is
measured against the intentions of a responsibly acting subject, and punishment is aimed not merely at compensating for disadvantageous consequences of action, but at blameworthy actions. At this stage of moral judgment, the consensual regulation of conflict is guided not by the idea of
restoring a violated status quo ante, but by that of making amends for a
wrong that has been responsibly committed, of healing an intentional
breach of norms. With this, the function of administering justice and the
position of the judge change in the minds of legal subjects. The judge protects the integrity of the legal order, and the force he avails himself of in
exercising this function derives its legitimacy from a legal order respected
as valid. Judicial power is no longer based on the prestige of one's status,
but on the legitimacy of a legal order in which the position of someone who
safeguards the law and is equipped with the required power of sanction
becomes structurally necessary. *Because judicial office is itself a source of
legitimate power, political domination can first crystallize around this office.*
Upon the basis of traditional law, the separation between penal and civil
law only implicitly drawn in archaic legal institutions is carried through
clearly. Civil law derives from converting arbitration proceedings under-

stood in preconventional terms over to the conventional stage of moral consciousness. Furthermore, law now has the position of a metainstitution; it serves as a kind of insurance against breakdown, covering situations in which the binding power of first-order institutions fails to work. The political order as a whole is constituted as a legal order, but it is laid like a shell around a society whose core domains are by no means legally organized throughout. Social intercourse is institutionalized much more in forms of traditional mores than through law. This changes in modern societies.

With an economy differentiated out via the medium of money; there emerges an ethically neutralized system of action that is institutionalized *directly* in forms of bourgeois private law. The system of social labor gets transferred from first-order institutions (which are themselves guaranteed by law) *directly* over to the norms of civil law. Insofar as actions are coordinated through a delinguistified medium such as money, normatively embedded interactions are turned into success-oriented transactions among private legal subjects. As civil law largely loses the position of a metainstitution, a functionally equivalent gradation of first-order and second-order norms takes shape within the legal system itself.

Beyond the differentiation of penal and civil law, there is now a separation of private and public law. Whereas civil society is institutionalized as a sphere of legally domesticated, incessant competition between strategically acting private persons, the organs of state, organized by means of public law, constitute the level on which consensus can be restored in cases of stubborn conflict. This helps clarify how the problem of justification is both displaced and intensified. Inasmuch as law becomes positive, the paths of legitimation grow longer. The legality of decisions, which is measured by adherence to formally unobjectionable procedures, relieves the legal system of justification problems that pervade traditional law in its entirety. On the other hand, these problems get more and more intensive where the critcizability and need for justification of legal norms are only the other side of their positivity—the principle of enactment and the principle of justification reciprocally require one another. The legal system *as a whole* needs to be anchored in basic principles of legitimation. In the bourgeois constitutional state these are, in the first place, basic rights and the principle of popular sovereignty; they embody postconventional structures of moral consciousness. Together with the moral-practical foundations of penal and civil law, they are in the bridges between a de-moralized and externalized legal sphere and a deinstitutionalized and internalized morality.

I have roughly sketched out these two stages in the evolution of law and morality to show that the transitions to conventional and postconventional legal and moral representations fulfill *necessary* conditions for the emergence of the institutional frameworks of political and economic class societies. I understand the connection between them as follows: new levels of system differentiation can establish themselves only if the rationalization of the lifeworld has reached a corresponding level. But then I have to explain why the development toward universalism in law and morality *both* expresses a rationalization of the lifeworld *and* makes new levels of integration possible. This becomes clearer in the light of two *countertendencies* that establish themselves on the level of interactions and action orientations in the wake of increasing "value generalization."

E.—Parsons applies the phrase "value generalization" to the tendency for value orientations that are institutionally required of actors to become more and more general and formal in the course of social evolution. This trend is the structurally necessary result of a legal and moral development that, as we saw, shifts the securing of consensus in cases of conflict to more and more abstract levels. Naturally, even the simplest interaction systems cannot function without a certain amount of *generalized* action orientations. Every society has to face the basic problem of coordinating action: how does ego get alter to continue interaction in the desired way? How does he avoid conflict that interrupts the sequence of action? If we begin with simple interactions within the framework of everyday communicative practice and inquire after *generalized motives* that might move alter to a *blanket* acceptance of ego's interaction offers, we come across trivial elements not tied to any special presuppositions: the prestige ego enjoys and the influence he exercises. When a prestigious or influential person takes the initiative, he can count on receiving a certain "advance" of trust or confidence, which may be paid out in a readiness for consensus and obedience that goes beyond any single situation. We might also say: the generalized action orientations of the other participants correspond to the prestige and influence disposed over by some persons.

In stratified tribal societies, the social structure is stamped by prestige and influence. The advance of trust is transferred from person to group. The situation-transcending readiness to accept extends now to dominant descent groups; members of higher-status groups meet with obedience to expectations that no longer need to be covered by their personal status. In politically constituted societies, the rulers' authority of office expands the scope for generalized value orientations; in certain spheres of action, they are detached from particular kinship relations. The readiness to agree and to follow is accorded in the first instance not to influential families but to the legal authorities of the state. Political rule means the competence to carry out decisions on the basis of binding norms; the political order is legitimate insofar as it is based on the citizens' fidelity to the law. This duty of obedience to officeholders is less particularistic than the readiness to follow members of a leading social stratum. Modern bourgeois society, finally, requires an even higher level of value generalization. Insofar as traditional morals [*Sittlichkeit*] split up into legality and morality, an autonomous application of general principles is required in private affairs, while in the occupational and public spheres obedience to positively enacted laws is demanded. Actors' motives were at first under the control of the concrete value orientations of kinship rules; in the end, the generalization of motives and values goes so far that *abstract obedience to law* becomes the only normative condition that actors have to meet in formally organized domains of action.

The trend toward value generalization gives rise to two tendencies on the plane of interaction. The further motive and value generalization advance, the more communicative action gets detached from concrete and traditional normative behavior patterns. This uncoupling shifts the burden of social integration more and more from religiously anchored consensus to processes of consensus formation in language. The transfer of action coordination to the mechanism of reaching understanding permits the structures of communicative action to appear in an even purer form. In this respect, value generalization is a necessary condition for releasing the rationality potential immanent in communicative action. This fact by itself would entitle us to understand the development of law and morality, from which value generalization originates, as an aspect of the rationalization of the lifeworld.

On the other hand, freeing communicative action from particular value orientations also forces the separation of action oriented to success from action oriented to mutual understanding. With the generalization of motives and values, space opens up for subsystems of purposive rational action. The coordination of action can be transferred over to delinguistified media of communication only when contexts of strategic action get differentiated out. While a deinstitutionalized, only internalized morality ties the regulation of conflict to the idea of justifying normative validity claims—to the procedures and presuppositions of moral argumentation—a demoralized, positive, compulsory law exacts a deferment of legitimation that makes it possible to steer social action via media of a different type.

This polarization reflects an uncoupling of system integration from social integration, which presupposes a differentiation on the plane of interaction not only between action oriented to success and to mutual understanding, but between the corresponding mechanisms of action coordination—the ways in which ego brings alter to continue interaction, and the bases upon which alter forms generalized action orientations. On the basis of increasingly generalized action orientations, there arises an ever denser network of interactions that do without directly normative steering and have to be coordinated in another way. To satisfy this growing need for coordination, there is either explicit communication or relief mechanisms that reduce the expenditure of communication and the risk of disagreement. In the wake of the differentiation between action oriented to mutual understanding and to success, two sorts of *relief mechanisms* emerge in the form of communication media that either condense or replace mutual understanding in language. We have already come across prestige and influence as primitive generators of a willingness to follow; the formation of media begins with them.

Prestige is attributed rather to the person, influence to the flow of communication itself. Although prestige and influence are interdependent variables—prestige enhances influence, influence enhances prestige—we can separate them analytically in respect to their sources. In the simplest case, prestige is based on personal attributes, influence on disposition over resources. In the catalog of qualities relevant to prestige, we find physical strength and attractiveness as well as technical-practical skills, intellectual abilities, as well as what I call the responsibility of a communicatively acting subject. By this I understand strength of will, credibility, and reliability, that is to say, cognitive, expressive, and moral-practical virtues of action oriented to validity claims. On the other hand, property and knowledge are the two most important sources of influence. The term 'knowledge' is used here in a broad sense covering anything that can be acquired through learning and appropriating cultural traditions, where the latter are understood to include both cognitive and socially integrative (i.e., expressive and moral-practical) elements.

Alter's generalized readiness to accept can now be traced to specific sources of ego's prestige or influence: in the cases of physical strength and attractiveness, cognitive-instrumental skills and disposition over property, it can be traced to ties that are motivated empirically, by inducement or intimidation; in the cases of interactive responsibility and disposition over knowledge, by contrast, it goes back to a trust or confidence that is rationally motivated, by agreement based on reasons. This yields a provisional classification of the generalized acceptability induced by prestige and influence (see figure 4).

I do not mean to raise a systematic claim with this schema; it is intended merely to illustrate that a differentiation along the lines of empirically motivated ties and rationally motivated trust can be found in the sources of prestige and influence. Alter takes up ego's offer either because he is oriented to the rewards and sanctions ego can dispense, or because he is confident that ego has the requisite knowledge and is sufficiently autonomous to guarantee the redemption of the validity claims he raises in communication.

The problem of reducing the expenditure of communication and the risk of dissensus can be resolved on the next level when prestige and influence no longer only induce a readiness for consensus and a willingness to follow, but are themselves generalized. They come to form generalized media.

One condition for the formation of different types of media is a differentiation of sources of influence, in particular, a separation of empirically motivated trust. Media such as money and power attach to empirically motivated ties, while generalized forms of communication such as professional reputation or "value commitment" (i.e., moral-practical leadership) rest on specific kinds of trust that are supposedly rationally motivated.

We can clarify the difference in type as follows. Everyday communicative practice is, as we have seen, embedded in a lifeworld context defined by cultural tradition, legitimate orders, and socialized individuals. Interpretive performances draw upon and advance consensus.[34] The rationality potential of mutual understanding in language is actualized to the extent that motive and value generalization progress and the zones of what is unprob-

Motivation / Attribution of prestige and influence	Attributes	Resources
Empirical	*Strength:* Deterrence through the fear of punishment, inducement through the expectation of protection *Know-how:* Inducement through the expectation of success *Physical attractiveness:* Emotional ties	*Property:* Inducement through the expectation of reward
Rational	*Responsibility:* Trust in autonomy	*Knowledge:* Trust in valid knowledge

FIGURE 4. Sources of Generalized Acceptability

lematic shrink. The growing pressure for rationality that a problematic lifeworld exerts upon the mechanism of mutual understanding increases the need for achieved consensus, and this increases the expenditure of interpretive energies and the risk of dissensus. It is these demands and dangers that can be headed off by media of communication. The way these media function differs according to whether they focus consensus formation in language through specializing in certain aspects of validity and hierarchizing processes of agreement, or whether they uncouple action coordination from consensus formation in language altogether, and neutralize it with respect to the alternatives of agreement or failed agreement.

The transfer of action coordination from language over to steering media means an uncoupling of interaction from lifeworld contexts. Media such as money and power attach to empirical ties; they encode a purposive-rational attitude toward calculable amounts of value and make it possible to exert generalized, strategic influence on the decisions of other participants while *bypassing* processes of consensus-oriented communication. Inasmuch as they do not merely simplify linguistic communication, but *replace* it with a symbolic generalization of rewards and punishments, the lifeworld contexts in which processes of reaching understanding are always embedded are devalued in favor of media-steered interactions; the lifeworld is no longer needed for the coordination of action.

Societal subsystems differentiated out via media of this kind can make themselves independent out of the lifeworld, which gets shunted aside into the system environment. Hence the transfer of action over to steering media appears from the lifeworld perspective both as reducing the costs and risks of communication and as conditioning decisions in expanded spheres of contingency—and thus, in this sense, as a *technicizing of the lifeworld*.

The generalization of the influence that attaches to rationally motivated trust in the possession of knowledge—whether cognitive-instrumental, moral-practical, or aesthetic-practical—cannot have the same effect. Where reputation or moral authority enters in, action coordination has to be brought about by means of resources familiar from consensus formation in language. Media of this kind cannot uncouple interaction from the lifeworld context of shared cultural knowledge, valid norms, and accountable motivations, because they have to make use of the resources of consensus formation in language. This also explains why they need no special institutional reconnection to the lifeworld and remain dependent upon rationalization of the lifeworld.

Influence that is specialized in cognitive matters—that is, scientific reputation—can take shape only insofar as cultural value spheres (in Weber's sense) have been differentiated out, making it possible to treat the cognitive tradition exclusively under the validity aspect of truth. Normatively specialized influence—for example, moral leadership—can take shape only insofar as moral and legal development have reached the postconventional level at which moral consciousness is anchored in the personality system through internal behavior controls. Both kinds of influence require, in addition, technologies of communication by means of which a public sphere can develop. Communicative action can be steered through specialized influence, through such media as professional reputation and value commitment, only to the extent that communicative utterances are, in their original appearance, already embedded in a virtually present web of communicative contents far removed in space and time but accessible in principle.

Writing, the printing press, and electronic media mark the significant innovations in this area; by these means speech acts are freed from spatiotemporal contextual limitations and made available for multiple and future contexts. The transition to civilization was accompanied by the invention of writing; it was used at first for administrative purposes, and later for the literary formation of an educated class. This gives rise to the role of the author who can direct his utterances to an indefinite, general public, the role of the exegete who develops a tradition through teaching and criticism, and the role of the reader who, through his choice of reading matter, decides in which transmitted communications he wants to take part. The printing press gained cultural and political significance only in modern society. It brought with it a freeing of communicative action from its original contexts; this was raised again to a higher power by the electronic media of mass communication developed in the twentieth century.

The more consensus formation in language is relieved by media, the more complex becomes the network of media-steered interaction. However, the two different kinds of relief mechanism promote quite different types of multiple communication. Delinguistified media of communication such as money and power, connect up interactions in space and time into more and more complex networks that no one has to comprehend or be responsible for. If by 'responsibility' we mean that one orients one's actions to criticizable validity claims, then a "deworlded" coordination of action that is unhinged from communicatively established consensus does not require that participants be responsible actors. By contrast, those media of communication such as reputation and value commitment, which decontextualize and focus, but do not replace, processes of reaching understanding, relieve interaction from yes/no positions of criticizable validity claims only *in the first instance*. They are dependent on technologies of communication, because these technologies make possible the formation of public spheres, that is, they see to it that even concentrated networks of communication are connected up to the cultural tradition and, *in the last instance*, remain dependent on the actions of responsible actors.

F.—These two contrary tendencies clearly mark a polarization between two types of action-coordinating mechanisms and an extensive uncoupling of system integration and social integration. In subsystems differentiated out via steering media, systemic mechanisms create their own, norm-free social structures jutting out from the lifeworld. These structures do, of course, remain linked with everyday communicative practice via basic institutions of civil or public law. We cannot directly infer from the mere fact that system and social integration have been largely uncoupled to linear dependency in one direction or the other. Both are conceivable: the institutions that anchor steering mechanisms such as power and money in the lifeworld could serve as a channel *either* for the influence of the lifeworld on formally organized domains of action *or,* conversely, for the influence of the system on communicatively structured contexts of action. In the one case, they function as an institutional framework that subjects system maintenance to the normative restrictions of the lifeworld, in the other, as a base that subordinates the lifeworld to the systemic constraints of material reproduction and thereby "mediatizes" it.

In theories of the state and of society, both models have been played through. Modern natural law theories neglected the inner logic of a functionally stabilized civil society in relation to the state; the classics of political economy were concerned to show that systemic imperatives were fundamentally in harmony with the basic norms of a polity guaranteeing freedom and justice. Marx destroyed this practically very important illusion; he showed that the laws of capitalist commodity production have the latent function of sustaining a structure that makes a mockery of bourgeois ideals. The lifeworld of the capitalist carrier strata, which was expounded in rational natural law and in the ideals of bourgeois thought generally, was devalued by Marx to a sociocultural superstructure. In his picture of base and superstructure he is also raising the methodological demand that we exchange the internal perspective of the lifeworld for an observer's perspective, so that we might grasp the systemic imperatives of an independent economy as they act upon the bourgeois lifeworld *a tergo*. In his view, only in a socialist society could the spell cast upon the lifeworld by the system be broken, could the dependence of the superstructure on the base be lifted.

In one way, the most recent systems functionalism is an heir-successor to Marxism, which it radicalizes and defuses at the same time. On the one hand, systems theory adopts the view that the systemic constraints of material production, which it understands as imperatives of self-maintenance of the general social system, reach right through the symbolic structures of the lifeworld. On the other hand, it removes the critical sting from the base-superstructure thesis by reinterpreting what was intended to be an empirical diagnosis as a prior analytical distinction. Marx took over from bourgeois social theory a presupposition that we found again in Durkheim: it is not a matter of indifference to a society whether and to what extent forms of social integration dependent on consensus are repressed and replaced by anonymous forms of system-integrative sociation. A theoretical approach that presents the lifeworld merely as one of several anonymously steered subsystems undercuts this distinction. Systems theory treats accomplishments of social and system integration as functionally equivalent and thus deprives itself of the standard of communicative rationality. And without that standard, increases in the complexity achieved *at the expense* of a rationalized lifeworld cannot be identified *as costs*. Systems theory lacks the analytic means to pursue the question that Marx (also) built into his base-superstructure metaphor and Weber renewed in his own way by inquiring into the paradox of societal rationalization. For us, this question takes on the form of whether the rationalization of the lifeworld does not become paradoxical with the transition to modern societies. The rationalization of the lifeworld makes possible the emergence and growth of subsystems whose independent imperatives turn back destructively upon the lifeworld itself.

I shall now take a closer look at the conceptual means by which this hypothesis might be given a more exact formulation. The assumption regarding a "mediatization" of the lifeworld refers to "interference" phenomena that arise when system and lifeworld have become differentiated from one another to such an extent that they can exert mutual influence upon one another. The mediatization of the lifeworld takes effect on and with the structures of the lifeworld; it is not one of those processes that are available as themes *within* the lifeworld, and thus it cannot be read off from the intuitive knowledge of members. On the other hand, it is also inaccessible from an external, systems-theoretical perspective. Although it comes about counterintuitively and cannot easily be perceived from the internal perspective of the lifeworld, there are indications of it in the formal conditions of communicative action.

The uncoupling of system integration and social integration means at first only a differentiation between two types of action coordination, one coming about through the consensus of those involved, the other through functional interconnections of action. System-integrative mechanisms attach to the effects of action. As they work through action orientations in a subjectively inconspicuous fashion, they may leave the socially integrative contexts of action which they are parasitically utilizing structurally unaltered—it is this sort of intermeshing of system with social integration that we postulated for the development level of tribal societies. Things are different when system integration intervenes in the very forms of social integration. In this case, too, we have to do with latent functional interconnections, but the subjective inconspicuousness of systemic constraints that *instrumentalize* a communicatively structured lifeworld takes on the character of deception, of objectively false consciousness. The effects of the system on the lifeworld, which change the structure of contexts in socially integrated groups, have to remain hidden. The reproductive constraints that instrumentalize a lifeworld without weakening the illusion of its self-sufficiency have to hide, so to speak, in the pores of communicative action. This gives rise to a *structural violence* that, without becoming manifest as such, takes hold of the forms of intersubjectivity of possible understanding. Structural violence is exercised by way of systemic restrictions on communication; distortion is anchored in the formal conditions of communicative action in such a way that the interrelation of the objective, social, and subjective world gets prejudged for participants in a typical fashion. In analogy to the cognitive a priori of Lukács's "forms of objectivity," I shall introduce the concept of a *form of understanding* [*Verständigungsform*].

Lukács defined forms of objectivity as principles that, through the societal totality, preform the encounters of individuals with objective nature, normative reality, and their own subjective nature. He speaks of a priori forms of objectivity because, operating within the framework of the philosophy of the subject, he starts from the basic relation of a knowing and acting subject to the domain of perceptible and manipulable objects. After the change of paradigm introduced by the theory of communication, the formal properties of the intersubjectivity of possible understanding can take the place of the conditions of the objectivity of possible experience. A form of mutual understanding represents a compromise between the general structures of communicative action and reproductive constraints unavailable as themes within a given lifeworld. Historically variable forms of understanding are, as it were, the sectional planes that result when systemic constraints of material reproduction inconspicuously intervene in the forms of social integration and thereby mediatize the lifeworld.

I shall now (a) illustrate the concept of a form of understanding with those civilizations in which religious-metaphysical worldviews take on ideological functions, in order (b) to gain an analytic perspective on the hypothetical sequence of forms of mutual understanding.

(a) In societies organized around a state, a need for legitimation arises that, for structural reasons, could not yet exist in tribal societies. In societies organized through kinship, the institutional system is anchored ritually, that is, in a practice that is interpreted by mythical narratives and that stabilizes its normative validity all by itself. By contrast, the authority of the laws in which a general political order is articulated has to be guaranteed, in the first instance, by the ruler's power of sanction. But political domination has socially integrating power only insofar as disposition over means of sanction does not rest on naked repression, but on the authority of an office anchored in turn in a legal order. For this reason, laws need to be intersubjectively recognized by citizens; they have to be legitimated as right and proper. This leaves culture with the task of supplying reasons why an existing political order deserves to be recognized. Whereas mythical narratives interpret and make comprehensible a ritual practice of which they themselves are part, religious and metaphysical worldviews of prophetic origin have the form of doctrines that can be worked up intellectually and that explain and justify an existing political order in terms of the world-order they explicate.[35]

The need for legitimation that arises, for structural reasons, in civilizations is especially precarious. If one compares the ancient civilizations with even strongly hierarchized tribal societies, one finds an unmistakable increase in social inequality. In the framework of state organization, units with different structures can be functionally specified. Once the organization of social labor is uncoupled from kinship relations, resources can be more easily mobilized and more effectively combined. But this expansion of material reproduction is gained at the price of transforming the stratified kinship system into a stratified class society. What presents itself from a system perspective as an integration of society at the level of an expanded material reproduction, means, from the perspective of social integration, an increase in social inequality, wholesale economic exploitation, and the juridically cloaked repression of dependent classes. The history of penal law provides unmistakable indicators of the high degree of repression required in all ancient civilizations. Social movements that can be analyzed as class struggles—although they were not carried on as such—pose a threat to social integration. For this reason, the functions of exploitation and repression fulfilled by rulers and ruling classes in the systemic nexus of material reproduction have to be kept latent as far as possible. Worldviews have to become ideologically efficacious.

Weber showed how the world religions were dominated by a basic question, namely, the legitimacy of the unequal distribution of earthly goods among humankind. Theocentric worldviews put forward theodicies so as to reinterpret the need for a religious explanation of suffering perceived as unjust into an individual need for salvation, and thus to satisfy it. Cosmocentric worldviews offered equivalent solutions to the same problem. What is common to religious and metaphysical worldviews is a more or less clearly marked, dichotomous structure that makes it possible to relate the sociocultural world to a world behind it. The world behind the visible world of this life, behind the world of appearances, represents a fundamental order; when it is possible to explain the orders of a stratified class society as homologous to that world-order, worldviews of this kind can take on ideological functions. The world religions pervaded both popular and high cultures; they owed their overwhelming efficacy to the fact that with the same set of assertions and promises they could satisfy the need for justification at very different levels of moral consciousness simultaneously.

At first glance, it strikes one as puzzling that ideological interpretations of the world and society could be sustained *against all appearances* of barbaric injustice. The constraints of material reproduction could not have reached so effectively and relentlessly through the class-specific lifeworlds of civilizations if cultural traditions had not been immunized against dissonant experiences. I would explain this unassailability by the systemic restrictions placed on communication. Although religious-metaphysical worldviews exerted a strong attraction on intellectual strata; although they provoked the hermeneutic efforts of many generations of teachers, theologians, educated persons, preachers, mandarins, bureaucrats, citizens, and the like; although they were reshaped by argumentation, given a dogmatic form, systematized and rationalized in terms of their own motifs, the basic religious and metaphysical concepts lay at a level of undifferentiated validity claims where the rationality potential of speech remains more tightly bound than in the profane practice of everyday life, which had not been worked through intellectually. Owing to the fusion of ontic, normative, and expressive aspects of validity, and to the cultically rooted fixation of a corresponding belief attitude, the basic concepts that carried, as it were, the legitimation load of ideologically effective worldviews were immunized against objections already within the cognitive reach of everyday communication. The immunization could succeed when an institutional separation between the sacred and the profane realms of action ensured that traditional foundations were not taken up "in the wrong place"; within the domain of the sacred, communication remained *systematically restricted* due to the lack of differentiation between spheres of validity, that is, *as a result of the formal conditions of possible understanding.*[36]

The mode of legitimation in civilizations is thus based on a form of understanding that systemically limits possibilities of communication owing to its failure to differentiate sufficiently among the various validity claims. Earlier we placed mythical, religious-metaphysical, and modern worldviews in a hierarchy, according to the degree of decentration of the world-understandings they make possible. Analogously, we can order action orientations, and the realms of action they define, according to the degree of differentiation of validity aspects, and in this way we can get at the relative a priori of the form of understanding dominant at a given time and place. These *forms of the intersubjectivity of mutual understanding* do not reflect the structures of dominant worldviews in any symmetrical manner, for established interpretive systems do not pervade all areas of action with the same intensity. As we have seen, in civilizations the immunizing power of the form of understanding derives from a peculiar, structurally describable differential between two realms of action: in comparison to profane action orientations, sacred ones enjoy a greater authority, even though validity spheres are less differentiated and the potential for rationality is less developed in sacred than in profane domains of action.

(*b*) With a systematic investigation of forms of understanding in mind, I shall distinguish four domains of action: (1) the domain of cultic practice; (2) the domain in which religious systems of interpretation have the power directly to orient everyday practice; and finally the profane domains in which the cultural shock of knowledge is utilized for (3) communication and (4) purposive activity, without the structures of the worldview directly taking effect in action orientations.

Since I regard (1) and (2) as belonging to the sacred realm of action, I can avoid difficulties that result from Durkheim's oversimplified division.

Magical practices carried on by individuals outside of the cultic community should not be demoted, as Durkheim proposed they should, to the profane realm. Everyday practice is permeated throughout with ceremonies that cannot be understood in utilitarian terms. It is better not to limit the sacred realm of action to cultic practice, but to extend it to the class of actions based on religious patterns of interpretation.[37]

Furthermore, there are internal relations between the structures of worldviews and the kinds of cultic actions: to myth there corresponds a *ritual* practice (and sacrificial actions) of tribal members; to religious-metaphysical worldviews a *sacramental* practice (and prayers) of the congregation; to the religion of culture [*Bildungsreligion*] of the early modern period, finally, a *contemplative* presentation of auratic works of art. Along this path, cultic practice gets "disenchanted," in Weber's sense; it loses the character of compelling the gods to some end, and it is less and less carried on in the consciousness that a divine power can be *forced* to do something.[38]

Within the realm of profane action I shall distinguish between communicative and purposive activity; I shall assume that these two *aspects* can be distinguished even when corresponding *types* of action (not to mention *domains* of action defined by these types) have not yet been differentiated. The distinction between communicative and purposive activity is not relevant to the sacred realm. In my view, there is no point in contrasting religious cults and magical practices from this perspective.[39]

The next step would be to place the practices in different domains of action in a developmental-logical order according to the degree to which aspects of validity have been differentiated from one another. At one end of the scale stands ritual practice, at the other end the practice of argumentation. If we further consider that between the sacred and the profane domains there are differentials in authority and rationality—and in the opposite directions—we then have the points of view relevant to ordering the forms of understanding in a systematic sequence. The following schema (figure 5) represents four forms of mutual understanding ordered along the line of a progressive unfettering of the rationality potential inherent in communicative action. The areas (1–2) and (3–4) stand for the form of understanding in archaic societies, the areas (5–6) and (7–8) for that in civilizations, the areas (9–10) and (11–12) for that in early modern societies.

Taking the archaic form of understanding as an example, I shall next give a somewhat more detailed account of the contrasting directions of the differentials in authority and rationality between the sacred and the profane domains of action. Following that I shall comment more briefly on the forms of understanding typical of civilizations (5–8) and of early modern societies (9–12).

(*ad 1* and *2*) We find ritualized behavior already in vertebrate societies; in the transitional field between primate hordes and paleolithic societies, social integration was probably routed primarily through those strongly ritualized modes of behavior we counted above as symbolically mediated interaction. Only with the transformation of primitive systems of calls into grammatically regulated, propositionally differentiated speech was the sociocultural starting point reached at which ritualized *behavior* changed into ritualized *action;* language opened up, so to speak, an interior view of rites. From this point on, we no longer have to be content with *describing* ritualized behavior in terms of its observable features and hypothesized functions; we can try to *understand* rituals—insofar as they have maintained a residual existence and have become known to us through field studies.

A modern observer is struck by the extremely irrational character of ritual practices. The aspects of action that we cannot help but keep apart today are merged in one and the same act. The element of purposive activity comes out in the fact that ritual practices are supposed magically to bring about states in the world; the element of normatively regulated action is noticeable in the quality of obligation that emanates from the ritually conjured, at once attracting and terrifying, powers; the element of expressive action is especially clear in the standardized expressions of feeling in ritual ceremonies; finally an assertoric aspect is also present inasmuch as ritual practice serves to represent and reproduce exemplary events or mythically narrated original scenes.

Domains of action / Differentiation of validity spheres	Sacred		Profane	
	Cultic practice	Worldviews that steer practice	Communication	Purposive activity
Confusion of relations of validity and effectiveness: performative-instrumental attitude	1. Rite (institutionalization of social solidarity)	2. Myth	—	—
Differentiation between relations of validity and effectiveness: orientation to success vs. to mutual understanding	5. Sacrament/prayer (institutionalization to paths to salvation and knowledge)	6. Religious and metaphysical worldviews	3. Communicative action bound to particular contexts and with a holistic orientation to validity	4. Purposive activity as a task-oriented element of roles (utilization of technical innovations)
Differentiation of specific validity claims at the level of action; objectivating vs. norm-conformative vs. expressive attitudes	9. Contemplative presentation of auratic art (institutionalization of the enjoyment of art)	10. Religious ethics of conviction, rational natural law, civil religion	7. Normatively regulated communicative action with an argumentative handling of truth claims	8. Purposive activity organized through legitimate power (utilization of specialized practical-professional knowledge)
Differentiation of specific validity claims at the level of discourse: communicative action vs. discourse	—	—	11. Normatively unbound communicative action with institutionalized criticism	12. Purposive activity as ethically neutral purposive-rational action (utilization of scientific technologies and strategies)

FIGURE 5. Forms of Mutual Understanding

Ritual practice is, of course, already part of a sociocultural form of life in which a higher form of communication has emerged with grammatical speech. Language in the strict sense breaks up the unity of teleological, normative, expressive, and cognitive aspects of action. Yet mythical thought shields ritual practice from the tendencies toward decomposition that appear at the level of language (with the differentiation between action oriented to mutual understanding and to success, and the transformation of adaptive behavior into purposive activity). Myth holds the same aspects together on the plane of interpretation that are fused together on the plane of practice. An interpretation of the world that confuses internal relations of meaning with external relations among things, validity with empirical efficacy, can protect ritual practice against rips in the fabric woven from communicative and purposive activity indistinguishably. This explains its coexistence with profane contexts of cooperation in which goal-oriented actions are effectively coordinated within the framework of kinship roles. The experience gained in everyday practice is worked up in myth and connected with narrative explanations of the orders of the world and of society. In this regard, myth bridges over the two domains of action.

We can see in the formal structures of the relevant action orientations that there is a rationality differential between sacred and profane domains. At the heart of the sacred realm is ritual practice, which stands or falls with the interweaving of purposive activity and communication, of orientations to success with orientations to mutual understanding. It is stabilized by a mythical understanding of the world that, while it develops in narrative form, that is, at the level of grammatical speech, nonetheless exhibits similar categorical structures. In the basic categories of myth, relations on validity are still confused with relations of effectiveness. On the other hand, the mythical worldview is opened to the flow of experience from the realm of profane action. Everyday practice already rests on a difference between aspects of validity and reality.

(*ad 3* and *4*) It is above all in the areas of production and warfare that cooperation based on a division of labor develops and requires action oriented to success. From the standpoint of developmental history as well, efficacy is the earliest aspect of the rationality of action. As long as truth claims could barely be isolated on the level of communicative action, the "know-how" invested in technical and strategic rules could not yet take the form of explicit knowledge. In contrast to magic, the profane practice of everyday life already calls for differentiating between orientations to success and to mutual understanding. However, within communicative action the claims to truth, to truthfulness, and to rightness likely flowed together in a whole that was first broken up in a methodical fashion when, with the advent of writing, a stratum of literati arose who learned to produce and process texts.

The normative scope of communicative action was relatively narrowly restricted by particularistic kinship relations. Under the aspect of fulfilling standardized tasks, goal-directed cooperative actions remained embedded in a communicative practice that itself served to fulfill narrowly circumscribed social expectations. These expectations issued from a social structure regarded as part of a mythically explained and ritually secured world-order. The mythical system of interpretation closed the circuit between profane and sacred domains.

(*ad 5* and *6*) When a holistic concept of validity was constituted, internal relations of meaning could be differentiated from external relations among things, though it was still not possible to discriminate among the various aspects of validity. As Weber has shown, it is at this stage that religious and metaphysical worldviews arise. Their basic concepts proved to be resistant to every attempt to separate off the aspects of the true, the good, and the perfect. Corresponding to such worldviews is a sacramental practice with forms of prayer or exercises and with demagicalized communication between the individual believer and the divine being. These worldviews are more or less dichotomous in structure; they set up a "world beyond" and leave a demythologized "this world" or a desocialized "world of appearances" to a disenchanted everyday practice. In the realm of profane action, structures take shape that break up the holistic concept of validity.

(*ad 7* and *8*) On the level of communicative action, the syndrome of validity claims breaks up. Participants no longer only differentiate between orientations to success and to mutual understanding, but between the different basic pragmatic attitudes as well. A polity with a state and conventional legal institutions has to rely on obedience to the law, that is, on a norm-conforming attitude toward legitimate order. The citizens of the state must be able to distinguish this attitude—in everyday actions as well—from an objectivating attitude toward external nature and an expressive attitude vis-à-vis their own inner nature. At this stage, communicative action can free itself from particularistic contexts, but it stays in the space marked out by solid traditional norms. An argumentative treatment of texts also makes participants aware of the differences between communicative action and discourse. But specific validity claims are differentiated only on the plane of action. There are not yet forms of argumentation tailored to specific aspects of validity.[40]

Purposive activity also attains a higher level of rationality. When truth claims can be isolated, it becomes possible to see the internal connection between the efficiency of action oriented to success and the truth of empirical statements, and to make sure of technical know-how. Thus practical professional knowledge can assume objective shape and be transmitted through teaching. Purposive activity gets detached from unspecific age and sex roles. To the extent that social labor is organized via legitimate power, special activities can define occupational roles.

(*ad 9* and *10*) That validity claims are not yet fully differentiated at this stage can be seen in the cultural tradition of the early modern period. Independent cultural value spheres do take shape, but to begin with only science is institutionalized in an unambiguous fashion, that is, under the aspect of exactly one validity claim. An autonomous art retains its aura and the enjoyment of art its contemplative character; both features derive from its cultic origins. An ethics of conviction remains tied to the context of religious traditions, however subjectivized; postconventional legal representations are still coupled with truth claims in rational natural law and form the nucleus of what Robert Bellah has called "civil religion." Thus, although art, morality, and law are already differentiated value spheres, they do not get wholly disengaged from the sacred domain so long as the internal development of each does not proceed unambiguously under precisely one specific aspect of validity. On the other hand, the forms of modern religiosity give up basic dogmatic claims. They destroy the metaphysical-religious "world beyond" and no longer dichotomously contrast this profane world to Transcendence, or the world of appearances to the reality of an underlying *Essence*. In domains of profane action, structures can take shape that are defined by an unrestricted differentiation of validity claims on the levels of action *and* argumentation.

(*ad 11* and *12*) It is here that discourse becomes relevant for profane spheres of action, too. In everyday communication, participants can keep apart not only different basic pragmatic attitudes, but also the levels of action and discourse. Domains of action normed by positive law, with posttraditional legal institutions, presuppose that participants are in a position to shift from naïvely performing actions to reflectively engaging in argumentation. To the extent that the hypothetical discussion of normative validity claims is institutionalized, the critical potential of speech can be brought to bear on existing institutions. Legitimate orders still appear to communicatively acting subjects as something normative, but this normativity has a different quality insofar as institutions are no longer legitimated per se through religious and metaphysical worldviews.

Purposive activity is freed from normative contexts in a more radicalized sense. Up to this point, action oriented to success remained linked with norms of action and embedded in communicative action within the framework of a task-oriented system of social cooperation. But with the legal institutionalization of the monetary medium, success-oriented action steered by egocentric calculations of utility loses its connection to action oriented by mutual understanding. This strategic action, which is disengaged from the mechanism of reaching understanding and calls for an objectivating attitude even in regard to interpersonal relations, is promoted to the model for methodically dealing with a scientifically objectivated nature. In the instrumental sphere, purposive activity gets free of normative restrictions to the extent that it becomes linked to flows of information from the scientific system.

The two areas on the left in the bottom row of figure 5 have been left empty because, with the development of modern societies, the sacred domain has largely disintegrated, or at least has lost its structure-forming significance. At the level of completely differentiated validity spheres, art sheds its cultic background, just as morality and law detach themselves from their religions and metaphysical background. With this *secularization of bourgeois culture,* the cultural value spheres separate off sharply from one another and develop according to the standards of the inner logics specific to the different validity claims. Culture loses just those formal properties that enabled it to take on ideological functions. Insofar as these tendencies—schematically indicated here—actually do establish themselves in developed modern societies, the structural force of system imperatives intervening in the forms of social integration can no longer hide behind the rationality differential between sacred and profane domains. The modern form of understanding is too transparent to provide a niche for this structural violence by means of inconspicuous restrictions on communication. Under these conditions it is to be expected that the competition between forms of system and social integration would become more visible than previously. In the end, systemic mechanisms suppress forms of social integration even in those areas where a consensus-dependent coordination of action cannot be replaced, that is, where the symbolic reproduction of the lifeworld is at stake. In these areas, the *mediatization* of the lifeworld assumes the form of a *colonization.*

In the concluding chapter I shall take the modern form of understanding, which has been crystallizing in the West since the eighteenth century, as my point of departure for a theory of modernity linked to Weber's rationalization thesis. Before doing so, I want to pick up again the thread of the history of social theory. Through the work of Talcott Parsons we can get clear about how to interrelate the basic concepts of systems theory and action theory, which we have until now merely conjoined in an abstract way. In the process we can also look at the present state of discussions concerning the foundations of social science, and we can take up the problem of reification once more, at the level of contemporary standards of theory formation, and reformulate it in terms of systemically induced lifeworld pathologies.

Part Three
THE ANALYSIS AND CRITIQUE OF MODERN SOCIETY

Chapter Ten
THE PUBLIC SPHERE

Concept

By "public sphere" we mean first of all a domain of our social life in which such a thing as public opinion can be formed. Access to the public sphere is open in principle to all citizens. A portion of the public sphere is constituted in every conversation in which private persons come together to form a public. They are then acting neither as business or professional people conducting their private affairs, nor as legal consociates subject to the legal regulations of a state bureaucracy and obligated to obedience. Citizens act as a public when they deal with matters of general interest without being subject to coercion; thus with the guarantee that they may assemble and unite freely, and express and publicize their opinions freely. When the public is large, this kind of communication requires certain means of dissemination and influence; today, newspapers and periodicals, radio and television are the media of the public sphere. We speak of a political public sphere (as distinguished from a literary one, for instance) when the public discussions concern objects connected with the practice of the state. The coercive power of the state is the counterpart, as it were, of the political public sphere, but it is not a part of it. State power is, to be sure, considered "public" power, but it owes the attribute of publicness to its task of caring for the public, that is, providing for the common good of all legal consociates. Only when the exercise of public authority has actually been subordinated to the requirement of democratic publicness does the political public sphere acquire an institutionalized influence on the government, by way of the legislative body. The term "public opinion" refers to the functions of criticism and control of organized state authority that the public exercises informally, as well as formally during periodic elections. Regulations concerning the publicness (or publicity [*Publizität*] in its original meaning) of state-related activities, as, for instance, the public accessibility required of legal proceedings, are also connected with this function of public opinion. To the public sphere as a sphere mediating between state and society, a sphere in which the public as the vehicle of public opinion is formed, there corresponds the principle of publicness—the publicness that once had to win out against the secret politics of monarchs and that since then has permitted democratic control of state activity.

It is no accident that these concepts of the public sphere and public opinion were not formed until the eighteenth century. They derive their specific meaning from a concrete historical situation. It was then that one learned to distinguish between opinion and public opinion, or *opinion publique*. Whereas mere opinions (things taken for granted as part of a culture, normative convictions, collective prejudices and judgments) seem to persist unchanged in their quasi-natural structure as a kind of sediment of history, public opinion, in terms of its very idea, can be formed only if a public that engages in rational discussion exists. Public discussions that are institutionally protected and that take, with critical intent, the exercise of political authority as their theme have not existed since time immemorial—they developed only in a specific phase of bourgeois society, and only by virtue of a specific constellation of interests could they be incorporated into the order of the bourgeois constitutional state.

History

It is not possible to demonstrate the existence of a public sphere in its own right, separate from the private sphere, in the European society of the High Middle Ages. At the same time, however, it is not a coincidence that the attributes of authority at that time were called "public." For a public representation of authority existed at that time. At all levels of the pyramid established by feudal law, the status of the feudal lord is neutral with respect to the categories "public" and "private"; but the person possessing that status represents it publicly; he displays himself, represents himself as the embodiment of a "higher" power, in whatever degree. This concept of representation has survived into recent constitutional history. Even today the power of political authority on its highest level, however much it has become detached from its former basis, requires representation through the head of state. But such elements derive from a pre-bourgeois social structure. Representation in the sense of the bourgeois public sphere, as in "representing" the nation or specific clients, has nothing to do with *representative publicness*, which inheres in the concrete existence of a lord. As long as the prince and the estates of his realm "are" the land, rather than merely "representing" it, they are capable of this kind of representation; they represent their authority "before" the people rather than for the people.

The feudal powers (the church, the prince, and the nobility) to which this representative publicness adheres disintegrated in the course of a long process of polarization; by the end of the eighteenth century they had decomposed into private elements on the one side and public on the other. The position of the church changed in connection with the Reformation; the tie to divine authority that the church represented, that is, religion, became a private matter. Historically, what is called the freedom of religion safeguarded the first domain of private autonomy; the church itself continued its existence as one corporate body under public law among others. The corresponding polarization of princely power acquired visible form in the separation of the public budget from the private household property of the feudal lord. In the bureaucracy and the military (and in part also in the administration of justice), institutions of public power became autonomous vis-à-vis the privatized sphere of the princely court. In terms of the estates, finally, elements from the ruling groups developed into organs of public power, into parliament (and in part also into judicial organs); elements from the occupational status groups, insofar as they had become established in urban corporations and in certain differentiations within the estates of the land, developed into the sphere of bourgeois society, which would confront the state as a genuine domain of private autonomy.

Representative publicness gave way to the new sphere of "public power" that came into being with the national and territorial states. Ongoing state activity (permanent administration, a standing army) had its counterpart in the permanence of relationships that had developed in the meantime with the stock market and the press, through traffic in goods and news. Public power became consolidated as something tangible confronting those who were subject to it and who at first found themselves only negatively defined by it. These are the "private persons" who are excluded from public power because they hold no office. "Public" no longer refers to the representative court of a person vested with authority; instead, it now refers to the competence-regulated activity of an apparatus furnished with a monopoly on the legitimate use of force. As those to whom this public power is addressed, private persons subsumed under the state form the public.

As a private domain, society, which has come to confront the state, as it were, is on the one hand clearly differentiated from public power; on the other hand, society becomes a matter of public interest insofar as with the rise of a market economy the reproduction of life extends beyond the confines of private domestic power. The *bourgeois public sphere* can be understood as the sphere of private persons assembled to form a public. They soon began to make use of the public sphere of informational newspapers, which was officially regulated, against the public power itself, using those papers, along with the morally and critically oriented weeklies, to engage in debate about the general rules governing relations in their own essentially privatized but publicly relevant sphere of commodity exchange and labor.

The Liberal Model of the Public Sphere

The medium in which this debate takes place—public discussion—is unique and without historical prototype. Previously the estates had negotiated contracts with their princes in which claims to power were defined on a case-by-case basis. As we know, this development followed a different course in England, where princely power was relativized through parliament, than on the Continent, where the estates were mediatized by the monarch. The "third estate" then broke with this mode of equalizing power, for it could no longer establish itself as a ruling estate. Given a commercial economy, a division of authority accomplished through differentiation of the rights of those possessing feudal authority (liberties belonging to the estates) was no longer possible—the power under private law of disposition of capitalist property is nonpolitical. The bourgeois are private persons; as such, they do not "rule." Thus their claims to power in opposition to public power are directed not against a concentration of authority that should be "divided" but rather against the principle of established authority. The principle of control, namely publicness, that the bourgeois public opposes to the principle of established authority aims at a transformation of authority as such, not merely the exchange of one basis of legitimation for another.

In the first modern constitutions the sections listing basic rights provide an image of the liberal model of the public sphere: they guarantee society as a sphere of private autonomy; opposite it stands a public power limited to a few functions; between the two spheres, as it were, stands the domain of private persons who have come together to form a public and who, as citizens of the state, mediate the state with the needs of bourgeois society, in order, as the idea goes, to thus convert political authority to "rational" authority in the medium of this public sphere. Under the presuppositions of a society based on the free exchange of commodities, it seemed that the general interest, which served as the criterion by which this kind of rationality was to be evaluated, would be assured if the dealings of private persons in the marketplace were emancipated from social forces and their dealings in the public sphere were emancipated from political coercion.

The political daily press came to have an important role during this same period. In the second half of the eighteenth century, serious competition to the older form of news writing as the compiling of items of information arose in the form of literary journalism. Karl Bücher describes the main outlines of this development: "From mere institutions for the publication of news, newspapers became the vehicles and guides of public opinion as well, weapons of party politics. The consequence of this for the internal organization of the newspaper enterprise was the insertion of a new function between the gathering of news and its publication: the editorial function. For the newspaper publisher, however, the significance of this development was that from a seller of new information he became a dealer in public opinion." Publishers provided the commercial basis for the newspaper without, however, commercializing it as such. The press remained an institution of the public itself, operating to provide and intensify public discussion, no longer a mere organ for the conveyance of information, but not yet a medium of consumer culture.

This type of press can be observed especially in revolutionary periods, when papers associated with the tiniest political coalitions and groups spring up, as in Paris in 1789. In the Paris of 1848 every halfway prominent politician still formed his own club, and every other one founded his own *journal:* over 450 clubs and more than 200 papers came into being there between February and May alone. Until the permanent legalization of a public sphere that functioned politically, the appearance of a political newspaper was equivalent to engagement in the struggle for a zone of freedom for public opinion, for publicness as a principle. Not until the establishment of the bourgeois constitutional state was a press engaged in the public use of reason relieved of the pressure of ideological viewpoints. Since then it has been able to abandon its polemical stance and take advantage of the earning potential of commercial activity. The ground was cleared for this development from a press of viewpoints to a commercial press at about the same time in England, France, and the United States, during the 1830s. In the course of this transformation from the journalism of writers who were private persons to the consumer services of the mass media, the sphere of publicness was changed by an influx of private interests that achieved privileged representation within it.

The Public Sphere in Mass Welfare-State Democracies

The liberal model of the public sphere remains instructive in regard to the normative claim embodied in institutionalized requirements of publicness; but it is not applicable to actual relationships within a mass democracy that is industrially advanced and constituted as a social-welfare state. In part, the liberal model had always contained ideological aspects; in part, the social presuppositions to which those aspects were linked have undergone fundamental changes. Even the forms in which the public sphere was manifested, forms which made its idea seem to a certain extent obvious, began to change with the Chartist movement in England and the February Revolution in France. With the spread of the press and propaganda, the public expanded beyond the confines of the bourgeoisie. Along with its social exclusivity the public lost the cohesion given it by institutions of convivial social intercourse and by a relatively high standard of education. Accordingly, conflicts which in the past were pushed off into the private sphere now enter the public sphere. Group needs, which cannot expect satisfaction from a self-regulating market, tend toward state regulation. The public sphere, which must now mediate these demands, becomes a field for competition among interests in the cruder form of forcible confrontation. Laws that have obviously originated under the "pressure of the streets" can scarcely continue to be understood in terms of a consensus achieved by private persons in public discussion; they correspond, in more or less undisguised form, to compromises between conflicting private interests. Today it is social organizations that act in relation to the state in the political public sphere, whether through the mediation of political parties or directly, in interplay with public administration. With the interlocking of the public and private domains, not only do political agencies take over certain functions in the sphere of commodity exchange and social labor; societal powers also take over political functions. This leads to a kind of "refeudalization" of the public sphere. Large-scale organizations strive for political compromises with the state and with one another, behind closed doors if possible; but at the same time they have to secure at least plebiscitarian approval from the mass of the population through the deployment of a staged form of publicity.

The political public sphere in the welfare state is characterized by a singular weakening of its critical functions. Whereas at one time publicness was intended to subject persons or things to the public use of reason and to make political decisions susceptible to revision before the tribunal of public opinion, today it has often enough already been enlisted in the aid of the secret policies of interest groups; in the form of "publicity" it now acquires public prestige for persons or things and renders them capable of acclamation in a climate of nonpublic opinion. The term "public relations" itself indicates how a public sphere that formerly emerged from the structure of society must now be produced circumstantially on a case-by-case basis. The central relationship of the public, political parties, and parliament is also affected by this change in function.

This existing trend toward the weakening of the public sphere, as a principle, is opposed, however, by a welfare-state transformation of the functioning of basic rights: the requirement of publicness is extended by state organs to all organizations acting in relation to the state. To the extent to which this becomes a reality, a no longer intact public of private persons acting as individuals would be replaced by a public of organized private persons. Under current circumstances, only the latter could participate effectively in a process of public communication using the channels of intra-party and intra-organizational public spheres, on the basis of a publicness enforced for the dealings of organizations with the state. It is in this process of public communication that the formation of political compromises would have to achieve legitimation. The idea of the public sphere itself, which signified a rationalization of authority in the medium of public discussions among private persons, and which has been preserved in mass welfare-state democracy, threatens to disintegrate with the structural transformation of the public sphere. Today it could be realized only on a different basis, as a rationalization of the exercise of social and political power under the mutual control of rival organizations committed to publicness in their internal structure as well as in their dealings with the state and with one another.

Chapter Eleven
TECHNOLOGY AND SCIENCE AS "IDEOLOGY"

For Herbert Marcuse on his seventieth birthday, July 19, 1968

Max Weber introduced the concept of "rationality" in order to define the form of capitalist economic activity, bourgeois private law, and bureaucratic authority. Rationalization means, first of all, the extension of the areas of society subject to the criteria of rational decision. Second, social labor is industrialized, with the result that criteria of instrumental action also penetrate into other areas of life (urbanization of the mode of life, technification of transport and communication). Both trends exemplify the type of purposive-rational action, which refers to either the organization of means or choice between alternatives. Planning can be regarded as purposive-rational action of the second order. It aims at the establishment, improvement, or expansion of systems of purposive-rational action themselves.

The progressive "rationalization" of society is linked to the institutionalization of scientific and technical development. To the extent that technology and science permeate social institutions and thus transform them, old legitimations are destroyed. The secularization and "disenchantment" of action-orienting worldviews, of cultural tradition as a whole, is the obverse of the growing "rationality" of social action.

Herbert Marcuse has taken these analyses as a point of departure in order to demonstrate that the formal concept of rationality—which Weber derived from the purposive-rational action of the capitalist entrepreneur, the industrial wage laborer, the abstract legal person, and the modern administrative official and based on the criteria of science as well as technology—has specific substantive implications. Marcuse is convinced that what Weber called "rationalization" realizes not rationality as such but rather, in the name of rationality, a specific form of unacknowledged political domination. Because this sort of rationality extends to the correct choice among strategies, the appropriate application of technologies, and the efficient establishment of systems (with *presupposed* aims in *given* situations), it removes the total social framework of interests in which strategies are chosen, technologies applied, and systems established, from the scope of reflection and rational reconstruction. Moreover, this rationality extends only to relations of possible technical control and therefore requires a type of action that implies domination, whether of nature or of society. By virtue of its structure, purposive-rational action is the exercise of control. That is why, in accordance with this rationality, the "rationalization" of the conditions of life is synonymous with the institutionalization of a form of domination whose political character becomes unrecognizable: the technical reason of a social system of purposive-rational action does not lose its political content. Marcuse's critique of Weber comes to the conclusion that

the very concept of technical reason is perhaps ideological. Not only the application of technology but technology itself is domination (of nature and men)—methodical, scientific, calculated, calculating control. Specific purposes and interests of domination are not foisted upon technology "subsequently" and from the outside; they enter the very construction of the technical apparatus. Technology is always a historical-social *project:* in it is projected what a society and its ruling interests intend to do with men and things. Such a "purpose" of domination is "substantive" and to this extent belongs to the very form of technical reason.[1]

As early as 1956 Marcuse referred in a quite different context to the peculiar phenomenon that in industrially advanced capitalist societies domination tends to lose its exploitative and oppressive character and become "rational," without political domination thereby disappearing: "domination is dependent only on the capacity and drive to maintain and extend the apparatus as a whole."[2] Domination is rational in that a system can be maintained which can allow itself to make the growth of the forces of production, coupled with scientific and technical progress, the basis of its legitimation although, at the same time, the level of the productive forces constitutes a potential in relation to which "the renunciations and burdens placed on individuals seem more and more unnecessary and irrational."[3] In Marcuse's judgment, the objectively superfluous repression can be recognized in the "intensified subjection of individuals to the enormous apparatus of production and distribution, in the deprivatization of free time, in the almost indistinguishable fusion of constructive and destructive social labor."[4] Paradoxically, however, this repression can disappear from the consciousness of the population because the legitimation of domination has assumed a new character: it refers to the "constantly increasing productivity and domination of nature which keeps individuals . . . living in increasing comfort."[5]

The institutionalized growth of the forces of production following from scientific and technical progress surpasses all historical proportions. From it the institutional framework draws its opportunity for legitimation. The thought that relations of production can be measured against the potential of developed productive forces is prevented because the existing relations of production present themselves as the technically necessary organizational form of a rationalized society. Here "rationality," in Weber's sense, shows its Janus face. It is no longer only a critical standard for the developmental level of the forces of production in relation to which the objectively super-fluous, repressive character of historically obsolete relations of production can be exposed. It is also an apologetic standard through which these same relations of production can be justified as a functional institutional frame-work. Indeed, in relation to its apologetic serviceability, "rationality" is weakened as a critical standard and degraded to a corrective *within* the system: what can still be said is at best that society is "poorly pro-grammed." At the stage of their scientific-technical development, then, the forces of production appear to enter a new constellation with the relations of production. Now they no longer function as the basis of a critique of prevailing legitimations in the interest of political enlightenment, but be-come instead the basis of legitimation. *This* is what Marcuse conceives of as world-historically new.

But if this is the case, must not the rationality embodied in systems of purposive-rational action be understood as specifically limited? Must not the rationality of science and technology, instead of being reducible to un-varying rules of logic and method have absorbed a substantive, historically derived, and therefore transitory a priori structure? Marcuse answers in the affirmative:

The principles of modern science were *a priori* structured in such a way that they could serve as conceptual instruments for a universe of self-propelling, productive control; theoretical operationalism came to correspond to practical operationalism. The scientific method which led to the ever-more-effective domination of nature thus came to provide the pure concepts as well as the instrumentalities for the ever-more-effective domination of man by man *through* the domination of nature. . . . Today, domination perpetuates and extends itself not only through technology but *as* technology, and the latter provides the great legitimation of the expanding polit-ical power, which absorbs all spheres of culture.

In this universe, technology also provides the great rationalization of the un-freedom of man and demonstrates the "technical" impossibility of being autono-mous, of determining one's own life. For this unfreedom appears neither as irratio-nal nor as political, but rather as submission to the technical apparatus which enlarges the comforts of life and increases the productivity of labor. Technological rationality thus protects rather than cancels the legitimacy of domination and the instrumentalist horizon of reason opens on a rationally totalitarian society.[6]

Weber's "rationalization" is not only a long-term process of the transfor-mation of social structures but simultaneously "rationalization" in Freud's sense: the true motive, the perpetuation of objectively obsolete domination, is concealed through the invocation of purposive-rational imperatives. This invocation is possible only because the rationality of science and technology is immanently one of control: the rationality of domination.

Marcuse owes this concept, according to which modern science is a his-torical formation, equally to Husserl's treatise on the crisis of European science and Heidegger's destruction of Western metaphysics. From the materialist position Ernst Bloch has developed the viewpoint that the rationality of modern science is, in its roots, distorted by capitalism in such a way as to rob modern technology of the innocence of a pure productive force. But Marcuse is the first to make the "political content of technical reason" the analytical point of departure for a theory of advanced capitalist society. Because he not only develops this viewpoint philosophically but also attempts to corroborate it through sociological analysis, the difficulties inherent in this conception become visible. I shall refer here to but one ambiguity contained in Marcuse's own conception.

If the phenomenon on which Marcuse bases his social analysis, i.e., the peculiar *fusion of technology and domination*, rationality and oppression, could not be interpreted otherwise than as a world "project," as Marcuse says in the language of Sartre's phenomenology, contained in the material a priori of the logic of science and technology and determined by class interest and historical situation, then social emancipation could not be conceived without a complementary revolutionary transformation of science and technology themselves. In several passages Marcuse is tempted to pursue this idea of a New Science in connection with the promise, familiar in Jewish and Protestant mysticism, of the "resurrection of fallen nature." This theme, well known for having penetrated into Schelling's (and Baader's) philosophy via Swabian Pietism, returns in Marx's *Paris Manuscripts,* today constitutes the central thought of Bloch's philosophy, and, in reflected forms, also directs the more secret hopes of Walter Benjamin, Max Horkheimer, and Theodor W. Adorno. It is also present in Marcuse's thought:

The point which I am trying to make is that science, *by virtue of its own method* and concepts, has projected and promoted a universe in which the domination of nature has remained linked to the domination of man—a link which tends to be fatal to this universe as a whole. Nature, scientifically comprehended and mastered, reappears in the technical apparatus of production and destruction which sustains and improves the life of the individuals while subordinating them to the masters of the apparatus. Thus the rational hierarchy merges with the social one. If this is the case, then the change in the direction of progress, which might sever this fatal link, would also affect the very structure of science—the scientific project. Its hypotheses, without losing their rational character, would develop in an essentially different experimental context (that of a pacified world); consequently, science would arrive at essentially different concepts of nature and establish essentially different facts.[7]

In a logical fashion Marcuse envisages not only different modes of theory formation but a different scientific methodology in general. The transcendental framework within which nature would be made the object of a new experience would then no longer be the functional system of instrumental action. The viewpoint of possible technical control would be replaced by one of preserving, fostering, and releasing the potentialities of nature: "there are two kinds of mastery: a repressive and a liberating one."[8] To this view it must be objected that modern science can be interpreted as a historically unique project only if at least one alternative project is thinkable. And, in addition, an alternative New Science would have to include the definition of a New Technology. This is a sobering consideration because technology, if based at all on a project, can only be traced back to a "project" of the human species *as a whole,* and not to one that could be historically surpassed.

Arnold Gehlen has pointed out in what seems to me conclusive fashion that there is an immanent connection between the technology known to us and the structure of purposive-rational action. If we comprehend the behavioral system of action regulated by its own results as the conjunction of rational decision and instrumental action, then we can reconstruct the history of technology from the point of view of the step-by-step objectivation of the elements of that very system. In any case technological development lends itself to being interpreted as though the human species had taken the elementary components of the behavioral system of purposive-rational action, which is primarily rooted in the human organism, and projected them one after another onto the plane of technical instruments, thereby unburdening itself of the corresponding functions.[9] At first the functions of the motor apparatus (hands and legs) were augmented and replaced, followed by energy production (of the human body), the functions of the sensory apparatus (eyes, ears, and skin), and finally by the functions of the governing center (the brain). Technological development thus follows a logic that corresponds to the structure of purposive-rational action regulated by its own results, which is in fact the structure of *work*. Realizing this, it is impossible to envisage how, as long as the organization of human nature does not change and as long therefore as we have to achieve self-preservation through social labor and with the aid of means that substitute for work, we could renounce technology, more particularly *our* technology, in favor of a qualitatively different one.

Marcuse has in mind an alternative *attitude* to nature, but it does not admit of the idea of a New Technology. Instead of treating nature as the object of possible technical control, we can encounter her as an opposing partner in a possible interaction. We can seek out a fraternal rather than an exploited nature. At the level of an as yet incomplete intersubjectivity we can impute subjectivity to animals and plants, even to minerals, and try to communicate with nature instead of merely processing her under conditions of severed communication. And the idea that a still enchained subjectivity of nature cannot be unbound until men's communication among themselves is free from domination has retained, to say the least, a singular attraction. Only if men could communicate without compulsion and each could recognize himself in the other, could mankind possibly recognize nature as another subject: not, as idealism would have it, as its Other, but as a subject of which mankind itself is the Other.

Be that as it may, the achievements of technology, which are indispensable as such, could surely not be substituted for by an awakened nature. The alternative to existing technology, the project of nature as opposing partner instead of object, refers to an alternative structure of action: to symbolic interaction in distinction to purposive-rational action. This means, however, that the two projects are projections of work and of language, i.e., projects of the human species as a whole, and not of an individual epoch, a specific class, or a surpassable situation. The idea of a New Science will not stand up to logical scrutiny any more than that of a New Technology, if indeed science is to retain the meaning of modern science inherently oriented to possible technical control. For this function, as for scientific-technical progress in general, there is no more "humane" substitute.

Marcuse himself seems to doubt whether it is meaningful to relativize as a "project" the rationality of science and technology. In many passages of *One-Dimensional Man,* revolutionizing technological rationality means only a transformation of the institutional framework which would leave untouched the forces of production as such. The structure of scientific-technical progress would be conserved, and only the governing values would be changed. New values would be translated into technically solvable tasks. The *direction* of this progress would be new, but the standard of rationality itself would remain unchanged: "Technics, as a universe of instrumentalities, may increase the weakness as well as the power of man. At the present stage, he is perhaps more powerless over his own apparatus than he ever was before."[10]

This sentence reinstates the political innocence of the forces of production. Here Marcuse is only renewing the classical definition of the relationship between the productive forces and the production relations. But in so doing, he is as far from coming to grips with the new constellation at which he is aiming as he was with the assertion that the productive forces are thoroughly corrupted in their political implications. What is singular about the "rationality" of science and technology is that it characterizes the growing potential of self-surpassing productive forces which continually threaten the institutional framework *and at the same time,* set the standard of legitimation for the production relations that restrict this potential. The dichotomy of this rationality cannot be adequately represented either by historicizing the concept or by returning to the orthodox view: neither the model of the original sin of scientific-technical progress nor that of its innocence do it justice. The most sensible formulation of the matter in question seems to me to be the following:

The technological *a priori* is a political *a priori* inasmuch as the transformation of nature involves that of man, and inasmuch as the "man-made creations" issue from and reenter a societal ensemble. One may still insist that the machinery of the technological universe is "as such" indifferent towards political ends—it can revolutionize or retard a society. An electronic computer can serve equally in capitalist or socialist administrations; a cyclotron can be an equally efficient tool for a war party or a peace party. . . . However, when technics becomes the universal form of material production, it circumscribes an entire culture; it projects a historical totality—a "world." [11]

The difficulty, which Marcuse has only obscured with the notion of the political content of technical reason, is to determine in a categorically precise manner the meaning of the expansion of the rational form of science and technology, i.e., the rationality embodied in systems of purposive-rational action, to the proportions of a life form, of the "historical totality" of a lifeworld. This is the same process that Weber meant to designate and explain as the rationalization of society. I believe that neither Weber nor Marcuse has satisfactorily accounted for it. Therefore I should like to attempt to reformulate Weber's concept of rationalization in another frame of reference in order to discuss on this new basis Marcuse's critique of Weber, as well as his thesis of the double function of scientific-technical progress (as productive force and as ideology). I am proposing an interpretative scheme that, in the format of an essay, can be introduced but not seriously validated with regard to its utility. The historical generalizations thus serve only to clarify this scheme and are no substitute for its scientific substantiation.

By means of the concept of "rationalization" Weber attempted to grasp the repercussions of scientific-technical progress on the institutional framework of societies engaged in "modernization." He shared this interest with the classical sociological tradition in general, whose pairs of polar concepts all revolve about the same problem: how to construct a conceptual model of the institutional change brought about by the extension of subsystems of purposive-rational action. Status and contract, *Gemeinschaft* and *Gesellschaft,* mechanical and organic solidarity, informal and formal groups, primary and secondary groups, culture and civilization, traditional and bureaucratic authority, sacral and secular associations, military and industrial society, status group and class—all of these pairs of concepts represent as many attempts to grasp the structural change of the institutional framework of a traditional society on the way to becoming a modern one. Even Parsons's catalog of possible alternatives of value-orientations belongs in the list of these attempts, although he would not admit it. Parsons claims that his list systematically represents the decisions between alternative value-orientations that must be made by the subject of any action whatsoever, regardless of the particular or historical context. But if one examines the list, one can scarcely overlook the historical situation of the inquiry on which it is based. The four pairs of alternative value-orientations,

affectivity versus *affective neutrality,*
particularism versus *universalism,*
ascription versus *achievement,*
diffuseness versus *specificity,*

which are supposed to take into account *all* possible fundamental decisions, are tailored to an analysis of *one* historical process. In fact they define the relative dimensions of the modification of dominant attitudes in the transition from traditional to modern society. Subsystems of purposive-rational action do indeed demand orientation to the postponement of gratification, universal norms, individual achievement and active mastery, and specific and analytic relationships, rather than to the opposite orientations.

In order to reformulate what Weber called "rationalization," I should like to go beyond the subjective approach that Parsons shares with Weber and propose another categorial framework. I shall take as my starting point the fundamental distinction between *work* and *interaction*.[12]

By "work" or *purposive-rational action* I understand either instrumental action or rational choice or their conjunction. Instrumental action is governed by *technical rules* based on empirical knowledge. In every case they imply conditional predictions about observable events, physical or social. These predictions can prove correct or incorrect. The conduct of rational choice is governed by *strategies* based on analytic knowledge. They imply deductions from preference rules (value systems) and decision procedures; these propositions are either correctly or incorrectly deduced. Purposive-rational action realizes defined goals under given conditions. But while instrumental action organizes means that are appropriate or inappropriate according to criteria of an effective control of reality, strategic action depends only on the correct evaluation of possible alternative choices, which results from calculation supplemented by values and maxims.

By "interaction," on the other hand, I understand *communicative action,* symbolic interaction. It is governed by binding *consensual norms,* which define reciprocal expectations about behavior and which must be understood and recognized by at least two acting subjects. Social norms are enforced through sanctions. Their meaning is objectified in ordinary language communication. While the validity of technical rules and strategies depends on that of empirically true or analytically correct propositions, the validity of social norms is grounded only in the intersubjectivity of the mutual understanding of intentions and secured by the general recognition of obligations. Violation of a rule has a different consequence according to type. *Incompetent* behavior, which violates valid technical rules or strategies, is condemned per se to failure through lack of success; the "punishment" is built, so to speak, into its rebuff by reality. *Deviant* behavior, which violates consensual norms, provokes sanctions that are connected with the rules only externally, that is by convention. Learned rules of purposive-rational action supply us with *skills,* internalized norms with *personality structures.* Skills put us in a position to solve problems; motivations allow us to follow norms. The diagram below summarizes these definitions. They demand a more precise explanation, which I cannot give here. It is above all the bottom column which I am neglecting here, and it refers to the very problem for whose solution I am introducing the distinction between work and interaction.

	Institutional framework: symbolic interaction	Systems of purposive-rational (instrumental and stragetic) action
action-orienting rules	social norms	technical rules
level of definition	intersubjectively shared ordinary language	context-free language
type of definition	reciprocal expectations about behavior	conditional predictions conditional imperatives
mechanisms of acquisition	role internalization	learning of skills and qualifications
function of action type	maintenance of institutions (conformity to norms on the basis of reciprocal enforcement)	problem-solving (goal attainment, defined in means-end relations)
sanctions against violation of rules	punishment on the basis of conventional sanctions: failure against authority	inefficacy: failure in reality
"rationalization"	emancipation, individuation; extension of communication free of domination	growth of productive forces; extension of power of technical control

In terms of the two types of action we can distinguish between social systems according to whether purposive-rational action or interaction predominates. The institutional framework of a society consists of norms that guide symbolic interaction. But there are subsystems such as (to keep to Weber's examples) the economic system or the state apparatus, in which primarily sets of purposive-rational action are institutionalized. These contrast with subsystems such as family and kinship structures, which, although linked to a number of tasks and skills, are primarily based on moral rules of interaction. So I shall distinguish generally at the analytic level between (1) the *institutional framework* of a society or the sociocultural lifeworld and (2) the *subsystems of purposive-rational action* that are "embedded" in it. Insofar as actions are determined by the institutional framework they are both guided and enforced by norms. Insofar as they are determined by subsystems of purposive-rational action, they conform to patterns of instrumental or strategic action. Of course, only institutionalization can guarantee that such action will in fact follow definite technical rules and expected strategies with adequate probability.

With the help of these distinctions we can reformulate Weber's concept of "rationalization."

The term "traditional society" has come to denote all social systems that generally meet the criteria of civilizations. The latter represent a specific stage in the evolution of the human species. They differ in several traits from more primitive social forms: (1) a centralized ruling power (state organization of political power in contrast to tribal organization); (2) the division of society into socioeconomic classes (distribution to individuals of social obligations and rewards according to class membership and not according to kinship status); (3) the prevalence of a central worldview (myth, complex religion) to the end of legitimating political power (thus converting power into authority). Civilizations are established on the basis of a relatively developed technology and of division of labor in the social process of production, which make possible a surplus product, i.e., a quantity of goods exceeding that needed for the satisfaction of immediate and elementary needs. They owe their existence to the solution of the problem that first arises with the production of a surplus product, namely, how to distribute wealth and labor both unequally and yet legitimately according to criteria other than those generated by a kinship system.[13]

In our context it is relevant that despite considerable differences in their level of development, civilizations, based on an economy dependent on agriculture and craft production, have tolerated technical innovation and organizational improvement only within definite limits. One indicator of the traditional limits to the development of the forces of production is that until about three hundred years ago no major social system had produced more than the equivalent of a maximum of two hundred dollars per capita per annum. The stable pattern of a precapitalist mode of production, preindustrial technology, and premodern science makes possible a typical relation of the institutional framework to subsystems of purposive-rational action. For despite considerable progress, these subsystems, developing out of the system of social labor and its stock of accumulated technically exploitable knowledge, never reached that measure of extension after which their "rationality" would have become an open threat to the authority of the cultural traditions that legitimate political power. The expression "traditional society" refers to the circumstance that the institutional framework is grounded in the unquestionable underpinning of legitimation constituted by mythical, religious or metaphysical interpretations of reality—cosmic as well as social—as a whole. "Traditional" societies exist as long as the development of subsystems of purposive-rational action keep within the limits of the legitimating efficacy of cultural traditions.[14] This is the basis for the "superiority" of the institutional framework, which does not preclude structural changes adapted to a potential surplus generated in the economic system but does preclude critically challenging the traditional form of legitimation. This immunity is a meaningful criterion for the delimitation of traditional societies from those which have crossed the threshold to modernization.

The "superiority criterion," consequently, is applicable to all forms of class society organized as a state in which principles of universally valid rationality (whether of technical or strategic means-ends relations) have not explicitly and successfully called into question the cultural validity of inter-subjectively shared traditions, which function as legitimations of the political system. It is only since the capitalist mode of production has equipped the economic system with a self-propelling mechanism that ensures long-term continuous growth (despite crises) in the productivity of labor that the introduction of new technologies and strategies, i.e., innovation as such, has been institutionalized. As Marx and Schumpeter have proposed in their respective theories, the capitalist mode of production can be comprehended as a mechanism that guarantees the *permanent* expansion of subsystems of purposive-rational action and thereby overturns the traditionalist "superiority" of the institutional framework to the forces of production. Capitalism is the first mode of production in world history to institutionalize self-sustaining economic growth. It has generated an industrial system that could be freed from the institutional framework of capitalism and connected to mechanisms other than that of the utilization of capital in private form.

What characterizes the passage from traditional society to society commencing the process of modernization is *not* that structural modification of the institutional framework is necessitated under the pressure of relatively developed productive forces, for that is the mechanism of the evolution of the species from the very beginning. What is new is a level of development of the productive forces that makes permanent the extension of subsystems of purposive-rational action and thereby calls into question the traditional form of the legitimation of power. The older mythic, religious, and metaphysical worldviews obey the logic of interaction contexts. They answer the central questions of men's collective existence and of individual life history. Their themes are justice and freedom, violence and oppression, happiness and gratification, poverty, illness, and death. Their categories are victory and defeat, love and hate, salvation and damnation. Their logic accords with the grammar of systematically distorted communication and with the fateful causality of dissociated symbols and suppressed motives.[15] The rationality of language games, associated with communicative action, is confronted at the threshold of the modern period with the rationality of means-ends relations, associated with instrumental and strategic action. As soon as this confrontation can arise, the end of traditional society is in sight: the traditional form of legitimation breaks down.

Capitalism is defined by a mode of production that not only poses this problem but also solves it. It provides a legitimation of domination which is no longer called down from the lofty heights of cultural tradition but instead summoned up from the base of social labor. The institution of the market, in which private property owners exchange commodities—including the market on which propertyless private individuals exchange their labor power as their only commodity—promises that exchange relations will be and are just owing to equivalence. Even this bourgeois ideology of justice, by adopting the category of reciprocity, still employs a relation of communicative action as the basis of legitimation. But the principle of reciprocity is now the organizing principle of the sphere of production and reproduction itself. Thus on the basis of a market economy, political domination can be legitimated henceforth "from below" rather than "from above" (through invocation of cultural tradition).

If we suppose that the division of society into socioeconomic classes derives from the differential distribution among social groups of the relevant means of production, and that this distribution itself is based on the institutionalization of relations of social force, then we may assume that in all civilizations this institutional framework has been identical with the system of political domination: traditional authority was political authority. Only with the emergence of the capitalist mode of production can the legitimation of the institutional framework be linked immediately with the system of social labor. Only then can the property order change from a *political relation* to a *production relation,* because it legitimates itself through the rationality of the market, the ideology of exchange society, and no longer through a legitimate power structure. It is now the political system which is justified in terms of the legitimate relations of production: this is the real meaning and function of rationalist natural law from Locke to Kant.[16] The institutional framework of society is only mediately political and immediately economic (the bourgeois constitutional state as "superstructure").

The superiority of the capitalist mode of production to its predecessors has these two roots: the establishment of an economic mechanism that renders permanent the expansion of subsystems of purposive-rational action, and the creation of an economic legitimation by means of which the political system can be adapted to the new requisites of rationality brought about by these developing subsystems. It is this process of adaptation that Weber comprehends as "rationalization." Within it we can distinguish between two tendencies: rationalization "from below" and rationalization "from above."

A permanent pressure for adaptation arises from below as soon as the new mode of production becomes fully operative through the institutionalization of a domestic market for goods and labor power and of the capitalist enterprise. In the system of social labor this institutionalization ensures cumulative progress in the forces of production and an ensuing horizontal extension of subsystems of purposive-rational action—at the cost of economic crises, to be sure. In this way traditional structures are increasingly subordinated to conditions of instrumental or strategic rationality: the organization of labor and of trade, the network of transportation, information, and communication, the institutions of private law, and, starting with financial administration, the state bureaucracy. Thus arises the substructure of a society under the compulsion of modernization. The latter eventually widens to take in all areas of life: the army, the school system, health services, and even the family. Whether in city or country, it induces an urbanization of the *form* of life. That is, it generates subcultures that train the individual to be able to "switch over" at any moment from an interaction context to purposive-rational action.

This pressure for rationalization coming from below is met by a compulsion to rationalize coming from above. For, measured against the new standards of purposive rationality, the power-legitimating and action-orienting traditions—especially mythological interpretations and religious worldviews—lose their cogency. On this level of generalization, what Weber termed "secularization" has two aspects. First, traditional worldviews and objectivations lose their power and validity *as* myth, *as* public religion, *as* customary ritual, *as* justifying metaphysics, *as* unquestionable tradition. Instead, they are reshaped into subjective belief systems and ethics which ensure the private cogency of modern value-orientations (the "Protestant ethic"). Second, they are transformed into constructions that do both at once: criticize tradition and reorganize the released material of tradition according to the principles of formal law and the exchange of equivalents (rationalist natural law). Having become fragile, existing legitimations are replaced by new ones. The latter emerge from the critique of the dogmatism of traditional interpretations of the world and claim a scientific character. Yet they retain legitimating functions, thereby keeping actual power relations inaccessible to analysis and to public consciousness. It is in this way that ideologies in the restricted sense first came into being. They replace traditional legitimations of power by appearing in the mantle of modern science and by deriving their justification from the critique of ideology. Ideologies are coeval with the critique of ideology. In this sense there can be no prebourgeois "ideologies."

In this connection modern science assumes a singular function. In distinction from the philosophical sciences of the older sort, the empirical sciences have developed since Galileo's time within a methodological frame of reference that reflects the transcendental viewpoint of possible technical control. Hence the modern sciences produce knowledge which through its *form* (and not through the subjective intention of scientists) is technically exploitable knowledge, although the possible applications generally are realized afterwards. Science and technology were not interdependent until late into the nineteenth century. Until then modern science did not contribute to the acceleration of technical development nor, consequently, to the pressure toward rationalization from below. Rather, its contribution to the modernization process was indirect. Modern physics gave rise to a philosophical approach that interpreted nature and society according to a model borrowed from the natural sciences and induced, so to speak, the mechanistic worldview of the seventeenth century. The reconstruction of classical natural law was carried out in this framework. This modern natural law was the basis of the bourgeois revolutions of the seventeenth, eighteenth, and nineteenth centuries, through which the old legitimations of the power structure were finally destroyed.[17]

By the middle of the nineteenth century the capitalist mode of production had developed so fully in England and France that Marx was able to identify the locus of the institutional framework of society in the relations of production and at the same time criticize the legitimating basis constituted by the exchange of equivalents. He carried out the critique of bourgeois ideology in the form of *political economy*. His labor theory of value destroyed the semblance of freedom, by means of which the legal institution of the free labor contract had made unrecognizable the relationship of social force that underlay the wage-labor relationship. Marcuse's criticism of Weber is that the latter, disregarding this Marxian insight, upholds an abstract concept of rationalization, which not merely fails to express the specific class content of the adaptation of the institutional framework to the developing systems of purposive-rational action, but conceals it. Marcuse knows that the Marxian analysis can no longer be applied as it stands to advanced capitalist society, with which Weber was already confronted. But he wants to show through the example of Weber that the evolution of modern society in the framework of state-regulated capitalism cannot be conceptualized if liberal capitalism has not been analyzed adequately.

Since the last quarter of the nineteenth century two developmental tendencies have become noticeable in the most advanced capitalist countries: an increase in state intervention in order to secure the system's stability, and a growing interdependence of research and technology, which has turned the sciences into the leading productive force. Both tendencies have destroyed the particular constellation of institutional framework and subsystems of purposive-rational action which characterized liberal capitalism, thereby eliminating the conditions relevant for the application of political economy in the version correctly formulated by Marx for liberal capitalism. I believe that Marcuse's basic thesis, according to which technology and science today also take on the function of legitimating political power, is the key to analyzing the changed constellation.

The permanent regulation of the economic process by means of state intervention arose as a defense mechanism against the dysfunctional tendencies, which threaten the system, that capitalism generates when left to itself. Capitalism's actual development manifestly contradicted the capitalist idea of a bourgeois society, emancipated from domination, in which power is neutralized. The root ideology of just exchange, which Marx unmasked in theory, collapsed in practice. The form of capital utilization through private ownership could only be maintained by the governmental corrective of a social and economic policy that stabilized the business cycle. The institutional framework of society was repoliticized. It no longer coincides immediately with the relations of production, i.e., with an order of private law that secures capitalist economic activity and the corresponding general guarantees of order provided by the bourgeois state. But this means a change in the relation of the economy to the political system: politics is no longer *only* a phenomenon of the superstructure. If society no longer "autonomously" perpetuates itself through self-regulation as a sphere preceding and lying at the basis of the state—and its ability to do so was the really novel feature of the capitalist mode of production—then society and the state are no longer in the relationship that Marxian theory had defined as that of base and superstructure. Then, however, a critical theory of society can no longer be constructed in the exclusive form of a critique of political economy. A point of view that methodically isolates the economic laws of motion of society can claim to grasp the overall structure of social life in its essential categories only as long as politics depends on the economic base. It becomes inapplicable when the "base" has to be comprehended as in itself a function of governmental activity and political conflicts. According to Marx, the critique of political economy was the theory of bourgeois society only as *critique of ideology.* If, however, the ideology of just exchange disintegrates, then the power structure can no longer be criticized *immediately* at the level of the relations of production.

With the collapse of this ideology, political power requires a new legitimation. Now since the power indirectly exercised over the exchange process is itself operating under political control and state regulation, legitimation can no longer be derived from the unpolitical order constituted by the relations of production. To this extent the requirement for direct legitimation, which exists in precapitalist societies, reappears. On the other hand, the resuscitation of immediate political domination (in the traditional form of legitimation on the basis of cosmological worldviews) has become impossible. For traditions have already been disempowered. Moreover, in industrially developed societies the results of bourgeois emancipation from immediate political domination (civil and political rights and the mechanism of general elections) can be fully ignored only in periods of reaction. Formally democratic government in systems of state-regulated capitalism is subject to a need for legitimation which cannot be met by a return to a prebourgeois form. Hence the ideology of free exchange is replaced by a substitute program. The latter is oriented not to the social results of the institution of the market but to those of government action designed to compensate for the dysfunctions of free exchange. This policy combines the element of the bourgeois ideology of achievement (which, however, displaces assignment of status according to the standard of individual achievement from the market to the school system) with a guaranteed minimum level of welfare, which offers secure employment and a stable income. This substitute program obliges the political system to maintain stabilizing conditions for an economy that guards against risks to growth and guarantees social security and the chance for individual upward mobility. What is needed to this end is latitude for manipulation by state interventions that, at the cost of limiting the institutions of private law, secure the private form of capital utilization *and bind the masses' loyalty to this form.*

Insofar as government action is directed toward the economic system's stability and growth, politics now takes on a peculiarly negative character.

For it is oriented toward the elimination of dysfunctions and the avoidance of risks that threaten the system: not, in other words, toward the *realization of practical goals* but toward the *solution of technical problems.* Claus Offe pointed this out in his paper at the 1968 Frankfurt Sociological Conference:

In this structure of the relation of economy and the state, "politics" degenerates into action that follows numerous and continually emerging "avoidance imperatives": the mass of differentiated social-scientific information that flows into the political system allows both the early identification of risk zones and the treatment of actual dangers. What is new about this structure is . . . that the risks to stability built into the mechanism of private capital utilization in highly organized markets, risks that can be manipulated, prescribe preventive actions and measures that *must* be accepted as long as they are to accord with the existing legitimation resources (i.e., substitute program).[18]

Offe perceives that through these preventive action-orientations, government activity is restricted to administratively soluble technical problems, so that practical questions evaporate, so to speak. *Practical substance is eliminated.*

Old-style politics was forced, merely through its traditional form of legitimation, to define itself in relation to practical goals: the "good life" was interpreted in a context defined by interaction relations. The same still held for the ideology of bourgeois society. The substitute program prevailing today, in contrast, is aimed exclusively at the functioning of a manipulated system. It eliminates practical questions and therewith precludes discussion about the adoption of standards; the latter could emerge only from a democratic decision-making process. The solution of technical problems is not dependent on public discussion. Rather, public discussions could render problematic the framework within which the tasks of government action present themselves as technical ones. Therefore the new politics of state interventionism requires a depoliticization of the mass of the population. To the extent that practical questions are eliminated, the public realm also loses its political function. At the same time, the institutional framework of society is still distinct from the systems of purposive-rational action themselves. Its organization continues to be a problem of *practice* linked to communication, not one of *technology,* no matter how scientifically guided. Hence, the bracketing out of practice associated with the new kind of politics is not automatic. The substitute program, which legitimates power today, leaves unfilled a vital need for legitimation: how will the depoliticization of the masses be made plausible to them? Marcuse would be able to answer: by having technology and science *also* take on the role of an ideology.

Since the end of the nineteenth century the other developmental tendency characteristic of advanced capitalism has become increasingly momentous: the scientization of technology. The institutional pressure to augment the productivity of labor through the introduction of new technology has always existed under capitalism. But innovations depended on sporadic inventions, which, while economically motivated, were fortuitous in character. This changed as technical development entered into a feedback relation with the progress of the modern sciences. With the advent of large-scale industrial research, science, technology, and industrial utilization were fused into a system. Since then, industrial research has been linked up with research under government contract, which primarily promotes scientific and technical progress in the military sector. From there information flows back into the sectors of civilian production. Thus technology and science become a leading productive force, rendering inoperative the conditions for Marx's labor theory of value. It is no longer meaningful to calculate the amount of capital investment in research and development on the basis of the value of unskilled (simple) labor power, when scientific-technical progress has become an independent source of surplus value, in relation to which the only source of surplus value considered by Marx, namely the labor power of the immediate producers, plays an ever smaller role.[19]

As long as the productive forces were visibly linked to the rational decisions and instrumental action of men engaged in social production, they could be understood as the potential for a growing power of technical control and not be confused with the institutional framework in which they are embedded. However, with the institutionalization of scientific-technical progress, the potential of the productive forces has assumed a form owing to which men lose consciousness of the dualism of work and interaction.

It is true that social interests still determine the direction, functions, and pace of technical progress. But these interests define the social system so much as a whole that they coincide with the interest in maintaining the system. *As such* the private form of capital utilization and a distribution mechanism for social rewards that guarantees the loyalty of the masses are removed from discussion. The quasi-autonomous progress of science and technology then appears as an independent variable on which the most important single system variable, namely economic growth, depends. Thus arises a perspective in which the development of the social system *seems* to be determined by the logic of scientific-technical progress. The immanent law of this progress seems to produce objective exigencies, which must be obeyed by any politics oriented toward functional needs. But when this semblance has taken root effectively, then propaganda can refer to the role of technology and science in order to explain and legitimate why in modern societies the process of democratic decision-making about practical problems loses its function and "must" be replaced by plebiscitary decisions about alternative sets of leaders of administrative personnel. This technocracy thesis has been worked out in several versions on the intellectual level.[20] What seems to me more important is that it can also become a background ideology that penetrates into the consciousness of the depoliticized mass of the population, where it can take on legitimating power.[21] It is a singular achievement of this ideology to detach society's self-understanding from the frame of reference of communicative action and from the concepts of symbolic interaction and replace it with a scientific model. Accordingly the culturally defined self-understanding of a social lifeworld is replaced by the self-reification of men under categories of purposive-rational action and adaptive behavior.

The model according to which the planned reconstruction of society is to proceed is taken from systems analysis. It is possible in principle to comprehend and analyze individual enterprises and organizations, even political or economic subsystems and social systems as a whole, according to the pattern of self-regulated systems. It makes a difference, of course, whether we use a cybernetic frame of reference for analytic purposes or *organize* a given social system in accordance with this pattern as a man-machine system. But the transferral of the analytic model to the level of social organization is implied by the very approach taken by systems analysis. Carrying out this intention of an instinct-like self-stabilization of social systems yields the peculiar perspective that the structure of one of the two types of action, namely the behavioral system of purposive-rational action, not only predominates over the institutional framework but gradually absorbs communicative action as such. If, with Arnold Gehlen, one were to see the inner logic of technical development as the step-by-step disconnection of the behavioral system of purposive-rational action from the human organism and its transferral to machines, then the technocratic intention could be understood as the last stage of this development. For the first time man can not only, as *Homo faber,* completely objectify himself and confront the achievements that have taken on independent life in his products; he can in addition, as *Homo fabricatus,* be integrated into his technical apparatus if the structure of purposive-rational action can be successfully reproduced on the level of social systems. According to this idea the institutional framework of society—which previously was rooted in a different type of action— would now, in a fundamental reversal, be *absorbed* by the subsystems of purposive-rational action, which were embedded in it.

Of course this technocratic intention has not been realized anywhere even in its beginnings. But it serves as an ideology for the new politics, which is adapted to technical problems and brackets out practical questions. Furthermore it does correspond to certain developmental tendencies that could lead to a creeping erosion of what we have called the institutional framework. The manifest domination of the authoritarian state gives way to the manipulative compulsions of technical-operational administration. The moral realization of a normative order is a function of communicative action oriented to shared cultural meaning and presupposing the internalization of values. It is increasingly supplanted by conditioned behavior, while large organizations as such are increasingly patterned after the structure of purposive-rational action. The industrially most advanced societies seem to approximate the model of behavioral control steered by external stimuli rather than guided by norms. Indirect control through fabricated stimuli has increased, especially in areas of putative subjective freedom (such as electoral, consumer, and leisure behavior). Sociopsychologically, the era is typified less by the authoritarian personality than by the destructuring of the superego. The increase in *adaptive behavior* is, however, only the obverse of the dissolution of the sphere of linguistically mediated interaction by the structure of purposive-rational action. This is paralleled subjectively by the disappearance of the difference between purposive-rational action and interaction from the consciousness not only of the sciences of man, but of men themselves. The concealment of this difference proves the ideological power of the technocratic consciousness.

In consequence of the two tendencies that have been discussed, capitalist society has changed to the point where two key categories of Marxian theory, namely class struggle and ideology, can no longer be employed as they stand.

It was on the basis of the capitalist mode of production that the struggle of social classes as such was first constituted, thereby creating an objective situation from which the class structure of traditional society, with its immediately political constitution, could be *recognized* in retrospect. State-regulated capitalism, which emerged from a reaction against the dangers to the system produced by open class antagonism, suspends class conflict. The system of advanced capitalism is so defined by a policy of securing the loyalty of the wage-earning masses through rewards, that is, by avoiding conflict, that the conflict still built into the structure of society in virtue of the private mode of capital utilization is the very area of conflict which has the greatest probability of remaining latent. It recedes behind others, which, while conditioned by the mode of production, can no longer assume the form of class conflicts. In the paper cited, Claus Offe has analyzed this paradoxical state of affairs, showing that open conflicts about social interests break out with greater probability the less their frustration has dangerous consequences for the system. The needs with the greatest conflict potential are those on the periphery of the area of state intervention. They are far from the central conflict being kept in a state of latency and therefore they are not seen as having priority among dangers to be warded off. Conflicts are set off by these needs to the extent that disproportionately scattered state interventions produce backward areas of development and corresponding disparity tensions:

The disparity between areas of life grows above all in view of the differential state of development obtaining between the actually institutionalized and the possible level of technical and social progress. The disproportion between the most modern apparatuses for industrial and military purposes and the stagnating organization of the transport, health, and educational systems is just as well known an example of this disparity between areas of life as is the contradiction between rational planning and regulation in taxation and finance policy and the unplanned, haphazard development of cities and regions. Such contradictions can no longer be designated accurately as antagonisms between classes, yet they can still be interpreted as results of the still dominant process of the private utilization of capital and of a specifically capitalist power structure. In this process the prevailing interests are those which, without being clearly localizable, are in a position, on the basis of the established mechanism of the capitalist economy, to react to disturbances of the conditions of their stability by producing risks relevant to the system as a whole.[22]

The interests bearing on the maintenance of the mode of production can no longer be "clearly localized" in the social system as class interests. For the power structure, aimed as it is at avoiding dangers to the system, precisely excludes "domination" (as immediate political or economically mediated social force) exercised in such a manner that one class subject *confronts* another as an identifiable group.

This means not that class antagonisms have been abolished but that they have become *latent*. Class distinctions persist in the form of subcultural traditions and corresponding differences not only in the standard of living and life style but also in political attitude. The social structure also makes it probable that the class of wage earners will be hit harder than other groups by social disparities. And finally, the generalized interest in perpetuating the system is still anchored today, on the level of immediate life chances, in a structure of privilege. The concept of an interest that has become *completely* independent of living subjects would cancel itself out. But with the deflection of dangers to the system in state-regulated capitalism, the political system has incorporated an interest—which transcends latent class boundaries—in preserving the compensatory distribution façade.

Furthermore, the displacement of the conflict zone from the class boundary to the underprivileged regions of life does not mean at all that serious conflict potential has been disposed of. As the extreme example of racial conflict in the United States shows, so many consequences of disparity can accumulate in certain areas and groups that explosions resembling civil war can occur. But unless they are connected with protest potential from other sectors of society no conflicts arising from such underprivilege can really overturn the system—they can only provoke it to sharp reactions incompatible with formal democracy. For underprivileged groups are not social classes, nor do they ever even potentially represent the mass of the population. Their *disfranchisement* and pauperization no longer coincide with *exploitation,* because the system does not live off their labor. They can represent at most a past phase of exploitation. But they cannot through the withdrawal of cooperation attain the demands that they legitimately put forward. That is why these demands retain an appellative character. In the case of long-term nonconsideration of their legitimate demands underprivileged groups can in extreme situations react with desperate destruction and self-destruction. But as long as no coalitions are made with privileged groups, such a civil war lacks the chance of revolutionary success that class struggle possesses.

With a series of restrictions this model seems applicable even to the relations between the industrially advanced nations and the formerly colonial areas of the Third World. Here, too, growing disparity leads to a form of underprivilege that in the future surely will be increasingly less comprehensible through categories of exploitation. Economic interests are replaced on this level, however, with immediately military ones.

Be that as it may, in advanced capitalist society deprived and privileged groups no longer confront each other *as* socioeconomic classes—and to some extent the boundaries of underprivilege are no longer even specific to groups and instead run across population categories. Thus the fundamental relation that existed in all traditional societies and that came to the fore under liberal capitalism is mediatized, namely the class antagonism between partners who stand in an institutionalized relationship of force, economic exploitation, and political oppression to one another, and in which communication is so distorted and restricted that the legitimations serving as an ideological veil cannot be called into question. Hegel's concept of the ethical totality of a living relationship which is sundered because one subject does not reciprocally satisfy the needs of the other is no longer an appropriate model for the mediatized class structure of organized, advanced capitalism. The suspended dialectic of the ethical generates the peculiar semblance of *post-histoire*. The reason is that relative growth of the productive forces no longer represents *eo ipso* a potential that points beyond the existing framework with emancipatory consequences, in view of which legitimations of an existing power structure become enfeebled. For the leading productive force—controlled scientific-technical progress itself—has now become the basis of legitimation. Yet this new form of legitimation has cast off the old shape of *ideology.*

Technocratic consciousness is, on the one hand, "less ideological" than all previous ideologies. For it does not have the opaque force of a delusion that only transfigures the implementation of interests. On the other hand today's dominant, rather glassy background ideology, which makes a fetish of science, is more irresistible and farther-reaching than ideologies of the old type. For with the veiling of practical problems it not only justifies a *particular class's* interest in domination and represses *another class's* partial need for emancipation, but affects the human race's emancipatory interest as such.

Technocratic consciousness is not a rationalized, wish-fulfilling fantasy, not an "illusion" in Freud's sense, in which a system of interaction is either represented or interpreted and grounded. Even bourgeois ideologies could be traced back to a basic pattern of just interactions, free of domination and mutually satisfactory. It was these ideologies which met the criteria of wish-fulfillment and substitute gratification; the communication on which they were based was so limited by repressions that the relation of force once institutionalized as the capital-labor relation could not even be called by name. But the technocratic consciousness is not based in the same way on the causality of dissociated symbols and unconscious motives, which generates both false consciousness and the power of reflection to which the critique of ideology is indebted. It is less vulnerable to reflection, because it is no longer *only* ideology. For it does not, in the manner of ideology, express a projection of the "good life" (which even if not identifiable with a bad reality, can at least be brought into virtually satisfactory accord with it). Of course the new ideology, like the old, serves to impede making the foundations of society the object of thought and reflection. Previously, social force lay at the basis of the relation between capitalist and wage-laborers. Today the basis is provided by structural conditions which predefine the tasks of system maintenance: the private form of capital utilization and a political form of distributing social rewards that guarantees mass loyalty. However, the old and new ideology differ in two ways.

First, the capital-labor relation today, because of its linkage to a loyalty-ensuring political distribution mechanism, no longer engenders uncorrected exploitation and oppression. The process through which the persisting class antagonism has been made virtual presupposes that the repression on which the latter is based first came to consciousness in history and *only then* was stabilized in a modified form as a property of the system. Technocratic consciousness, therefore, cannot rest in the same way on collective repression as did earlier ideologies. Second, mass loyalty today is created only with the aid of rewards for *privatized needs*. The achievements in virtue of which the system justifies itself may not in principle be interpreted politically. The acceptable interpretation is immediately in terms of allocations of money and leisure time (neutral with regard to their use), and mediately in terms of the technocratic justification of the occlusion of practical questions. Hence the new ideology is distinguished from its predecessor in that it severs the criteria for justifying the organization of social life from any normative regulation of interaction, thus depoliticizing them. It anchors them instead in functions of a putative system of purposive-rational action.

Technocratic consciousness reflects not the sundering of an ethical situation but the repression of "ethics" as such as a category of life. The common, positivist way of thinking renders inert the frame of reference of interaction in ordinary language, in which domination and ideology both arise under conditions of distorted communication and can be reflectively detected and broken down. The depoliticization of the mass of the population, which is legitimated through technocratic consciousness, is at the same time men's self-objectification in categories equally of both purposive-rational action and adaptive behavior. The reified models of the sciences migrate into the sociocultural lifeworld and gain objective power over the latter's self-understanding. The ideological nucleus of this consciousness is *the elimination of the distinction between the practical and the technical*. It reflects, but does not objectively account for, the new constellation of a disempowered institutional framework and systems of purposive-rational action that have taken on a life of their own.

The new ideology consequently violates an interest grounded in one of the two fundamental conditions of our cultural existence: in language, or more precisely, in the form of socialization and individuation determined by communication in ordinary language. This interest extends to the maintenance of intersubjectivity of mutual understanding as well as to the creation of communication without domination. Technocratic consciousness makes this practical interest disappear behind the interest in the expansion of our power of technical control. Thus the reflection that the new ideology calls for must penetrate beyond the level of particular historical class interests to disclose the fundamental interests of mankind as such, engaged in the process of self-constitution.[23]

If the relativization of the field of application of the concept of ideology and the theory of class be confirmed, then the category framework developed by Marx in the basic assumptions of historical materialism requires a new formulation. The model of forces of production and relations of production would have to be replaced by the more abstract one of work and interaction. The relations of production designate a level on which the institutional framework was anchored only during the phase of the development of liberal capitalism, and not either before or after. To be sure, the productive forces, in which the learning processes organized in the subsystems of purposive-rational action accumulate, have been from the very beginning the motive force of social evolution. But, they do not appear, as Marx supposed, *under all circumstances* to be a potential for liberation and to set off emancipatory movements—at least not once the continual growth of the productive forces has become dependent on scientific-technical progress that has *also* taken on functions of *legitimating political power*. I suspect that the frame of reference developed in terms of the analogous, but more general relation of institutional framework (interaction) and subsystems of purposive-rational action ("work" in the broad sense of instrumental and strategic action) is more suited to reconstructing the sociocultural phases of the history of mankind.

There are several indications that during the long initial phase until the end of the Mesolithic period, purposive-rational actions could only be motivated at all through ritual attachment to interactions. A profane realm of subsystems of purposive-rational action seems to have separated out from the institutional framework of symbolic interaction in the first settled cultures, based on the domestication of animals and cultivation of plants. But it was probably only in civilizations, that is under the conditions of a class society organized as a state that the differentiation of work and interaction went far enough for the subsystems to yield technically exploitable knowledge that could be stored and expanded relatively independently of mythical and religious interpretations of the world. At the same time social norms became separated from power-legitimating traditions, so that "culture" attained a certain independence from "institutions." The threshold of the modern period would then be characterized by that process of rationalization which commenced with loss of the "superiority" of the institutional framework to the subsystems of purposive-rational action. Traditional legitimations could now be criticized against the standards of rationality of means-ends relations. Concurrently, information from the area of technically exploitable knowledge infiltrated tradition and compelled a reconstruction of traditional world interpretations along the lines of scientific standards.

We have followed this process of "rationalization from above" up to the point where technology and science themselves in the form of a common positivistic way of thinking, articulated as technocratic consciousness, began to take the role of a substitute ideology for the demolished bourgeois ideologies. This point was reached with the critique of bourgeois ideologies. It introduced ambiguity into the concept of rationalization. This ambiguity was deciphered by Horkheimer and Adorno as the dialectic of enlightenment, which has been refined by Marcuse as the thesis that technology and science themselves become ideological.

From the very beginning the pattern of human sociocultural development has been determined by a growing power of technical control over the external conditions of existence on the one hand, and a more or less passive adaptation of the institutional framework to the expanded subsystems of purposive-rational action on the other. Purposive-rational action represents the form of *active* adaptation, which distinguishes the collective *self-*preservation of societal subjects from the preservation of the species characteristic of other animals. We know how to bring the relevant conditions of life under control, that is, we know how to adapt the environment to our needs culturally rather than adapting ourselves to external nature. In contrast, changes of the institutional framework, to the extent that they are derived immediately or mediately from new technologies or improved strategies (in the areas of production, transportation, weaponry, etc.) have not taken the same form of active adaptation. In general such modifications follow the pattern of *passive* adaptation. They are not the result of planned purposive-rational action geared to its own consequences, but the product of fortuitous, undirected development. Yet it was impossible to become conscious of this disproportion between active and passive adaptation as long as the dynamics of capitalist development remained concealed by bourgeois ideologies. Only with the critique of bourgeois ideologies did this disproportion enter public consciousness.

The most impressive witness to this experience is still the *Communist Manifesto*. In rapturous words Marx eulogizes the revolutionary role of the bourgeoisie: "The bourgeoisie cannot exist without constantly revolutionizing the instruments of production, and thereby the relations of production, and with them the whole relations of society." In another passage he writes:

The bourgeoisie, during its role of scarce one hundred years, has created more massive and more colossal productive forces than have all preceding generations together. Subjection of nature's forces to man, machinery, application of chemistry to industry and agriculture, steam navigation, railways, electric telegraphs, clearing of whole continents for cultivation, canalization of rivers, whole populations conjured out of the ground. . . .

Marx also perceives the reaction of this development back upon the institutional framework:

All fixed, fast-frozen relations, with their train of ancient and vulnerable prejudices and opinions, are swept away, all new-formed ones become antiquated before they can ossify. All that is solid melts into air, all that is holy is profaned, and man is at last compelled to face with sober senses his real conditions of life and his relations with his kind.

It is with regard to the disproportion between the passive adaptation of the institutional framework and the "active subjection of nature" that the assertion that men make their history, but not with will or consciousness, was formulated. It was the aim of Marx's critique to transform the secondary adaptation of the institutional framework as well into an active one, and to bring under control the structural change of society itself. This would overcome a fundamental condition of all previous history and complete the self-constitution of mankind: the end of prehistory. But this idea was ambiguous.

Marx, to be sure, viewed the problem of making history with will and consciousness as one of the *practical* mastery of previously ungoverned processes of social development. Others, however, have understood it as a *technical* problem. They want to bring society under control in the same way as nature by reconstructing it according to the pattern of self-regulated systems of purposive-rational action and adaptive behavior. This intention is to be found not only among technocrats of capitalist planning but also among those of bureaucratic socialism. Only the technocratic consciousness obscures the fact that this reconstruction could be achieved at no less a cost than closing off the only dimension that is essential, because it is susceptible to humanization, *as* a structure of interactions mediated by ordinary language. In the future the repertoire of control techniques will be considerably expanded. On Herman Kahn's list of the most probable technical innovations of the next thirty years I observe among the first fifty items a large number of techniques of behavioral and personality change:

30. new and possibly pervasive techniques for surveillance, monitoring and control of individuals and organizations;
33. new and more reliable "educational" and propaganda techniques affecting human behavior—public and private;
34. practical use of direct electronic communication with and stimulation of the brain;
37. new and relatively effective counterinsurgency techniques;
39. new and more varied drugs for control of fatigue, relaxation, alertness, mood, personality, perceptions, and fantasies;
41. improved capability to "change" sex;
42. other genetic control or influence over the basic constitution of an individual.[24]

A prediction of this sort is extremely controversial. Nevertheless, it points to an area of future possibilities of detaching human behavior from a normative system linked to the grammar of language-games and integrating it instead into self-regulated subsystems of the man-machine type by means of immediate physical or psychological control. Today the psychotechnic manipulation of behavior can already liquidate the old fashioned detour through norms that are internalized but capable of reflection. Behavioral control could be instituted at an even deeper level tomorrow through biotechnic intervention in the endocrine regulating system, not to mention the even greater consequences of intervening in the genetic transmission of inherited information. If this occurred, old regions of consciousness developed in ordinary-language communication would of necessity completely dry up. At this stage of human engineering, if the end of psychological manipulation could be spoken of in the same sense as the end of ideology is today, the spontaneous alienation derived from the uncontrolled lag of the institutional framework would be overcome. But the self-objectivation of man would have fulfilled itself in planned alienation—men would make their history with will, but without consciousness.

I am not asserting that this cybernetic dream of the instinct-like self-stabilization of societies is being fulfilled or that it is even realizable. I do think, however, that it follows through certain vague but basic assumptions of technocratic consciousness to their conclusion as a negative utopia and thus denotes an evolutionary trend that is taking shape under the slick domination of technology and science as ideology. Above all, it becomes clear against this background that *two concepts of rationalization* must be distinguished. At the level of subsystems of purposive-rational action, scientific-technical progress has already compelled the reorganization of social institutions and sectors, and necessitates it on an even larger scale than heretofore. But this process of the development of the productive forces can be a potential for liberation if and only if it does not replace rationalization on another level. *Rationalization at the level of the institutional framework* can occur only in the medium of symbolic interaction itself, that is, through *removing restrictions on communication*. Public, unrestricted discussion, free from domination, of the suitability and desirability of action-orienting principles and norms in the light of the sociocultural repercussions of developing subsystems of purposive-rational action—such communication at all levels of political and repoliticized decision-making processes is the only medium in which anything like "rationalization" is possible.

In such a process of generalized reflection institutions would alter their specific composition, going beyond the limit of a mere change in legitimation. A rationalization of social norms would, in fact, be characterized by a decreasing degree of repressiveness (which at the level of personality structure should increase average tolerance of ambivalence in the face of role conflicts), a decreasing degree of rigidity (which should multiply the chances of an individually stable self-presentation in everyday interactions), and approximation to a type of behavioral control that would allow role distance and the flexible application of norms that, while well-internalized, would be accessible to reflection. Rationalization measured by changes in these three dimensions does not lead, as does the rationalization of purposive-rational subsystems, to an increase in technical control over objectified processes of nature and society. It does not lead per se to the better functioning of social systems, but would furnish the members of society with the opportunity for further emancipation and progressive individuation. The growth of productive forces is not the same as the intention of the "good life." It can at best serve it.

I do not even think that the model of a technologically possible surplus that cannot be used in full measure within a repressively maintained institutional framework (Marx speaks of "fettered" forces of production) is appropriate to state-regulated capitalism. Today, better utilization of an unrealized potential leads to improvement of the economic-industrial apparatus, but no longer *eo ipso* to a transformation of the institutional framework with emancipatory consequences. The question is not whether we completely *utilize* an available or creatable potential, but whether we *choose* what we want for the purpose of the pacification and gratification of existence. But it must be immediately noted that we are only posing this question and cannot answer it in advance. For the solution demands precisely that unrestricted communication about the goals of life activity and conduct against which advanced capitalism, structurally dependent on a depoliticized public realm, puts up a strong resistance.

A new conflict zone, in place of the virtualized class antagonism and apart from the disparity conflicts at the margins of the system, can only emerge where advanced capitalist society has to immunize itself, by depoliticizing the masses of the population, against the questioning of its technocratic background ideology: in the public sphere administered through the mass media. For only here is it possible to buttress the concealment of the difference between progress in systems of purposive-rational action and emancipatory transformations of the institutional framework, between technical and practical problems. And it is necessary for the system to conceal this difference. Publicly administered definitions extend to *what* we want for our lives, but not to *how* we would like to live if we could find out, with regard to attainable potentials, how we *could* live.

Who will activate this conflict zone is hard to predict. Neither the old class antagonism nor the new type of underprivilege contains a protest potential whose origins make it tend toward the repoliticization of the desiccated public sphere. For the present, the only protest potential that gravitates toward the new conflict zone owing to identifiable interests is arising among groups of university, college, and high school students. Here we can make three observations:

1. Protesting students are a privileged group, which advances no interests that proceed immediately from its social situation or that could be satisfied in conformity with the system through an augmentation of social rewards. The first American studies of student activists conclude that they are predominantly not from upwardly mobile sections of the student body, but rather from sections with privileged status recruited from economically advantaged social strata.[25]

2. For plausible reasons the legitimations offered by the political system do not seem convincing to this group. The welfare-state substitute program for decrepit bourgeois ideologies presupposes a certain status and achievement orientation. According to the studies cited, student activists are less privatistically oriented to professional careers and future families than other students. Their academic achievements, which tend to be above average, and their social origins do not promote a horizon of expectations determined by anticipated exigencies of the labor market. Active students, who relatively frequently are in the social sciences and humanities, tend to be immune to technocratic consciousness because, although for varying motives, their primary experiences in their own intellectual work in neither case accord with the basic technocratic assumptions.

3. Among this group, conflict cannot break out because of the extent of the discipline and burdens imposed, but only because of their quality. Students are not fighting for a larger share of social rewards in the prevalent categories: income and leisure time. Instead, their protest is directed against the very category of reward itself. The few available data confirm the supposition that the protest of youth from bourgeois homes no longer coincides with the pattern of authority conflict typical of previous generations. Student activists tend to have parents who share their critical attitude. They have been brought up relatively frequently with more psychological understanding and according to more liberal educational principles than comparable inactive groups.[26] Their socialization seems to have been achieved in subcultures freed from immediate economic compulsion, in which the traditions of bourgeois morality and their petit-bourgeois derivatives have lost their function. This means that training for switching over to value-orientations of purposive-rational action no longer includes fetishizing this form of action. These educational techniques make possible experiences and favor orientations that clash with the conserved life form of an economy of poverty. What can take shape on this basis is a lack of understanding in principle for the reproduction of virtues and sacrifices that have become superfluous—a lack of understanding why despite the advanced stage of technological development the life of the individual is still determined by the dictates of professional careers, the ethics of status competition, and by values of possessive individualism and available substitute gratifications: why the institutionalized struggle for existence, the discipline of alienated labor, and the eradication of sensuality and aesthetic gratification are perpetuated. To this sensibility the structural elimination of practical problems

from a depoliticized public realm must become unbearable. However, it will give rise to a political force only if this sensibility comes into contact with a problem that the system cannot solve. For the future I see *one* such problem. The amount of social wealth produced by industrially advanced capitalism and the technical and organizational conditions under which this wealth is produced make it ever more difficult to link status assignment in an even subjectively convincing manner to the mechanism for the evaluation of individual achievement.[27] In the long run therefore, student protest could permanently destroy this crumbling achievement-ideology, and thus bring down the already fragile legitimating basis of advanced capitalism, which rests only on depoliticization.

Chapter Twelve
WHAT DOES A CRISIS MEAN TODAY?
LEGITIMATION PROBLEMS IN
LATE CAPITALISM

The expression "late capitalism" implicitly asserts that, even in state-regulated capitalism, social developments are still passing through "contradictions" or crises. I would therefore like to begin by elucidating the concept of *crisis*.

Prior to its use in economics, we are familiar with the concept of crisis in medicine. It refers to that phase of a disease in which it is decided whether the self-healing powers of the organism are sufficient for recovery. The critical process, the disease, seems to be something objective. A contagious disease, for instance, affects the organism from outside. The deviations of the organism from what it should be—i.e., the patient's normal condition—can be observed and, if necessary, measured with the help of indicators. The patient's consciousness plays no part in this. *How* the patient feels and *how* he experiences his illness is at most a symptom of events that he himself can barely influence. Nevertheless, we would not speak of a crisis in a medical situation of life or death if the patient were not trapped in this process with all his subjectivity. A crisis cannot be separated from the victim's inner view. He experiences his impotence toward the objectivity of his illness only because he is a subject doomed to passivity and temporarily unable to be a subject in full possession of his strength.

Crisis suggests the notion of an objective power depriving a subject of part of his normal sovereignty. If we interpret a process as a crisis, we are tacitly giving it a normative meaning. When the crisis is resolved, the trapped subject is liberated.

This becomes clearer when we pass from the medical to the dramaturgical notion of crisis. In classical aesthetics from Aristotle to Hegel, crisis signifies the turning point of a fateful process which, although fully objective, does not simply break in from the outside. There is a contradiction expressed in the catastrophic culmination of a conflict of action, and that contradiction is inherent in the very structure of the system of action and in the personality systems of the characters. Fate is revealed in conflicting norms that destroy the identities of the characters unless they in turn manage to regain their freedom by smashing the mythical power of fate.

The notion of crisis developed by classical tragedy has its counterpart in the notion of crisis to be found in the doctrine of salvation. Recurring throughout the philosophy of history in the eighteenth century, this figure of thought enters the evolutionary social theories of the nineteenth century. Marx is the first to develop a sociological concept of system crisis. It is against that background that we now speak of social or economic crises. In any discussion of, say, the great economic crisis in the early 'thirties, the Marxist overtones are unmistakable.

Since capitalist societies have the capacity of steadily developing technological productive forces, Marx conceives an economic crisis as a *crisis-ridden process of economic growth*. Accumulation of capital is tied to the acquisition of surplus. This means for Marx that economic growth is regulated by a mechanism that both establishes and conceals a power relationship. Thus the model of rising complexity is contradictory in the sense that the economic system keeps creating new and more problems as it solves others. The total accumulation of capital passes through periodic devaluations of capital components: this forms the cycle of crises, which Marx in his time was able to observe. He tried to explain the classical type of crisis by applying the theory of value with the help of the law of the tendential fall of the rate of profit. But that is outside my purpose at the moment. My question is really: Is late capitalism following the same or similar self-destructive pattern of development as classical—i.e., competitive—capitalism? Or has the organizing principle of late capitalism changed so greatly that the accumulation process no longer generates any problems jeopardizing its existence?

My starting point will be a rough descriptive model of the most important structural features of late-capitalist societies. I will then mention three crisis tendencies which today, though not specific to the system, are major topics of discussion. And finally, I will deal with various explanations of the crisis tendencies in late capitalism.

Structural Features of Late-Capitalist Societies

The expression "organized or state-regulated capitalism" refers to two classes of phenomena both of which can be traced back to the advanced stage of the accumulation process. One such class is the process of economic concentration (the creation of national and by now even multinational corporations) and the organization of markets for goods, capital, and labor. On the other hand, the interventionist state keeps filling the increasing functional gaps in the market. The spread of oligopolistic market structures certainly spells the end of competitive capitalism. But no matter how far companies may see into the future or extend their control over the environment, the steering mechanism of the market will continue to function as long as investments are determined by company profits. At the same time, by complementing and partially replacing the market mechanism, government intervention means the end of liberal capitalism. But no matter how much the state may restrict the owner of goods in his private autonomous activity, there will be no political planning to allocate scarce resources as long as the overall societal priorities develop naturally—i.e., as indirect results of the strategies of private enterprise. In advanced capitalist societies, the economic, the administrative, and the legitimation systems can be characterized as follows.

The economic system. During the 1960s, various authors, using the example of the United States, developed a three-sector model based on the distinction between the private and public areas. Private production is market-oriented, one sector still regulated by competition, another by the market strategies of the oligopolies that tolerate a competitive fringe. However, the public area, especially in the wake of armament and space-travel production, has witnessed the rise of great industries which, in their investment decisions, can operate independently of the market. These are either enterprises directly controlled by the government or private firms living on government contracts. The monopolistic and the public sectors are dominated by capital-intensive industries; the competitive sector is dominated by labor-intensive industries. In the monopolistic and the public sectors, the industries are faced with powerful unions. But in the competitive sector, labor is not as well organized, and the salary levels are correspondingly different. In the monopolistic sector, we can observe relatively rapid progress in production. However, in the public sector, the companies do not *need* to be, and in the competitive sector they *cannot* be, that efficient.

The administrative system. The state apparatus regulates the overall economic cycle by means of global planning. On the other hand, it also improves the conditions for utilizing capital.

Global planning is limited by private autonomous use of the means of production (the investment freedom of private enterprises cannot be restricted). It is limited on the other hand by the general purpose of crisis management. There are fiscal and financial measures to regulate cycles, as well as individual measures to regulate investments and overall demand (credits, price guarantees, subsidies, loans, secondary redistribution of income, government contracts based on business-cycle policies, indirect labor-market policies, etc.). All these measures have the reactive character of avoidance strategies within the context of a well-known preference system. This system is determined by a didactically demanded compromise between competing imperatives: steady growth, stability of money value, full employment, and balance of trade.

Global planning manipulates the marginal conditions of decisions made by private enterprise. It does so in order to *correct* the market mechanism

by neutralizing dysfunctional side effects. The state, however, *supplants* the market mechanism wherever the government creates and improves conditions for utilizing excess accumulated capital. It does so:
- by "strengthening the competitive capacity of the nation," by organizing supranational economic blocks, by an imperialistic safeguarding of international stratification, etc.;
- by unproductive government consumption (armament and space-travel industry);
- by politically structured guidance of capital in sectors neglected by an autonomous market;
- by improving the material infrastructure (transportation, education and health, vocation centers, urban and regional planning, housing, etc.);
- by improving the immaterial infrastructure (promotion of scientific research, capital expenditure in research and development, intermediary of patents, etc.);
- by increasing the productivity of human labor (universal education, vocational schooling, programs of training and reeducation, etc.);
- by paying for the social costs and real consequences of private production (unemployment, welfare; ecological damage).

The legitimation system. With the functional weaknesses of the market and the dysfunctional side effects of the market mechanism, the basic bourgeois ideology of fair exchange also collapsed. Yet there is a need for even greater legitimation. The government apparatus no longer merely safeguards the prerequisites for the production process. It also, on its own initiative, intervenes in that process. It must therefore be legitimated in the growing realms of state intervention, even though there is now no possibility of reverting to the traditions that have been undermined and worn out in competitive capitalism. The universalistic value systems of bourgeois ideology have made civil rights, including suffrage, universal. Independent of general elections, legitimation can thus be gotten only in extraordinary circumstances and temporarily. The resulting problem is resolved through formal democracy.

A wide participation by the citizens in the process of shaping political will—i.e., genuine democracy—would have to expose the contradiction between administratively socialized production and a still private form of acquiring the produced values. In order to keep the contradiction from being thematized, one thing is necessary. The administrative system has to be sufficiently independent of the shaping of legitimating will. This occurs in a legitimation process that elicits mass loyalty but avoids participation. In the midst of an objectively politicized society, the members enjoy the status of passive citizens with the right to withhold their acclaim. The private autonomous decision about investments is complemented by the civil privatism of the population.

Class structure. The structures of late capitalism can be regarded as a kind of reaction formation. To stave off the system crisis, late-capitalist societies focus all socially integrative strength on the conflict that is structurally most probable. They do so in order all the more effectively to keep that conflict latent.

In this connection, an important part is played by the quasi-political wage structure, which depends on negotiations between companies and unions. Price fixing, which has replaced price competition in the oligopolistic markets, has its counterpart in the labor market. The great industries almost administratively control the prices in their marketing territories. Likewise, through wage negotiations, they achieve quasi-political compromises with their union adversaries. In those industrial branches of the monopolistic and public sectors that are crucial to economic development, the commodity known as labor has a "political" price. The "wage-scale partners" find a broad zone of compromise, since increased labor costs can be passed on into the prices, and the middle-range demands made by both sides against the government tend to converge. The main consequences of immunizing the original conflict zone are as follows: (1) disparate wage developments; (2) a permanent inflation with the corresponding short-lived redistribution of incomes to the disadvantage of unorganized wage earners and other marginal groups; (3) a permanent crisis in government finances, coupled with public poverty—i.e., pauperization of public transportation, education, housing, and health; (4) an insufficient balance of disproportionate economic developments, both sectoral (e.g., agriculture) and regional (marginal areas).

Since World War II, the most advanced capitalist countries have kept the class conflict latent in its essential areas. They have extended the business cycle, transforming the periodic pressures of capital devaluation into a permanent inflationary crisis with milder cyclical fluctuations. And they have filtered down the dysfunctional side effects of the intercepted economic crisis and scattered them over quasi-groups (such as consumers, school children and their parents, transportation users, the sick, the elderly) or divided groups difficult to organize. This process breaks down the social identity of the classes and fragments class consciousness. In the class compromise now part of the structure of late capitalism, nearly everyone both participates and is affected as an individual—although, with the clear and sometimes growing unequal distribution of monetary values and power, one can well distinguish between those belonging more to the one or to the other category.

Three Developing Crises

The rapid growth processes of late-capitalist societies have confronted the system of world society with new problems. These problems cannot be regarded as crisis phenomena specific to the system, even though the possibilities of coping with the crises *are* specific to the system and therefore limited. I am thinking of the disturbance of the ecological balance, the violation of the personality system (alienation), and the explosive strain on international relations.

The ecological balance. If physically economic growth can be traced back to the technologically sophisticated use of more energy to increase the productivity of human labor, then the societal formation of capitalism is remarkable for impressively solving the problem of economic growth. To be sure, capital accumulation originally pushes economic growth ahead, so there is no option for the conscious steering of this process. The growth imperatives originally followed by capitalism have meanwhile achieved a global validity by way of system competition and worldwide diffusion (despite the stagnation or even retrogressive trends in some Third World countries).

The mechanisms of growth are forcing an increase of both population and production on a worldwide scale. The economic needs of a growing population and the productive exploitation of nature are faced with material restrictions: on the one hand, finite resources (cultivable and inhabitable land, fresh water, metals, minerals, etc.); on the other hand, irreplaceable ecological systems that absorb pollutants such as fallout, carbon dioxide, and waste heat. Forrester and others have estimated the limits of the exponential growth of population, industrial production, exploitation of natural resources, and environmental pollution. To be sure, their estimates have rather weak empirical foundations. The mechanisms of population growth are as little known as the maximum limits of the earth's potential for absorbing even the major pollutants. Moreover, we cannot forecast technological development accurately enough to know what raw materials will be replaced or renovated by future technology.

However, despite any optimistic assurances, we are able to indicate (if not precisely determine) *one* absolute limitation on growth: the thermal strain on the environment due to consumption of energy. If economic growth is necessarily coupled with increasing consumption of energy, and if all natural energy that is transformed into economically useful energy is ultimately released as heat, it will eventually raise the temperature of the atmosphere. Again, determining the deadline is not easy. Nevertheless, these reflections show that an exponential growth of population and production—i.e., an expanded control over external nature—will some day run up against the limits of the biological capacity of the environment.

This is not limited to complex societal systems. Specific to these systems are the possibilities of warding off dangers to the ecology. Late-capitalist societies would have a very hard time limiting growth without abandoning their principle of organization, because an overall shift from spontaneous capitalist growth to qualitative growth would require production planning in terms of use-values.

The anthropological balance. While the disturbance of the ecological balance points out the negative aspect of the exploitation of natural resources, there are no sure signals for the capacity limits of personality systems. I doubt whether it is possible to identify such things as psychological constants of human nature that inwardly limit the socialization process. I do, however, see a limitation in the kind of socializing that societal systems have been using to create motives for action. Our behavior is oriented by norms requiring justification and by interpretative systems guaranteeing identity. Such a communicative organization of behavior can become an obstacle in complex societies for a simple reason. The adaptive capacity in organizations increases proportionately as the administrative authorities become independent of the particular motivations of the members. The choice and achievement of organization goals in systems of high intrinsic complexity have to be independent of the influx of narrowly delimited motives. This requires a generalized willingness to comply (in political systems, such willingness has the form of legitimation). As long as socialization brings inner nature into a communicative behavioral organization, no legitimation for norms of action could conceivably secure an unmotivated acceptance of decisions. In regard to decisions whose contents are still undetermined, people will comply if convinced that those decisions are based on a legitimate norm of action. If the motives for acting were no longer to pass through norms requiring justification, and if the personality structures no longer had to find their unity under interpretative systems guaranteeing identity, then (and only then) the unmotivated acceptance of decisions would become an irreproachable routine, and the readiness to comply could thus be produced to any desirable degree.

The international balance. The dangers of destroying the world system with thermonuclear weapons are on a different level. The accumulated potential for annihilating is a result of the advanced stage of productive forces. Its basis is technologically neutral, and so the productive forces can also take the form of destructive forces (which has happened because international communication is still undeveloped). Today, mortal damage to the natural substratum of global society is quite possible. International communication is therefore governed by a historically new imperative of self-limitation. Once again, this is not limited to all highly militarized societal systems, but the possibilities of tackling this problem have limits specific to the systems. An actual disarmament may be unlikely because of the forces behind capitalist and postcapitalist class societies. Yet regulating the arms race is not basically incompatible with the structure of late-capitalist societies if it is possible to increase technologically the use-value of capital to the degree that the capacity effect of the government's demand for unproductive consumer goods can be balanced.

Disturbances Specific to the System

I would now like to leave these three global consequences of late-capitalist growth and investigate disturbances specific to the system. I will start with a thesis, widespread among Marxists, that the basic capitalist structures continue unaltered and create economic crises in altered manifestations. In late capitalism, the state pursues the politics of capital with other means. This thesis occurs in two versions.

Orthodox state-theory maintains that the activities of the interventionist state, no less than the exchange processes in liberal capitalism, obey economic laws. The altered manifestations (the crisis of state finances and permanent inflation, growing disparities between public poverty and private wealth, etc.) are due to the fact that the self-regulation of the realization process is governed by power rather than by exchange. However, the crisis tendency is determined, as much as ever, by the law of value, the structurally forced asymmetry in the exchange of wage labor for capital. As a result, state activity cannot permanently compensate for the tendency of falling rates of profit. It can at best mediate that trend—i.e., consummate it with political means. The replacement of market functions by state functions does not alter the unconscious nature of the overall economic process. This is shown by the narrow limits of the state's possibilities for manipulation. The state cannot substantially intervene in the property structure without causing an investment strike. Neither can it manage to permanently avoid cyclical stagnation tendencies of the accumulation process—i.e., stagnation tendencies that are created endogenously.

A revisionist version of the Marxist theory of the state is current among leading economists in the German Democratic Republic. According to this version, the state apparatus, instead of naturally obeying the logic of the law of value, is consciously supporting the interests of united monopoly capitalists. This agency theory, adapted to late capitalism, regards the state not as a blind organ of the realization process but as a potent supreme capitalist who makes the accumulation of capital the substance of his political planning. The high degree of the socialization of production brings together the individual interests of the large corporations and the interest in maintaining the system. And all the more so because its existence is threatened internally by forces transcending the system. This leads to an overall capitalist interest, which the united monopolies sustain with the aid of the state apparatus.

I consider both versions of the theory of economic crises inadequate. One version underestimates the state, the other overestimates it.

In regard to the orthodox thesis, I wonder if the state-controlled organization of scientific and technological progress and the system of collective bargaining (a system producing a class compromise, especially in the capital- and growth-intensive economic sectors) have not altered the mode of production. The state, having been drawn into the process of production, has modified the determinants of the process of utilizing capital. On the basis of a partial class compromise, the administrative system has gained a limited planning capacity. This can be used within the framework of the democratic acquisition of legitimation for purposes of reactive avoidance of crises. The cycle of crises is deactivated and rendered less harmful in its social consequences. It is replaced by inflation and a permanent crisis of public finances. The question as to whether these surrogates indicate a successful halting of the economic crisis or merely its temporary shift into the political system is an empirical one. Ultimately, this depends on whether the indirectly productive capital invested in research, development, and education can continue the process of accumulation. It can manage to do so by making labor more productive, raising the rate of surplus value, and cheapening the fixed components of capital.

The revisionist theory has elicited the following reservations. For one thing, we cannot empirically support the assumption that the state apparatus, no matter in whose interest, can actively plan, as well as draft and carry through, a central economic strategy. The theory of state-monopoly capitalism (akin to Western theories of technocracy) fails to recognize the limits of administrative planning in late capitalism. Bureaucracies for planning always reactively avoid crises. The various bureaucracies are not fully coordinated, and because of their limited capacity for perceiving and steering, they tend to depend largely on the influence of their clients. It is because of this very inefficiency that organized partial interests have a chance to penetrate the administrative apparatus. Nor can we empirically support the other assumption that the state is active as the agent of the united monopolists. The theory of state-monopoly capitalism (akin to Western elite theories) overrates the significance of personal contacts and direct influence. Studies on the recruiting, make-up, and interaction of the various power elites fail to cogently explain the functional connections between the economic and administrative systems.

In my opinion, the late-capitalist state can be properly understood neither as the unconscious executive organ of economic laws nor as a systematic agent of the united monopoly capitalists. Instead, I would join Claus Offe in advocating the theory that late-capitalist societies are faced with two difficulties caused by the state's having to intervene in the growing functional gaps of the market. We can regard the state as a system that uses legitimate power. Its output consists in sovereignly executing administrative decisions. To this end, it needs an input of mass loyalty that is as unspecific as possible. Both directions can lead to crisislike disturbances. Output crises have the form of the efficiency crisis. The administrative system fails to fulfill the steering imperative that it has taken over from the economic system. This results in the disorganization of different areas of life. Input crises have the form of the legitimation crisis. The legitimation system fails to maintain the necessary level of mass loyalty. We can clarify this with the example of the acute difficulties in public finances, with which all late-capitalist societies are now struggling.

The government budget, as I have said, is burdened with the public expenses of an increasingly socialized production. It bears the costs of international competition and of the demand for unproductive consumer goods (armament and space travel). It bears the costs for the infrastructural output (transportation and communication, scientific and technological progress, vocational training). It bears the costs of the social consumption indirectly concerned with production (housing, transportation, health, leisure, general education, social security). It bears the costs of providing for the unemployed. And finally, it bears the externalized costs of environmental damage caused by private production. Ultimately, these expenses have to be met by taxes. The state apparatus thus has two simultaneous tasks. It has to levy the necessary taxes from profits and income and employ them so efficiently as to prevent any crises from disturbing growth. In addition the selective raising of taxes, the recognizable priority model of their utilization, and the administrative performance have to function in such a way as to satisfy the resulting need for legitimation. If the state fails in the former task, the result is a deficit in administrative efficiency. If it fails in the latter task, the result is a deficit in legitimation.

Theorems of the Legitimation Crisis

I would like to restrict myself to the legitimation problem. There is nothing mysterious about its genesis. Legitimate power has to be available for administrative planning. The functions accruing to the state apparatus in late capitalism and the expansion of social areas treated by administration increase the need for legitimation. Liberal capitalism constituted itself in the forms of bourgeois democracy, which is easy to explain in terms of the bourgeois revolution. As a result, the growing need for legitimation now has to work with the means of political democracy (on the basis of universal suffrage). The formal democratic means, however, are expensive. After all, the state apparatus does not just see itself in the role of the supreme capitalist facing the conflicting interests of the various capital factions. It also has to consider the generalizable interests of the population as far as necessary to retain mass loyalty and prevent a conflict-ridden withdrawal of legitimation. The state has to gauge these three interest areas (individual capitalism, state capitalism, and generalizable interests), in order to find a compromise for competing demands. A theorem of crisis has to explain not only why the state apparatus encounters difficulties but also why certain problems remain unsolved in the long run.

First, an obvious objection. The state can avoid legitimation problems to the extent that it can manage to make the administrative system independent of the formation of legitimating will. To that end, it can, say, separate expressive symbols (which create a universal willingness to follow) from the instrumental functions of administration. Well known strategies of this sort are: the personalizing of objective issues, the symbolic use of inquiries, expert opinions, legal incantations, etc. Advertising techniques, borrowed from oligopolistic competition, both confirm and exploit current structures of prejudice. By resorting to emotional appeals, they arouse unconscious motives, occupy certain contents positively, and devalue others. The public, which is engineered for purposes of legitimation, primarily has the function of structuring attention by means of areas of themes and thereby of pushing uncomfortable themes, problems, and arguments below the threshold of attention. As Niklas Luhmann put it: The political system takes over tasks of *ideology planning*.

The scope for manipulation, however, is narrowly delimited, for the cultural system remains peculiarly resistant to administrative control. There is no administrative creation of meaning, there is at best an ideological erosion of cultural values. The acquisition of legitimation is self-destructive as soon as the mode of acquisition is exposed. Thus, there is a systematic limit for attempts at making up for legitimation deficits by means of well aimed manipulation. This limit is the structural dissimilarity between areas of administrative action and cultural tradition.

A crisis argument, to be sure, can be constructed out of these considerations only with the viewpoint that the expansion of state activity has the side effect of disproportionately increasing the need for legitimation. I regard such an overproportionate increase as likely because things that are taken for granted culturally, and have so far been external conditions of the political systems, are now being drawn into the planning area of administration. This process thematizes traditions which previously were not part of public programming, much less of practical discourse. An example of such direct administrative processing of cultural tradition is educational planning, especially the planning of the curriculum. Hitherto, the school administration merely had to codify a given naturally evolved canon. But now the planning of the curriculum is based on the premise that the tradition models can also be different. Administrative planning creates a universal compulsion for justification toward a sphere that was actually distinguished by the power of self-legitimation.

In regard to the direct disturbance of things that were culturally taken for granted, there are further examples in regional and urban planning (private ownership of land), health planning ("classless hospital"), and family planning and marriage-law planning (which are shaking sexual taboos and facilitating emancipation).

An awareness of contingency is created not just for contents of tradition but also for the techniques of tradition—i.e., socialization. Among preschool children, formal schooling is already competing with family upbringing. The new problems afflicting the educational routine, and the widespread awareness of these problems, are reflected by, among other indications, a new type of pedagogical and psychological writing addressed to the general public.

On all these levels, administrative planning has unintentional effects of disquieting and publicizing. These effects weaken the justification potential of traditions that have been forced out of their natural condition. Once they are no longer indisputable, their demands for validity can be stabilized only by way of discourse. Thus, the forcible shift of things that have been culturally taken for granted further politicizes areas of life that previously could be assigned to the private domain. However, this spells danger for bourgeois privatism, which is informally assured by the structures of the public. I see signs of this danger in strivings for participation and in models for alternatives, such as have developed particularly in secondary and primary schools, in the press, the church, theaters, publishing, etc.

These arguments support the contention that late-capitalist societies are afflicted with serious problems of legitimation. But do these arguments suffice to explain why these problems cannot be solved? Do they explain the prediction of a crisis in legitimation? Let us assume the state apparatus could succeed in making labor more productive and in distributing the gains in productivity in such a way as to assure an economic growth free of crises (if not disturbances). Such growth would nevertheless proceed in terms of priorities independent of the generalizable interests of the population. The priority models that Galbraith has analyzed from the viewpoint of "private wealth vs. public poverty" result from a class structure which, as always, is still being kept latent. This structure is ultimately the cause of the legitimation deficit.

We have seen that the state cannot simply take over the cultural system and that, in fact, the expansion of areas for state planning creates problems for things that are culturally taken for granted. "Meaning" is an increasingly scarce resource. Which is why those expectations that are governed by concrete and identifiable needs—i.e., that can be checked by their success—keep mounting in the civil population. The rising level of aspirations is proportionate to the growing need for legitimation. The resource of "value," siphoned off by the tax office, has to make up for the scanty resource of "meaning." Missing legitimations have to be replaced by social rewards such as money, time, and security. A crisis of legitimation arises as soon as the demands for these rewards mount more rapidly than the available mass of values, or if expectations come about that are different and cannot be satisfied by those categories of rewards conforming with the present system.

Why, then, should not the level of demands keep within operable limits? As long as the welfare state's programming in connection with a widespread technocratic consciousness (which makes uninfluenceable system-restraints responsible for bottlenecks) maintains a sufficient amount of civil privatism, then the legitimation emergencies do not have to turn into crises. To be sure, the democratic form of legitimation could cause expenses that cannot be covered if that form drives the competing parties to outdo one another in their platforms and thereby raise the expectations of the population higher and higher. Granted, this argument could be amply demonstrated empirically. But we could still have to explain why late-capitalist societies even bother to retain formal democracy. Merely in terms of the administrative system, formal democracy could just as easily be replaced by a variant—a conservative, authoritarian welfare state that reduces the political partici- pation of the citizens to a harmless level; or a Fascist authoritarian state that keeps the population toeing the mark on a relatively high level of per- manent mobilization. Evidently, both variants are in the long run less com- patible with developed capitalism than a party state based on mass democ- racy. The sociocultural system creates demands that cannot be satisfied in authoritarian systems.

This reflection leads me to the following thesis: Only a rigid sociocultural system, incapable of being randomly functionalized for the needs of the administrative system, could explain how legitimation difficulties result in a legitimation crisis. This development must therefore be based on a *moti- vation crisis*—i.e., a discrepancy between the need for motives that the state and the occupational system announce and the supply of motivation offered by the sociocultural system.

Theorems of the Motivation Crisis

The most important motivation contributed by the sociocultural system in late-capitalist societies consists in syndromes of civil and family/vocational privatism. Civil privatism means strong interests in the administrative sys- tem's output and minor participation in the process of will-formation (high- output orientation vs. low-input orientation). Civil privatism thus corre- sponds to the structures of a depoliticized public. Family and vocational privatism complements civil privatism. It consists of a family orientation with consumer and leisure interests, and of a career orientation consistent with status competition. This privatism thus corresponds to the structures of educational and occupational systems regulated by competitive perform- ance.

The motivational syndromes mentioned are vital to the political and eco- nomic system. However, bourgeois ideologies have components directly rel- evant to privatistic orientations, and social changes deprive those compo- nents of their basis. A brief outline may clarify this.

Performance ideology. According to bourgeois notions which have re- mained constant from the beginnings of modern natural law to contempo- rary election speeches, social rewards should be distributed on the basis of individual achievement. The distribution of gratifications should correlate to every individual's performance. A basic condition is equal opportunity to participate in a competition which is regulated in such a way that exter- nal influences can be neutralized. One such allocation mechanism was the market. But ever since the general public realized that social violence is practiced in the forms of exchange, the market has been losing its credibility as a mechanism for distributing rewards based on performance. Thus, in the more recent versions of performance ideology, market success is being replaced by the professional success mediated by formal schooling. However, *this* version can claim credibility only when the following conditions have been fulfilled:

- equal opportunity of access to higher schools;
- nondiscriminatory evaluation standards for school performance;
- synchronic developments of the educational and occupational systems;
- work processes whose objective structure permits evaluation according to performances that can be ascribed to individuals.

"School justice" in terms of opportunity of access and standards of evaluation has increased in all advanced capitalist societies at least to some degree. But a countertrend can be observed in the two other dimensions. The expansion of the educational system is becoming more and more independent of changes in the occupational system, so that ultimately the connection between formal schooling and professional success will most likely loosen. At the same time, there are more and more areas in which production structures and work dynamics make it increasingly difficult to evaluate individual performance. Instead, the extrafunctional elements of occupational roles are becoming more and more important for conferring occupational status.

Moreover, fragmented and monotonous work processes are increasingly entering sectors in which previously a personal identity could be developed through the vocational role. An intrinsic motivation for performance is getting less and less support from the structure of the work process in market-dependent work areas. An instrumentalist attitude toward work is spreading even in the traditionally bourgeois professions (white-collar workers, professionals). A performance motivation coming from outside can, however, be sufficiently stimulated by wage income only:

- if the reserve army on the labor market exercises an effective competitive pressure;
- if a sufficient income differential exists between the lower wage groups and the inactive work population.

Both conditions are not necessarily met today. Even in capitalist countries with chronic unemployment (such as the United States), the division of the labor market (into organized and competitive sectors) interferes with the natural mechanism of competition. With a mounting poverty line (recognized by the welfare state), the living standards of the lower income groups and the groups temporarily released from the labor process are mutually assimilating on the other side in the subproletarian strata.

Possessive individualism. Bourgeois society sees itself as an instrumental group that accumulates social wealth only by way of private wealth—i.e., guarantees economic growth and general welfare through competition between strategically acting private persons. Collective goals, under such cir-

cumstances, can be achieved only by way of individual utility orientations. This preference system, of course, presupposes:
• that the private economic subjects can with subjective unambiguity recognize and calculate needs that remain constant over given time periods;
• that this need can be satisfied by individually demandable goods (normally, by way of monetary decisions that conform to the system).

Both presuppositions are no longer fulfilled as a matter of course in the developed capitalist societies. These societies have reached a level of societal wealth far beyond warding off a few fundamental hazards to life and the satisfying of basic needs. This is why the individualistic system of preference is becoming vague. The steady interpreting and reinterpreting of needs is becoming a matter of the collective formation of the will, a fact which opens the alternatives of either free and quasi-political communication among consumers as citizens or massive manipulation—i.e., strong indirect steering. The greater the degree of freedom for the preference system of the demanders, the more urgent the problem of sales policies for the suppliers—at least if they are to maintain the illusion that the consumers can make private and autonomous decisions. Opportunistic adjustment of the consumers to market strategies is the ironical form of every consumer autonomy, which is to be maintained as the façade of possessive individualism. In addition, with increasing socialization of production, the quota of collective commodities among the consumer goods keeps growing. The urban living conditions in complex societies are more and more dependent on an infrastructure (transportation, leisure, health, education, etc.) that is withdrawing further and further from the forms of differential demand and private appropriation.

Exchange-value orientation. Here I have to mention the tendencies that weaken the socialization effects of the market, especially the increase of those parts of the population that do not reproduce their lives through income from work (students, welfare recipients, social security recipients, invalids, criminals, soldiers, etc.) as well as the expansion of areas of activity in which, as in civil service or in teaching, abstract work is replaced by concrete work. In addition, the relevance that leisure acquires with fewer working hours (and higher real income), compared with the relevance of issues within the occupational sphere of life, does not in the long run privilege those needs that can be satisfied monetarily.

The erosion of bourgeois tradition brings out normative structures that are no longer appropriate to reproducing civil and family and professional privatism. The now dominant components of cultural heritage crystalize around a faith in science, a "postauratic" art, and universalistic values. Irreversible developments have occurred in each of these areas. As a result, functional inequalities of the economic and the political systems are blocked by cultural barriers, and they can be broken down only at the psychological cost of regressions—i.e., with extraordinary motivational damage. German

Fascism was an example of the wasteful attempt at a collectively organized regression of consciousness below the thresholds of fundamental scientistic convictions, modern art, and universalistic law and morals.

Scientism. The political consequences of the authority enjoyed by the scientific system in developed societies are ambivalent. The rise of modern science established a demand for discursive justification, and traditionalistic attitudes cannot hold out against that demand. On the other hand, short-lived popular syntheses of scientific data (which have replaced global interpretations) guarantee the authority of science *in the abstract.* The authority known as "science" can thus cover both things: the broadly effective criticism of any prejudice, as well as the new esoterics of specialized knowledge and expertise. A self-affirmation of the sciences can further a positivistic common sense on the part of the depoliticized public. Yet scientism establishes standards by which it can also be criticized itself and found guilty of residual dogmatism. Theories of technocracy and of democratic elitism, asserting the necessity of an institutionalized civic privatism, come forth with the presumption of theories. But this does not make them immune to criticism.

Postauratic art. The consequences of modern art are somewhat less ambivalent. The modern age has radicalized the autonomy of bourgeois art in regard to the external purposes for which art could be used. For the first time, bourgeois society itself produced a counterculture against the bourgeois life style of possessive individualism, performance, and practicality. The *Bohème,* first established in Paris, the capital of the nineteenth century, embodies a critical demand that had arisen, unpolemically still, in the aura of the bourgeois artwork. The alter ego of the businessman, the "human being," whom the bourgeois used to encounter in the lonesome contemplation of the artwork, soon split away from him. In the shape of the artistic avant-garde, it confronted him as a hostile, at best seductive force. In artistic beauty, the bourgeoisie had been able to experience its own ideals and the (as always) fictitious redemption of the promise of happiness which was merely suspended in everyday life. In radicalized art, however, the bourgeois soon had to recognize the negation of social practice as its complement.

Modern art is the outer covering in which the transformation of bourgeois art into a counterculture was prepared. Surrealism marks the historical moment when modern art programmatically destroyed the outer covering of no-longer-beautiful illusion in order to enter life desublimated. The leveling of the different reality degrees of art and life was accelerated (although not, as Walter Benjamin assumed, introduced) by the new techniques of mass reproduction and mass reception. Modern art had already sloughed off the aura of classical bourgeois art in that the art work made the production process visible and presented itself as a made product. But art enters the ensemble of utility values only when abandoning its autonomous status. The process is certainly ambivalent. It can signify the degeneration of art into a propagandistic mass art or commercialized mass culture, or else its transformation into a subversive counterculture.

Universalist morality. The blockage which bourgeois ideologies, stripped of their functional components, create for developing the political and economic system, is even clearer in the moral system than in the authority of science and the self-disintegration of modern art. The moment traditional societies enter a process of modernization, the growing complexity results in steering problems that necessitate an accelerated change of social norms. The tempo inherent in natural cultural tradition has to be heightened. This leads to bourgeois formal law which permits releasing the norm contents from the dogmatic structure of mere tradition and defining them in terms of intention. The legal norms are uncoupled from the corps of privatized moral norms. In addition, they need to be created (and justified) according to principles. Abstract law counts only for that area pacified by state power. But the morality of bourgeois private persons, a morality likewise raised to the level of universal principles, encounters no barrier in the continuing natural condition between the states. Since principled morality is sanctioned only by the purely inward authority of the conscience, its claim to universality conflicts with public morality, which is still bound to a concrete state-subject. This is the conflict between the cosmopolitanism of the human being and the loyalties of the citizen.

If we follow the developmental logic of overall societal systems of norms (leaving the area of historical examples), we can settle that conflict. But its resolution is conceivable only under certain conditions. The dichotomy between inner and outer morality has to disappear. The contrast between morally and legally regulated areas has to be relativized. And the validity of *all* norms has to be tied to the discursive formation of the will of the people potentially affected.

Competitive capitalism for the first time gave a binding force to strictly universalistic value systems. This occurred because the system of exchange had to be regulated universalistically and because the exchange of equivalents offered a basic ideology effective in the bourgeois class. In organized capitalism, the bottom drops out of this legitimation model. At the same time, new and increased demands for legitimation arise. However, the system of science cannot intentionally fall behind an attained stage of cumulative knowledge. Similarly, the moral system, once practical discourse has been admitted, cannot simply make us forget a collectively attained stage of moral consciousness.

I would like to conclude with a final reflection.

If no sufficient concordance exists between the normative structures that still have some power today and the politicoeconomic system, then we can still avoid motivation crises by uncoupling the cultural system. Culture would then become a nonobligatory leisure occupation or the object of professional knowledge. This solution would be blocked if the basic convictions of a communicative ethics and the experience complexes of countercultures (in which postauratic art is embodied) acquired a motive-forming power determining typical socialization processes. Such a conjecture is supported by several behavior syndromes spreading more and more among young people—either retreat as a reaction to an exorbitant claim on the personality-resources; or protest as a result of an autonomous ego organization that cannot be stabilized without conflicts under given conditions. On the activist side we find: the student movement, revolts by high-school students and apprentices, pacifists, women's lib. The retreatist side is represented by hippies, Jesus people, the drug subculture, phenomena of undermotivation in schools, etc. These are the primary areas for checking our hypothesis that late-capitalist societies are endangered by a collapse of legitimation.

Chapter Thirteen

THE CRISIS OF THE WELFARE STATE AND THE EXHAUSTION OF UTOPIAN ENERGIES

1

Since the late eighteenth century a new time consciousness has been developing in Western culture.[1] Whereas in the Christian West the "new age" [*neue Zeit*] designated the future period that would dawn on Judgment Day, from the late eighteenth century on the "modern age" [*Neuzeit*] has meant one's own period, the present. The present is understood at each point as a transition to something new; it lives with an awareness that historical events are accelerating and an expectation that the future will be different. The epochal new beginning that marked the modern world's break with the world of the Christian Middle Ages and antiquity is repeated, as it were, in every present moment that brings forth something new. The present perpetuates the break with the past in the form of a continual renewal. The horizon of anticipations opening onto the future and referring to the present also governs the way the past is grasped. Since the end of the eighteenth century, history has been conceived as a process that is world-encompassing and problem-generating. In that process, time is thought of as a scarce resource for the future-oriented mastery of problems left us by the past. Exemplary periods in the past that the present might have been able to use unhesitatingly to orient itself have faded into insignificance. Modernity can no longer derive the standards it uses to orient itself from models offered by other epochs. Modernity sees itself as exclusively dependent on itself; it must draw on itself for its normativity. From now on the authentic present is the locus in which innovation and the continuation of tradition are intertwined.

This devaluation of an exemplary past and the necessity to extract substantive normative principles from one's own modern experiences and forms of life accounts for the altered structure of the *Zeitgeist*. The *Zeitgeist* becomes the medium in which political thought and discussion will henceforth move. The *Zeitgeist* receives impulses from two contrary but interdependent and mutually interpenetrating currents of thought: it is fueled by the clash of historical and utopian thought.[2] At first these two modes of thought seem mutually exclusive. *Historical thought,* saturated with actual experience, seems destined to criticize utopian schemes; the function of *utopian thought* with its exuberance seems to be opening up alternatives for action and margins of possibility that push beyond historical continuities. But in fact modern time consciousness has opened up a horizon in which utopian thought fuses with historical thought. Certainly the movement of utopian energies into historical consciousness characterizes the *Zeitgeist* that has stamped the political public sphere of modern people since the days of the French Revolution. Infected by the *Zeitgeist*'s focus on the significance of the current moment and attempting to hold firm under the pressure of current problems, political thought becomes charged with utopian energies—but at the same time this excess of expectations is to be controlled by the conservative counterweight of historical experience.

Since the early nineteenth century, "utopia" has become a polemical political concept that everyone uses against everyone else. The accusation was first advanced against the abstract thought of the Enlightenment and its liberal heirs, then, naturally, against socialists and communists, but also against the conservative Ultras—against the former because they evoked an abstract future, against the latter because they evoked an abstract past. Because all are infected with utopian thought, no one wants to be a utopian.[3] Thomas More's *Utopia,* Campanella's *Sun State,* Bacon's *New Atlantis*— these spatial utopias conceived during the Renaissance could appropriately be called "novels of the state" because their authors never left any doubt about the fictitious character of the narratives. They translated notions of paradise back into historical spaces and earthly antiworlds; they transformed eschatological expectations back into profane life-possibilities. As Fourier noted, the classical utopias of a better life, a less threatened life, were presented as a "dream of the good—without the means to realize the dream, without a method." Despite their critical relationship to their times, they had as yet no contact with history. That situation did not change until Mercier, a follower of Rousseau, in a novel of the future about Paris in the year 2440, shifted the Fortunate Isles from spatially distant regions into a distant future—thus depicting eschatological expectations for a future restoration of paradise in terms of a secular axis of historical progress.[4] But as soon as utopia and history came into contact in this way, the classical form of utopia changed; the novel of the state lost its novelistic features. From now on those who were the most sensitive to the utopian energies of the *Zeitgeist* would be the ones who most energetically pursued the fusion of utopian with historical thought. Robert Owen and Saint-Simon, Fourier and Proudhon emphatically rejected utopianism; and they in turn were accused by Marx and Engels of being "utopian socialists." Not until this century did Ernst Bloch and Karl Mannheim purge the term "utopia" of its association with "utopianism" and rehabilitate it as a legitimate medium for depicting alternative life possibilities that are inherent in the historical process itself. A utopian perspective is thus inscribed within politically active historical consciousness itself.

This, in any case, is how things seemed to stand—until recently. Today it seems as though utopian energies have been used up, as if they have retreated from historical thought. The horizon of the future has contracted and has changed both the *Zeitgeist* and politics in fundamental ways. The future is negatively cathected; on the threshold of the twenty-first century we see outlined the horrifying panorama of a worldwide threat to general life interests: the spiraling arms race, the uncontrolled spread of nuclear weapons, the structural impoverishment of developing nations, environmental problems, and the nearly catastrophic operations of high technology are the catchwords that have penetrated public consciousness through the mass media. The responses of the intellectual community reflect as much bewilderment as those of the politicians. It is by no means only realism when we increasingly replace attempts at orientation to the future with a bewilderment we simply accept. The situation may be objectively obscure. Obscurity is nonetheless also a function of a society's assessment of its own readiness to take action. What is at stake is Western culture's confidence in itself.

2

Granted, there are good reasons for this exhaustion of utopian energies. The classical utopias depicted the conditions for a life of dignity, for socially organized happiness; the social utopias that merged with historical thought, the utopias that have influenced political discussion since the nineteenth century, awaken more realistic expectations. They present science, technology, and planning as promising and unerring instruments for the rational control of nature and society. Since then, this very expectation has been shaken by massive evidence. Nuclear energy, weapons technology, the penetration of space, genetic research and biotechnical intervention in human behavior, information processing, data management, and new communications media are technologies which by their very nature have conflicting consequences. The more complex the systems that require steering become, the greater the probability of dysfunctional secondary effects. We experience on a daily basis the transformation of productive forces into destructive forces, of planning capacities into the potential for disruption. It is no wonder, then, that the theories gaining in influence today are primarily those that try to show how the very forces that make for increasing power, the forces from which modernity once derived its self-consciousness and its utopian expectations, are in actuality turning autonomy into dependence, emancipation into oppression, and reason into irrationality. Derrida concludes from Heidegger's critique of modern subjectivity that we can escape from the treadmill of Western logocentrism only through aimless provocation. Instead of trying to master foreground contingencies *in* the world, he says, we should surrender to the mysteriously encoded contingencies through which the world discloses itself. Foucault radicalizes Horkheimer's and Adorno's critique of instrumental reason to make it a theory of the Eternal Return of power. His proclamation of a cycle of power that is always the same returning in discourse formations that are always new cannot help but extinguish the last spark of utopia and destroy the last traces of Western culture's self-confidence.

On the intellectual scene the suspicion is spreading that the exhaustion of utopian energies is not just an indication of a transitory mood of cultural pessimism but instead goes deeper. It could indicate a change in modern time consciousness as such. Perhaps the amalgam of historical and utopian thought is disintegrating; perhaps the structure of the *Zeitgeist* and the overall situation of politics are changing. Perhaps historical consciousness is being *relieved* of its utopian energies: just as at the end of the eighteenth century, with the temporalization of utopias, hopes for paradise moved into the mundane sphere, so today, two hundred years later, utopian expectations are losing their secular character and once again assuming religious form.

I consider this thesis of the onset of the postmodern period to be unfounded. Neither the structure of the *Zeitgeist* nor the mode of debating future life possibilities has changed; utopian energies as such are not withdrawing from historical consciousness. Rather, what has come to an end is a particular utopia that in the past crystallized around the potential of a society based on social labor.

The classical social theorists from Marx to Max Weber agreed that the structure of bourgeois society was characterized by abstract labor, by the type of labor for payment that is regulated by market forces, valorized in capitalistic form, and organized in the form of business enterprise. Because the form of this abstract labor displayed such an ability to penetrate all spheres and put its stamp on them, utopian expectations too could be directed toward the sphere of production, in short, to the emancipation of labor from external control. The utopias of the early socialists took concrete form in the image of the phalanstery, a labor-based social organization of free and equal producers. The communal form of life of workers in free association was supposed to arise from the proper organization of production itself. This idea of worker self-management continued to inspire the protest movement of the late 1960s.[5] For all his critique of early socialism, Marx, too, in the first part of *The German Ideology,* was pursuing the same utopian idea of a society based on social labor:

Thus things have now come to such a pass that . . . individuals must appropriate the existing totality of productive forces . . . to achieve self-activity. . . . The appropriation of these forces is itself nothing more than the development of the individual capacities corresponding to the material instruments of production. . . . Only at this stage does self-activity coincide with material life, which corresponds to the development of individuals into complete individuals and the casting-off of natural limitations.[6]

The utopian idea of a society based on social labor has lost its persuasive power—and not simply because the forces of production have lost their innocence or because the abolition of private ownership of the means of production clearly has not led in and of itself to workers' self-management. Rather, it is above all because that utopia has lost its point of reference in reality: the power of abstract labor to create structure and give form to society. Claus Offe has compiled convincing "indications of the objectively decreasing power of matters of labor, production, and earnings to determine the constitution and development of society as a whole."[7]

Anyone who looks at one of the rare pieces of writing that dares to make a utopian reference in its title today (I am thinking of André Gorz's *Paths to Paradise*) will find this diagnosis confirmed. Gorz bases his proposal to disengage labor and income through a guaranteed minimum income on the ending of the Marxian expectation that self-directed activity and material life could still become one and the same.

But why should the diminishing persuasive power of a utopia of social labor be of significance to the broader public, and why should it help to explain a *general* exhaustion of utopian impulses? We should remember that it was not only intellectuals whom this utopia attracted. It inspired the European labor movement, and in our century it left its traces in three very different but historically influential programs. The political movements corresponding to these programs were established in reaction to the consequences of World War I and the ensuing economic crisis: Soviet communism in Russia, authoritarian corporatism in fascist Italy, in Nazi Germany, and in Falangist Spain; and social-democratic reformism in the mass democracies of the West. Only this latter project of a social welfare state has adopted the legacy of the bourgeois emancipation movements, namely, the democratic constitutional state. Although this project emerged from the social-democratic tradition, it has by no means been pursued only by social-democratic governments. Since World War II, all the governing parties in the Western countries have won their majorities more or less explicitly under the banner of welfare state objectives. Since the middle of the 1970s, however, awareness of the limitations of the welfare state project has been growing, without as yet a clear alternative in view. Thus I will formulate my thesis as follows: the new obscurity is part of a situation in which a welfare-state program that continues to be nourished by a utopia of social labor is losing its power to project future possibilities for a collectively better and less threatened way of life.

3

In the welfare state project, of course, the utopian core, liberation from alienated labor, took a different form. Emancipated living conditions worthy of human beings are no longer to emerge directly from the revolutionizing of labor conditions, that is, from the transformation of alienated labor into self-directed activity. Nevertheless, reformed conditions of employment retain a position of central importance in this project as well.[8] They remain the reference point not only for measures designed to humanize labor, which continues to be largely heteronomous, but also and especially for compensatory measures designed to assume the burden of the fundamental risks of wage labor (accident, illness, loss of employment, lack of provision for old age). As a result, all those who are able to work must be incorporated into this streamlined and cushioned system of employment—hence the goal of full employment. The compensatory process functions only if the role of the full-time wage earner becomes the norm. For the burdens that continue to be connected with the cushioned status of dependent wage labor, citizens are compensated in their role as clients of the welfare state bureaucracies with legal claims, and in their role as consumers of mass-produced goods, with buying power. The lever for the pacification of class antagonism thus continues to be the neutralization of the conflict potential inherent in the status of the wage laborer.

This goal is to be reached through social welfare legislation and collective bargaining on wage scales by independent parties. Welfare state policies derive their legitimation from general elections and find their social base in autonomous labor unions and labor parties. It is of course the power and the capacity for action of an interventionist state apparatus that ultimately determine the success of the project. This apparatus is supposed to intervene in the economic system with the aim of protecting capitalist growth, smoothing out crises, and safeguarding simultaneously both jobs and the competitiveness of business in the international marketplace, so that increases are generated from which redistributions can be made without discouraging private investors. This throws some light on the *methodological* side of the project: the welfare state compromise and the pacification of class antagonism are to be achieved by using democratically legitimated state power to protect and restrain the quasi-natural process of capitalist growth. The *substantive* side of the project is nourished by the residues of a utopia of social labor: as the status of the employee is normalized through rights to political participation and social ownership, the general population gains the opportunity to live in freedom, social justice, and increasing prosperity. The presupposition here is that peaceful coexistence between democracy and capitalism can be ensured through state intervention.

In the developed industrial societies of the West this precarious condition could, by and large, be fulfilled, at least under the favorable constellation of factors in the postwar and reconstruction periods. But I want to deal here not with the changed constellation that has existed since the 1970s, not with external circumstances, but with the internal difficulties that arise for the welfare state as a result of its own successes.[9] In this regard two questions arise repeatedly. First, does the interventionist state have sufficient power at its disposal, and can it operate efficiently enough to keep the capitalist system under control as intended in its program? Second, is the use of political power the correct method for reaching the substantive goal of promoting and safeguarding emancipated forms of life worthy of human beings? Thus we are concerned first with the question of the degree to which capitalism and democracy can be reconciled, and second with the question whether new forms of life can be created through legal-bureaucratic means.

On question 1: From the beginning, the national state has proved too narrow a framework to adequately guarantee Keynesian economic policies against external factors—against the imperatives of the world market and the investment policies of business enterprises operating on a worldwide scale. But the limits of the state's power and capacity to intervene internally are still more evident. Here, the more successfully the welfare state enacts its programs, the more clearly it runs into the opposition of private investors. There are many causes, of course, for a decreasing profitability of business, for declining willingness to invest, and for falling rates of growth. But conditions for the valorization of capital do not, in actual fact, remain unaffected by the results of social welfare policies, and especially not in the subjective perception of business enterprises. In addition, rising costs for wages and benefits strengthen the tendency to invest in rationalizing production, investments which—under the banner of a second industrial revolution—so substantially increase the productivity of labor and so substantially decrease the labor time necessary to society as a whole that despite the secular trend toward shortening the work week more and more labor power is unused. Be that as it may, in a situation in which reluctance to invest, economic stagnation, increasing unemployment, and the crisis in public budgets can be suggestively connected in the public's perception with the costs of the welfare state, the structural limitations under which the welfare state compromise was worked out and maintained become quite evident. Because the welfare state may not interfere with the economic system's mode of functioning, it has no possibility of influencing private investment activity other than through interventions that conform to the economic system. Nor would it have the power to do so, because the redistribution of income is essentially limited to a horizontal reshuffling within the group of the dependently employed and does not touch the class-specific structure of wealth, in particular the distribution of ownership of the means of production. Thus it is precisely the successful welfare state that skids into a situation in which it becomes apparent, as Claus Offe has shown, that the welfare state itself is not an autonomous "source of prosperity" and cannot guarantee employment security as a civil right.

In such a situation the welfare state is immediately in danger of its social base slipping away. In times of crisis the upwardly mobile groups of voters who have received the greatest direct benefits from the welfare state development can develop a mentality concerned with maintaining their standard of living and may ally themselves with the old middle class, and in general with the strata concerned with "productivity," to form a defensive coalition opposing underprivileged or marginalized groups. Such a regrouping of the electoral base threatens primarily parties like the Democrats in the United States, the English Labor Party, or the German Social-Democratic Party, which for decades have been able to count on a firm welfare state clientele. At the same time, labor unions come under pressure through the changed situation in the labor market; their power to make effective threats is diminished, they lose members and contributions and see themselves forced into a politics of alliances tailored to the short-term interests of those who are still employed.

On question 2: Even if under more favorable conditions the welfare state could retard or completely avoid the side-effects of its own success that are jeopardizing the very conditions of its functioning, a further problem would remain unresolved. Advocates of the welfare state project had always looked in only one direction. In the foreground was the task of controlling quasi-natural economic power and diverting the destructive consequences of crisis-prone economic growth from the lifeworld of dependent workers. Government power achieved by parliamentary means seemed both an innocent and an indispensable resource; faced with the systemic inner logic of the economy, the interventionist state had to draw on that power for its strength and its capacity for action. The reformers had seen active state intervention, not only in the economic cycle but also in the life cycle of its citizens, as completely unproblematic—reforming the conditions of life of the employed was, after all, the goal of the welfare state program. And in fact a relatively high degree of social justice has been achieved in this way.

But the very people who acknowledge this historical achievement on the part of the welfare state and who refrain from cheap criticism of its weaknesses have come to recognize the one failure that derives not from any particular obstacle or from a half-hearted realization of the project but from a specific narrowness of vision on the part of the project itself. All skepticism about the medium of power, which may be indispensable but is only seemingly innocent, has been removed from awareness. Social welfare programs need a great deal of power to achieve the force of law financed by public budgets—and thus to be implemented within the lifeworld of their beneficiaries. Thus an ever denser net of legal norms, or governmental and para-governmental bureaucracies, is spread over the daily life of its potential and actual clients.

Extensive discussions of excessive legal regulation and bureaucratization in general and the counterproductive effects of government social-welfare policy in particular, and of the professionalization and scientization of social services, have made one thing clear: the legal and administrative means through which welfare state programs are implemented are not a passive medium with no properties of its own. On the contrary, they are linked with a practice that isolates individual facts, a practice of normalization and surveillance. Foucault has traced the reifying and subjectivizing power of this practice down to its very finest capillary ramifications in everyday communication. Certainly the deformations of a lifeworld that is regimented, dissected, controlled, and watched over are more subtle than the obvious forms of material exploitation and impoverishment; but social conflicts that have been shifted over into the psychological and physical domains and internalized are no less destructive for all that. In short, a contradiction between its goal and its method is inherent in the welfare state project as such. Its goal is the establishment of forms of life that are structured in an egalitarian way and that at the same time open up arenas for individual self-realization and spontaneity. But evidently this goal cannot be reached via the direct route of putting political programs into legal and administrative form. Generating forms of life exceeds the capacities of the medium of power.

4

I have discussed the obstacles that the successful welfare state puts in its own path in the context of two problems. I do not mean to say thereby that the development of the welfare state has been a misguided specialization. On the contrary, the institutions of the welfare state represent as much of an advance in the political system as those of the democratic constitutional state, an advance to which there is no identifiable alternative in societies of our type—either with regard to the functions that the welfare state fulfills or with regard to the normatively justified demands that it satisfies. In particular, nations that have lagged behind in the development of the social welfare state have no plausible reason for deviating from this path. It is precisely this lack of alternatives, and perhaps even the irreversibility of these compromise structures that are still being debated, that now confronts us with the dilemma that the developed forms of capitalism can no more live without the welfare state than they can live with its further expansion. The more or less bewildered reactions to this dilemma indicate that the potential of the utopian idea of a laboring society to stimulate new developments in the political sphere has been exhausted.

Following Claus Offe, one can distinguish three patterns of response to this dilemma in countries like the Federal Republic of Germany and the United States.[10] The more conservative wing of the social-democratic parties, which *defends the legitimacy of industrial society and the welfare state,* finds itself on the defensive. I intend this characterization in a broad sense, so that it can be applied, for example, both to the liberal wing of the Democratic Party in the United States and to the second government under Mitterrand in France. The legitimists delete from the welfare state project precisely the components it had derived from the utopian idea of a laboring society. They renounce the goal of overcoming heteronomous labor so that the status of a free citizen with equal rights extends into the sphere of production and can become the nucleus around which autonomous forms of life crystallize. Today the legitimists are the true conservatives, who want to stabilize what has been achieved. They hope to find a point of equilibrium between the development of a welfare state and modernization based on a market economy. The disturbed balance between orientations to democratic use-values and a toned-down version of the intrinsic capitalist dynamic is to be restored. This program focuses on preserving the existing achievements of the welfare state. It fails to recognize, however, the potentials for resistance accumulating in the wake of progressive bureaucratic erosion of communicatively structured lifeworlds that have been emancipated from quasi-natural contexts. Nor does it take seriously the shifts in the social and labor union base on which welfare state policies have hitherto been able to rely. With shifts in the structure of the electorate and a weakening of the position of the labor unions, these policies are threatened with a desperate race against time.

On the rise is *neoconservatism,* which is also oriented to industrial society but decidedly critical of the social welfare state. The Reagan administration and the government of Margaret Thatcher made their entrance under its banner; the conservative government in the Federal Republic of Germany has moved into the same position. Basically, neoconservatism is characterized by three components.

First: A supply-side economic policy is supposed to improve conditions for the valorization of capital and set the process of capital accumulation back in motion. It is willing to accept a relatively high unemployment rate, which is intended to be only temporary. As statistics in the United States show, the shifts in income are to the disadvantage of the poorer groups in the population, while only those who possess large amounts of capital realize definite increases in income. Hand in hand with this come definite reductions in social-welfare services. Second: The costs of legitimating the political system are to be reduced. "Inflation of rising expectations" and "ungovernability" are the slogans of a policy that aims at a greater detachment of administration from the formation of public will. In this context, neocorporatist developments are promoted, hence an activation of the non-governmental steering potential of large-scale organizations, primarily business organizations and labor unions. The transfer of normatively regulated parliamentary powers to systems that merely function, without normative regulation, turns the state into one partner among others in the negotiation. The displacement of jurisdiction onto the neocorporate gray areas withdraws more and more social matters from a decision-making process that is obligated by constitutional norms to give equal consideration to all who are concerned in any specific matter.[11] Third: Cultural policy, finally, is assigned the task of operating on two fronts. On the one hand, it is to discredit intellectuals as the social bearers of modernism, who are at once obsessed with power and unproductive; for postmaterial values, especially expressive needs for self-realization and the critical judgments of a universalistic Enlightenment morality, are seen as a threat to the motivational bases of a functioning society of social labor and a depoliticized public sphere. On the other hand, traditional culture and the stabilizing forces of conventional morality, patriotism, bourgeois religion, and folk culture are to be cultivated. Their function is to compensate the private lifeworld for personal burdens and to cushion it against the pressures of a competitive society and accelerated modernization.

Neoconservative policy has a certain chance to gain ascendancy if it finds a base in the bipartite segmented society it is promoting. The groups that have been excluded or marginalized have no veto power, since they represent a segregated minority that has been isolated from the production process. The pattern of relations between the metropolises and the underdeveloped peripheral areas that has increasingly become established in the international arena seems to be repeating itself within the developed capitalist societies: the established powers are less and less dependent for their own reproduction on the labor and willingness to cooperate of those who are impoverished and disenfranchised. But a policy has to be able to function as well as simply to gain acceptance. A *definite* termination of the welfare state compromise, however, would necessarily leave gaps in functioning that could be closed only through repression or demoralization.

A third and contrasting pattern of reaction is shown in the *dissidence of the critics of growth,* who have an ambivalent attitude toward the welfare state. Thus in the New Social Movements of the Federal Republic of Germany, for instance, minorities of the most diverse origins have joined in an "antiproductivist alliance"—the old and the young, women and the unemployed, gays and the handicapped, believers and nonbelievers. What unites them is their rejection of the productivist vision of progress that the legitimists share with the neoconservatives. For those two parties, the key to a modernization of society as free as possible from crises lies in correctly distributing the burden of problems between the two subsystems, the state and the economy. The one group sees the cause of crises in the unfettered inner dynamic of the economy; the other sees it in the bureaucratic restraints imposed on that dynamic. The corresponding therapies are the social restraint of capitalism on the one hand, or the transfer of problems from the planning body back to the market on the other hand. The one group sees the source of the disturbances in a monetarized labor force; the other, in the bureaucratic crippling of private enterprise. But both sides agree that the interactive domains of the lifeworld that are in need of protection can adopt only a passive role vis-à-vis the actual motors of social modernization, the state and the economy. Both sides are convinced that the lifeworld can be sufficiently decoupled from those two subsystems and protected from encroachments by the system if the state and the economy can be brought into the proper complementary relationship and can provide each other with mutual stabilization.

Only the dissident critics of industrial society start from the premise that the lifeworld is equally threatened by commodification *and* bureaucratization; neither of the two media, power and money, is by nature "more innocent" than the other. But the dissidents also consider it necessary to strengthen the autonomy of a lifeworld that is threatened in its vital foundations and its communicative infrastructure. Only they demand that the inner dynamic of subsystems regulated by power and money be broken, or at least checked, by forms of organization that are closer to the base and self-administered. In this context, concepts of a dual economy and proposals for the decoupling of social security and employment come into play.[12] This dedifferentiation is to apply not only to the role of the wage earner but also to that of the consumer, the citizen, and the client of the welfare state bureaucracies. The dissident critics of industrial society thus inherit the welfare state program in the radical-democratic components abandoned by the legitimists. But insofar as they do not go beyond mere dissidence, insofar as they remain caught in the fundamentalism of the Great Refusal and offer no more than the negative program of dedifferentiation and a halt to growth, they fall back behind *one* insight of the welfare state project.

The formula of the social containment of capitalism held more than just resignation in the face of the fact that the framework of a complex market economy could no longer be broken up from within and restructured democratically by means of the simple recipes of workers' self-management. That formula also contained the insight that an external and indirect attempt to gain influence on mechanisms of self-regulation requires something new, namely, a highly innovative combination of power and intelligent self-restraint. At first this insight was based on the notion that society could act upon itself without risk, using the neutral means of political and administrative power. If not only capitalism but the interventionist state itself is now to be "socially contained," the task becomes considerably more complicated. For then that combination of power and intelligent self-restraint can no longer be entrusted to the state's planning capacity.

If curbs and indirect regulation are now to be directed against the internal dynamics of public administration as well, the necessary potentials for reflection and steering must be sought elsewhere, namely, in a completely altered relationship between autonomous, self-organized public spheres on the one hand and domains of action regulated by money and administrative power on the other. This leads to the difficult task of making possible a democratic generalization of interest positions and a universalistic justification of norms *below* the threshold of party apparatuses that have become independent complex organizations and have, so to speak, migrated into the political system. Any naturally generated pluralism of defensive subcultures arising only on the basis of spontaneous refusal would have to develop separately from norms of civil equality. It would then constitute only a sphere that was a mirror image of the neocorporatist gray areas.

5

The development of the welfare state has reached an impasse. With it, the energies of the utopian idea of a laboring society have exhausted themselves. The responses of the legitimists and the neoconservatives move within the medium of a *Zeitgeist* which at this point can only be defensive; they are the expression of a historical consciousness that has been robbed of its utopian dimension. The dissident critics of a growth-oriented society also remain on the defensive. Their response could be turned to the offensive only if the welfare state project were neither simply maintained nor simply terminated but rather continued on a higher level of reflection. A welfare state project that has become reflective, that is directed not only to restraining the capitalist economy but to controlling the state itself, would, of course, lose labor as its central point of reference. For it is no longer a question of protecting full employment, which has been raised to the status of a norm. A reflective welfare state project could not even limit itself to introducing a guaranteed minimum income in order to break the spell that the labor market casts on the life history of all those capable of working— including the growing and increasingly marginalized potential of those who only stand to reserve. This step would be revolutionary, but not revolutionary enough—not even if the lifeworld could be protected not only against all the inhuman imperatives of the employment system but also against the counterproductive side-effects of an administrative system designed to provide for the whole of existence.

Such limits to the range within which barriers to the interchange between system and lifeworld are operative would prove functional only if a new distribution of power arose at the same time. Modern societies have at their disposal three resources with which to satisfy the need for steering: money, power, and solidarity. The respective spheres of influence of these three resources would have to be brought into a new balance. By this I mean that the integrative social force of solidarity would have to be able to maintain itself in the face of the "forces" of the other two regulatory resources, money and administrative power. The domains of life that specialize in the transmission of traditional values and cultural knowledge, in the integration of groups and the socialization of new generations, have always been dependent on solidarity. But a political formation of will that was to have an influence on the boundaries and the interchange between these communicatively structured spheres of life on the one hand and the state and the economy on the other would have to draw from the same source. That, by the way, is not so different from the normative ideas of our social studies textbooks, according to which society influences itself and its development through democratically legitimated authority.

According to this official version, political power springs from public formation of will and flows, as it were, through the state apparatus via legislation and administration, returning to a Janus-faced public that takes the form of a public of citizens at the entrance to the state and a public of clients at its exit. This is approximately how the citizens and the clients of public administration see the cycle of political power from their perspective. From the perspective of the political system, the same cycle, purged of all normative admixtures, presents itself differently. In this unofficial version, which systems theory keeps reminding us of, citizens and clients are members of the political system. In this description it is above all the meaning of the legitimation process that has changed. Interest groups and parties use their organizational power to create assent and loyalty to their organizational goals. The administration not only structures but also largely controls the legislative process; it in turn has to make compromises with powerful clients. Parties, legislative bodies, and bureaucracies must take account of the undeclared pressure of functional imperatives and bring them into accord with public opinion; the result is "symbolic politics." The government too must be concerned with supporting the masses and supporting the private investors at the same time.

In trying to fit these two contrary descriptions together into a realistic image, one can use the model, current in political science, of different arenas superimposed on one another. Claus Offe, for instance, distinguishes three such arenas. In the first, easily identifiable political elites within the state apparatus make their decisions. Beneath this lies a second arena in which a multitude of anonymous groups and collective agents influence one another, form coalitions, control access to the means of production and communication, and, already less visibly, preestablish through their social power the margins within which political questions can be thematized and decided. Beneath them, finally, lies a third arena in which subtle communication flows determine the form of political culture and, with the help of definitions of reality, compete for what Gramsci called cultural hegemony; this is where shifts in the trend of the *Zeitgeist* take place. The interaction among these arenas is not easily grasped. Up to now processes in the middle arena seem to have had priority. Wherever the empirical answer turns out to be, our *practical problem* can in any case be seen more readily now: any project that wants to shift the balance in favor of regulation through solidarity has to mobilize the lower arena against the two upper ones.

In the lower arena conflicts are not directly for money or power but rather for definitions. At issue are the integrity and autonomy of life-styles, perhaps the protection of traditionally established subcultures or changes in the grammar of traditional forms of life. Regionalist movements are examples of the former, feminist or ecological movements examples of the latter. For the most part these battles remain latent; they take place within the microsphere of everyday communication, and only now and then do they consolidate into public discourses and higher-level forms of intersubjectivity. These forms permit the formation of autonomous public spheres, which also enter into communication with one another as soon as the potential for self-organization and the self-organized employment of communications media is made use of. Forms of self-organization strengthen the collective capacity for action beneath the threshold at which organizational goals become detached from the orientations and attitudes of members of the organization and dependent instead on the interest of autonomous organizations in maintaining themselves. In organizations that remain close to the base, the capacity for action will always fall short of the capacity for reflection. That need not be an obstacle to accomplishing the task that occupies the foreground in continuing the welfare state project. The autonomous public spheres would have to achieve a combination of power and intelligent self-restraint that could make the self-regulating mechanisms of the state and the economy sufficiently sensitive to the goal-oriented results of radical democratic formation of will. Presumably, that can happen only if political parties relinquish *one* of their functions without replacing it, that is, without simply making room for a functional equivalent—the function of *generating* mass loyalty.

These reflections become more provisional, indeed vaguer, the more they approach the no-man's-land of the normative. There it is already easier to mark off negative boundaries. When the welfare state project becomes reflective it takes leave of the utopian idea of a laboring society. The latter used the contrast between living and dead labor, the idea of self-determined activity, to orient itself. In doing so, it had to presuppose that the subcultural forms of life of industrial workers were a source of solidarity. It had to presuppose that cooperative relationships within the factory would even intensify the naturally operative solidarity of the workers' subculture. But since then these subcultures have largely disintegrated. And it is somewhat doubtful whether their power to create solidarity can be regenerated in the workplace. Be that as it may, what was previously a presupposition or a condition of the utopian idea of a laboring society has now become a theme for discussion. And with this theme the utopian accents have moved from the concept of labor to the concept of communication. I speak only of "accents" because with the shift of paradigm from a society based on social labor to a society based on communication the form of linkage to the utopian tradition has also changed.

Of course, the utopian dimension of historical consciousness and political debate has by no means been completely closed off with the departure of the utopian contents of a laboring society. As utopian oases dry up, a desert of banality and bewilderment spreads. I hold to my thesis that the self-reassurance of modernity is spurred on, as before, by a consciousness of the significance of the present moment in which historical and utopian thought are fused with one another. But with the disappearance of the utopian contents of the laboring society, two illusions that have cast a spell over the self-understanding of modernity disappear as well. The first illusion stems from an inadequate differentiation.

In utopian conceptions of a well-ordered society, the dimensions of happiness and emancipation coincided with the dimensions of increasing power and the production of social wealth. Sketches of rational forms of life entered into a deceptive symbiosis with the rational domination of nature and the mobilization of societal energies. The instrumental reason released in the forces of production, and the functionalist reason developed in capacities for organization and planning, were to pave the way for a life that was at once humane, egalitarian, and libertarian. Ultimately, the potential for consensual relationships was to issue directly from the productivity of work relationships. The persistence of this confusion is reflected even in its critical reversal, as, for example, when the normalizing achievements of complex centralized organizations are lumped together with the generalizing achievements of moral universalism.[13]

Still more fundamental is the abandonment of the methodological illusion that was connected with projections of a concrete totality of future life-possibilities. The utopian content of a society based on communication is limited to the formal aspects of an undamaged intersubjectivity. To the extent to which it suggests a concrete form of life, even the expression "the ideal speech situation" is misleading. What can be outlined normatively are the necessary but general conditions for the communicative practice of everyday life and for a procedure of discursive formation of will that would put participants *themselves* in a position to realize concrete possibilities for a better and less threatened life, on *their own* initiative and in accordance with *their own* needs and insights.[14] From Hegel through Carl Schmitt down to our own day, the critique of utopia that has posted a warning sign against Jacobinism has been wrong in denouncing the supposedly unavoidable marriage of utopia and terror. Nevertheless, it is utopian in the negative sense to confuse a highly developed communicative infrastructure of *possible* forms of life with a specific totality, in the singular, representing the successful life.

Notes

INTRODUCTION

1. Jürgen Habermas, "Modernity versus Post-Modernity." *New German Critique* 22 (1981); also see Habermas, *Lectures on the Philosophical Discourse of Modernity* (Cambridge, Mass.: MIT Press, 1987).

2. See James Schmidt, "Jürgen Habermas and the Difficulties of Enlightenment," *Social Research* 49 (Spring 1982).

3. For example, see Peter Gay, *The Enlightenment: An Interpretation,* 2 vols. (New York: W. W. Norton, 1977).

4. Jürgen Habermas, *Theory and Practice* (Boston: Beacon Press, 1973); See chapters 1 and 2 of the present volume.

5. See Karl Marx, "A Contribution to the Critique of Hegel's Philosophy of Right, Introduction" in *Early Writings* (New York: Vintage Books, 1975).

6. Theodor Adorno and Max Horkheimer, *Dialectic of Enlightenment* (New York: Herder and Herder, 1972).

7. Several useful overviews of the critical theory of the Frankfurt School are available. See David Held, *Critical Theory* (Berkeley: University of California Press, 1980); Martin Jay, *The Dialectical Imagination* (Boston: Little, Brown and Company, 1973); Albrecht Wellmer, *Critical Theory of Society* (New York: Herder and Herder, 1971).

8. Regarding the link between Marx, the Frankfurt School, and Habermas, see, in particular, Albrecht Wellmer, *Critical Theory of Society* and Wellmer, "Reason, Utopia, and the *Dialectic of Enlightenment* " in *Habermas and Modernity,* ed. Richard Bernstein (Cambridge, Mass.: MIT Press, 1985). Also useful is the piece by P. Hohendahl, "The Dialectic of Enlightenment Revisited: Habermas' Critique of the Frankfurt School," *New German Critique* 35 (Spring/Summer 1985).

9. See, in particular, Thomas McCarthy, *The Critical Theory of Jürgen Habermas* (Cambridge, Mass.: MIT Press, 1978), and Rudiger Bubner, "Habermas's Concept of Critical Theory", in *Habermas: Critical Debates,* ed. John Thompson and David Held, (Cambridge, Mass.: MIT Press, 1982).

10. Quoted in McCarthy, *Critical Theory of Habermas,* 183. Also, see Jürgen Habermas, *Zur Logik der Sozialwissenschaften* (Frankfurt/Main, 1970), and "A Review of Gadamer's Truth and Method," in *Understanding and Social Inquiry,* ed. Fred Dallmayr and Thomas McCarthy (Notre Dame: University of Notre Dame Press, 1977).

11. See chapter 3 of the present volume.

12. See David Ingram, *Habermas and the Dialectic of Reason* (New Haven: Yale University Press, 1987), and Rick Roderick, *Habermas and the Foundations of Critical Theory* (London: Macmillan, 1986).

13. See Habermas, *Knowledge and Human Interests,* (Boston: Beacon Press, 1971), chapters 2 and 3. See also chapter 11 of the present volume.

14. Habermas, *Communication and the Evolution of Society* (Boston: Beacon Press, 1977).

15. Ibid., 153.

16. Ibid., 148.

17. Several excellent overviews of *The Theory of Communicative Action* (Boston: Beacon Press, 1984 and 1987) are available. Most impressive are David Ingram, *Habermas and the Dialectic of Reason;* Seyla Benhabib, *Critique, Norm, and Utopia* (New York: Columbia University Press, 1986).

18. See chapters 7 and 11 of the present volume.

19. See Habermas, *The Theory of Communicative Action,* vol. 1, chap. 2.

20. See chapter 8 of the present volume.

21. See chapter 4 of the present volume.

22. Jürgen Habermas, *Strukturwandel der Offentlichkeit* (Berlin, 1962). See chapter 10 of the present volume.

23. Jürgen Habermas, *Toward a Rational Society* (Boston: Beacon Press, 1970). See chapter 11 of the present volume.

24. Jürgen Habermas, *Legitimation Crisis* (Boston: Beacon Press, 1975). See chapter 12 of the present volume. See also the fine critical overviews by David Held, "Crisis Tendencies, Legitimation and the State," in *Habermas: Critical Debates,* and McCarthy, *The Critical Theory of Habermas.*

25. See chapters 4 and 11 of the present volume.

Chapter One
DOGMATISM, REASON, AND DECISION

1. I have since treated this subject in *Erkenntnis and Interesse* (Frankfurt, 1968; English translation: *Knowledge and Human Interests* [Boston: Beacon Press, 1971]).

2. See my study *Tehnik and Wissenschaft als "Ideologie"* (Frankfurt, 1968). The essay of that title appears as "Technology and Science as Ideology" in *Toward a Rational Society* (Boston: Beacon Press, 1970).

3. *Mündigkeit* has complex meanings in the German idealist tradition. It can refer to independence of judgment, the ability of an individual to use his or her reason, or individual responsibility—ED.

4. Paul Thiry d'Holbach, *Nature and Her Laws* (London, 1816), 1. On Holbach, see G. Mensching, *Totalität und Autonomie: Untersuchungen zur philosophischen Gesellschaftstheorie des französischen Materialismus* (Frankfurt, 1971).

5. Holbach, 5–6. The 1816 version has a slightly different translation.

6. Ibid., 5.

7. Johann G. Fichte, *Werke,* ed. Medicus (Darmstatt, 1962), 3:17.

8. Ibid.

9 Schelling, *Werke,* Münchner Jubiläumsausgabe, 1:236.

10. Ibid., 229.

11. On Fichte, see W. Schulz, *J. G. Fichte, Vernunft und Freiheit* (Pfullingen, 1962); W. Weischedel, *Der Zwiespalt im Denken Fichtes* (Berlin, 1962).

12. Fichte, *Werke*, 3:17.

13. An insight developed by Horkheimer and Adorno in their *Dialektik der Aufklärung* (Amsterdam, 1947; English translation: *Dialectic of Enlightenment*, New York, 1972). See my discussion of Adorno's philosophy in my *Philosophisch-politische Profile* (Frankfurt, 1971; English translation: *Philosophical-Political Profiles*, Cambridge, Mass., 1983), 176–99 (99–109 in the English translation).

14. See my *Knowledge and Human Interests*.

15. On the semiotics of Charles Morris, see K. O. Apel, "Sprache und Wahrheit," in *Philosophische Rundschau* 8 (1959):161ff; "Szientismus oder tranzendentale Hermeneutik?" in R. Bubner et al., *Hermeneutik und Dialektik* (Tübingen, 1970), 1:105–44.

16. With the exception of values immanent in science as specified by logical and methodological rules.

17. Ontological doctrines as well as dialectical ones fall into this category, and classical natural law as well as modern philosophies of history. It is no accident that Popper places Hegel and Marx next to Plato in the ranks of the great dogmatists—as so-called historicists.

18. E. Topitsch, *Sozialphilosophie zwischen Ideologie und Wissenschaft* (Neuwied, 1962), 279.

19. See G. Gäfgen, *Theorie der wissenschaftlichen Entscheidung* (Tübingen, 1963).

20. Cf. Gäfgen: "The result of the decision by no means has to appear 'rational' in the everyday sense of the term, since the actor can have a value system that, though it is coherent in itself, appears absurd in comparison to that of other actors. Absurdity of this kind can be defined only through comparison to a standard of normality of values and goals. . . . This kind of irrationality refers to the content and not to the form of the decisions" (26–27).

21. Ibid., 99.

22. Ibid., 176ff.

23. John Dewey, *The Quest for Certainty* (New York, 1960), 43.

24. H. Rittel, "Überlegungen zur wissenschaftlichen und politischen Bedeutung der Entscheidungstheorien," Studiengruppe für Systemforschung, Heidelberg, MS, 29–30; "Instrumentelles Wissen in der Politik," in *Wissenschaft ohne Politik*, ed. H. Krauch (Heidelberg, 1966), 183–209.

25. Cf. Niklas Luhmann, *Zweckbegriff und Systemrationalität* (Tübingen, 1968).

Chapter Two
BETWEEN PHILOSOPHY AND SCIENCE: MARXISM AS CRITIQUE

1. My discussion here is based on Reinhart Kosselleck's remarks on the history of these concepts in his *Kritik und Krise* (Freiburg, 1959; English translation *Critique and Crisis: Enlightenment and the Pathogenesis of Modern Society* [Cambridge, Mass., 1988]), 189ff., n. 155.

2. For the relationship between mysticism and the dialectic in intellectual history, see most recently Ernst Topitsch, "Marxism und Gnosis," in *Sozialphilosophie zwischen Ideologie und Wissenschaft* (Neuwied, 1962), 235ff.

3. Karl Marx, *Writings of the Young Marx on Philosophy and Society* (Garden City, N.J., 1967), 62.

4. G. W. F. Hegel, *Heidelberger Enzyklopädie*, ed. Glockner, § 391, p. 275.

5. Karl Marx, "Critique of Hegelian Philosophy," in *Economic and Philosophical Documents of 1844*, ed. D. J. Struik, trans. M. Milligan (New York: International Publishing, 1964), 177.

6. Alfred Schmidt, in his introduction to Ludwig Feuerbach, *Anthropologischer Materialismus* I (Frankfurt, 1967), 1:5–65.

7. Karl Marx, *Capital*, trans. Eden and Cedar Paul (New York, 1928), 1:45. For a recent work on this point, see H. Reichelt, *Zur logischen Struktur des Kapitalbegriffs bei Marx* (1970).

8. Ibid., 1:49.

9. Ibid., 154.

Chapter Three
SELF-REFLECTION AS SCIENCE

1. Karl-Otto Apel, *Analytic Philosophy of Language and the Geisteswissenschaften*, trans. Harald Holstelitie (Dordrecht: D. Reidel, 1967), and "Szientifik, Hermeneutik, Ideologiekritik," in *Man and World I* (1968):37ff.

2. The *Standard Edition of the Complete Psychological Works of Sigmund Freud*, translated from the German under the general editorship of James Strachey, in collaboration with Anna Freud, assisted by Alix Strachey and Alan Tyson (London: The Hogarth Press, 1967). All subsequent quotations and references are from this edition.

3. *Gesammelte Schriften*, 7:261.

4. Ibid.

5. Ibid.

6. Ibid., 3:260.

7. "New Introductory Lectures on Psychoanalysis," 22:57.

8. "The Claims of Psychoanalysis to Scientific Interest," 13:176 (translation altered).

9. See *The Psychopathology of Everyday Life*. See "The Interpretation of Dreams," vols. 4 and 5; "On Dreams," vol. 5.

10. See especially "'Wild' Psychoanalysis," vol. 11; "Remembering, Repeating, and Working-Through," vol. 12; "Lines of Advance in Psycho-Analytic Therapy," vol. 17; "Constructions in Analysis," vol. 23; "Analysis Terminable and Interminable," ibid.

11. "Introductory Lectures on Psychoanalysis," 16:435.

12. "Freud's Psychoanalytic Procedure," 7:252–53.

13. "'Wild' Psychoanalysis," 11:225.

14. "Constructions in Analysis," 23:265.

15. "An Outline of Psycho-Analysis," 23:178.

16. "The Dynamics of Transference," 12:108.

17. "Remembering, Repeating, Working-Through," 12.

18. "Lines of Advance in Psycho-Analytic Therapy," 17:161.

19. Ibid., 163.

20. "Some Additional Notes on Dream-Interpretation as a Whole," 19:133.

21. The official translation of Freud's concepts *das Ich* and *das Es* as the ego and the id was a serious mistake that both reflects and has contributed to the scientistic self-misunderstanding of metapsychology. *Das Ich* means the I and *das Es* the it. That is, they refer to the antithesis between reflexive, personal subjectivity and reified, impersonal objectivity. Freud's famous statement of the goal of psychoanalysis, "Wo Es war, soll Ich werden," should read in English, "Where it was, I shall become," or perhaps, "Where it-ness was, I-ness shall come into being." The choice of scientific Latin reifies the I into an object by making it into an "ego," which is not

the word used to express reflexivity, self-consciousness, and agency in English. As an "ego," the I is already an it, and the qualitative distinction between I and it is not visible in comparing the terms ego and id. At the same time, this scientistic terminology obscures the connection between the models of reflection of psychoanalysis and German Idealism. All this notwithstanding, the weight of recent tradition has made it seem advisable to retain "ego" and "id" in this translation—TRANS.

22. Alfred Lorenzer, *Kritik des psychoanalytischen Symbolbegriffs* and *Sprachzerstörung und -Rekonstruktion* (Frankfurt am Main: Suhrkamp Verlag, 1970).

23. Alasdair McIntyre's separation of motive and cause in *The Unconscious* (London: Routledge, 1958) makes this relationshiop unrecognizable.

24. *Vorgriff,* here translated as "anticipation," means an interpretive concept or model that prestructures that to which it is applied—TRANS.

25. See Arthur Danto, *Analytical Philosophy of History* (Cambridge: Cambridge University Press, 1965), 143ff. TRANSLATOR'S NOTE: The German *Geschichte,* like the French *histoire,* means both "history" and "story."

26. "Lines of Advance in Psycho-Analytic Therapy," 17:167.

27. "Constructions in Analysis," 23:262–63.

28. "Remarks on the Theory and Practice of Dream-Interpretation," 19:115.

29. See McIntyre, *The Unconscious,* 112ff.

30. "Constructions in Analysis," 23:262.

31. "In short, we conduct ourselves on the model of a familiar figure in one of Nestroy's farces—the manservant who has a single answer on his lips to every question or objection: 'It will all become clear in the course of future developments'" (ibid., 265).

32. "Introductory Lectures on Psychoanalysis," 16:436.

33. See Danto, *Analytical Philosophy of History,* chaps. 10 and 11.

Chapter Four
THE TASKS OF A CRITICAL THEORY OF SOCIETY

1. A. Gouldner, *The Coming Crisis of Western Sociology* (New York, 1970), pp. 25ff; B. Gruenberg, "The Problem of Reflexivity in the Sociology of Science," *Philosophy of Social Science* 8 (1978):321ff.

2. See the contributions by K. O. Hondrich, K. Eder, J. Habermas, N. Luhmann, J. Matthes, K. D. Opp, and K. H. Tjaden to "Theorienvergleich in der Soziologie," in *Zwischenbilanz der Soziologie,* ed. R. Lepsius (Stuttgart, 1976), 14ff.

3. W. Mayrl, "Genetic Structuralism and the Analysis of Social Consciousness," *Theory and Society* 5 (1978): 20ff.

4. See the nine-volume reprint of *Zeitschrift für Sozialforschung* by Kösel Verlag (Munich, 1979).

5. The state of the program is discussed in *Sozialforschung als Kritik,* ed. W. Bonss and A. Honneth (Frankfurt, 1982).

6. H. Dubiel, *Theory and Politics: Studies in the Development of Critical Theory* (Cambridge, Mass., 1985), pt. 2.

7. On what follows, see H. Dubiel and A. Söllner, "Die Nationalsozialismusforschung des Instituts für Sozialforchung," in *Recht und Staat im Nationalsozialismus* ed. Dubiel and Söllner (Frankfurt, 1981), 7ff.

8. As Marcuse presented it even then: "Social Implications of Modern Technology," *Zeitschrift für Sozialforschung* 9 (1941):414ff.

9. E. Fromm, "Über Methode und Aufgabe einer analytischen Sozialpsychologie," *Zeitschrift für Sozialforschung* 1 (1932): 28ff. English translation in E. Fromm, *The Crisis of Psychoanalysis* (Greenwich, Conn. 1971).

10. H. Dahmer, *Libido und Gesellschaft* (Frankfurt, 1973); *Analytische Sozialpsychologie,* ed. H. Dahmer (Frankfurt, 1980).

11. They did not change their position. See T. W. Adorno, "Sociology and Psychology," *New Left Review* 46 (1967):67–80 and 47 (1968):79–90; H. Marcuse, *Eros and Civilization* (Boston, 1955); and idem, *Five Lectures* (Boston, 1970).

12. E. Fromm, *Escape from Freedom* (New York, 1942).

13. E. Fromm, *Arbeiter und Angestellte am Vorabend des Dritten Reiches: Eine sozialpsychologische Untersuchung,* ed. W. Bonss (Stuttgart, 1980).

14. E. M. Lange, "Wertformanalyse, Geldkritik und die Konstruktion des Fetischismus bei Marx," *Neue Philosophische Hefte* 13 (1978):1ff.

15. H. Marcuse, "Philosophy and Critical Theory," in *Negations* (Boston, 1968), 134–58; here 135.

16. Ibid., 147.

17. Ibid., 158.

18. Ibid.

19. See J. Habermas, *Communication and the Evolution of Society* (Boston, 1979), esp. chaps. 3 and 4.

20. On the discussion of the breakdown of Keynesian economic policy in the West, see P. C. Roberts, "The Breakdown of the Keynesian Model," *Public Interest* (1978):20ff; J. A. Kregel, "From Post-Keynes to Pre-Keynes," *Social Research* 46 (1979):212ff; J. D. Wisman, "Legitimation, Ideology-Critique and Economics," *Social Research* 46 (1979): 219ff.; P. Davidson "Post Keynesian Economics," *Public Interest* (1980): 151ff.

21. A. Arato, "Critical Sociology and Authoritarian State Socialism," in *Habermas: Critical Debates,* ed. D. Held and J. Thompson (Cambridge, Mass., 1982), 196–218.

22. L. Löwenthal, *Gesammelte Schriften,* vol. 2 (Frankfurt, 1981).

23. H. Kohut, *Narzissmus, eine Theorie der Behandlung narzistischer Persönlichkeitsstörungen* (Frankfurt, 1973); and idem, *Die Heilung des Selbst* (Frankfurt, 1979).

24. Christopher Lasch, *The Culture of Narcissism* (New York, 1978).

25. P. Blos, *On Adolescence* (New York, 1962); Erik Erikson, *Identity and the Life Cycle* (New York, 1959).

25. See R. Döbert and G. Nunner-Winkler, *Adoleszenzkrise und Identitätsbildung* (Frankfurt, 1975); T. Ziehe, *Pubertät und Narzissmus* (Frankfurt, 1975); R. M. Merelman, "Moral Development and Potential Radicalism in Adolescence," *Youth and Society* 9 (1977):29ff; C. A. Rootes, "Politics of Moral Protest and Legitimation Problems of the Modern Capitalist State," *Theory and Society* 9 (1980):473ff.

27. See J. Habermas, *Knowledge and Human Interests* (Boston, 1971), esp. chaps. 10–12; A. Lorenzer, *Sprachzerstörung und Rekonstruktion* (Frankfurt, 1970); K. Menne, M. Looser, A. Osterland, K. Brede, and E. Moersch, *Sprache, Handlung und Unbewusstes* (Frankfurt, 1976).

28. J. Habermas, "Moral Development and Ego Identity," in *Communication and the Evolution of Society,* 69–94; R. Keagan, *The Evolving Self* (Cambridge, Mass., 1981).

29. W. R. D. Fairbane, *An Object Relations Theory of Personality* (London, 1952); D. W. Winnicott, *The Maturational Process and the Facilitating Environment* (New York, 1965).

30. See E. Jacobson, *The Self and the Object World* (New York, 1964); M. Mahler, *Symbiose und Individuation,* 2 vols. (Stuttgart, 1972); Kohut, *Narzissmus;* H. Kohut, *Introspektion, Empathie und Psychoanalyse* (Frankfiurt, 1976); O. Kernberg, *Borderline-Störungen und pathologischer Narzissmus* (Frankfurt, 1978).

31. A. Freud, *The Ego and the Mechanisms of Defense* (New York, 1946); D. R. Miller and G. E. Swanson, *Inner Conflict and Defense* (New York, 1966); L. B. Murphy, "The Problem of Defense and the Concept of Coping," in *The Child in His Family* ed. E. Antyony and C. Koipernik (New York, 1970); N. Haan, "A Tripartite Model of Ego-Functioning," *Journal of Neurological Mental Disease* 148 (1969):14ff.

32. *Entwicklung des Ichs,* ed. R. Dobert, G. Nunner-Winkler, and J. Habermas (Cologne, 1977); R. L. Selman, *The Growth of Interpersonal Understanding* (New York, 1980).

33. *New Directions for Child Development,* ed. W. Damon, 2 vols. (San Francisco, 1978); H. Furth, *Piaget and Knowledge* (Chicago, 1981).

34. See *The Theory of Communicative Action* (Boston, 1988), 2:277ff.

35. C. W. Mills, *Politics, Power and People* (New York, 1963); *Mass Culture,* ed. B. Rosenberg and D. White (Glencoe, Ill., 1957); A. Gouldner, *The Dialectics of Ideology and Technology* (New York, 1976); E. Barnouw, *The Sponser* (New York, 1977); D. Smythe, "Communications: Blind Spot of Western Marxism," *Canadian Journal of Political and Social Theory* 1 (1977); T. Gitlin, "Media Sociology: The Dominant Paradigm," *Theory and Society* 6 (1978):205ff.

36. D. Kellner, "Network Television and American Society: Introduction to a Critical Theory of Television," *Theory and Society* 10 (1981):31ff.

37. Ibid., 38ff.

38. A. Swinglewood, *The Myth of Mass Culture* (London, 1977).

39. D. Kellner, "TV, Ideology and Emancipatory Popular Culture," *Socialist Review* 45 (1979):13ff.

40. D. Kellner, "Kulturindustrie und Massenkommunikation: Die kritische Theorie und ihre Folgen," in *Sozialforschung als Kritik* ed. W. Bonss and A. Honneth (Frankfurt, 1982), 482–515.

41. From Lazarfeld's early radio studies on the dual character of communication flows and the role of opinion leaders, the independent weight of everyday communication in relation to mass communication has been confirmed again and again: "In the last analysis it is people talking with people more than people listening to, or reading, or looking at the mass media that really causes opinions to change." Mills, *Power, Politics and People,* 590. See P. Lazarsfeld, B. Berelson, and H. Gaudet, *The People's Choice* (New York, 1948); P. Lazarsfeld and E. Katz, *Personal Influence* (New York, 1955). Compare O. Negt and A. Kluge *Öffentlichkeit und Erfahrung* (Frankfurt, 1970), and, by the same authors, *Geschichte und Eigensinn* (Munich, 1981).

42. H. M. Enzenberger, "Baukasten zu einer Theorie der Meiden," in *Palaver* (Frankfurt, 1974), 91ff.

43.S. Benhabib, "Modernity and the Aporias of Critical Theory," *Telos* 49 (1981):38–60.

44. R. Inglehart, "Wertwandel und politisches Verhalten," in *Sozialer Wandel in Westeuropa* ed. J. Matthes (Frankfurt, 1979).

45. K. Hildebrandt and R. J. Dalton, "Die neue Politik," *Politische Vierteljahresschrift* 18 (1977): 230ff; S. H. Barnes, M. Kaase, et al., *Political Action* (Beverly Hills/London, 1979).

46. J. Hirsch, "Alternativbewegung: Eine politische Alternative," in *Parlamentarisches Ritual und politische Alternativen,* ed. R. Roth (Frankfurt, 1980).

47. On this point I found a manuscript by K. W. Brand very helpful: "Zur Diskussion um Entstehung, Funktion and Perspektive der "Ökologie- und Alternativbewegung," Munich, 1980.

48. Hirsch, "Alternativbewegung"; J. Huber, *Wer soll das alles ändern?* (Berlin, 1980).

49. J. Rraschke, "Politik und Wertwandel in den westlichen Demodratien," supplement to the weekly paper *Das Parlament,* September 1980, 23ff.

50. On the dual economy, see A. Gorz, *Abschied vom Proletariat* (Frankfurt, 1980); J. Huber, *Wer soll das alles ändern?* Concerning the effects of democratic mass parties on the lifeworld contexts of voters, see Claus Offe, "Konkurrenzpartei und kollektive politische Identität," in Roth, *Paralmentarisches Ritual.*

51. See, for example, B. Guggenberger, *Bürgerinitiativen in der Parteindemokratie* (Stuttgart, 1980).

52. See, for example, P. Berger, B. Berger, and H. Kellner, *Das Unbehagen in der Modernität* (Frankfurt, 1975).

53. J. Habermas, "Modernity versus Postmodernity," *New German Critique* 22 (1981):3–14; L. Baier, "Wer unsere Köpfe kolonisiert," in *Literaturmagazin* 9 (1978).

54. R. Bernstein, *The Restructuring of Social and Political Theory* (Philadephia, 1976).

55. In "The Methodological Illusions of Modern Political Theory," *Neue Hefte für Philosophie* 21 (1982):47–74, Seyla Benhabib stresses the fact that the discourse theory of ethics proposed by K. O. Apel and myself treats calculations of consequences and, above all, interpretations of needs as essential elements of moral argumentation. See K. O. Apel, "Sprechakttheorie und transzendentale Sprachpragmatik, zur Frage ethischer Normen," in *Sprachpragmatik und Philosophie,* ed. K. O. Apel (Frankfurt, 1976), 10–173; J. Habermas, *Moralbewusstsein und kommunikatives Handeln* (Frankfurt, 1983).

56. On this point, Max Horkheimer's essay "Materialismus und Moral," *Zeitschrift für Sozialforschung* 2 (1933):263ff., is still worth reading.

57. P. Bürger, *Theory of the Avant-Garde* (Minneapolis, 1984).

58. R. Rorty, *Philosophy and the Mirror of Nature* (Princeton, 1979).

59. R. F. Kitchener, "Genetic Epistemology, Normative Epistemology, and Psychologism," *Synthese* 45 (1980):257ff.; T. Kesselring, *Piagets genetische Erkenntnistheorie und Hegels Dialektik* (Frankfurt, 1981). I have examined the methodological peculiarities of reconstructive sciences in connection with the division of labor between philosophy and psychology in Kohlberg's theory of the development of moral consciousness, in "Interpretive Sociale Wetenschap versus Radicale Hermeneutiek," *Kennis en Method* 5 (1981):4ff.

60. In M. Horkheimer, *Critical Theory* (New York, 1972), 188–243, here p. 197.

61. Ibid., 205.

62. Ibid., 196. I once characterized the relation between social theory and social practice in the same way: "Historical materialism aims at achieving an explanation of social evolution which is so comprehensive that it encompasses the theory's own contexts of origin and application. The theory specifies the conditions under which a self-reflection of the history of the species has become objectively possible. At the same time it names those to whom the theory is addressed, who can with its help gain enlightenment about themselves and their emancipatory role in the process of history. With this reflection on the context of its origin and this anticipation of the context of its application, the theory understands itself as a necessary catalytic mo-

ment in the very complex of social life that it analyzes; and it analyzes this complex as an integral network of coercion, from the viewpoint of its possible transformation." *Theory and Practice* (Boston, 1973), 2–3.
65. K. Marx, *Grundrisse* (Harmondsworth, Eng., 1973), 104–5.
64. Ibid., 105.
65. Ibid.

Chapter Five
PSYCHOANALYSIS AND SOCIAL THEORY

1. "New Introductory Lectures," 22:179.
2. The German *Kultur* means both culture and civilization—TRANS.
3. "An Outline of Psychoanalysis," 17:195.
4. "Civilization and Its Discontents," 21:144.
5. "Introductory Lectures on Psychoanalysis," 16:312.
6. "The Claims of Psychoanalysis to Scientific Interest," 13:186.
7. Ibid.
8. "Civilization and Its Discontents," 21:89ff.
9. "The Future of an Illusion," 21:5–6.
10. Ibid., 6.
11. Ibid., 10.
12. Ibid., 31.
13. Ibid., 12.
14. Ibid., 46.
15. Freud developed this idea with reference to the taboo on killing. See ibid., 40ff.

Chapter Six
TOWARD A RECONSTRUCTION OF HISTORICAL MATERIALISM

1. In the first part of *The German Ideology* and in the preface to *A Contribution to the Critique of Political Economy.*
2. On the relationship of the assessments of historical materialism by Marx and Engels, cf. L. Krader, *Ethnologie und Anthropologie bei Marx* (München, 1973).
3. J. Stalin, *Dialectical and Historical Materialism* (New York, 1940).
4. I. S. Kon, *Die Geschichtsphilosophie des 20. Jahrhunderts,* vol. 2 (Berlin, 1966); E. M. Zukov, "Über die Perodisierung der Weltgeschichte," *Sowetwissenschaft* 3 (1961):241–54; E. Engelberg, "Fragen der Evolution und der Revolution in der Weltgeschichte," *Zeitschrift für Geschichtswissenschaft* 13 (1965):9–18; E. Hoffman, "Zwei aktuelle Probleme der geschichtlichen Entwicklungsfolge fortschreitender Gesellschaftsformationen," *Zeitschrift für Geschichtswissenschaft,* 16 (1968):1265–81; G. Lewin, "Zur Diskussion über die marxistische Lehre von den Gessellschaftsformationen," *Mitteilungen des Instituts für Orientforschung* (1969):137–51; and E. Engelberg, ed., *Probleme der marxistischen Geschichtswissenschaft* (Köln, 1972).
5. Marx and Engels, *The German Ideology,* in *Writings of the Young Marx on Philosophy and Society,* ed. L. Easton and K. Guddat (New York, 1967), 409.
6. On the delimitation of action types, cf. J. Habermas, *Toward a Rational Society* (Boston, 1970), 91ff.
7. Marx and Engels, *German Ideology,* 421.

8. Ibid., 409.

9. Ibid., 402.

10. B. Rensch, *Homo Sapiens: From Man to Demi-God* (New York, 1972); E. morin, *Das Rätsel des Humanen* (München, 1974).

11. C. F. Hockett and R. Ascher, "The Human Revolution," *Current Anthropology* (Feb. 1964):135–47; G. W. Hewes, "Primate Communication and the Gestural Origin of Language," *Current Anthropology* (Feb. 1973):5–29.

12. On incest barriers among vertebrates, cf. N. Bischoff, "The Biological Foundations of the Incest-taboo," *Social Science Information* 6 (1972):7–36. Ethological investigations do not take into account that it is the incest barrier between father and daughter that first clears the culturally innovative way to the family structure. Cf. Meyer Fortes, "Kinship and the Social Order," *Current Anthropology* (April 1972):285–96.

13. E. W. Count, *Being and Becoming: Essays on the Biogram* (New York, 1973).

14. J. Habermas, "Entwicklung der Interaktionskompetenz," unpubl. MS (Starnberg, 1974).

15. Morin, *Das Rätsel des Humanen,* 115 ff. On the ontogenesis of time consciousness, cf. J. Piaget, *The Child's Conception of Time* (New York, 1970).

16. D. Claessens, *Instinkt, Psyche, Geltung* (Opladen, 1967). Durkheim has already investigated the obligatory character of action norms, which to begin with generate their own power of sanction, under the aspect of the binding of feeling ambivalence; cf. E. Durkheim, *Sociology and Philosophy* (New York, 1974): "Furthermore there is another concept that exhibits the same duality, namely that of the holy. The holy object instills in us, if not fear, then certainly respect, which keeps us at a distance from it. At the same time it is an object of love and desire; we aspire to get closer to it, we strive toward it. Thus we have to do here with a double feeling." Cf. also A. Gehlen's theses on "indeterminate obligations" in *Urmensch und Spätkultur* (Bonn, 1956), 154ff.

17. On the concepts of "internal" and "external" nature, cf. J. Habermas, *Knowledge and Human Interests* (Boston, 1971), and *Legitimation Crisis* (Boston, 1975), 8ff.

18. Stalin, *Dialectical and Historical Materialism.*

19. J. Pecirka, "Von der asiatischen Produktionsweise zu einer marxistischen Analyse der frühen Klassengesellschaften," *Eirene* 6 (Prague, 1967), 141–74; and L. V. Danilova, "Controversial Problems of the Theory of Precapitalist Societies," *Soviet Anthropology and Archeology* 9 (Spring 1971):269–327.

20. M. Godelier, *Perspectives in Marxist Anthropology* (Cambridge, 1976).

21. Recently, O. Marquardt, *Schwierigkeiten mit der Geschichtsphilosophie* (Frankfurt, 1973).

22. In an unpublished manuscript on the theory of evolution, Niklas Luhmann expresses doubts about the applicability of the concept of motion in this connection.

23. Luhmann points this out in the manuscript mentioned in n. 22.

24. Cf. my critique of Luhmann in J. Habermas, N. Luhmann, *Theorie der Gesellschaft* (Frankfurt, 1971), 150ff; cf. also R.Döbert, *Systemtheorie und die Entwicklung religiöser Deutungssysteme* (Frankfurt, 1973), 66ff.

25. For example, H. Gericke, in "Zur Dialektik von Produktivkraft und Produktionsverhältnis im Feudalismus," *Zeitschrift für Geschichtswissenschaft,* 16 (1966):914–32, distinguishes the "increasingly higher degree of mastery of nature" from the "increasingly maturer forms of corporate social life": "The most important criteria and the decisive factors in historical progress are improvement of productive forces, especially the increase in conscious, goal-directed, success-oriented activity of immediate producers, as well as altered productive relations, which per-

mit an ever increasing number of people to participate competently and actively in economic, social, political, and cultural processes" (918–19).

26. K. Marx, *A Contribution to the Critique of Political Economy,* ed. M. Dobb (New York, 1970), Preface, 20–21.

27. K. Kautsky, *Die materialistische Geschichtsauffassung,* 2 vols. (Berlin, 1927), 1:817–18.

28. Cf. A. Touraine, *La Société post-industrielle* (Paris, 1969); and D. Bell, *The Coming of Postindustrial Society* (New York, 1973).

29. Godelier, *Perspectives in Marxist Anthropology.*

30. Marx, *A Contribution,* Preface, 21.

31. Stalin, *Dialectical and Historical Materialism.*

32. Godelier, *Perspectives in Marxist Anthropology.*

33. Marx and Engels, *Manifesto of the Communist Party,* in *Marx and Engels: Basic Writings on Politics and Philosophy,* ed. L. Feuer (New York, 1959), 19.

34. I. Sellnow, "Die Auflösung der Urgemeinschaftsordnung," in *Die Entstehung von Klassengesellschaften,* ed. K. Eder (Frankfurt, 1973), 69–112.

35. S. Moscovici, *The Human History of Nature* (New York, 1977).

36. Marx, *A Contribution,* Preface, 21.

37. A. Gehlen, "Anthropologische Ansicht der Technik," in Gehlen, *Technik im technischen Zeitalter* (Düsseldorf, 1965); and cf. my remarks in *Toward a Rational Society,* 87ff.

38. J. Piaget, *The Principles of Genetic Epistemology* (New York, 1972).

39. E. C. Welskopf, "Schauplatzwechsel und Pulsation des Fortschritts," in *Universalgeschichte,* ed. E. Schulin (Köln, 1974), 122–23.

40. Hoffmann, "Zwei aktuelle Probleme."

41. V. G. Childe, *What Happened in History* (London, 1964), 55ff; C. M. Cipolla, "Die zwei Revolutionen," in *Universalgeschichte,* 87–95.

42. Danilova, "Controversial Problems," 282–83.

43. E. R. Service, *Primitive Social Organization* (New York, 1962).

44. K. Eder, *Die Entstehung staatlich organisierter Gesellschaften* (Frankfurt, 1976).

45. Pecirka, "Von der asiatischen Produktionsweise."

46. R. Gunther, "Herausbildung und Systemcharakter der vorkapitalistischen Gesellschaftsformationen," *Zeitschrift für Geschichtswissenschaft* 16 (1968): 1204–11.

47. Gericke, "Zur Dialektik."

48. These phenomena stimulated Karl Jaspers to construct his notion of an "axial period"; cf. his *The Origin and Goal of History* (New York, 1976).

49. F. Tökei, *Zur Frage der asiatischen Produktionsweise* (Neuwied, 1965).

50. M. Finley, "Between Slavery and Freedom," *Comparative Studies in Society and History* 6 (April, 1964).

51. J. Habermas, *Legitimation Crisis,* 17ff.; K.Eder, "Komplexität, Evolution and Geschichte," in *Theorie der Gesellschaft, Supplement I* (Frankfurt, 1973).

52. L. Kohlberg, "Stage and Sequence," in *Handbook of Socialization Theory and Research,* ed. D. Goslin (Chicago, 1969), and "From Is to Ought," in *Cognitive Development and Epistemology,* ed. T. Mischel (New York, 1971), 151–236.

53. Eder, *Die Entstehung staatlich organisierter Gesellschaften.*

54. L. Krader, *Formation of the State* (New York, 1968).

55. The most important respresentatives of this theory are F. Ratzel, P. W. Schmidt, F. Oppenheimer, and A. Rüstow.

56. W. E. Mühlmann, "Herrschaft und Staat," in *Rassen, Ethnien, Kulturen* (Neuwied, 1964), 248–96.

57. This view, first developed by Marx and Engels in *The German Ideology,* has had many adherents; V. G. Childe is a good representative, originally in *Old World Prehistory* (London, 1938).

58. G. E. Lenski, *Power and Privilege* (New York, 1966). Earlier I too defended this view; cf. *Toward a Rational Society,* 94, and *Theorie der Gesellschaft,* 153–75.

59. R. L. Carneiro, "A Theory of the Origin of the State," *Science* 169 (1970): 733–38.

60. K. A. Wittfogel, *History of Chinese Society* (Philadelphia, 1946), and *Oriental Despotism: A Comparative Study of Total Power* (New Haven, 1957).

61. R. Coulborn, "Structure and Process in the Rise and Fall of Civilized Societies," *Comparative Studies in History and Society* 8 (1965–66); Carneiro, "A Theory of the Origin of the State."

62. I am drawing on a sketch presentved by Klaus Eder at the *16. Deutschen Soziologentag* in Kassel, 1974.

63. Ibid., 14.

64. Ibid., 15.

65. Ibid.

66. "The deep-seated contradiction was that the mastery of nature and the self-realization of man sometimes had to come into opposition, since the former process required for its increasing efficacy servitude as a means of realizing the organization and mobility (of labor power), while the latter had freedom as its goal and basis. Indeed in the final analysis the mastery of nature makes sense only if the self-realization of man, the humanizing of relations among men, succeeds." Welskopf, "Schauplatzwechsel," 131.

Chapter Seven
SOCIAL ACTION AND RATIONALITY

1. R. Bubner, *Handlung, Sprache und Vernunft* (Frankfurt, 1976), 66ff.

2. On decision theory, see H. Simon, *Models of Man* (New York, 1957); G. Gäfgen, *Theorie der wirtschaftlichen Entscheidung* (Tübingen, 1968). On game theory, see R. D. Luce and H. Raiffa, *Games and Decisions* (New York, 1957); M. Shubik, *Spieltheorie und Sozialwissenschaften* (Frankfurt, 1965). On exchange-theoretical approaches in social psychology, see P. P. Ekeh, *Social Exchange Theory* (London, 1964).

3. T. R. Sarbin, "Role Theory," in *Handbook of Social Psychology,* ed. G. Lindsey (Cambridge, Mass., 1954), 223–58; Talcott Parsons, "Social Interaction," in *International Encyclopedia of Social Science* 7:1429–41; Hans Joas, *Die gegenwärtige Lage der Rollentheorie* (Frankfurt, 1977), 68ff.

4. G. J. McCall and J. L. Simmons, *Identity and Interactions* (New York, 1966); E. Goffman, Frame Analysis (Harmondsworth, 1975), *Relations in Public* (Harmondsworth, 1971), *Interaction Ritual* (Harmondsworth, 1957); R. Harré and P. F. Secord, *Explanation of Behavior* (Totowa, N.J., 1972); R. Harré, *Social Being* (Oxford, 1979).

5. One can get an overview of symbolic interactionism and ethnomethodology from, for instance, the reader put together by the Arbeitsgruppe Bielefelder Soziologen, *Alltagswissen, Interaktion und gesellschaftliche Wirklichkeit,* 2 vols. (Hamburg, 1973); see also H. Steinert, "Das Handlungsmodell des symbolischen Interaktionismus," in *Handlungstheorien* 4, ed. H. Lenk (Munich, 1977):79ff.

6. G. H. von Wright, *Explanation and Understanding* (London, 1971), 96ff. Von Wright's point of departure is G. E. M. Anscombe, *Intention* (Oxford, 1957).

7. J. L. Austin speaks of the "direction of fit" or the "onus of match," which Anthony Kenny elaborates as follows: "Any sentence whatever can be regarded as—*inter alia*—a description of a state of affairs. . . . Now let us suppose that the possible state of affairs described in the sentence does not, in fact, obtain. *Do we fault the sentence or do we fault the facts?* If the former, then we shall call the sentence assertoric, if the latter, let us call it for the moment imperative" *Will, Freedom and Power* (Oxford, 1975), 38. If we conceive of intention sentences as imperatives that a speaker addresses to himself, then assertoric and intention sentences represent the two possibilities of agreement between sentence and state of affairs that are open to objective appraisal.

8. G. Gaefgen, "Formale Theorie des strategischen Handelns," in *Handlungstheorien* 1, ed. H. Lenk (Munich, 1980):249ff.

9. Compare Ottfried Höffe, *Strategien der Humanität* (Munich, 1975): "A strategic game is composed of four elements:

"1) The *players,* the sovereign units of decision, who pursue their ends and act according to their own deliberations and guiding principles;

"2) The *rules,* which fix the variables that each player can control: information conditions, resources and other relevant aspects of the environment; the system of rules fixes the type of game, the totality of behavioral possibilities, and in the end the gains or losses of every player; a change in the rules creates a new game;

"3) The end result of *payoffs,* the utility or value correlated with the alternative results of plays (in chess: win, lose, draw; in politics: public prestige, power and money, for instance);

"4) The *strategies,* the encompassing, alternatively possible plans of action. They are constructed with a view both to heeding and exploiting the rules and to taking account of the possible alternatives open to the opponent. Strategies represent a system of instructions that determine in advance, and often only in a rather global way, how, in every possible game situation, one chooses a move from the set of those allowed by the rules of the game. In the game-theoretical interpretation of social reality, certain strategies are often favorable only for a segment of the contest; new strategies then have to be developed for other segments; individual strategies have the significance of substrategies within the framework of an encompassing overall strategy.

"The rationality criterion of game theory refers not to the choice of individual moves but to the choice of strategies. Stated in the form of a maxim for decision, the basic pattern runs as follows: 'Choose the strategy which, in the framework of the rules of the game and in view of your opponents, promises to bring the greatest success'" (77–78).

10. H. Gerth and C. W. Mills, *Character and Social Structure* (New York, 1953).

11. This does not prejudge the question of whether we, as social scientists and philosophers, adopt a cognitive or a sceptical position in regard to moral-practical questions; that is, whether we hold a justification of action norms that is not relative to given ends to be possible. For example, Talcott Parsons shares with Weber a position of value skepticism; but when we use the concept of normatively regulated action we have to describe the actors *as if* they consider the legitimacy of action norms to be basically open to objective appraisal, no matter in which metaphysical, religious, or theoretical framework. Otherwise they would not take the concept of a world of legitimately regulated interpersonal relations as the basis of their action and could not orient themselves to valid norms but only to social facts. Acting in a norm-conformative attitude requires an intuitive understanding of normative validity; and this concept presupposes *some* possibility or other of normative grounding.

It cannot be a priori excluded that this conceptual necessity is a deception embedded in linguistic meaning conventions and thus calls for enlightenment—for example, by reinterpreting the concept of normative validity in emotivist or decisionistic terms and redescribing it with the help of other concepts like expressions of feeling, appeals, or commands. But the action of agents to whom such categorially "purified" action orientations can be ascribed could no longer be described in concepts of normatively regulated action.

12. E. Goffman, *The Presentation of Self in Everyday Life* (New York, 1959). On p. xi of the preface he writes: "The perspective employed in this report is that of the theatrical performance; the principles derived are dramaturgical ones. I shall consider the way in which the individual in ordinary work situations presents himself and his activity to others, the ways in which he guides and controls the impression they form of him, and the kinds of things he may and may not do while sustaining his performance before them. In using this model I will attempt not to make light of its obvious inadequacies. The stage presents things that are make-believe; presumably life presents things that are real and sometimes not well rehearsed. More important, perhaps, on the stage one player presents himself in the guise of a character to characters projected by other players; the audience constitutes a third party to the interaction—one that is essential and yet, if the stage performance were real, one that would not be there. In real life, the three parties are compressed into two; the part one individual plays is tailored to the parts played by the others present, and yet these others also constitute the audience."

13. Harré and Secord, *Explanation of Behavior*, 215–16.

14. Goffman, *Presentation of Self*, 31.

15. For the sake of simplicity, I am confining myself to *intentional* experiences (including weakly intentional moods) in order not to have to deal with the complicated limit case of sensations. The complication consists in the fact that here the misleading assimilation of experiential sentences to propositions is particularly tempting. Experiential sentences that express a sensation have almost the same meaning as propositional sentences that refer to a corresponding inner state brought about by stimulation of the senses. [Habermas uses the term *intentional experience* in the way that Husserl does, but without wanting thereby to subscribe to the phenomenological concept of intentionality—TRANS.] On the extended discussion of expressions of pain that has been sparked by Wittgenstein's remarks on this topic, see H. J. Giegel, *Zur Logik seelischer Ereignisse* (Frankfurt, 1969); P. M. S. Hacker, *Illusion and Insight* (Oxford, 1972), 251ff.

16. Compare the analysis of desires and feelings by Charles Taylor, "Explaining Action," *Inquiry* 13 (1970):54–89.

17. Richard Norman, *Reasons for Actions,* 65ff.

18. Goffman, *Presentation of Self*, 17–18.

19. Benjamin Lee Whorf, *Language, Thought and Reality* (Cambridge, Mass., 1956); H. Gipper, *Gibt es ein sprachliches Relativitätsprinzip?* (Frankfurt, 1972); P. Henle, ed., *Sprache, Denken, Kultur* (Frankfurt, 1969).

20. Harré and Secord, *Explanation of Behavior*, 215ff.; see especially Charles Taylor, *Language and Human Nature* (Carleton, Montreal, 1978).

21. F. Schütze, *Sprache*, 2 vols. (Munich, 1975).

22. For similar reasons, M. Roche insists on the distinction between linguistic and social conventions: "The school of conceptual analysis has characteristically seen no contrast between intention and convention; in their view the latter includes the former and vice versa" (M. Roche, "Die Philosophische Schule der Begriffsanalyse," in *Sprachanalyse und Soziologie,* ed. R. Wiggershaus [Frankfurt, 1975], 187). One could say, Roche allows, "that communicative conventions are a very special kind of social convention, that the life of ordinary language and its use in social situations

can be described independently of social interactions in social situations. But it would be difficult to ground this assertion, and conceptual analysis has no interest in clarifying it. Normally it assumes, rightly, that the analysis of concepts requires an analysis of 'language games' and social 'forms of life' (Wittgenstein), or that the analysis of speech acts requires an analysis of social acts (Austin). But it then mistakenly infers from this that the conventions of communication are paradigms of the social conventions surrounding them and that a use of language stands in the same relation to communication conventions as a social action does to social conventions" (188–89).

23. Arthur C. Danto, "Basic Actions," *American Philosophical Quarterly* 2 (1965):141–48, and *Analytical Philosophy of Action* (Cambridge, 1973).

24. The false impression that bodily movements coordinated with actions are themselves basic actions might be sustained perhaps by looking to certain exercises in which we intend nonindependent actions *as such*. In therapy or sports training, for purposes of anatomical display, in singing lessons, or foreign language lessons, or to illustrate action-theoretic assertions, every speaking and acting subject can, upon request, certainly raise his left arm, bend his right index finger, spread open his hand, repeat vocal sounds in a certain rhythm, make hissing noises, execute circular or linear movements with a drawing pencil, trace a wavy line, enunciate a German *ü*, straighten up his body, roll his eyes, stress a sentence according to a certain meter, raise or lower his voice, stretch his legs, and so on. But the fact that such bodily movements can be carried out intentionally does not contradict the thesis that they represent nonindependent actions. This can be seen in the fact that with these intentionally executed bodily movements the normal structure of mediation of action (as represented in 1 below) breaks down:

1. *S* is opening the window by executing a circular motion with his hand.

For it would be artificial to say:

2. *S* is (intentionally) raising his right arm by raising his right arm.

Of course, an intentionally executed bodily movement can be understood as part of a *practice*.

2.' During the gym lesson, in raising his right arm, *S* is carrying out the teacher's instruction to raise his right arm.

Nonindependent actions typically have to be embedded in a demonstration or training practice if they are to be able to appear *as* actions. Instructions of this type always appear in connection with a practice that demonstrates or exercises nonindependent elements of action as such. The exercises may belong to the normal education of growing children; but they may also belong to a training practice that prepares one for special actions, for *skills*.

25. A. I. Goldmann, *A Theory of Action* (Englewood Cliffs, N.J., 1970).

26. R. Bubner, *Handlung, Sprache und Vernunft,* 168ff.

27. J. L. Austin, *How to Do Things with Words* (Oxford, 1962).

28. I shall leave aside the development that speech act theory underwent in the hands of Austin himself (see my "What Is Universal Pragmatics?," 44ff.) and take as my point of departure the interpretation that Searle has given to this theory. John Searle, *Speech Acts* (London, 1969); and D. Wunderlich, *Studien zur Sprechakttheorie* (Frankfurt, 1976).

29. Austin, *How to Do Things with Words,* 101.

30. B. Schlieben-Lange, *Linguistische Pragmatik* (Stuttgart, 1975), 86ff.

31. D. S. Schwayder, *The Stratification of Behavior* (London, 1965), 287ff.

32. M. Meyer, *Formale und handlungstheoretische Sprachbetrachtungen* (Stuttgart, 1976).

33. M. Schwab, *Redehandeln* (Königstein, 1908), 28ff.

34. Austin, *How to Do Things with Words,* 118.

35. P. Strawson, "Intention and Convention in Speech Acts," *Philosophical Review* 73 (1964):439ff.

36. Compare J. Habermas, "What Is Universal Pragmatics?": "With institutionally bound speech actions, specific institutions are always involved. With institutionally unbound speech actions, only conditions of a generalized context must typically be met for a corresponding act to succeed. . . . To explain what acts of betting or christening mean, I must refer to the institutions of betting or christening. By contrast, commands or advice or questions do not represent institutions but types of speech acts that can fit very different institutions. To be sure, 'institutional bond' is a criterion that does not always permit an unambiguous classification. Commands can exist wherever relations of authority are institutionalized; appointments presuppose special, bureaucratically developed organizations; and marriages require a single institution (which is, however, found universally). But this does not destroy the usefulness of the analytic point of view. Institutionally unbound speech actions, insofar as they have any regulative meaning at all, are related to various aspects of action norms in general; they are not essentially fixed by particular institutions" (38–39).

Chapter Eight
THE CONCEPT OF THE LIFEWORLD AND THE HERMENEUTIC IDEALISM OF INTERPRETIVE SOCIOLOGY

1. On the phenomenological concept of the lifeworld, see L. Landgrebe, *Phänomenologie und Metaphysik* (Heidelberg, 1949), 10ff.; and idem, *Philosophie der Gegenwart* (Bonn, 1952), 65ff.; A. Gurwitsch, *The Field of Consciousness* (Pittsburgh, 1964); G. Brand, *Welt, Ich und Zeit* (The Hague, 1955); H. Hohl, *Lebenswelt und Geschichte* (Freiburg, 1962); W. Lippitz, "Der phänomenologische Begriff der Lebenswelt," *Zeitschrift für Philosophische Forschung* 32 (1978): 416ff.; K. Ulmer, *Philosophie der modernen Lebenswelt* (Tübingen, 1972).

2. On the sociological analysis of forms of life, see P. Winch, *The Idea of a Social Science* (London, 1958); R. Rhees, *Without Answers* (New York, 1969); D. L. Phillips and H. O. Mounce, *Moral Practices* (London, 1970); H. Pitkin, *Wittgenstein and Justice* (Berkeley, 1972); P. McHugh et al., *On the Beginning of Social Inquiry* (London, 1974).

3. Alfred Schutz, *Collected Papers I: The Problem of Social Reality*, ed. M. Natanson (The Hague, 1962).

4. Cf. H. Kuhn, "The Phenomenological Concept of Horizon," in *Philosophical Essays in Memory of E. Husserl*, ed. M. Faber (Cambridge, Mass., 1940), 106ff.

5. E. Husserl, *Experience and Judgment* (Evanston, 1973). For a critique of the foundation in consciousness of Schutz's phenomenological ontology of the social, see Michael Theunissen, *The Other: Studies in the Social Ontology of Husserl, Heidegger, Sartre and Buber* (Cambridge, Mass., 1984), 345–52.

6. L. Weisgerber, *Die Muttersprache im Aufbau unserer Kultur* (Düsseldorf, 1957); R. Hoberg, *Die Lehre vom sprachlichen Feld* (Düsseldorf, 1970); H. Gipper, *Gibt es ein sprachliches Relativitätsprinzip?* (Frankfurt, 1972).

7. Arthur Danto, *Analytical Philosophy of History* (Cambridge, 1968). See also P. Gardiner, ed., *The Philosophy of History* (Oxford, 1974). For the German discussion, see H. M. Baumgartner, *Kontinuität und Geschichte* (Frankfurt, 1972); R. Koselleck and W. Stempel, eds., *Geschichte, Ereignis und Erzählung* (Munich, 1973); K. Acham, *Analytische Geschichtsphilosophie* (Freiberg, 1974); J. Rüsen, *Für eine erneuerte Historik* (Stuttgart, 1976); H. Baumgartner and J. Rüsen, eds., *Geschichte und Theorie* (Frankfurt, 1976).

8. P. Berger and T. Luckmann, *The Social Construction of Reality* (Garden City, N.Y., 1967), 1.

9. Cf. A. M. Rose, ed., *Human Behavior and Social Processes* (Boston, 1962). The above-mentioned debate between ethnomethodology and symbolic interactionism can be traced back to the competition between one-sided, culturalistic and socialization-theoretical concepts of the lifeworld; see N. K. Denzin, "Symbolic Interactionism and Ethnomethodology," in *Understanding Everyday Life*, ed. Jack D. Douglas (London, 1971), 259–84, versus D. H. Zimmerman and D. L. Wieder, "Ethnomethodology and the Problem of Order," ibid., 285–98.

10. G. H. Mead, *Selected Writings*, ed. A. Reck (Chicago, 1964), 296.

11. Between the world wars this tradition was represented by such thinkers as Heidegger, Gehlen, Konrad Lorenz, and Carl Schmitt; today it is continued at a comparable level only in French post-structuralism.

12. See J. Habermas, *Zur Logik der Sozialwissenschaften* (Frankfurt, 1970), English trans. forthcoming, MIT Press; A. Ryan, "Normal Science or Political Ideology?" in *Philosophy, Politics and Society*, ed. P. Laslett, W. G. Runciman, and Q. Skinner, vol. 4 (Cambridge, 1972).

13. W. Schapp, *In Geschichten Verstrickt* (Wiesbaden, 1976).

14. T. Parsons, "Some Problems of General Theory," in *Theoretical Sociology*, ed. J. C. McKinney and E. A. Tiryakian (New York, 1970), 34. See also H. Willke, "Zum Problem der Interpretation komplexer Sozialsysteme," *Kölner Zeitschrift für Soziologie und Sozialpsychologie* 30 (1978): 228ff.

15. A. Etzione, "Elemente einer Makrosoziologie," in *Theorien des Sozialen Wandels*, ed. W. Zapf (Cologne, 1969), 147ff; and idem, *The Active Society* (New York, 1968), 135ff.

Chapter Nine
THE UNCOUPLING OF SYSTEM AND LIFEWORLD

1. N. Luhmann, "Interaction, Organization, and Society," in *The Differentiation of Society* (New York, 1982), 69–89.

2. "Segmentary societies are not 'primitive societies,' nor are they simple; it does not make sense to think of them as societies in the beginning stages of development. On the other hand, neither are they in some dead-end of societal development. They are dynamic in respect both to their structural reproduction and to their geographical expansion." Christian Sigrist, "Gesellschaften ohne Staat und die Entdeckungen der Sozialanthopologie," in *Gesellschaften ohne Staat, ed. F. Kramer and C. Sigrist (Frankfurt, 1978),* 1:39.

3. K. Gabriel, *Analysen der Organisationsgesellschaft* (Frankfurt, 1979), 151–52. Cf. P. Berger, *Zur Dialektik von Religion und Gesellschaft* (Frankfurt, 1973), 60ff.; T. Luckmann, "Zwänge und Freiheiten im Wandel der Gesellschaftsstruktur," in H. G. Gadamer and P. Vogler, *Neue Anthropologie* (Stuttgart, 1972), 3:168ff.

4. M. Fortes, *Kinship and Social Order* (Chicago, 1969), 234.

5. Ibid.

6. Ibid., 104.

7. T. Luckmann, "On the Boundaries of the Social World," in *Phenomenology and Social Reality*, ed. M. Natanson (The Hague, 1970).

8. A summary account can be found in L. Mair, *An Introduction to Social Anthropology*, rev. ed. (Oxford, 1972), 54ff.

9. On the elements of social organization in tribal societies, see R. Firth, *Elements of Social Organization* (London, 1971), 35ff.

10. On segmental dynamics, see C. Sigrist, *Regulierte Anarchie* (Frankfurt, 1979), 21ff.

11. B. Malinowski, "The Circulation Exchange of Valuables in the Archipelago of Eastern New Guinea," *Man* (1920):97ff.

12. Cf. the classical study by M. Mauss, *The Gift* (London, 1954), with an introduction by E. E. Evans-Pritchard.

13. Mair, *Social Anthropology*, 115.

14. E. Leach, *Political Systems of Highland Burma* (London, 1964).

15. M. Gluckmann, "Rituals of Rebellion in South East Africa," in *Order and Rebellion in Tribal Africa* (London, 1963), 110ff.

16. F. Steiner, "Notiz zer vergleichenden Ökonomie," in Kramer and Sigrist, *Gesellschaften ohne Staat*, 85ff.

17. Cf. the interpretation by Mair in *Social Anthropology*, 237–38.

18. This sequence explains the evolutionary content of the basic sociological concepts: role, status, office, formal law. They become blunt, or at least in need of sharpening, when used to analyze phenomena that do not appertain to the corresponding social formation. For example, the concept of role is central to explaining socialization processes, since the child grows into its social world by appropriating the system of familial roles. And yet it is precisely research into socialization that has given the strongest impulse to reformulating the role concept. This concept is not only derived from the kinship system, it can be *smoothly* applied only to phenomena in societies organized along kinship lines; socialization processes in modern societies escape the grasp of a social psychology tailored to the internalizing of roles. Cf. L. Krappmann, *Soziologische Dimensionen der Identität* (Stuttgart, 1971). On the historicity of basic sociological concepts, see D. Zaret, "From Weber to Parsons and Schütz: The Eclipse of History in Modern Social Theory," *American Journal of Sociology* 85 (1980):1180ff.

19. J. Habermas, *Communication and the Evolution of Society* (Boston, 1979), 143–44.

20. M. Godelier, *Perspectives in Marxist Anthropology* (Cambridge, 1976), and idem, "Infrastructures, Societies, and History," *Current Anthropology* 19 (1978): 763ff.

21. Luckmann, "Zwänge und Freiheiten," 191–92.

22. *African Political Systems*, ed. M. Fortes and E. Evans-Pritchard (Oxford, 1970).

23. Ibid., 14.

24. On this concept, see R. Goldscheid and O. Schumpeter, *Die Finanzkrise des Steuerstaats*, ed. R. Hickel (Frankfurt, 1976).

25. N. Luhmann, *Zweckbegriff und Systemrationalität* (Tübingen, 1969), 339.

26. N. Luhmann, "Allgemeine Theorie organisierter Sozialsysteme," in *Soziologische Aufklärung*, vol. 2 (Opladen, 1975).

27. L. Kohlberg, *Essays on Moral Development*, vols. 1 and 2 (San Francisco, 1981, 1984).

28. K. Eder, *Die Entstehung staatlich organisierter Gesellschaften* (Frankfurt, 1976).

29. W. Schluchter, *The Rise of Western Rationalism* (Berkeley, 1981).

30. I developed this thesis in more detail in *Communication and the Evolution of Society* (Boston, 1979), chaps. 3 and 4.

31. Mair, *Social Anthropology*, 145–46.

32. Ibid., 146.

33. Ibid., 148–49.

Table N. 1

Everyday Speech Acts	Formalized Speech Acts
Choice of loudness	Fixed loudness patterns
Choice of intonation	Extremely limited choice of intonation
All syntactic forms available	Some syntactic forms excluded
Complete vocabulary	Partial vocabulary
Flexibility of sequencing of speech acts	Fixity of sequencing of speech acts
Few illustrations from a fixed body of accepted parallels	Illustrations only from certain limited sources, e.g., scriptures, proverbs
No stylistic rules consciously held to operate	Stylistic rules consciously applied at all levels

Source: M. Bloch, "Symbols, Song, Dance and Features of Articulation," *Archives Europeénnes de Sociologie* 15 (1974):55 ff.

34. "Normally we do not have to think about the foundations of our corporate life or the conditions of its continued existence, nor to justify actions or expressly to find and display appropriate motives. Problematizing and thematizing are not excluded; they are always possible; but normally this non-actualized possibility already suffices as a basis for interaction. If no one calls it into question, then 'everything's o.k.'" N. Luhmann, *Macht* (Stuttgart, 1975).

35. N. Eisenstadt, "Cultural Traditions and Political Dynamics: The Origins and Modes of Ideological Politics," *British Journal of Sociology* 32 (1981):155ff. Naturally, the world religions appear only relatively late. Other bases of legitimation are required in archaic societies that have attained the level of state organization. In this connection M. Bloch's studies of kingdoms in central Madagascar are of particular interest: M. Bloch, "The Disconnection of Power and Rank as a Process," in *The Evolution of Social Systems,* ed. S. Friedman and M. J. Rowland (London, 1977); and idem, "The Past and the Present in the Present," *Man* 13 (1978):278ff. Bloch shows that in the transition from stratified tribal societies to class societies organized by a state, certain rites and ritually secured social rank-orderings get refunctionalized for purposes of legitimation. The hierarchical structures of the superseded tribal societies remain standing as a facade behind which the class structures of the new state-organized kingdoms hide, so to speak.

36. M. Bloch also uses a communications-theoretical approach to explain the ideological functions that actions passed down from the period of tribal society can take on in class societies. The formalism according to which ritual practices can assume such functions may be characterized in terms of restrictions on communication, as table N. 1 illustrates.

37. See for example Mair, *Social Anthropology,* 229: "In fact Leach's distinction between the technical and the ritual—between acts that we, as observers with some knowledge of scientific principles, can see produce the ends they aim at and those which do not—though it is not the same as Durkheim's distinction between sacred and profane, is the one that all anthropologists have made in distinguishing the magico-religious from the field of everyday life. As we see it, there is an aspect of life in which people seek to attain ends that are either not attainable by any human action or not attainable by the means they are using. They purport to be calling in aid beings or forces which *we* consider to be outside the course of nature as we understand it, and so call 'supernatural.' To this field of activity belong both the religious and the magical."

38. On the contrast between ritual and sacramental practice see Mary Douglas, *Natural Symbols* (London, 1973), 28l: "Ritualism is taken to be a concern that efficacious symbols be correctly manipulated and that the right words be pronounced in the right order. When we compare the sacraments to magic there are two kinds of view to take into account: on the one hand the official doctrine, on the other the popular form it takes. On the first view the Christian theologian may limit the efficacy of sacraments to the internal working of grace in the soul. But by this agency external events may be changed since decisions taken by a person in a state of grace will presumably differ from those of others. Sacramental efficacy works internally; magical efficacy works externally."

39. Mair, *Social Anthropology*, 229.

40. Strictly speaking, not even the philosophical discourse of Greek philosophy was specialized about the isolated validity claim of propositional truth.

Chapter Eleven
TECHNOLOGY AND SCIENCE AS "IDEOLOGY"

1. Herbert Marcuse, "Industrialization and Capitalism in the Work of Max Weber," in *Negations: Essays in Critical Theory*, trans. Jeremy J. Shapiro (Boston, 1968), 223–24.

2. Herbert Marcuse, "Freedom and Freud's Theory of the Instincts," in *Five Lectures*, trans. Jeremy J. Shapiro and Shierry M. Weber (Boston, 1970), 16.

3. Ibid., 3.

4. Ibid.

5. Ibid.

6. Herbert Marcuse, *One-Dimensional Man* (Boston, 1964).

7. Ibid., 166–67.

8. Ibid., 236.

9. "This law expresses an intratechnical occurrence, a process that man has not willed as a whole. Rather, it takes place, as it were, behind his back, instinctively extending through the entire history of human culture. Furthermore, in accordance with this law, technology cannot evolve beyond the stage of the greatest possible automation, for there are no further specifiable regions of human achievement that could be objectified." Arnold Gehlen, "Anthropologische Ansicht der Technik," in *Technik im technischen Zeitalter*, ed. Hans Freyer et al. (Düsseldorf, 1965).

10. Marcuse, *One-Dimensonal Man*, 235.

11. Ibid., 154.

12. On the context of these concepts in the history of philosophy, see my essay "Labor and Interaction: Remarks on Hegel's Jena *Philosophy of Mind*," in *Theory and Practice* (Boston, 1974), 142.

13. Gerhard E. Lenski, *Power and Privilege: A Theory of Social Stratification* (New York, 1966).

14. See Peter L. Berger, *The Sacred Canopy* (New York, 1967).

15. See my study *Knowledge and Human Interests* (Boston, 1971).

16. See Leo Strauss, *Natural Right and History* (Chicago, 1963); C. B. MacPherson, *The Political Theory of Possessive Individualism* (London, 1962); and Jürgen Habermas, "The Classical Doctrine of Politics in Relation to Social Philosophy," in *Theory and Practice*, 41.

17. See Jürgen Habermas, "Natural Law and Revolution," in *Theory and Practice*, 82.

18. Claus Offe, "Politische Herrschaft und Klassenstrukturen," in *Politikwissenschaft,* ed. Gisela Kress and Dieter Senghaas (Frankfurt am Main, 1969). The quotation in the text is from the original manuscript, which differs in formulation from the published text.

19. The most recent explication of this is Eugen Lobl, *Geistige Arbeit—die wahre Quelle des Reichtums,* trans. Leopold Grünwald (Vienna, 1968).

20. See Helmut Schelsky, *Der Mensch in der wissenschaftlichen Zivilisation* (Cologne-Opladen, 1961); Jacques Ellul, *The Technological Society* (New York, 1967); and Arnold Gehlen, "Über kulturelle Kristalisationen," in *Studien zur Anthropologie und Soziologie* (Berlin, 1963) and "Über kulturelle Evolution," in *Die Philosophie und die Frage nach dem Fortschritt,* ed. M. Hahn and F. Wiedmann (Munich, 1964).

21. To my knowledge there are no empirical studies concerned with the propagation of this background ideology. We are dependent on extrapolations from the findings of other investigations.

22. Offe, "Politische Herrschaft."

23. See my essay, "Knowledge and Human Interests," in the volume of the same title, 301.

24. Herman Kahn and Anthony J. Wiener, "The Next Thirty-three Years: A Framework for Speculation," in *Toward the Year 2000: Work in Progress,* ed. Daniel Bell (Boston, 1969), 80–81.

25. Seymour Martin Lipset and Philip G. Altbach, "Student Politics and Higher Education in the U.S.A.," in *Student Politics,* ed. Seymour Martin Lipset (New York, 1967); Richard W. Flacks, "The Liberated Generation: An Exploration of the Roots of Student Protest," *Journal of Social Issues* 23, no. 2:52–75; and Kenneth Keniston, "The Sources of Student Dissent," ibid., 108ff.

26. In Flacks's words, "Activists are more radical than their parents; but activists' parents are decidedly more liberal than others of their status. . . . Activism is related to a complex of values, not ostensibly political, shared by both the students and their parents. . . . Activists' parents are more 'permissive' than parents of nonactivists."

27. See Robert L. Heilbroner, *The Limits of American Capitalism* (New York, 1960).

Chapter Thirteen

THE CRISIS OF THE WELFARE STATE AND
THE EXHAUSTION OF UTOPIAN ENERGIES

1. I am following here the outstanding work of Reinhart Koselleck, *Vergangene Zukunft* (Frankfurt, 1979), translated as *Futures Past: On the Semantics of Historical Time* (Cambridge, Mass., 1985).

2. On this theme see J. Rüsen, "Utopie und Geschichte," in *Utopieforschung* (Stuttgart, 1982), ed. W. Vosskamp, 1:356ff.

3. L. Holscher, "Der Begriff der Utopie als historische Kategorie," in Vosskamp, *Utopieforschung,* 1:402ff.

4. Reinhart Koselleck, "Die Verzeitlichung der Utopie," in Vosskamp, *Utopieforschung,* 3:1ff.; R. Trousson, "Utopie, Geschichte, Fortschritt," ibid., 3:15ff.

5. Oskar Negt has recently published another noteworthy study from this perspective: *Lebendige Arbeit, enteignete Zeit* (Frankfurt, 1984).

6. Karl Marx and Friedrich Engels, *The German Ideology,* ed. C. J. Arthur (New York, 1970), 92–93.

7. Claus Offe, "Arbeit als soziologische Schlüsselkategorie," in his *Arbeitsgesellschaft—Strukturprobleme und Zukunftsperspektiven* (Frankfurt, 1984), 20.

8. From this perspective see also the recent work of H. Kern and M. Schumann, *Das Ende der Arbeitsteilung?* (Munich, 1984).

9. On this theme see Claus Offe, "Zu einigen Widersprüchen des modernen Sozialstaates," in his *Arbeitsgesellschaft,* 323ff.; and John Keane, *Public Life and Late Capitalism* (Cambridge, 1984), chap. 1, 10ff.

10. Claus Offe, "Perspektiven auf die Zukunft des Arbeitsmarktes," in his *Arbeitsgesellschaft,* 340ff.

11. Claus Offe, "Korporatismus als System nichtstaatlicher Machtsteuerung," in *Geschichte und Gesellschaft* 10 (1984):243ff.; on the system-theoretical justification of neocorporatism see H. Wilke, *Entzauberung des Staates* (Königstein, 1983).

12. T. Schmid, *Befreiung von falscher Arbeit: Thesen zum garantierten Mindesteinkommen* (Berlin, 1984).

13. See on this Jean-Francois Lyotard, *The Postmodern Condition: A Report on Knowledge* (Minneapolis, 1984). For a critical perspective, see Axel Honneth, "Der Affekt gegen das Allgemeine," *Merkur* 430 (December 1984):893ff.

14. Karl-Otto Apel, "Ist die Ethik der idealen Kommunikationsgemeinschaft einer Utopie?" in Vosskamp, *Utopieforschung,* 1:325ff.

Credits

Chapter 1, "Dogmatism, Reason, and Decision: On Theory and Practice in a Scientific Civilization," originally published as "Dogmatismus, Vernunft und Entscheidung—Zu Theorie und Praxis in der verwissenschaftlichen Zivilisation," and chapter 2, "Between Philosophy and Science: Marxism as Critique," originally published as "Zwischen Philosophie und Wissenschaft: Marxismus als Kritik," both translated by Shierry Weber Nicholsen, first appeared in Jürgen Habermas, *Theorie und Praxis,* © 1963 by Luchterhand Literaturverlag, Darmstadt.

Chapter 3, "Self-Reflection as Science: Freud's Psychoanalytic Critique of Meaning," and chapter 5, "Psychoanalysis and Society Theory: Nietzsche's Reduction of Cognitive Interests," originally appeared in Jürgen Habermas, *Knowledge and Human Interests,* translated by Jeremy J. Shapiro, © 1971 by Beacon Press, Boston.

Chapter 4, "The Tasks of a Critical Theory of Society," chapter 8, "The Concept of the Lifeworld and the Hermeneutic Idealism of Interpretive Sociology," and chapter 9, "The Uncoupling of System and Lifeworld," originally appeared in Jürgen Habermas, *The Theory of Communicative Action,* volume 2, *Lifeworld and System: A Critique of Functionalist Reason,* translated by Thomas McCarthy, © 1987 by Beacon Press, Boston.

Chapter 6, "Toward a Reconstruction of Historical Materialism," originally appeared in Jürgen Habermas, *Communication and the Evolution of Society,* translated by Thomas McCarthy, © 1979 by Beacon Press, Boston.

Chapter 7, "Social Action and Rationality," originally appeared in Jürgen Habermas, *The Theory of Communicative Action,* volume 1, *Reason and the Rationalization of Society,* translated by Thomas McCarthy, © 1984 by Beacon Press, Boston.

Chapter 10, "The Public Sphere," translated by Shierry Weber Nicholsen, was originally published as "Öffentlichkeit" in Jürgen Habermas, *Kultur und Kritik,* © 1973 by Suhrkamp Verlag, Frankfurt am Main. The translator wishes to thank MIT Press for permission to consult Thomas Burger's translation of *Strukturwandel der Öffentlichkeit* (*The Structural Transformation of the Public Sphere,* forthcoming), of which this article is a summary. Burger's translations of key terms have been followed as far as possible.

Chapter 11, "Technology and Science as 'Ideology,'" originally appeared in Jürgen Habermas, *Toward a Rational Society,* translated by Jeremy J. Shapiro, © 1970 by Beacon Press, Boston.

Chapter 12, "What Does a Crisis Mean Today? Legitimation Problems in Late Capitalism," originally appeared in *Social Research* 40, no. 4 (Winter 1973), © 1973 by *Social Research*.

Chapter 13, "The Crisis of the Welfare State and the Exhaustion of Utopian Energies," translated by Shierry Weber Nicholsen, will appear in *The New Obscurity*, MIT Press, Cambridge, Mass., in press. Reprinted by permission of MIT Press.